T0366843

A list of books in the series appears at the back of this book.

International Nietzsche Studies

Nietzsche has emerged as a thinker of extraordinary importance, not only in the history of philosophy but in many fields of contemporary inquiry. Nietzsche studies are maturing and flourishing in many parts of the world. This internationalization of inquiry with respect to Nietzsche's thought and significance may be expected to continue.

International Nietzsche Studies is conceived as a series of monographs and essay collections that will reflect and contribute to these developments. The series will present studies in which responsible scholarship is joined to the analysis, interpretation, and assessment of the many aspects of Nietzsche's thought that bear significantly upon matters of moment today. In many respects Nietzsche is our contemporary, with whom we do well to reckon, even when we find ourselves at odds with him. The series is intended to promote this reckoning, embracing diverse interpretive perspectives, philosophical orientations, and critical assessments.

The series is also intended to contribute to the ongoing reconsideration of the character, agenda, and prospects of philosophy itself. Nietzsche was much concerned with philosophy's past, present, and future. He sought to affect not only its understanding but also its practice. The future of philosophy is an open question today, thanks at least in part to Nietzsche's challenge to the philosophical traditions of which he was so critical. It remains to be seen—and determined—whether philosophy's future will turn out to resemble the "philosophy of the future" to which he proffered a prelude and of which he provided a preview, by both precept and practice. But this is a possibility we do well to take seriously. International Nietzsche Studies will attempt to do so, while contributing to the understanding of Nietzsche's philosophical thinking and its bearing upon contemporary inquiry.

—Richard Schacht

Nietzsche

NIETZSCHE

His Philosophy of Contradictions and the
Contradictions of His Philosophy

Wolfgang Müller-Lauter

Translated from the German by David J. Parent

Foreword by Richard Schacht

University of Illinois Press

Urbana and Chicago

Publication of this book was supported by a grant from Inter Nationes, Bonn.

Nietzsche: Seine Philosophie der Gegensätze und die Gegensätze Seiner Philosophie © 1971 by Walter de Gruyter & Co., Berlin and New York
English-language translation © 1999 by the Board of Trustees of the University of Illinois
Published by the University of Illinois Press by agreement with
Walter de Gruyter & Co., Berlin and New York
Manufactured in the United States of America
1 2 3 4 5 C P 6 5 4 3 2

This book is printed on acid-free paper.

Library of Congress Cataloging-in-Publication Data
Müller-Lauter, Wolfgang.
[Nietzsche. English]
Nietzsche : his philosophy of contradictions and the contradictions of
his philosophy / Wolfgang Müller-Lauter ; translated from the German
by David J. Parent ; foreword by Richard Schacht.
p.   cm. — (International Nietzsche studies)
Includes bibliographical references.
ISBN-13: 978-0-252-02452-8 (alk. paper)
ISBN-10: 0-252-02452-4 (alk. paper)
ISBN-13: 978-0-252-06758-7 (pbk. : alk. paper)
ISBN-10: 0-252-06758-4 (pbk. : alk. paper)
1. Nietzsche, Friedrich Wilhelm, 1844–1900. I. Title. II. Series.
B3317.M813   1999
193—dc21   98-25391
CIP

Contents

Foreword

The publication of this book in its original German form in 1971 was a major event in the development of Nietzsche studies in Germany. Heidegger's massive and highly idiosyncratic treatment of Nietzsche had appeared ten years previously and had become enormously influential, giving the interpretation of Nietzsche a direction and style that moved markedly away from traditional norms of scholarship. Müller-Lauter's book provided a much-needed counterweight to it, reaffirming the primacy of Nietzsche's texts (both published and unpublished) in the understanding of his thought and so serving as a rallying point for those in German-language Nietzsche studies who were not prepared to yield Nietzsche to those on both sides of the Rhine for whom Heidegger's way with Nietzsche was their point of departure.

Through his book, together with his subsequent contributions to the Nietzsche literature and other contributions to Nietzsche studies (particularly through his longtime stewardship of *Nietzsche Studien*), Müller-Lauter also played a crucial role in holding the fort against wider social and intellectual forces on both the right and the left that threatened the very existence and future of Nietzsche studies in both parts of Germany. His efforts and accomplishments were recognized publicly and movingly in a ceremony held October 1996 in Naumburg (Nietzsche's home town), in a part of Germany in which Nietzsche was long vilified and Nietzsche studies discouraged. In this well-attended official and media event, Müller-Lauter was awarded the first Friedrich Nietzsche Prize given by the State of Sachsen-Anhalt, honoring him for his long career as a Nietzsche scholar, of which this book is the single most salient accomplishment.

The debates carried on in the book with other German philosophers and scholars whose treatments of Nietzsche were taken by Müller-Lauter to call for attention and response are themselves illuminating. They both illustrate the kinds of interpretive issues that were at the forefront in Germany during this crucial pe-riod—at a time when Anglo-American Nietzsche studies were only beginning to gain philosophical respectability and to attain intellectual maturity—and also are indicative of the ways in which they were being addressed. Both Germanic and Anglo-American Nietzsche studies have evolved considerably in the inter-val, during which time the waters have also been roiled mightily by the influx into both philosophical and intellectual communities of the currents of Nietz-sche interpretation flowing from France and French-inspired circles in both ar-eas. A generation later one cannot help being struck by the unself-consciousness with which Müller-Lauter then felt able—and indeed impelled—to make use of Nietzsche's texts, both published and unpublished. And yet the spirit of his ef-fort remains no less salutary than his interpretation remains deserving of atten-tion; for it stands in resolute opposition to all those who would ignore what Nietzsche actually says in favor of their often questionable glosses on his mean-ing and the upshot of his thought.

To be sure, Müller-Lauter himself can be, has been, and perhaps should be faulted for himself ignoring important considerations pertaining to the texts he draws upon so extensively here—notably, considerations of context, of period, and of the status of the writings in question themselves (published or from Nietz-sche's notebooks and other *Nachlaß*). Indeed, his own sensitivity to such issues increased markedly even between the writing of the original version of this book and the time—just a few years later—of his writing of the two essays incorpo-rated into the present version of it, as its last two chapters. These chapters were not part of the original German edition of the book but will be included in fu-ture German editions. Chapter 8, "Nietzsche's 'Doctrine' of the Will to Power," first appeared as "Nietzsches 'Lehre' vom Willen zur Macht" in *Nietzsche-Studien* volume 3 (1974): 1–60. Chapter 9, "The Organism as Inner Struggle," first ap-peared as "Der Organismus als Innerer Kampf: Der Einfluss von Wilhelm Roux auf Friedrich Nietzsche" in *Nietzsche-Studien* volume 7 (1978): 189–223, 233–35. They are incorporated into the book—at the request of the author, who himself controls the rights to them—here for the first time.

In these essays, in the course of extending his interpretation to several further aspects of Nietzsche's thought, Müller-Lauter both attempts to justify his gen-eral manner of using Nietzsche's published and unpublished texts (while allow-ing that it may have been less guarded than it should have been) and to show how his mode of interpretive endeavor might be carried on more judiciously. Readers with a critical-scholarly sensibility refined by the attention given to this matter in recent years, and who may be taken aback by Müller-Lauter's way of availing himself of Nietzsche's texts, should thus not only be prepared to make some allowances for the state of the art when the book was written but also refer to his discussion of the matter and modified practice in the last two chapters.

Müller-Lauter surely is on firm ground, however, in insisting that it is at least a necessary (if not a sufficient) condition of the soundness of an interpretation of Nietzsche's thinking on some matter that it accord with what he actually says about it and that passages can be found in which he says things along the lines of the interpretation being offered. And he sought to make it as clear as he could that (unlike a number of his interpretive rivals) his interpretation amply satisfies this condition. If we today set the bar higher in this respect, we do so by way of basic agreement with him about how one ought to proceed in Nietzsche interpretation.

The interest and merit of Müller-Lauter's interpretation, moreover, are quite independent of the manner of its presentation. He may make extensive use of language extracted from Nietzsche's published and unpublished writings to set it out; but if this practice is thought to sever (or at least loosen) the links between the material extracted and the contexts in which its meaning alone can be properly discerned, then for that very reason this appropriated language may be read as that of Müller-Lauter himself as interpreter. What it loses in Nietzschean authority when viewed with these concerns in mind, it gains back when regarded simply as a part of Müller-Lauter's interpretive-expository vocabulary (for which he is heavily indebted to Nietzsche as well as to the German language more generally). The quotation marks used and citations given are not essential to understanding what he is saying; and one does better to focus upon the latter than to concern oneself with whether, in the Nietzschean text in which some phrase appeared, it is best construed in just the same way.

Matters are quite different, of course, when some full sentences or even paragraphs are cited in support or illustration of some interpretive point being made. In such cases the relation between them and the interpretation Müller-Lauter is offering is an important issue. And if one is to do justice to him, as well as to benefit from one's encounter with his discussion, one will do best to focus one's attention upon the latter sort of issue, without allowing concerns of the former sort to get in one's way.

The leitmotiv of Müller-Lauter's interpretation is that, while there are indeed significant "contradictions" or tensions and conflicts in Nietzsche's thinking with respect to a good many of the most important matters he discusses, they at least very often relate in interesting and important ways to what he believes to be "contradictory" states of affairs in these matters themselves. Before we criticize Nietzsche for his failure to achieve (or even to be particularly concerned with) the kind of consistency we might wish a philosopher's thinking to exhibit, therefore, he challenges us to suspend the assumption that things ought to be that way and to look with him at whether they might not actually be otherwise—or at any rate, at whether they might be more complicated, ambiguous, and "contradictory" than we can do justice to with the kinds of concepts and analytical tools at our disposal. The thinking he is (and we are) able to do when making this attempt will inevitably be difficult, tentative, and unstable; and we can never be sure what to make of many of the most intriguing "contradictions" we come up with. But we can no more dismiss out of hand the claims upon us of such thinking than we can be assured of its soundness.

Müller-Lauter leaves us with the question of the ultimate tenability of Nietzsche's thought, in view of the "contradictions" that are so fundamental to it—a question that all who take Nietzsche seriously must confront and deal with in some way. If something must give, he does not say what he thinks it ought to be. He does make it clear, however, that it was for very powerful reasons that Nietzsche's thinking pulled in such contrary directions and that it is as unsatisfactory to abandon one line of thought or the other as it is difficult to reconcile them. Müller-Lauter's Nietzsche can be neither easily embraced nor lightly dismissed. It is high time, however, that his interpretation enter the fray of English-language discussion of how to understand what Nietzsche was up to and what to make of it.

A note on notes and references: In the original edition Müller-Lauter's hundreds of footnotes were printed at the bottoms of the pages and often filled a substantial portion of the page. A fair number of these notes were simply identifications of cited material. These have been integrated into the main text, following the standard practice of using readily identifiable English-translation acronyms and Nietzsche's part and section numbers whenever possible, in the interest of making this information readily available in a manner with which English-speaking readers will be familiar. A key to these and other references is provided on pages xvii–xviii. Other notes have been renumbered and gathered together at the end of the book. It is hoped that this deviation from the original will not inconvenience many readers and will allow the main arguments to emerge more clearly. The extensive scholarship and further argumentation in the notes do warrant their consultation, however; and readers should be sure at least to locate them and consult them as may be appropriate to their interests and concerns.

❖ ❖ ❖

The appearance of this translation owes much to many who have had a hand in it at one point or another, including Jörg Salaquarda of the University of Vienna, who first proposed undertaking the project; Hans-Robert Cram of De Gruyter, whose cooperation made it possible; Richard Martin of the University of Illinois Press, whose interest and assistance have been crucial; and my research assistant, Craig Matarrese, who was very helpful in the final stages of the preparation of the manuscript. But the greatest debt is owed to the translator, the late David J. Parent of Illinois State University, who agreed to undertake the project without promise of any compensation other than its intrinsic worth and who produced a very fine translation indeed in a remarkably short time. Sadly, Parent did not live to see the book's publication, suffering a massive heart attack not long after the translation was completed and dying several months later, on Christmas Eve 1997. He was a true scholar and gentleman, to whom the existence of this volume will stand as a lasting tribute.

—Richard Schacht

Preface

This book is the result of investigations into the history of modern nihilism. Reflections on Nietzsche's significance for the problematic of nihilism compelled me to rethink the basic questions of his philosophical thought. In this endeavor Nietzsche's thematization of contradictions turned out to be a fruitful point of departure. The elaboration of Nietzsche's questions and answers, in my opinion, throws a great deal of light on this philosopher's actual and merely apparent contradictions, which his interpreters have noted repeatedly.

The present book uses the procedure of an immanent portrayal and critique of Nietzsche's philosophy. The effort to grasp a thinker in his innermost concerns seems to me unavoidable even when one wishes to consider him "from the outside"—from any vantage point whatsoever. For this makes it possible to avoid overhasty interpretations and evaluations, of which Nietzsche scholarship offers a great number of examples. Although any attempt at an immanent critique may be guided by a preconcepton, this preconception undergoes corrections imposed by the object of the critique, leading to a more adequate understanding.

In view of these remarks, this book's restriction to an immanent-critical portrayal of Nietzsche's philosophy has two implications. First, Nietzsche's significance within the history of modern nihilism is not the theme of this investigation, although, of course, the preliminary studies required for such an investigation were undertaken. And secondly, I forego a critique whose standpoint lies outside of Nietzsche's philosophy. The ideas presented in this book merely present the preconditions for such a critique. My last word on Nietzsche's philosophy is thus not stated here—assuming that it is possible at all to say one's last word on so rich and open a philosophy.

At this time [1971], any study of Nietzsche faces the difficulty that a considerable number of important posthumous manuscripts have not yet been published.

Only eight of the probable thirty volumes of the *Kritische Gesamtausgabe,* which will remedy this deficiency, have appeared to date. Therefore I have had to rely on and quote from the *Großoctavausgabe,* which is problematic in many respects. However, I also consulted the volumes of the *Kritische Gesamtausgabe* that have appeared in print so far. Moreover, I am grateful to Professor Mazzino Montinari, of Florence, for important suggestions, mainly with regard to yet unpublished texts. Dr. Montinari was so kind as to read the proofs of this book. Since the publication process meanwhile was nearly finished, I was no longer able to include a few interesting posthumous fragments in my discourse. In any case, they did not call for a modification of the views I express.

I owe some ideas, suggestions, and references, especially to secondary literature, to my assistant, Jörg Salaquarda. In addition he provided formal guidance for this work from the beginning and he also assembled the bibliography and the index of names that appears in the German edition.

—Wolfgang Müller-Lauter
  Berlin, March 1971

Abbreviations

English-language versions of citations from Nietzsche's writings generally follow the listed translations and are identified in the customary fashion, by section number after the indicated English-language acronyms:

AC   *The Anti-Christ,* trans. R. J. Hollingdale. Penguin Books: London, 1990.

BT   *The Birth of Tragedy,* trans. W. Kaufmann. Random House: New York, 1967.

BGE   *Beyond Good and Evil,* trans. W. Kaufmann. Random House: New York, 1966.

CW   *The Case of Wagner,* trans. W. Kaufmann. Random House: New York, 1967.

D   *Daybreak,* trans. R. J. Hollingdale. Cambridge University Press: New York, 1982.

EH   *Ecce Homo,* trans. W. Kaufmann. Random House: New York, 1967.

GS   *The Gay Science,* trans. W. Kaufmann. Random House: New York, 1974.

GM   *On the Genealogy of Morals,* trans. W. Kaufmann. Random House: New York, 1989.

HA   *Human, All Too Human,* trans. R. J. Hollingdale. Cambridge University Press: New York, 1986.

HL   *"On the Uses and Disadvantages of History for Life,"* Second *Untimely Meditation;* see UM below.

TI   *Twilight of the Idols,* trans. R. J. Hollingdale. Penguin Books: London, 1968.

UM   *Untimely Meditations,* trans. R. J. Hollindale. Cambridge University Press: New York, 1983.

WP   *The Will to Power,* trans. W. Kaufmann and R. J. Hollingdale. Random House: New York, 1968.

WS   *The Wanderer and His Shadow,* the second part of the second volume of *Human, All Too Human* (originally published separately, and preserving its original separate section numbering).

Z   *Thus Spoke Zarathustra,* trans. W. Kaufmann. Viking Penguin: New York, 1966.

German-language editions of Nietzsche's writings used are referred to by volume and page number and other data as may be appropriate:

BAW   *Friedrich Nietzsche Werke und Briefe. Historisch-Kritische Gesamtausgabe, Werke,* 5 vols. Munich (Beck), 1933ff.

GA   *Großoktavausgabe,* ed. by the Nietzsche Archive, 19 vols. in three divisions. Leipzig, 1894–1912. "*Nachlaß*" (unpublished notes) when not otherwise identified, refers to GA.

Ges. Br.   *Friedrich Nietzsches Gesammelte Briefe,* 5 vols. Leipzig, 1905ff.

KGW   *Kritische Gesamtausgabe: Werke,* ed. by G. Colli and M. Montinari, ca. 30 vols. in 8 divisions. Berlin, 1967ff.

Nietzsche

Introduction

It is equally disastrous for the mind to have a system and to have none. Surely, then, it will have to decide to combine the two.
—Friedrich Schlegel, *Athenäum*-Fragment, 53

The contradictions inherent in Nietzsche's works have given his interpreters a great deal of trouble from the first. In many cases these inconsistencies can be arranged in a temporal sequence and regarded as phases in Nietzsche's philosophical development. The most drastic changes or reorientations can usually be divided into three to five phases. Upon closer examination other contradictions in this philosopher's thinking prove to be merely apparent, resulting from his use of the same general term to designate differently valued specifications of a single state of affairs,[1] to judge one state of affairs in terms of its varying relationships to other states of affairs,[2] or to characterize it with regard to its own different intrinsic aspects.[3]

Yet inconsistencies in Nietzsche's fundamental discourse remain. Nietzsche scholars have displayed a broad range of reactions. Some have held that because of his confusing statements Nietzsche cannot be ranked among the great philosophical thinkers.[4] Others have valued him as an artist who should not be mistaken for a philosopher,[5] a philosophical poet from whom conceptual rigor cannot be expected,[6] or an over-imaginative writer who did not subject the "ethereal offspring" ['*luftigen Kinder*'] of his mind to "critique and control by reality" and therefore achieved no "harmony" either with reality or with himself.[7] He has also been misused as a writer of aphorisms whose thinking offers "a random selection of timely sayings."[8] Finally, various scholars have attempted either to show that Nietzsche's thinking is coherent in its essential lines or to systematize him after the fact.

The scholars who seek overall coherence in Nietzsche's works differ in their approach to the problem. The most extreme position denies that any significant contradictions can be found in Nietzsche. Thus Hans Vaihinger states that Nietzsche's ideas, "despite their aphoristic form and unsystematic sequence, form a

strictly coherent, logically satisfactory whole; they flow with immanent necessity from a single basic principle and combine into a seamless circle."[9] Vaihinger
sees his task as to assemble "the splinters scattered in apparent disorder, the *disjecta
membra,* into a strictly coherent system."[10] Of course, he must admit that besides
the "main stream" elaborated by himself all sorts of "secondary sub-currents" can
be found in Nietzsche. However, when he adds that this is the case with other
thinkers too,[11] he trivializes the nearly incomparable difficulties faced by Nietzsche-interpretation.

Alfred Baeumler, although no less concerned than Vaihinger with demonstrating the coherence of Nietzsche's work, expresses himself somewhat more cautiously. According to him, "Nietzsche's intuitions" form a system as long as one
knows how "to distinguish essential writings from fleeting notes."[12] To be sure,
the criterion for such a distinction seems ultimately to reside in Baeumler's own
"intuition." Since he sees the idea of eternal recurrence as contradicting Nietzsche's fundamental doctrine of the will to power, he is compelled to rank it among
the "fleeting" remarks that cannot be fitted into "the system." He marginalizes it
as the "expression of a highly personal experience," that is, of a religious nature.[13]

The insight that contradictory lines of thought do exist in Nietzsche's works
does not necessarily require that one renounce "systematization." One can, as
Georg Simmel did, select from the totality of Nietzsche's statements "those which
provide a concise, unified, and meaningful intellectual whole." Simmel admits
that statements of Nietzsche's can be cited that are "irreconcilably contrary" to
the interpretation he presents.[14] Yet, despite his more cautious estimate of his own
interpretation compared with Vaihinger and Baeumler, Simmel too brackets out
the problem of contradiction.

Another possibility is to try to keep the "whole" Nietzsche in view with all his
contradictions while still asserting the intrinsic, original unity of his work. This
has been done by positing as the innermost core something not expressed by
Nietzsche himself, at least not in the sense of grounding the contradictions. Attempts to lay bare the hidden roots of Nietzsche's thinking have led to crude
simplifications as well as to profound interpretations.

Georg Lukács, for instance, writes that "the system" of Nietzsche's "colorfully
scintillating, mutually contradictory myths" consists in their all being "myths of
the imperialistic bourgeoisie to mobilize against its main enemy," socialism.[15] Karl
Jaspers, however, says that "the contradictions and circularity in the movement
of Nietzsche's thought" are "in the last analysis merely the means of treating *indirectly* something that lies beyond form, law, and what is sayable," namely, the
most hidden ground of being.[16] Martin Heidegger foregoes seeking out "the various discrepancies, contradictions, and oversights, the overhasty and often also

superficial and accidental in Nietzsche's representations" in order to discover, "*on the contrary, the realm of his real inquiry.*"[17] Heidegger thus seeks to penetrate into what is left unsaid by Nietzsche, hidden from his own self, although it supplies the implicit underpinnings of his entire work, that is, a metaphysics of forgotten being.

Such interpretations disregard the problem of contradictions in favor of an uncontradictory foundation of Nietzsche's philosophical thinking that is not elaborated or even considered by Nietzsche himself. The various interpreters identify very different things as that foundation, depending on their own standpoints. Orienting oneself by the multiplicity of such interpretations, one sinks into the quagmire of contradictory Nietzsche-interpretations without having adequately examined Nietzsche's philosophy of contradictions in its specificity.

Attempts to derive his way of thinking from his particular personality seem to do more justice to its specific content. The philosopher's self-testimonials suggest such a psychological grounding. "I would have perished from each single one of my affects," he writes, "I always played one off against the other."[18] Looking back upon his work, Nietzsche in *Ecce Homo* speaks of a "dual series of experiences," an "accessibility to apparently separate worlds," that is repeated "in every respect" in his nature. For he is *both* a decadent, *and* "its opposite: *one who has turned out well*."[19] Even Lou Andreas-Salomé tried to grasp as the basis of Nietzsche's philosophy his "complex personality," which fell into an "ever deeper *disharmony*" as a result of the "inner warfare of his drives."[20] In the course of its development, she writes, his philosophy became more and more "a monstrous reflection of his self-image"; Nietzsche generalized "his soul into the world soul."[21] Ernst Bertram, too, in his striving for a mythic transfiguration of Nietzsche, starts from his "duality of soul."[22] While Andreas-Salomé stresses that Nietzsche strove futilely for the unity of his personality, Bertram ascribes to the philosopher the "task of reconciliation, of the unification of the incompatible."[23] Apparently myth-formation is to take on and advance this task. It seems to Bertram "as if the whole development of the Nietzsche-image has run its course to a myth of the believing doubter, a legend of the God-seeking blasphemer, a figure of the prophetic beginning of the end."[24]

But whether the contradictions are deduced from psychology or obfuscated by myths, the reduction to Nietzsche's particular personality that underlies such approaches always begins by eliminating the *philosophical* state of the question. If Nietzsche's assertions are understood merely as emanating from his individual temperament, the truth claim of these conflicting series of ideas can no longer be examined seriously in terms of objective contents discussed by Nietzsche. Things are different if, with Michael Landmann, one seeks to understand Nietzsche's contradictions as stemming "not from personal eccentricity," but rather as the "fateful expression of a late epoch."[25] This late epoch is characterized by awareness of increasing discrepancies because since the Renaissance "cultural fields have acquired autonomy," shattering the coherence of the cosmos that had previously been "possible."[26] That being the case, Nietzsche's self-contradictions are not essentially personal. They express, rather, the contradictoriness of the modern world. And Landmann rightly observes that Nietzsche's inner strife is "common to us all" and that preoccupation with his thought therefore has a more than antequarian significance.[27]

Nietzsche understands himself essentially as a critic of his time. Yet he states: "Whoever attacks his time, can attack only *himself:* what, then, can he see if not himself?"[28] But for one's own time to be attacked in the self, that self must have been exposed to the various spiritual movements of the time and thus expanded to complete awareness of the time. So Nietzsche's ambition, his torment, and also his happiness consist in this: "To explore the whole sphere of the modern soul, to have sat in its every nook" (WP 1031). Though "impassioned for independence" he still has the "most dependent soul" because he is so exposed to the present age and "more tormented by all the smallest ropes . . . than others are by chains."[29]

Reflecting on himself, that is, on his own time, he finds that "all of us have unconsciously, involuntarily in our bodies values, words, formulas, moralities of *opposite* origin" (CW).[30] He discovers that "the problem of the nineteenth century" consists in the "difference between its ideals and their contradiction." He is preoccupied with the question whether this contradictoriness must be merely the expression of weakness, "sickness" or decay, which he sees in so many forms in the phenomena of his time, or whether it also contains the seeds of future strength and health, of a synthesis. And he concludes that it "could be the *precondition of greatness* to grow to such an extent in violent tension" (WP 111). What Nietzsche here calls only a possibility, he expresses in various contexts as his conviction, namely, that the contradictions in culture and society must be enhanced and deepened, because only through them can something higher be reached. He also states, conversely, that when opposites approximate each other, this must lead to their degeneration (cf. WP 885).

General references to the *origin* of contradictions in Nietzsche's thinking can, however, as little free us from the real philosophical problem as can allusions to their overcoming in any *future.* The inconsistencies must be examined closely. Nietzsche scholarship has hitherto concentrated mainly on the contradiction between the doctrines of the will to power, or of the overman, and the theory of the eternal recurrence of the same. Karl Löwith sees this as Nietzsche's "fundamental contradiction," stemming "from a basic conflict in the relation between man and the world—without God and a common order of creation." This is Nietzsche's major contradiction, and it lies on a different plane than the many resolvable "inconsistancies" found in his works.[31] According to Löwith, at the very zenith of modernity, Nietzsche, with his idea of eternal recurrence, revives antiquity's view of the world but remains unable to harmonize this notion with his remarks on the overman. With a penetrating analysis of Nietzschean texts, Löwith ascribes particular significance to the origin of the idea of eternal recurrence and confronts it with the "modern" idea of the overman.

Eugen Fink, on the contrary, emphasizes the future of both of Nietzsche's theories. As Fink claims, "in his concept of Dionysos" Nietzsche thinks "the two Janus-faces together"; he does not resort to "mythical memory" only when he wants "to express his recalcitrant unitary basic conception of life"; rather, he stands in the "morning twilight of a new myth of the divinity of the world." Nietzsche does not suppress the contradiction between the will to power and eternal recurrence; rather, he combines the two in a unity. Of course, he himself did not comprehend "the peculiar nature of this unity."[32]

The inherent deficiency in these and other attempts to reconcile the *contradictions* [*Gegensätze*] *in Nietzsche's philosophy* is that they do not take *Nietzsche's philosophy of contradictions* sufficiently into account. Nietzsche sought to underscore contradictoriness [*Gegensatz*] as constitutive of the world even more fundamentally than his above-cited remarks suggest. For Nietzsche, the whole of reality is determined from the outset by the "struggle" of opposites. In the course of his philosophizing he sees himself compelled to describe the antitheses in detail with complete sharpness. His goal, to be sure, is to synthesize things that stand in a peculiar relationship by their very opposition. But again and again what Nietzsche tries to articulate into a unity ultimately breaks apart. Incompatibility replaces mere opposition. The more drastically he seeks to overcome it, the more clearly it emerges. His philosophy of contradictions leads to insurmountable contradictions in his philosophical thinking.

Nietzsche repeatedly thematized the problem of "contradictoriness" [*Gegensätzlichkeit*]. The present book will examine the scope of this thematization and the grounds and abysses to which it leads. Inquiring into the nature of "real" oppositions, Nietzsche destroys metaphysical convictions and logical validity-claims and fashions his theory of "*wills to power*" (this use of the plural is deliberate) that interrelate in their play of forces. Seeking the origin of the value-conflicts rampant in his century, he is forced to elaborate his historico-philosophical ideas, which are oriented primarily on the phenomenon of morality. His inquiry into the wills to power that collapse under the struggle of contradictions opens up for him the *problem of nihilism*. The contradictoriness of wills to power as the ultimate reality transforms his understanding of truth. But the two factors that constitute his "new truth" turn out to be incompatible.

As Nietzsche tries to envisage the human being who will be able to master the contradictions, he creates the image of the *overman* [*Übermensch*]. But this figure splits into two mutually incompatible images. The one type of overman he imagines is the synthesis of all opposites, the *Yes* to everything that was, is, and will be, and so must be exposed to the claim of the *theory of eternal recurrence,* which this *Yes* without restriction requires. The other type of overman, the relentless strong man, also experiences his highest development in confrontation with the theory of eternal recurrence. This theory itself, moreover, turns out to be *intrinsically* contradictory, so that it cannot possibly be thought of as the valid expression of the one world complex generated by contradictions.

This book might seem to some, in the end, to reach the same results as prior Nietzsche scholarship. That is not the case, as the book itself will show. For example, the often repeated allegation that the theory of the will to power, or that of the overman, is incompatible with eternal recurrence will be shown to be merely apparent, while on the other hand essential inconsistencies not previously noted by Nietzsche-interpreters will become evident.

The following chapters will seek to elucidate Nietzsche's work in terms of his own philosophical point of departure and to trace it from there to the highest developments of his reasoning. Only in this way can the interconnections of his ideas, as well as his repeated failure on various levels of thought, be brought to light. The question remains whether a philosopher inevitably fails if he succumbs repeatedly to the "fascination of the opposing point of view" and refuses to be deprived of the "stimulus of the enigmatic" character of existence (WP 470).

1

Apparent Contradictions and
Real Contradictions of the Will to Power

The will to power can manifest itself only
against resistances. —*The Will to Power*, 656

Discussion of the problem of contradictions in Nietzsche's thought encounters a peculiar difficulty: his statements about the *existence* of contradictions seem themselves to be contradictory. On the one hand, he says that "one is fruitful only at the cost of being rich in contradictions" (TI 5:3). "To be *classical*, one must possess all strong, seemingly contradictory gifts and desires" (WP 848). What he admires about Händel, Leibniz, Goethe, and Bismarck—who are "characteristic of the *strong German type*"—is the relentlessness of life "among antitheses, full of that supple strength that guards against convictions and doctrines by employing one against the other and reserving freedom for itself" (WP 884). It is Nietzsche's basic "insight . . . that with every growth of man, his other side must grow too" (WP 881). If one seeks to abolish the reverse side, then the ideal of the front side, which one would precisely like to preserve, also disappears.[1] Opposites belong together as complementary. Therefore, counter-tensions must be promoted in the direction toward emergence of the *highest man*. He could represent "the *antithetical character of existence* most strongly." And it should find in him its "glory and sole justification" (WP 881).

   This sounds all the more bewildering when Nietzsche, on the other hand, denies that any opposites at all can be found in reality. "There are no opposites: only from those of logic do we have the concept of the opposites—and falsely transfer it to things" (WP 552). Accordingly, he demands that one "remove antitheses from things after comprehending that we have projected them there" (WP 124). On closer inspection, however, the contradiction occurring here proves to be only apparent. To make this clear, logic's role in establishing opposites must first be inquired into. It must be noted, too, that for Nietzsche logic itself is something that has become. Its principles are not an ultimate, irreducible given, prior to all world interpretation. They arise from the "compulsion to arrange a world for ourselves in which *our existence* is made possible" (WP 521). This compulsion is a "subjective" one, that is, it arises from man's particular vital conditions; hence it is "a biological compulsion" (WP 515).[2] In the original "realm of illogic"— he writes in *The Gay Science*—those beings "who made inferences in a way different from ours perished."

> Those, for example, who did not know how to find often enough what is "equal" as regards both nourishment and hostile animals—those, in other words, who subsumed things too slowly and cautiously—were favored with a lesser probability of survival than those who guessed immediately upon encountering similar instances that they must be equal. The dominant tendency, however, to treat as equal what is merely similar—an illogical tendency, for nothing is really equal—is what first created any basis for logic. (GS 111)[3]

In reality the similar has nothing to do with a supposed identicalness. There "is no degree of the same: but something completely different from the same." Precisely speaking, of course nothing is intrinsically similar any more than anything is intrinsically identical: similarity is always merely similarity "*for us.*"[4]

Previously, in *Human, All Too Human*, Nietzsche had gone even further in his striving to discover what logic could derive from: "It is from the lower organisms that man had inherited the belief that there are *identical things*" (HA I:18).[5] In these as well as in later investigations into the genealogy of the logical he was convinced that the act preceding and grounding all logic consists in making the same out of what intrinsically is not the same.[6]

This "identification," by which living creatures preserve themselves, is, then, a falsification of what is real. And only on the basis of falsification can "the will to *logical truth*" be implemented. It is *one* "drive" that rules in both: in the underlying falsification and in the logic erected upon it (WP 512). But reality is not only falsified by regarding what is different as identical. Such equation has as its basis the deceptive conviction that each of the equated things is and remains self-identical. Equation also always involves a fixation. In reality there is nothing fixed, nothing constant, but only the stream of incessant becoming and decaying. This basic idea of Nietzsche's stands most sharply contrary to the "Eleatism" that is deeply rooted in the needs of living creatures. Thus Nietzsche states that for plants every thing is not only "identical with itself," but also "in repose," indeed "eternal." Understanding both equation and fixation in their most extreme possibilities, he suspects finally that the "original belief of everything organic" may, from the very beginning, have been "that all the rest of the world is one and unmoving" (HA I:18).

Humans "constitute" things by means of acts of equation and fixation. The assumption of things resulting from such constitution is "the precondition for belief in logic." The "A" of logic is "a reconstruction of the thing" (WP 515). And the logical principles are merely imperatives "to posit and arrange a world" (WP 516). To be sure, we always find ourselves already in a "logically" ordered reality. But this is only because "long before logic itself entered our consciousness we did nothing but *introduce its postulates into events*" (WP 521).

That logic is inadequate to reality by no means makes it dispensable. It was originally "intended as *facilitation*" (WP 538) and has meanwhile become habitual. To that extent we are "*necessitated* to error" (TI 3:5) Nietzsche also grants its validity within such limits. Man could not live without its fictions (BGE 4). Its falsehood does not derogate from its usefulness to life (BGE 4). His critique is directed only at the fact that it "later acquired the effect of *truth*" (WP 538). Although logic is merely "a kind of backbone of vertebrates" but is "nothing true in-itself,"[7] it does not doubt "its ability to assert something about the true-in-itself" (WP 516). It amounts to the same whether it believes to find alleged truths in the things themselves or in archetypes of them, or whether it regards them as pure knowledge prior to all experience. In either case it fails to realize that its principles are merely "*regulative articles of belief* " (WP 530). A merely apparent world is presented as the true one and superimposed upon reality: logic degenerates into a two-world theory, into metaphysics.

What impelled humans to expand the vitally useful functions of logic into metaphysical "truths" will be discussed below. The foregoing remarks were meant simply to demarcate the horizon for the question of the origin of "opposites" from logic. Now this origin can be elaborated. Equation and fixation constitute logic. Its essential expression for the problem of "opposites" is found in the law of contradiction. This law excludes the possibility that one and the same "thing" can have opposite predicates at the same time. In it "reigns" the prejudice, characterized by Nietzsche as crude and false, "that one cannot have two opposite sensations at the same time" (WP 516), just as in the principle of identity we have "the 'apparent fact' of things that are the same" (WP 520). That we "are unable" to affirm and deny the same thing at the same time is only "a subjective empirical law" without any objective necessity (WP 516). "Not being able to contradict is proof of incapacity, not of 'truth'" (WP 515). In any case, it cannot be presupposed that the law of contradiction applies to "things," "which are something different, opposite."[8]

Thus Nietzsche defends contradiction against the claims of logic, for he sees it as inherent in reality itself. Yet he realizes that the logical postulate of non-contradiction [*Widerspruchlosigkeit*] gives rise to a merely apparent contradictoriness [*Gegensätzlichkeit*] that obscures the actual contradictory nature [*Gegensatzcharakter*] of life. The exclusion of opposite determinations from a state of affairs cannot simply deny what is excluded, since this is actually present or repeatedly makes its presence felt. It merely separates it off from what is supposedly self-identical. What is separated off can then be further articulated internally according to the pattern of identity. Thus a multiplicity of things posited as separate is conceived. Logic is now elevated to the "criterion of *true being*" and transformed into metaphysics, and the originally subjective means of expression are projected into reality. "All those hypostases: substance, attribute, object, subject, action, etc.," are posited "as realities" (WP 516). Reality is torn apart and only after the fact is a *commercium* of what allegedly rests in itself constructed—by means of a pattern of causality, for example. But "cause and effect: such a duality probably never exists; in truth we are confronted by a *continuum* out of which we isolate a couple of pieces" (GS 112). What underlies it is "the separation of the 'deed' from the 'doer,' of the event from someone *who produces* events, of the process from a something that is not process but enduring *substance,* thing, body, soul, etc." (WP 631, cf. 55ff., and GM I:13).

Where apparent realities cannot without further ado be placed into a context, they stand out as opposites "for a certain measure of optics." But in truth that is not what is involved: the complexes of event perceived as things and compared with one another display merely a *difference of degree,* for example, "a difference in the tempo of the event," as in the case of the supposed opposites: motion—rest (WP 552). And since it is "easier to think opposites than degrees,"[9] a "bad habit" leads us moreover "into wanting to comprehend and analyze the inner world, too, the spiritual-moral world, in terms of such opposites" (HA, "WS" 67). Thus at last "the fundamental faith of the metaphysicians" arises: "*faith in opposite values*" (BGE 2).

So much about the origin of the supposed opposites that are believed real from "those of logic" (WP 552). Nietzsche's critique is directed not at the use of the logical opposites, whose life-facilitating functions are indispensable for man, but rather at their assumed objectivity. It has already been pointed out that he counters the law of contradiction with the reality of opposites. Nonetheless we do not encounter here anything incompatible. More precisely seen, what Nietzsche contests is only any antithesis that is understood as *absolute* and in which separately existing entities are supposed to be direct opposites. Yet he does indeed assert an immanent contradictoriness of world reality, based on the concrete polarities in which the one world has always been developing and continues to develop. This is the basic motif of his thinking once he has overcome the influence especially of Schopenhauerian metaphysics, and it comes into play here: to assert the uniqueness of the world versus every kind of metaphysical dualism. The real "opposites" that his philosophical thinking admits are not mutually exclusive; they can be derived from one another.

The second aphorism of the final chapter of *Beyond Good and Evil* makes Nietzsche's view stand out even more clearly than his earlier statements (in HA I:1). Here he opposes the appearance that the will to truth could not originate from the will to deception, the selfless act not from selfishness, disinterested contemplation not from lust. He counters the metaphysical conclusion that "the things of highest value must have another origin *of their own*," which lay "in the lap of Being, the intransitory, the hidden god, the 'thing-in-itself'" with the argument that the "values of the good and revered things" could consist precisely in their being "insidiously related, tied to, and involved with these wicked, seemingly opposite things—maybe even one with them in essence" (BGE 2).

Nietzsche, as is known, made copious use of the method of deriving a state of affairs from its opposite. The genealogy of the logical from the illogical, which we have come upon, is just one example. In general he considers the will to ignorance, to untruth, to be the ground of all will to knowledge. The will to truth is only a "refinement," but not the absolute opposite of the will to untruth (BGE 24). Nietzsche's genealogies, especially those of his moral-critical unmasking psychology, were to no slight extent a reason for the fascination his thinking aroused in the early decades of the twentieth century. As a reaction, reference was often made to their questionable aspects, especially their simplifications and forced readings. Yet critiques of Nietzsche, however justified they may be on specific points, mostly do not get beyond the surface. It is more essential to give full value to the basic effort of Nietzsche's philosophizing: to accept the contradictory character of existence as a fact, indeed as an ultimate given (though in its concretion, it repeatedly withdraws when one seeks to apprehend it) without thereby succumbing to a metaphysical dualism or systematic thinking in Hegel's manner.

Can Nietzsche still speak seriously of opposites if he reduces them to differences of degree? Is the affirmative use of the concept "opposite"—a few examples of which we have cited above—perhaps merely a figurative mode of expression for which he should not be held accountable? Does his doctrine of the continuum of ceaseless happening [*haltosen Geschehens*] as what is truly real leave any room for anything truly antithetical?

What Nietzsche wants to exhibit, however, is precisely the *real oppositions* at the ground of what happens, indeed as what makes it possible for anything to happen, to begin with. In order to uncover these oppositions, one must first show the consequences that follow from his denial of the constant in favor of pure process. The fiction of the constant results from making-equal and -determinate

[*Gleich- und Fest-machen*]. The being that performs these acts, however, does not originally have a fixed intrinsic identity, although it understands itself as such. The only reason for this self-understanding is that it determines itself as self-identical. Here too it is true that "*not* similarity," which must be "denied," but rather "our adjusting them and making them similar" is the fact (WP 485). Nietzsche once even says that we have "invented the reality of *things* and projected them into the medley of sensations" (WP 552).[10]

How do we go about constituting our self-understanding? We *believe* "in a *unity* under all the various moments of the highest sense of reality" that are given to us. We trace back this unity to a ground common to the multifariousness of such experiences. That ground is understood as the one cause out of which everything encompassed by that belief is supposed to emerge. Since the reality of feelings seems to indicate one cause, they themselves are posited as the same. We give the cause itself the name, for example, of "subject." "'Subject' is the fiction that many *similar* states in us are the effect of *one* substratum: but it is *we* who have first *created* the 'similarity' of these states" (WP 485). How, then, can we characterize this "we" that believes in its unity and exists prior to all self-identification? The "individual" is as inappropriate for this original thing as is that of "subject." This too is a matter of our secondary and "false autonomy . . . as *atom*" (WP 785). But can a personal pronoun be applied to something pre-individual? Is it, then, truly a "we" or an "I"?

This I, or ego, "our oldest article of faith" (WP 635), is, in Nietzsche's view, another word for the subject. As he says of the subject that it is "not something given, but something added and invented and projected behind what there is" (WP 481), so he says of the "ego" that it is thought of and invented by thinking "as an adjunct to the multiplicity of its processes" (WP 574). "Through thought the 'ego' is posited" (WP 483). The multitude of thought-processes is, however, itself only an "*outside*": "a symptom of much more internal and more fundamental events."[11]

So again we must refer to what Nietzsche means by "events." Even what misunderstands itself as an "individual" must be understood as an event. The "individual" is in truth "the *entire process* in its entire course" (WP 785). It is something incessantly changing. Change occurs "pervasively": there is nothing permanent at the basis, *to which* it happens. In such an insight the "individual" dissolves into countless individuals that follow one another in infinitesimally small moments.[12] This characterization is, of course, not the whole picture. For it must be asked: what, nonetheless, holds this multiplicity together in that context that allows one to speak of a process? What makes it possible at all to speak of events in their sequence?

The sequence is constituted by the antagonism of a multiplicity of forces. Nietzsche repeatedly depicts man as such a multiplicity: "The *ego* is a multitude of person-like forces, of which now these, now those stand in the foreground as *ego* and look upon the others as a subject looks upon an influential and determinative outside world. The subject point leaps around; probably we sense the degrees of forces and drives as near and far and interpret as a plain landscape what in truth is a multitude of quantitative degrees."[13] Within the interplay of a multiplicity of forces and drives some specific one always takes command. But since each of them is "a kind of lust to rule," with its own particular "perspective that it would like to compel all the other drives to accept as a norm" (WP 481), rulership can be acquired and defended only in struggle. "Even the relationship of the ruler with those who are ruled" must still be understood "as a conflict, and the relationship of the obedient to the rulers as a resistance," that is, a struggle.[14]

The resulting conflict of the drives or forces is thus the condition for all events.[15] This conflict can never come to a standstill, "for every drive also incites its counter-drive."[16] "One drive stimulates the other; each one fantasizes (i.e., interprets, develops *its* perspective) and wants to impose its own kind of error, but each of these errors immediately again becomes the pretext for another drive (for example, contradiction, analysis, etc.)."[17] Thus man "has cultivated an abundance of *contrary* drives and impulses in himself" (WP 966). The contrary drives cause additional drives to be "moved."[18] "Each of these drives feels itself impeded or promoted, flattered, with regard to every other one; each has its own law of development (its rise and decline, its tempo, etc.)—and one is dying off when the other ascends."[19] In their "For and Against" (WP 481), in "the competition between affects" (WP 618), alliances form and break apart again; rulers replace one another; the subject-point leaps around.

"Interaction and struggle" in such a multiplicity lie at "the basis of our thought and our consciousness in general" (WP 490). Here the present study has penetrated through to the real contradictions that, in Nietzsche's view, antecede all logic. Even its axioms are merely the expression of the power constellations of impulses or forces to one another. "The *origin of the logical functions*" is first derived from their antagonism.[20] "The course of logical ideas and inferences in our brain today corresponds to a process and a struggle among impulses that are, taken singly, very illogical and unjust. We generally experience only the result of this struggle because this primeval mechanism now runs its course so quickly and is so well concealed" (GS 111).

If we pause to examine more closely the results of Nietzsche's deconstructions thus far, the suspicion arises that they were futile. Is what is destroyed not always restored? The "individual" was multiplied into a great number of "individuals";

the ego of the person proved to be a multitude of person-like forces; the subject split apart into "a multiplicity of subjects" (WP 490). Do not the rejected metaphysical apparent realities, which were traced back to logic, in the end comprise the sphere of true reality? The Cartesian substantiality of the thinking ego, against which Nietzsche repeatedly polemicizes,[21] has indeed proven untenable. But doesn't the ego, according to Nietzsche, consist in a multiplicity of substances?

Such a critique would take Nietzsche at his word when words fail him: "Unfortunately we have no words to designate what really exists."[22] If, despite his repeatedly stated conviction of the "immediacy of ultimate insights,"[23] he wants to give information about them, he has to use both the words of everyday language[24] and the traditional language of the metaphysics he opposes. He adopts its terminology, though without believing it can serve to "comprehend" anything. "No path leads from the concept to the essence of things."[25] The fundamental references to his critique of logic have already made this clear. The concept fails in two respects concerning the truth of what really exists: *first,* it fixates, whereas fleeting events are what really take place;[26] *secondly,* it subsumes many "unequal" cases as equal. The concept first arises "by equating what is unequal."[27] Nietzsche therefore rejects all words insofar as they lay claim to the concept, and he uses them merely as "*signs.*" They are supposed only to refer to states of fact. One must follow their referential character [*Hinweisungscharakter*], and not focus exclusively upon them; the conceptual must be left behind in order to arrive at what is "really present."

Nietzsche uses words such as "subject," "ego," "individual," "person" as *signs* for the elusive content of naming. And he rejects them as soon as he reflects on them as concepts. The same thing holds for words with which he characterizes the *mode of being* of what is truly real: impulse, force, affect. The word "*Trieb* ['impulse' or 'drive'] is only a translation into the language of feeling from the non-feeling."[28] Nor has "a *force* ever been demonstrated," but rather there are always only "*effects* translated into a completely foreign language" (WP 620, cf. 664). And even affects are nothing but "an *invention of causes* that do not exist." We should "*deny* them and treat them as *errors of the intellect*" (WP 670).

Occasionally, after such deconstruction of metaphysical concepts, Nietzsche draws back to largely formalized definitions of the real: for instance, when he characterizes reality as "dynamic quanta" that "stand in a relation of tension to all other dynamic quanta" (WP 635). Of course, such a way of speaking must not be understood "as concepts." From this starting point the peculiarities of real contradictions in Nietzsche's sense can now be elaborated more completely. The characteristics discovered in analyzing the "ego" apply—it must be noted—to the real as such. Perspectivism, as described above, is operative even in the "domain of the inorganic" (WP 637). Or, as Nietzsche formulates it more radically: there is "no inorganic world."[29] There is only *life,* that is, incessant processes of the establishment of force (cf. WP 642). The complex of events that we call "ego" is nothing but a particular concretion of life.

The relation of tension between the dynamic quanta constitutes their "essence" (WP 635). They do not first exist for themselves and then enter a relationship with one another. They exist only in the (incessantly changing) referentiality of all to all. The tension within the field of reference results from the antagonism of the quanta. Quanta stand opposed to one another; herewith an original qualitative difference of opposites is denied; for behind their assertion Nietzsche always sees the metaphysical dualism he opposes rearing its head. "We have a hard time breaking free of *qualities.*"[30] So we feel that "mere *quantitative differences* are something fundamentally distinct from quantity, namely . . . *qualities* which can no longer be reduced to one another" (WP 565). But what we there call quality is only "a *perspective* truth for *us;* not an 'in itself'" (WP 563).[31] The mere quantitative differences result only in a *difference of degree* of reality, which term Nietzsche, in his critique of logic and metaphysics, contrasts with the idea of "opposites."

Nietzsche sees, on the other hand, that the reduction of the qualitative to quanta is insufficient for the interpretation of "events": "In a purely quantitative world everything would be dead, stiff, motionless" (WP 964). The world is, however, in constant motion. The dynamics of quanta are understandable only under the assumption of a particular *quale.* Hence all qualities are not reducible to quantities (WP 564). "*Dynamis* still has an inner quality" (WP 618). This quality must be the only one there is at all, if indeed only quantitative differences of degree are discoverable in reality.

All events presuppose an antagonism. So what comprises this antagonism must be the sought-for *quale.* If Nietzsche defines it as force, then it holds true that "there is only one kind of force" (WP 814). The use of this term leads one to think of the concept of force in mechanics. But the mechanical concept is for Nietzsche just "an empty word" (WP 621). It is supposed to name the cause of changes in the motion and form of bodies, although it cannot express what is really at work there. Hence it needs at least "to be completed: an inner will must be ascribed to it" (WP 619). This inner will must, however, not be taken in the sense of the Aristotelian tradition: it does not involve the mere realization of something always pregiven as a disposition. Nietzsche seeks to "eliminate" pregiven "purposes" from willing.[32] Therefore he opposes most emphatically the teleological thinking of earlier philosophers. And he discovers "a disguised teleology"[33] even in Schopenhauer's doctrine of the blind will that is nonetheless capable of inventing an intellect for its service.

The next task is to remove the possibility of further misunderstandings that could arise when Nietzsche attaches the name "will" to the sole quality. References to his critique of Schopenhauer's theory of will can help clarify this issue. He rejects with particular emphasis the thesis of the *simplicity of the will*. Schopenhauer by this theory, as Nietzsche states, merely "adopted a popular prejudice and exaggerated it" (BGE 19). In truth, the will is not "something simple, a brute datum, underivable, and intelligible by itself" (GS 127), but rather "something *complicated,* something that is a unit only as a word" (BGE 19). The doer believes in the immediacy and undeceivability of his willing; he understands it as something that produces an effect, as a faculty (TI 3:5). But he is deceiving himself. He does not notice anything "of the mechanism of events and of the hundredfold fine work that needs to be done" so that any action can take place. And he has no idea "of the incapacity of the will in itself to do even the tiniest part of this work" (GS 127).

Thus, what Schopenhauer, appealing to "what is directly known to everyone,"[34] calls will, is not the *quale* Nietzsche seeks. It is so far from being so for him that he can deny the very existence of such a will. "*There is no such thing as will*": namely, when it is conceived as something simple, belonging to an ego-substance that could underlie our actions as their cause (WP 488).[35] We have "added" it too "to certain phenomena of consciousness."[36] As such a fabrication it is itself "an *effect,* and *not* the beginning and the cause."[37]

"The will," then, shares the lot of other self-definitions of the truly complex event "man," which were treated above. Nietzsche understands it as the mere appearance of a simplicity that is caused by a multiplicity hiding behind it in this way. The multiplicity is real; the "unity, *imagined.*"[38] The appearance remains hidden from consciousness; for consciousness itself is nothing more than such an appearance, insofar as it appears to be an irreducible intellect. Nietzsche's "critique of modern philosophy" in general is aimed at its having taken as its starting point the alleged "facts of consciousness" without seeing through the "*phenomenalism in introspection*" (WP 475). For what underlies "consciousness," which is "usually thought of as unique," is the countless multiplicity in the experiences of "many consciousnesses,"[39] as Nietzsche describes it, in view of the "tremendous association of living creatures"[40] that comprise the human body.[41] In the "interplay of many very unequivalent intelligences,"[42] the intellect is presented with "only a *selection* of experiences . . . moreover experiences that are utterly simplified, clearly arranged, made comprehensible, hence *falsified*—so that it in turn may continue with this simplifying and clear arranging, i.e., falsifying."[43]

What purpose does this falsifying simplification serve? We discovered a similar process when examining Nietzsche's genealogy of logic: to regard the dissimilar as similar is one of the conditions for preserving life. If the living being, man, must simplify and falsify the reality he encounters, the question remains why the multiplicity, which he always is, hides behind fictional unities, thus simplifying and falsifying his own being in his own view. It is easy to see the need for this. A multiplicity can survive the struggle against another one only by presenting itself as a simple phenomenon, that is, by hiding the struggles for domination immanent within itself not only from other multiplicities but even from itself; the "simple" must remain "protected and shut off" from its own truth. For only so can it fulfill the task it faces: to represent toward the outside the multiplicity constituted as a homogeneous whole by antitheses. Only in this way can something be prepared "that is generally called 'one will'": the act of willing.[44] In the shielded-off consciousness of the intellect this then appears to be an underivable given, although it is only "a resultant, a kind of individual reaction which necessarily follows a host of partly contradictory, partly congruous stimuli" (AC 14).

Behind consciousness and will, indeed "in every complicated organic being,"[45] "a crowd of consciousnesses and wills" thus emerges. Only in such underlying wills can Nietzsche's sole quality be found. Ultimately he coined for it the expression "will to power." He traces back to this the previously drawn characterizations of what is truly real: not only *force* must in the last analysis be understood as will to power (cf. WP 619), but the *affects*, too, are nothing but developments of the will to power, which is "the primitive form of affect" (WP 688, cf. 692), and the drives too are said to be traceable to the will to power. For in one of the plans from the 1882–85 period, Nietzsche notes: "Our intellect, our will, as well as our sensations, are dependent on our valuations: these correspond to our drives and their conditions for existing. Our drives are reducible to the *will to power*. The will to power is the ultimate fact we come down to."[46]

And this is not only the result of Nietzsche's analysis of the human self, as must be emphasized again and again. The will to power, as the ultimate "ground and character of all change" (WP 685), is the "essence" (BGE 186) of the world: it is the only *quale* that in its manifold gradations constitutes the world. The "radiation of power wills" stands behind everything that appears as force. A quantum of force is in reality a "power quantum," or more acutely: "a quantum of 'will to power.'" The quality of what is quantitatively different, its essence, can be defined more closely as a "will to violate and to defend oneself against violation" (WP 634). The "meaning" of violation is the domination characterized above. But the exercise of domination presupposes power. Insofar as all willing wants power, it is a "willing something." This something cannot be removed from the will. Where this happens, the will is no longer thought as what it is (WP 668, cf. 692).

But even the term "will to power" gives occasion for such misinterpretations as were already mentioned above in the discussions of other determinations Nietz-sche draws upon for what is ultimately there. Perhaps that is not the least reason why Nietzsche did not publish a book under this "not undangerous title":[47] it got no further than plans, drafts, and collections of material. The following pages will deal with misunderstandings against which Nietzsche's doctrine must be guarded. Essential features of the will to power will be brought out in the process.

In Part II of the posthumous (*Nachlaß*) Volume XIV of the *Gesamtausgabe,* edited by Peter Gast and Elisabeth Förster-Nietzsche, in the context of a passage in which Nietzsche writes that the Germans of today are no longer thinkers, there occurs the sentence: "The will to power as principle would be readily understand-able [*schon verständlich*] to them" (i.e., the Germans).[48] What is said there must come as a surprise after what has been said in this chapter. The will to power is a principle? Moreover, one that is apparently not all too difficult for the unthink-ing Germans to understand? Doesn't this statement militate against the interpre-tation of the will to power presented above? Isn't this will to power, then, after all a "more precise definition" of Schopenhauer's will to life, as E. Horneffer maintained?[49]

The text of the statement printed in the *Gesamtausgabe,* Volume XIV goes back to a deciphering by the brothers E. and A. Horneffer, which P. Gast adopted in preparing the edition.[50] Later, after his definitive break with Elizabeth Förster-Nietzsche, when rechecking the sentence once more, he discovered that one word had been deciphered falsely, changing the meaning of the sentence into its op-posite. M. Montinari, in KGW VIII/2 p. 114, confirms this reading, according to which the sentence reads: "The will to power as principle would be hard [*schwer*] for them to understand."[51] What is this supposed to mean?

For the unthinking Germans, talk of the will to power, insofar as power is spo-ken of, could seem to be "a confirmation of some *Reichs*-German aspirations."[52] Besides, they are accustomed to using the term "will" in the sense of Schopenhauer and his successors. Therefore, what Nietzsche says of the will to power must be *hard* for them to understand. Is the will to power, then, precisely not a "principle" in the sense of traditional metaphysics? Nietzsche does speak of a "principle" in the cited sentence, but like all other words with which he seeks to designate what is ultimately given, this term too must not be misunderstood in the sense of a con-cept. The word "principle," too, is used by Nietzsche merely as a vehicle by means of which he tries to penetrate through to something yet unsaid.

Nietzsche's will to power is certainly not a more precise determination of Schopenhauer's principle of the will to life. It also is not a will *in miniature* that now would stand as what is truly simple behind the supposedly simple will as conceived by Schopenhauer. If that were Nietzsche's line of argument, he would still remain caught in the metaphysical pattern of thought that he rejects. For he definitely does not seek to deduce the multiple from one principle; on the contrary, he sees everything simple as the product of a real multiplicity. Nietzsche's thinking was clarified, above, when we described his deconstruction of the subject and was taken up again concerning the deconstruction of our allegedly simple consciousness of will. The point here is to exclude the misunderstanding that multiplicity ultimately still refers, after all, to an ultimate "unity" in the sense of an arche, from which it stems. Nietzsche notes, for example, that it is "not necessary" to posit a unity behind the multiplicity of affects.[53] If the affects in turn are "reducible" to the will to power, still the will to power is not the one thing they are grounded on. For from the outset there is a "*multiplicity of 'wills to power'*: each with a multiplicity of means of expression and forms."[54]

What Nietzsche says in such statements about man also applies to the whole of reality: "*This world is the will to power—and nothing besides!*" It is "as a play of forces and waves of force at the same time one and many, increasing here and at the same time decreasing there, a sea of forces flowing and pushing together" (WP 1067). In talking of the unity of the many, Nietzsche is not envisaging a metaphysical root, but a reciprocal relation, indeed dependence of the many on one another, a dependence that brings them into the context of the one world. In that world everything is so tightly interwoven "that every displacement of power at any point would affect the whole system" (WP 638). In principle the following is true: "All unity is a unity *only as organization and cooperation*—just as a human community is a unity—as opposed to an atomistic anarchy, as a pattern of domination that *signifies* a unity but *is* not a unity" (WP 561).

That such a unity of organization and cooperation is formed and constantly transformed only by the multiply gradated antagonism of the many and their struggle with one another has been made sufficiently clear. What does this mean for understanding the will to power? Nietzsche points out that the will to power must rely on what offers it resistance; "it seeks that which resists it" (WP 656, cf. 693).[55] Therefore the will to power can be assessed by "how much resistance, pain, torture it endures and knows how to turn to its advantage" (WP 382). But if will to power is supposed to be the only reality, what can offer resistance to it can likewise be only will to power. Every expression of wills to power thus already presupposes a multitude of wills to power. The reality that Nietzsche finally comes upon is the multiplicity of wills to power relating to one another antithetically and forming the one world by such a relationship. *The* will to power is, in effect, the quality common to what is different quantitatively (in terms of power). But this commonness must not be reduced to the simplicity of a grounding principle: this quality exists only in the multiplicity of quantitative difference. Otherwise it could not be will to power, because there would be nothing opposed that would permit the overpowering. To speak of quality as if it existed in some way "in itself," "prior" to the quantitative particularizations, is to misunderstand Nietzsche in the sense of a metaphysics he opposed most determinedly.

Martin Heidegger's interpretation of the will to power could be cited as an example of such an interpretation. For Nietzsche, as Heidegger reads him, life does not have only "the drive to maintain itself," as Darwinism thinks; rather, it is "self-assertion."[56] But life can *assert* itself only when it constantly *overpowers* itself. The will to power is this "self-overpowering."[57] The "character of enhancement in will"[58] thus displayed causes it to advance from one stage of power to the next.[59] It exceeds and heightens "respectively itself." Thus, for Heidegger, "will to power" finally means: "the self-empowering of power for its own overpowering."[60] According to this interpretation, the will to power is not directed against other power-quanta, other wills to power, but rather develops intrinsically in its uniqueness. It moves self-sufficiently in the realm of its own being. In his interpretation, Heidegger sets off quality by itself, whereas according to Nietzsche it occurs only in the quanta. For Heidegger, then, the designated "self-assertion" is nothing other than "original assertion of essence."[61] All the will to power's "willing out beyond itself" is, in his interpretation, a "coming to itself to find and assert itself in the circumscribed simplicity of its essence."[62]

Heidegger has thus made the will to power a metaphysical principle unfolding out of itself, although remaining by itself and indeed ultimately returning to its own origin.[63] He seeks thereby to demonstrate "the inner relation of Nietzsche's will to power to Aristotle's *dynamis, energeia,* and *entelecheia.*"[64] He thinks he rediscovers in Nietzsche's concept of power, first, potency in the sense of *dynamis;* secondly, the exercise of power in the sense of *energeia;* and thirdly, the above-mentioned coming-to-itself (in the simplicity of essence) in the sense of *entelecheia.*

Heidegger does not believe that Nietzsche "can be interpreted directly with the help of Aristotelian teaching." He demands, rather, that both be taken back "to a more original context of questions."[65] What he sees as this context is the history of metaphysics interpreted as the history of being of the will and he sees metaphysics as reaching its perfection in Nietzsche's thought. Here we cannot go any further into Heidegger's design. But attention must be called to the fact that the attempt to insert Aristotle's highest determinations of being into Nietzsche's "will to power" blocks access to Nietzsche's particular way of thinking. Nietzsche draws no distinction—however hidden—in terms of *dynamis* and *energeia.* And the thought of a coming-to-itself in the sense of *entelecheia* is expressly rejected by Nietzsche for the will to power.[66]

Above all, Heidegger's thesis that the will to power always is "essential will . . . never the willing of a particular actual entity"[67] must be contradicted decisively. Certainly, this will never actually exists separate and in isolation, but only in the multiplicity of wills related to one another antithetically. In view of this fact, a problem arises. The wills to power do not occur in isolation, and yet the individuals who are powerful on their own do so—precisely in their relation to one another. What are they, then, in themselves? This question becomes even more acute when it is recalled that for Nietzsche they represent the ultimate givens. They neither stem from a metaphysical principle, nor can be derived from the whole of the world. For they constitute first of all the intrinsically flooding sea, which the world is, in Nietzsche's view. They can be neither atoms nor substances: for Nietzsche strives to demolish these concepts, as well as all related ones. The question "*Who* wants power?" (WP 693), so we hear him say, is absurd if it is asking for an ultimate bearer of the will to power.

But what, then, is that which is powerful on its own supposed to be? Nietzsche once wrote: "There is no will: there are only points of will [*Punktation*] that are constantly increasing or losing their power" (WP 715).[68] In the same passage, he speaks of "monads": to be sure, one may speak of them as of "atoms" only "relatively," because "a cruder world of the permanent" is thereby posited. In fact, Nietzsche's "points of will" remind one of Leibniz's immaterial "*points méta-physiques.*" Even his remarks on "*perspectivism,* by virtue of which every center of force—and not only man—construes all the rest of the world from *its own viewpoint*" (WP 636),[69] call to mind Leibnizian monadology.

To be sure, this relationship should not be overemphasized. Nietzsche's monads are neither constant, nor "windowless," nor are they at all "entelechies" in the Leibnizian sense. Although "the smallest world is the most durable" (WP 715), it still is not of temporally unlimited duration. Thus, it is also not correct to ascribe to Nietzsche's will to power substantiality (in the Leibnizian sense). The "struggle of the atoms" leads, "given certain differences of strength," to "two atoms" becoming one. "Likewise one becomes two when the inner state brings about a disgregation of the power-center."[70] "The 'number' of beings is itself in flux" (WP 520). That which is powerful on its own is thus itself something constantly changing, increasing power or decreasing it. Nietzsche's talk of multiplicities of will to power does not presuppose fixed units. The philosophical ultimate he discovers is never an actual (quantitative) ultimate. Every quantum of will to power can decrease as well as increase, not only incorporating new quanta in itself but also steadily disintegrating further.[71]

To the question of what it is that brings and holds together the incessantly changing organizations of will to power in itself, and also allows them to flow apart, the final answer is: it is contradictions that make possible all aggregation [*Aggregation*] as well as all disintegration [*Disgregation*]; indeed, such contradictions are both immanent in every organization and they confront it "from outside," from other organizations. The will to power requires contradictions, which of course also can themselves be only will to power. Contradiction first makes it into will to power.[72] By such dependence on contradiction, the will to power is, as Nietzsche says, originally "not a being, not a becoming, but a *pathos*," out of which "a becoming and effecting first emerge" (WP 635).

2

The Problem of Contradictions in Nietzsche's Philosophy of History

Goals do not exist, ideals contradict one another . . . —Nachlaß, GA XIV, 335

In chapter 1 we traced Nietzsche's philosophy of the contradictions inherent in the world down to their underlying determinations. This brought to light the constitutive character of contradictions for human existence understood as a process. But the general ideas considered so far left open the question of the particular concrete realities in which organization and disorganization of wills to power occur in the human individual and in the interhuman realms.

Nietzsche's philosophy of contradictions took its departure, no doubt, from the living experience of such "concrete realities." This kind of experience is what first raised for him the problem of man as a "being of contradictions." And Nietzsche's attempt to work out dependence on antitheses as a basic trait of the real as such, as evidenced in aspects of the doctrine of the will to power described above, must be understood both as a differentiation of human self-understanding and as an expansion of the content of that experience to the whole of existence. Against the background of what was depicted in chapter 1, Nietzsche's critique of his time and his observations on the history of philosophy must appear rather crude. Yet he believes he does not succumb to the "*basic error* of all historians," who do not realize that the "facts are all . . . much too small to be grasped."[1] He also knows that he often cannot speak differently than those to whom brute facts mean ultimate truth. Crudeness in description cannot be avoided anywhere, not even in describing "lawful" processes in the natural world, not to mention in the realm of history. In truth, facts everywhere point to constitutive processes of increasing or decreasing power. The components constantly escape final observation. They refer to a multiplicity that is never fully imaginable. Yet they find expression in what they constitute.[2] Whatever in Nietzsche evokes the impression of irreducible simplicity is constantly meant as something complex held together by a dominant "drive" or whose manifest "elements" are striving apart.

Nietzsche, who circles around the "modern soul" and settles in "its every nook," discovers signs of *disintegration* in coherent complexes. The modern age is the time of disintegration characterized by "*disorganizing* principles" (WP 65). Disorganization is shown in the heterogeneity of mutually contradictory valuations.[3] "We are living in the period when different views of life coexist; therefore this age is so instructive as rarely any other; therefore it is so sick, because it suffers at once from the evils of all trends."[4] The human being of the nineteenth century is "the *multifarious* man, perhaps the most interesting chaos there has ever been" (WP 883). He lacks the standard that would allow him to affirm one thing and condemn the other. The "universality in understanding" he strives for leads to "amenability to experience of whatever kind"; this results, in turn, in his "not knowing which way to turn" (TI 9:50). Where every claim, even the most diametrically opposite, is justified, no "new ideal" can form.[5] But our time really would need such a "new ideal," whose rule could restrain the centrifugal forces and direct them toward a unifying goal.

The question of the possibility of such a future cannot be answered without first examining the *origin* of current trends toward disintegration. The heterogeneity of the views of life is rooted in the diversity of *traditional* valuations. "A very precise thinking back leads to the insight that we are a multiplication of many pasts."[6] Tradition itself thus becomes the problem. Nietzsche studied this problem very early, most impressively in his inquiry into *The Uses and Disadvantages of History for Life*.

The answers he obtained in this second of his *Untimely Meditations*[7] are only provisional. In this essay—which is easy to read but not easy to interpret, due to the diverse tendencies it combines[8]—Nietzsche is just starting on the road to knowledge of the one and only world's continuum of becoming (described in chapter 1). At this point he is still trying to avoid the consequences he will later draw.[9] Later he will understand the "historical sickness" discussed in the early work as a symptom of decadence and will grasp decadence itself in its historical origin. He will try to fulfill what he had demanded in the second *Untimely Meditation:* that the origin of historical culture must itself be known historically (HL 8).[10] Despite the provisional character of its findings, however, and despite (in a certain sense: precisely because of) some ambivalences, *Uses and Disadvantages* highlights most sharply the facts that provide the point of departure for Nietzsche's philosophy of contradictions.[11] Therefore we will scrutinize some of the most important aspects of that work in the following pages.

In that treatise Nietzsche describes how "the young man" of the nineteenth century is "swept along through all the millennia" (HL 7) as a consequence "of the mighty historical movement . . . as has been in evidence among the Germans particularly for the past two generations" (HL, "Foreword"). An ever growing deluge of the past and the foreign is pouring into the soul of modern humans. They seek in vain to get the "flood" (HL 10)[12] under control: "Memory opens all its gates and yet is not open wide enough . . . to receive, arrange, and honor these strange guests" (HL 4).[13]

Formerly things were different. History stood in the service of life, whose needs restrained the diversity of the past. But now the constellation has been changed completely, namely "by science, by the demand that history should be a science." Science has intervened like a new, gleaming and glorious star between knowledge of the past and life (HL 4).[14] It exercises its rule by objectifying the past. It is in the nature of such objectivization for the most variegated things to be all the same for it.[15] Historical science pays no less attention to the most remote facts than to matters that still concern its contemporaries.

Thus the quantity of material grows incessantly, but it is of no concern to the persons who live and act. What is made the object by history seems closed off in itself. Characteristically, all knowledge is based on "separation, delimitation, restriction."[16] Objectivization isolates, permits no practical expansion. Thus historical science guards history, "to see that nothing comes out of it except more history, but certainly no real events" (HL 5).[17] Separated from the present and the future, the past can be "resolved into a phenomenon of knowledge" (HL 1).[18] What it shows is that the person acting in history was blind. He was driven forward by something he did not himself see through. He thought he was acting, yet the action was merely passing through him. Now his activity is moved into the bright light of cognition by the scientific historian. "The truly historical *connexus* of cause and effect" (HL 2) is discovered. A self-contained and transparent "historical phenomenon, known clearly and completely . . . is, for the one who has perceived it, dead" (HL 1). It no longer carries life in it; the illusions (HL 7) that fed the action that constituted it have been destroyed. Nor can what is intrinsically dead impart any life to the present and the future. Rather, whoever succumbs to the danger of historical empathy himself takes on a "corpse-like odor."[19] The result is "the mere scholar" who—like Mommsen, in Nietzsche's opinion—"mummifies" everything.[20] History conceived as a "pure, sovereign science" would be for mankind no more than "a sort of conclusion of life and a settling of accounts with it" (HL 1).

This is, of course, only one of the points of view from which young Nietzsche sees historical science. He could not judge it more harshly than by counterposing it to life as something lethal. But this antithesis proves to be too drastic. If it is the only line of thinking, it remains incomprehensible why the present can suffer from the historical disease to the extent described by Nietzsche. Life, as it moves on, surely need not bother with what is dead. And if the past stands in the way of the living, they can eliminate it, as the "most audacious one" demands in his posthumous notes for the second *Untimely Meditation:* "Away with everything past; into the fire with the archives, libraries, art galleries! Let the present itself produce what it needs, for it is worthy only of what it can do itself. Do not torment it by mummifying what once was valid and necessary in a remote time, and remove the dead bones, so that the living can enjoy their day and deeds!"[21]

But the past cannot be dismissed even in this way: precisely the scientific mode of perception leads to this insight. The person presently living also belongs in the "truly historical *connexus.*" "Any beginning afresh is always a delusion."[22] We are "as a matter of fact the outcome of . . . earlier aberrations, passions, and errors, indeed . . . crimes; it is not possible wholly to free oneself from this chain." The best we can do is start a conflict "against the inherited traditions," and occasionally a newly implanted "second nature" achieves "victory" over the first, inherited one (HL 3).

If, however, one submits to the scientific point of view, the victory proves to be merely apparent: in fact, then, the very conflict with the past is its necessary consequence. "The drive for historical knowledge" has the goal "of understanding man in his becoming." By dissolving everything constant it deprives "the cultural drive of its greatest strength."[23] For the "doctrines of sovereign becoming" (HL 9), which stem from the hypertrophy of the historical sense, destroy the sense of responsibility that is indispensable for the man of action. His will is, so he must tell himself, necessitated by the past. If he inquires into it in order to understand his willing with regard to its real determining causes, he is driven further and further back in the series of causes. He cannot stop even at the beginning of the "history of mankind." For the radicalized historical perspective this is "only the continuation of the history of animals and plants" (HL 9).[24] And as the origin of the process into which he knows he is inserted eludes him, so also its destination. He feels like a helpless link in an endless chain. But not only the conviction of man's own power is destroyed by the doctrine of "sovereign becoming." If he understands himself as a link in a chain, he still ascribes a certain stability to himself. But this is dissolved away if process is considered to be the only reality. In that case, self-identity is reduced to a mere fiction.

Let us, with Nietzsche of the second *Untimely Meditation,* posit as the most extreme example "a man condemned to see everywhere a state of becoming" or "who wanted to feel historically through and through" (HL 1). Of him we would have to say that he "would no longer believe in his own being, would no longer believe in himself, would see everything flowing asunder in moving points and would lose himself in this stream of becoming" (HL 1). This image of the stream seems to Nietzsche particularly suitable to express the mobility of the real. In 1872 he noted: "From one time to the other a stream flows over; each adds something new; each swallows and evaporates a great deal of the water it receives. The stream does not always get larger: for some ages add little and destroy a great deal."[25]

Radically performed "historicizing" leads to a "shattering and dismantling of all foundations, their dissolution into a continual evolving that flows ceaselessly away" (HL 9). But, Nietzsche continues, man needs belief "in the enduring and eternal." This is the ultimate "foundation of all his rest and security" (HL 10). Nietzsche therefore in the second *Untimely Meditation* opposes the claims of scientific-historical thinking with the suprahistorical forces of art and religion. They are to "lead the eye away from becoming towards that which bestows upon existence the character of the eternal and stable" (HL 10).

Nietzsche's justification of this need is alluded to here to call attention to the second antithesis that he brings out in the course of his discussions of historical science: the antithesis between becoming and being. Here being is the name for what escapes restless becoming and perishing and remains constant. In his early writing Nietzsche still considers belief in a suprahistorical reality to be vitally necessary. "The excesses of the historical sense" operate "at the expense of being and life" (HL 9). Nietzsche here still praises the suprahistorical because it is a dam against the "infinite and unbounded sea of light whose light is knowledge of all becoming" (HL 10).

The "disadvantages" of scientific history thus consist not only in the fact that it kills the traditional past by seeing through it. Insight into the sovereignty of becoming turns out to be deadly in yet another respect (HL 9). It also destroys the self-confidence of the person acting in his present for the future. And finally it dissolves the self into the process of becoming. Only if man leaps out of this process and clings to something constant can he assert himself in the realm of the inconstant. Nietzsche of course sees through belief in something constant: it is an illusion. But what if it were indispensable? If only it permitted man to gain a footing in the stream of becoming and perishing? Would it not be justified thereby?[26]

Even this second antithesis does not exhaust what Nietzsche has to say on the "historical sickness" of modern man. In the third antithesis that he discovers, Nietzsche goes beyond the one-sidedness in which the two previously discussed antitheses left the past. For the past neither dies completely under the Medusan gaze of knowledge, nor can it be adequately grasped in the image of a chain to which present and future are linked. Human history is not a mere flowing away of events. In his introductory distinction between human consciousness of time and the animal's,[27] Nietzsche writes: "The chain runs with him. And it is a matter for wonder: a moment, now here and then gone, nothing before it came, again nothing after it has gone, nonetheless [it] returns as a ghost and disturbs the peace of a later moment. A leaf flutters from the scroll of time, floats away—and suddenly floats back again and falls into the man's lap" (HL 1). Here the known past is neither what is "dead" nor what has flowed away in the stream of becoming that draws all the present after it. It is, rather, precisely the present living as past.

For Nietzsche there is no doubt: "Only through this power of employing the past for the purposes of life and of again introducing into history what has been done and is gone does man become man" (HL 1). Life needs "the service of history" (HL 2). Its service: for history must subordinate itself to life. The claim that history must be a science is thus definitively rejected; it should not itself be "the goal." "Accumulation of knowledge" should not happen "for its own sake," but "only for the ends of life and thus also under the domination and supreme direction of these ends" (HL 4). What is useless for life "is not true history."[28] Nietzsche elaborates three kinds of such history: the monumental, the antiquarian, and the critical. We need not here go into this distinction, nor into the uses and disadvantages for life of each of these three kinds of history.

For in the context of this study we are interested mainly in the question of what happens when knowledge of the past overflows the boundaries set by life's needs. It was already pointed out that this "flooding" by the "traditional" is, according to Nietzsche, characteristic of the nineteenth century: a multitude of "foreign guests" invades the present. The memory seeks in vain to classify them.

The development of this question leads to the third antithesis of the early Nietzsche's philosophy of history. In this antithesis he counterposes the life-weakening disintegration [*Disgregation*] of the drives, which can stem from an excess of history, especially in its scientific form, to life's need for organization.[29] This makes it quite clear that "our historical education leads to the death of every culture,"[30] since culture is based on the "unity of artistic style in all the expressions of the life of a people" (HL 4). Nietzsche sees that the diversity of historical knowledge can shatter the unity of willing. "Should one not have to atone," he remarks, "if one lives in the precious picture-galleries of all times and the gaze always returns comparingly to the observer with the question what he really was looking for in these rooms."[31] Nietzsche cites Goethe's statement: "Had I known as clearly as I do now, how many wonderful things have existed for centuries, I would not have written a line, but have done something else."[32] Hence Nietzsche's call for the *unhistorical*, "the art and power of *forgetting* and of enclosing oneself within a bounded horizon" (HL 10), that is, of excluding whatever will not fit within that horizon. Only in this way can "the health of a people undermined by the study of history" be restored (HL 4, cf. 10).

Why can the many "strange guests" not be "integrated"? Because they are "in conflict with one another" (HL 4). Each contradicts the other. None of them therefore acquires genuine authority.[33] Their influence on their host changes depending on his mood: "One now handles the standards of the most varied cultures simultaneously and can thereby evaluate almost everything as moral or immoral, as one wishes, that is, depending on our good or bad will toward our fellowmen or toward ourselves."[34] The "continually shifting horizons," to which the above-described "excess of history" leads, can cause a human being to retreat "from an infinite horizon . . . to himself, to the smallest egoistic enclosure." Because the most variegated perspectives open up to him, he cannot entrust himself completely to any. He believes in nothing anymore, but he needs everything that is presented to him for the limited purposes of the moment. So he becomes "clever": "He 'listens to reason,' calculates, and accommodates himself to the facts, keeps calm, blinks, and knows how to seek his own or his party's advantage in the advantage and disadvantage of others" (HL 9).

This egoism is only one of the possible consequences of the "simultaneity of standards of the most varied cultures." The multiplicity of traditions can also be oppressive. Those who experience themselves only as "antiquarians" and "late descendents" "live an ironic existence." "Embodied memory" that they are, they are only too aware of the unproductiveness of their knowledge and of their lack of future (HL 8). The young persons exposed to historical education become accustomed "no longer to be very much surprised at anything, finally to be pleased with everything." In the end, their "only refuge is in an intentional stupidity." They fall into a state of mental paralysis. And "where there has been stronger and more subtle consciousness, another emotion has, no doubt, also appeared: disgust. The young man has become so homeless and doubts all concepts and all customs. He now knows: every age is different; it does not matter what you are like. In melancholy indifference he lets opinion after opinion pass him by" (HL 7).

Indifference, with its air of "objectivity" (HL 6), which historical science demands, can also lead to apathy. Or to the habit of "embracing the too great abundance . . . as lightly as possible so as quickly to expel it again and have done with it." Here too nothing is taken seriously any more. The result is the "weak personality," on whom "the real and existent makes only a slight impression" (HL 4). The individual grows "fainthearted and unsure and dares no longer believe in himself: he sinks . . . into the accumulated jumble of what he has learned but which has no outward effect, of instruction which does not become life" (HL 5).

Nietzsche thus sees the historical scholars of his time as "a race of eunuchs," of "neuters," who also take "history too as a neuter" (HL 5).[35] As a consequence of driving out the instincts by history, humans are reshaped almost into mere abstractions and shadows. What seems to give them a real profile turns out, on closer inspection, to be a mask. If "one takes hold of these masks, one suddenly has nothing but rags and tatters in one's hands" (HL 5). Nietzsche later uses the image of a masquerade to characterize the effects of the historical mentality; man now "requires history as a storage room for costumes. To be sure, he soon notices that not one fits him very well—so he keeps changing." The "changes of the style masquerade" are accompanied by "moments of despair over the fact that 'nothing is becoming.' It is no use to parade as romantic or classical, Christian or Florentine, baroque or 'national,' *in moribus et artibus:* it 'does not look good'" (BGE 223).[36]

Why does no costume fit nineteenth-century man? Because he cannot quite fill one. If, for example, he acts Florentine, he is at the same time also otherwise—and so he is not convincing as a Florentine, not even as a mask that could give the illusion of a Florentine. The patches in his clothing cannot be overlooked. He no longer can represent anything credibly, because he is too much: "the man who appreciates everything, the insatiable stomach which nonetheless does not know what honest hunger and thirst are" (HL 10).

Compared with the person lost in the multiplicity of traditions, who "is ailing and collapses because the lines of his horizon are constantly shifting again restlessly," Nietzsche can even recognize as positive the limited mentality of the person whose horizon is as "narrow as that of a dweller in the Alps"; for in spite of all "injustice and error" he stands there "in superlative health and vigour, a joy to all who see him" (HL 1). Indeed, the unassailable firm grip on a standpoint once acquired is even praised in the second *Untimely Meditation* as the truly philosophical attitude, although of course it can no longer be found: no one dares any longer "to fulfill the philosophical law in himself, no one lives philosophically with that simple loyalty that constrained a man of antiquity to bear himself as a Stoic wherever he was, whatever he did, once he had affirmed his loyalty to the Stoa" (HL 5).

The early Nietzsche finds "the natural antidotes to the stifling of life by the historical, by the malady of history" (HL 10) in the unhistorical[37] and in the suprahistorical, described above. The antidote of the suprahistorical is abandoned as Nietzsche's philosophical thinking develops into his critique of metaphysics.[38] He can no longer cling to illusions.[39] Even later, however, the unhistorical, the power of forgetting, is still emphasized by him as useful to life. In *On the Genealogy of Morals* he states that "forgetfulness" is "not a mere *vis inertiae,*" but rather "an active, in the strictest sense positive faculty of repression." It is, as it were, "a doorkeeper," a "preserver of psychic order" (GM II:1). In *Beyond Good and Evil* he considers the need for "limited horizons," for "the *narrowing of perspectives*" to be "a condition of life and growth" (BGE 188). But besides the tendency to eliminate what could disturb the "healthy closedness" [*Geschlossenheit*] of the horizon, another factor then also crops up: to accept even the opposite, to live in a dangerous openness of one's feeling and thinking.

Nietzsche in the interval became convinced that the historical sense, this sixth sense of the nineteenth century (BGE 224), does not have to be a sickness. It does not have to degenerate into a cultural barbarity. It could even become the virtue of the age. In *The Gay Science* he regards it as "the beginning of something altogether new and strange in history." As Nietzsche looks at the multiplicity of things mediated through the historical sense, it seem to him almost "as if it were not a matter of a new feeling but rather a decrease of all old feelings" (GS 337). But the thought "that we are a multiplication of many pasts,"[40] is now given a positive turn. To live a new kind of life could then mean: "If one could burden one's soul with all this—the oldest, the newest, losses, hopes, conquests, and the victories of humanity; if one could finally contain all this in one soul and crowd it into a single feeling—this would surely have to result in a *happiness* that humanity has not known so far—the happiness of a god full of power and love, full of tears and laughter" (GS 337). Understanding himself historically, Nietzsche is proud of his "origin": "In what moved Zarathustra, Moses, Mohammed, Jesus, Plato, Brutus, Spinoza, Mirabeau, I too already live, and in some things there first emerges fully mature to daylight what took a few millennia embryonically."[41] But can the inconsistencies opened up by the juxtaposition of these names actually be mediated? That question will have to be asked.

First, it should be pointed out that Nietzsche's efforts to master the various problems posed for him by his "revaluation" of the historical are of many kinds. They extend from continued discussion of the consequences of his historical perspectivism, which he had dealt with in *Uses and Disadvantages,* consisting in arranging the past for one's present life,[42] all the way to attempts at a grand synthesis of the traditional opposites that clash together in the present, which we will discuss below. In addition, there is also the tendency to transform history into a work of art (cf. HL 7)[43] and the related tendency to allow "the myth-creating force" to become effective "instead of the historical."[44]

Although the last-mentioned strivings still betray certain reservations toward the historical sense and Nietzsche repeatedly warns of the dangers of the "usual view of history,"[45] from *Human, All Too Human* on he takes seriously the thesis presented there, that "the whole of philosophy is henceforth forfeit to history" (HA II:10). Having "recovered" from the historical sickness "slowly and toilsomely," he is "in no way prepared to give up 'history' thereafter because he had once suffered from it" (HA II).[46] He now no longer wants to close his eyes to its knowledge, as had happened in the second *Untimely Meditation*.[47] Now he reproaches earlier philosophers for lacking a historical sense. In this regard he often speaks in generalities (TI 3:1, cf. WP 408); only occasionally does he become specific.[48]

This change in his estimation of the value of studying history leaves Nietzsche's understanding of history essentially intact. Human history is the continuation of the history of the organic, which itself has no beginning. What happens in it, happens with necessity. After the destruction of the concept of causality, history can of course no longer involve a *connexus* of causes and effects. Rather, the continuum of becoming, which replaces causality, excludes the mechanistic interpretation of that necessity. It must, however, also not be understood teleologically. History has neither a goal imposed on it from the outside nor an immanent one. There can, then, also not be any forward movement in it. The illusion of historical progress forms in us only because we experience time as running forward.

In truth, not even man is a "progress compared with the animal"; all the less so "the nineteenth century . . . compared with the sixteenth." In his observations on the history of mankind, Nietzsche, on the contrary, repeatedly discovers movements of declining vital energy. "The civilized tenderfoot is an abortion compared to the Arab and Corsican"; "the German spirit of 1888 represents a regress from the German spirit of 1788" (WP 90).[49] But even such retrogressive movements contain no hidden meaning. Everything "proceeds blindly and stupidly. As a leaf runs its course in a brook, although it is held up here and there."[50] History is a dice-game of chance, Nietzsche had written in the second *Untimely Meditation* (HL 2, cf. Z III:5).[51] Later on, this sentence undergoes a significant restriction. Previously chance ruled in the history of mankind, he writes.[52] "A few successes are scored" in it, "scattered throughout all ages, while there are untold failures," since it lacks order and meaningful coherence (WP 90).[53] "That gruesome dominion of nonsense and accident that has so far been called 'history,'" can be brought to "an end" (BGE 203)[54] by our laying claim to what is intrinsically senseless as material for the creative power of our will. Nietzsche, by delineating possibilities for such a new beginning, can understand himself as the person upon whose appearance the history of mankind is broken into two parts (EH).[55] It will be shown below that he believes that nihilism, which took shape in previous history, can be overcome by liberating the human will.

If absurdity is not to have the last word after the destruction of the suprahistorical, then meaning must be established by man from the outset in history itself, which is the only remaining realm of reality. "If no goal resides in the entire history of human destinies, then we must insert one."[56]

The desire to insert a goal in history does not exempt one from looking back at prior history. For precisely this prior history would give rise to the necessity of a goal being set by man. Only after he has been made fully aware of the chaos of conflicting valuations in his background by developing the historical sense can he learn to feel that he is "the *shaper* who neither merely looks on, nor wants to."[57] The breaking of history into two sections can thus not mean that every connection between the accidental past and the planned future is torn apart. The future is linked with the past. But now the future must express its antithetical relation to the past. Nietzsche, in his contemplation of the history of mankind, therefore seeks to combine the two: he must elaborate both the future's connection with the past and the opposition of the two.[58] This effort again presupposes Nietzsche's conviction, depicted in chapter 1 above, that real opposites are not absolute, but rather can be derived from one another.

These general characteristics are, of course, not sufficient to clarify Nietzsche's particular view of history. For it gets its impulses from the disintegration phenomena that he discovered in his own time. The answer he had given in the second *Untimely Meditation* to the question of the origin of such disorganization necessarily proved to be inadequate as his philosophical thinking progressed. If the star of science, radiant but hostile to life, is supposed to have conjured up the contemporary chaos of convictions, then a further question has to be asked: How did that star originate? From what does it draw its power over life?

In his published writings after *Thus Spoke Zarathustra,* Nietzsche answers that the rule of scientific thought is, in the last analysis, merely a symptom of a deeper-reaching sickness of the human will to life.[59] The historical malady, in turn, is traced back to this sickness.[60] The basis for disintegration in the modern period is already laid down before strivings for historical objectivity have begun. History in its chance form has long been a history of decline and retrogression. To be sure, there was also "many a favorable element"[61] among the accidental occurrences. There were counter-movements, although in the long run these could not prevail. The Romans, the great men of the Renaissance, Napoleon—these are the examples cited most frequently by Nietzsche. They were, however, unable to hold back the decline.

Yet what declines must start from a height; the healthy human being stands at the beginning of the history of every culture. The will to power, "the primordial fact of all history,"[62] is refracted in him without inhibition; his trajectory paralyzes the "sick" person's will to power or diverts it from its natural goals. "Let us admit to ourselves, without trying to be cautious," Nietzsche exclaims, "how every higher culture on earth so far has begun! Human beings whose nature was still natural, barbarians in every terrible sense of the word, men of prey, who were still in possession of unbroken strength of will and lust for power, hurled themselves upon weaker, more civilized, more peaceful races, perhaps traders or cattle raisers, or upon mellow old cultures whose last vitality was even then flaring up in splendid fireworks of spirit and corruption" (BGE 257). Those who were victorious initially were always the healthiest "of all tropical beasts and plants," man the beast of prey, the man of prey (BGE 197, cf. GM I:11), the "beast in deed" (GM II:22), for example, the notorious "blond beast" (GM I:11). Zoology continues powerfully in man. But how could it happen that finally the weak, the sickly, seized, exercised, and expanded their power?

The precondition for this is that the strong weakened themselves. This self-debilitation can go as far as their self-destruction. Driven by the will to ever greater power, they risk their life too rashly. "The experiences of history" show Nietzsche this: "The strong races decimate one another; they ruin one another"; at least after such struggles "periods of profound exhaustion and torpor supervene" (WP 864). A self-debilitation of the strong, however, also ensues when their rule remains uncontested. "The victors mostly become stupid," Nietzsche notes as early as 1879.[63] The strong need enemies, constant battle "with neighbors or with the oppressed who rebel or threaten rebellion." Generally speaking, they need "*unfavorable* conditions." And only when these remain essentially the "same" is their cohesion as a ruling caste assured. If "fortunate conditions" begin, so that neither wars nor uprising are to be feared, the prior hardships of life are eliminated, and finally an undisturbed enjoyment of life becomes possible, then the community, which had previously been held together by common interest, falls apart (BGE 262).[64]

The strong, if they are to remain strong, are dependent on certain conditions to intensify the will to power that formerly existed in history only accidentally and temporarily. An excess or a lack of struggle destroys their rule. After ruinous wars the strong are "weaker, more devoid of will, more absurd than the weak average" (WP 864). And if the common opponent is completely absent, the accumulated energy pits the individuals against one another to such an extent that after a brief blossoming of individualism "a tremendous perishing and mutual annihilation begins, so that only the mediocre survive" (BGE 262).

It was only against strong men weakened in one way or another that the originally repressed counter-will of the weaker men could win out. Till then the strong had been "value-creative." In their values they glorified everything they knew about themselves (BGE 260). Above all, what expressed itself in their virtues, as Nietzsche likes to say, was a "pathos of distance"; it served to "hold down and keep away" their inferiors (BGE 257).[65] The defeated had to despise themselves if they based their own self-evaluation on the standards of the strong. But if they now strove to rule over those who were originally strong, they needed opposing values, in which their hatred of the strong counteracted their contempt for the weak. "The slave revolt in morality begins when *ressentiment* itself becomes creative and gives birth to values" (GM I:10).

How could it happen that the *ressentiment*-values won? Nietzsche asks again and again. "Why did life and physiological well-constitutedness everywhere succumb? (WP 401). "How did those come to power who are last?" (WP 54). And furthermore how could the weak maintain their domination in the course of history, once they had acquired it? Or else regain it despite all (temporarily successful) counter-movements of the strong? "We modern men" are indeed "the heirs of the self-torture of millennia," as required by the values of the weak (GM II:24).

Nietzsche's first answer is: the weak triumphed through their number. They had "great fruitfulness and duration" on their side, whereas among the strong we find, for the reasons treated above, "rapid wastage, speedy reduction in numbers" (WP 685). The weak were "stronger numerically" (WP 401). Now, greater numbers do not necessarily mean power. The *ressentiment*-values did not become the ruling values simply because they were held by many. To impose them against the values of the strong, indeed first of all to *invent* them, it was necessary to activate a medium that those who first ruled had available to only a slight degree because they did not need it: *cleverness*. For the weak, however, this had been "a condition of existence of the first importance." The men of *ressentiment* employed their spirituality against the "unconscious instincts" or the bold reckless imprudence of the strong (GM I:10). They achieved and preserved supremacy not merely "through their numbers," but rather—and that is Nietzsche's second answer—"through their shrewdness, their cunning" (WP 685, cf. TI 9:14). Cleverness and cunning presuppose knowledge of the inner drives of the person who is to be outwitted. This knowledge is obtained by means of *self*-knowledge. The clever application of this acquired knowledge to the strong enabled the weak to re-channel the instincts of the strong.

The victorious campaign of the *ressentiment*-values determined the history of Europe. It begins with the history of the Jewish people. Israel, "with its vengefulness and revaluation of all values, has hitherto triumphed again and again over all other ideals, over all *nobler* ideals" (GM I:8). It was the Jews who, with frightening consistency, dared to invert the aristocratic value-equation (good = noble = powerful = beautiful = happy = beloved of God): "The wretched alone are the good; the poor, impotent, lowly alone are the good; the suffering, deprived, sick, ugly alone are pious, alone are blessed by God; blessedness is for them alone— and you, the powerful and noble, are on the contrary the evil, the cruel, the lustful, the insatiable, the godless to all eternity; you will be in all eternity the unblessed, accursed, and damned!" (GM I:7).

Christianity merely expands this "lie" of Judaism: "it is actually its logical consequence" (AC 24). In Christianity "as the art of holy lying, the whole of Judaism, a schooling and technique pursued with the utmost seriousness for hundreds of years attains its ultimate perfection. The Christian, that *ultima ratio* of the lie, is the Jew once more—even thrice more" (AC 44). Through Christianity the triumph of the weak over the strong first becomes a historical disaster. It could attain power only because the Roman rulers were degenerate (WP 874). Since then it continued to consolidate its power; it is to blame that "the history of Europe since the time of the Roman Empire" has been "a slave uprising."[66] Although for Nietzsche Christianity is merely a continuation of Judaism, on the other hand he emphasizes the difference between the two. The Jews, "a nation of the toughest vital energy," were not yet weak-willed like the Christians. They utilized the "decadence-instincts" only for self-preservation under the most difficult conditions. They were not dominated by these instincts; rather, they used them as a *means* to prevail against the world (AC 24). Of course, they had already outlived their originally strong instincts; their toughness had grown "old and tame" (WP 156).

These first references to the history of the Judeo-Christian revolution can serve to bring out the pattern of Nietzsche's view of history. In all previous history, driven by chance, two phases can be distinguished. In the initial phase, the strong and healthy ruled; in the second phase, the weak and sick. Their supremacy shall be abolished in the future. To accomplish this, a new revaluation of the leading values is needed. Through it the strong will again come to power. Their power, consolidated by measures yet to be discussed, will be withdrawn from the blind action of chance. Nietzsche's genealogical method now seeks repeatedly to delineate or to prognosticate the three phases into which history must be articulated when it is regarded under the aspect of the two drastic transformations of the fundamental values into their opposites.[67]

The history of valuation is a history of the conflicting moralities of the strong and the weak. However, usually Nietzsche uses the term morality only to designate the *ressentiment*-valuation. Thus, he distinguishes "the *pre-moral* period of mankind," which spans "the longest part of human history, the prehistoric times," from the moral period, which gradually replaced the first one "in the last ten thousand years . . . in a few large regions of the earth." In this second period, man's "first attempt at self-knowledge" took place. We men of today stand "at the threshold" of a new, third period, "which should be designated negatively, to begin with, as the *extra-moral* one."[68] Another "self-reflection" and "profundity" of man will cause him "once again" to perform a "reversal and fundamental shift in values" (BGE 32).

Moral self-knowledge is, however, not simply contemplation. Man does not merely turn toward himself, he turns against himself. Nietzsche's genealogy of the conscience tries to make this clear. In the first period of human history, when the "semi-animals, well-adapted to wilderness, to war, to prowling, to adventure," finally "were enclosed with the walls of society and of peace," their instincts suddenly lost their natural field of activity. They could no longer, as before, penetrate outward in uninhibited and healthy strength. The pressure of a society of already weakened humans redirected the impulses of those who had originally been strong. The repressed delight in persecution and destruction turned inward against the possessors of these instincts. Such sickly "*internalization* of man" engendered "bad conscience" (GM II:16). Even selflessness, self-denial and self-sacrifice—contradictory terms for Nietzsche, because the self is not at all discarded in such modes of behavior—are nothing but manifestations of the cruel violation of the self by the self, which are expressed in the bad conscience. Only the completely selfish "will to self-maltreatment provides the conditions for the *value* of the unegoistic" (GM II:18).

The development of bad conscience, indeed, initiated "the gravest and uncanniest illness, from which humanity has not yet recovered." Yet this should not obscure the fact that with this phenomenon, as with the moral period generally, something happened "the end of which is not yet in sight." The enigmatic and contradictory nature of the moral person contains a "promise for the future." It is "as if with him something were announcing and preparing itself, as if man were not a goal but only a way, an episode, a bridge, a great promise" (GM II:16). In fact, in the context of a genealogy of faith in God, Nietzsche assumes "that we have practically entered upon the reverse course." The "decline of faith in the Christian God," in which "the maximum feeling of guilty indebtedness on earth" was produced, is accompanied by a considerable "decline of mankind's feeling of guilt." Nietzsche foresees "a kind of *second innocence*," brought about by "the complete and definitive victory of atheism" (GM II:20).

The second innocence will not, however, consist in a mere restoration of the first one. History is irreversible. "A reversion, a turning back in any sense and to any degree is quite impossible" (TI 9:43). The moral period, too, cannot simply be reversed. The new morality must, despite all antitheticalness [*Gegensätzlichkeit*] to this period, grow out of it. On the other hand, Nietzsche often disregards this historicalness of the strong human of the future. His image then takes on the features of man in the pre-moral era. Nietzsche rather often gives the impression that he considers a return to pre-history (which in any case was not fully extinguished in us) not only possible (GM II:9), but even desirable.[69] But more frequently, the man of the future appears as the one who not only seeks to wander through the past of the moral period, but rather assimilates it in order to transform it into something new.

Nietzsche's genealogy of *objectivity* can give a first impression of this possibility. How the needs of life's self-preservation and intensification could at the outset give rise to the fiction of "things," of "objects" was described in chapter 1. The will constituting these fictions was later to a certain extent diminished by the weak-willed, whereby object-"knowledge" was given the rank of independent *truths*. Finally, a "pure, will-less, painless, timeless knowing subject" was posited, to whom these truths were accessible: in reality, a new fiction, in order to obscure the more original one from oneself (GM III:12).[70] Thus one achieved an objectivity that employed "such contradictory concepts as 'pure reason,' 'absolute spirituality,' 'knowledge in itself'" (GM III:12).

But the multitude of supposedly objective interpretations—especially in the study of history, which Nietzsche preferred to draw upon as a model for his reflections on scientific theory—revealed the underlying active and interpretative forces that were only apparently held in check. "The same text allows countless interpretations: there is no single 'right' interpretation."[71] Behind the diverse conflicting interpretations, the objectivity that was striven for emerges as "disgregation of the will" (WP 444). But Nietzsche at this point does not demand that this disintegration of the will be abrogated in favor of the naive, unreflective practice of the pre-moral era. For the unnatural objectivity of the second man is "no small discipline and preparation of the intellect for its future 'objectivity.'" Although it remains bound to the forces from which it tries to break free, still it has produced a *distance* between them and their objects.

This distancing can be made productive. The future "objectivity" in Nietzsche's sense will grow out of the prior one as man's faculty "to *control* his 'pro' and 'con' and to dispose of them." In contrast with the former claim to objectivity, it should be realized that there is "*only* a perspectival 'knowing.'" The point is precisely to employ "a *variety* of perspectives and affective interpretations." "The *more* affects we allow to speak about one thing, the *more* eyes, different eyes, we can use to observe one thing, the more complete our 'concept' of this thing, our 'objectivity' will be" (GM III:12).[72] This completeness will, of course, in line with Nietzsche's presuppositions, always be only a relative one. Nor does such a sum of perspectives lead to a perspective-free knowledge. And finally the adoption of manifold vantage-points into one consciousness cannot remove the conflict in which these vantage points are locked.

The call for a new "objectivity" opens an unlimited scope for claims of a perspectival diversity, a scope denied by Nietzsche in the second *Untimely Meditation,* with regard to history. Yet he was convinced he was not thereby succumbing to the spirit of the times, which he so strongly opposed. He believed he could overcome it by radicalizing its tendencies. To what extent he contradicts his statements in the earlier work can be shown by comparing the above-cited "defense of the Stoics"[73] with a later note that states: "When a person contradicts himself a thousand times and goes many ways and wears many masks and finds within himself no end, no final horizon-line: is it probable that such a person experiences less 'truth' than a virtuous Stoic, who has taken his position once and for all like a pillar and with the hard skin of a pillar? But such prejudices sit at the threshold of all previous philosophies."[74]

Yet in the second *Untimely Meditation* Nietzsche had planted the seed for his later view, insofar as he had called whatever people could assimilate only a question of a person's *plastic strength:* "The most powerful and tremendous nature would be characterized by the fact that it would know no boundary at all at which the historical sense began to overwhelm it; it would draw to itself and incorporate into itself all the past, its own and that most foreign to it, and as it were transform it into blood" (HL 1). Nietzsche had added however: "That which such a nature cannot subdue, it knows how to forget" (HL 1). But in principle the possibility of harmonizing within oneself in a positive sense the diverse contradictions of tradition is here already conceded.[75] Hence also the possibility of combining the various perspectives focused on one and the same object, while at the same time they must be understood in their historicalness.

The thought that only the most powerful nature can do this persists into Nietzsche's latest work. What appeared as a fiction in the early work becomes for Nietzsche the ideal he strives to realize. He needs "the production of a *synthetic, summarizing, justifying* man" (WP 866). That man does not yet exist: "The great synthetic man is lacking" (WP 883). But "with a certain elevation of the type man a new force, which we knew nothing of until now, can be revealed (namely a synthesis of opposites!)."[76] The "European of the future," whom the important men of the nineteenth century sought "to prepare . . . and anticipate experimentally" in the "mysterious workings of their soul" (BGE 256) will put all prior knowledge in the service of his passion.[77] "For anyone who grows up into the heights of humanity *the world* becomes ever fuller; ever more fishhooks are cast in his direction to capture his interest; the number of things that stimulate him grows constantly" (GS 301).

Such over-flooding of stimuli constitutes modern man's sickness. But though the strong man may "have all the morbid traits of the century," he is able to "balance them through a superabundant, shaping recuperative strength" (WP 1014). He who is to "valuate reversely" to what was done before must "have *all* qualities of the modern soul," but be "strong enough to transform them into sheer good health."[78] A note written by Nietzsche at the time of writing *Daybreak* now applies only to the weak: "Develop all your forces—but that means: develop anarchy! Perish!"[79]

To put an end to the contingency of prior events, the strong man needs more than a healthy will to life. He must also have available the cleverness that the weak have cultivated. "Human history would be altogether too stupid a thing without the spirit that the impotent have introduced into it" (GM I:7).[80] "Let us not think meanly of that which two thousand years of morality have bred in our spirit!" Nietzsche exclaims (WP 267). The moral epoch of mankind thus falls into a double meaning: on the one hand, it seems to be a time of decline;[81] on the other, a time of preparation for a richer humanity, which would be impossible without it. To cite an example: Is bad conscience the illness of weariness of life, driving one to self-destruction, or is it an illness only in the same sense "as pregnancy is an illness"? (GM II:19). Can it be *both,* as Nietzsche's statements would suggest? Is his thought of the development of opposites out of one another still tenable here? Can the event of dissolution produce out of itself the opposite tendency to unity?

Such questions will be studied in the following chapters, and the concept of nihilism will be drawn into the investigation. The issue of nihilism was already an implicit theme in this chapter. For, in the late Nietzsche's view, the history of nihilism is nothing more than the pathological history of moral man. The disintegrating tendencies of historical science[82] are, then, interpreted as the symptoms of the late phase of nihilism (GM III:26; cf. also WP 1 and 69). The attempt to overcome nihilism was already taking shape in previous references to the strong man of the future. Before we can in this context discuss Nietzsche's call for a genuine synthesis of the many contradictions presented in his doctrine of the overman, the movement of nihilistic disintegration must be analyzed in its full significance.

3

Nihilism as Will to Nothingness

Man would rather will nothingness *than*
not *will.* —*Genealogy of Morals* III:28

Nietzsche no doubt came across the term "nihilism," which he began using in the 1880s, in a series of contemporary writers. Due to its use by the Russian anarchists, the term had acquired widespread popularity in the German-speaking region, too.[1] The picture Nietzsche formed of those anarchists was mostly determined by his reading of Dostoevsky's novels;[2] but he also read, for example, publications of Ivan Turgenev and Alexander Herzen (in Sorrento, by 1877 at the latest)[3] and he perhaps excerpted Peter Kropotkin.[4] According to Charles Andler,[5] Nietzsche's use of the word "nihilism" resulted from his reading of Paul Bourget's *Essais de psychologie contemporaine.*[6]

Bourget, it should be noted, speaks of nihilism mainly with the Russian anarchists in mind. Yet he also relates this nihilism closely with other, in part very diverse kinds of phenomena of his time, all pointing to *one* basic evil: disgust with the world. In his Baudelaire essay, Bourget seeks to discover the origin of this feeling. He identifies it as the discrepancy between the *needs* of the modern age that accompany the development of civilization and the *inadequacies* of existing reality. The universal outbreak of world-nausea in the nineteenth century was, he believed, caused by this outbreak. It manifested itself in different ways. Among the Slavs it was expressed as nihilism, among the Germanic nations as pessimism, and among the Romanic nations in an unusual nervous irritability.[7] In all this, however, Bourget finds the same "spirit of the negation of life, which darkens Western civilization more and more each day."[8]

Nietzsche recognized a kindred spirit in Bourget. Like Bourget he was concerned with diagnosing the "sickness" of the century and developing a "theory" of decadence. The horizon within which this happened in Bourget could, of course, not seem broad enough for him; the discrepancy between need and reality offered him no satisfactory explanation of the spirit of the negation of life.

What supposedly comprised the background for that spirit, according to the "discrete psychologist" Bourget,[9] had to be accounted merely foreground by Nietzsche.

More distinctly than Bourget, Nietzsche sums up the various "symptoms of sickness" under the name of nihilism. How far back he traces the pathological history of the modern European was described in our comments on his philosophy of history. In retrospect it can be said that the birth of moral man marks the beginning of Western nihilism.

Nietzsche, then, reaches further back than others who spoke of nihilism before him. And he no longer understands nihilism primarily as the result of reason's exaggerated self-glorification, as it appeared in critiques of the philosophy of German Idealism by F. H. Jacobi, Franz von Baader, Christian H. Weisse, and Immanuel H. Fichte—of which critiques Nietzsche probably had no knowledge. Nihilism, detectable even *prior* to all reflection and speculation, cannot be refuted by merely rational arguments: "The real refutations are physiological."[10] For if reason wages war on decadence, it does not thereby extract itself from decadence. Reason can, at best, change the *expression* of decadence, as Nietzsche tries to show by the example of Socrates (TI 2:10; cf. WP 435).

All consciousness is, as the last and latest phase of the development of the organic, much too unfinished and weak (GS 11) to be of any avail against what it stems from. "The growth of consciousness" often does appear to be a "danger," indeed a "disease" (GS 354)—e.g. in a genealogy of self-consciousness attempted by Nietzsche—yet he does not carry to extremes what the discussion of nihilism had discovered before him. He wants to seek the disease at its place of origin. The "weak, delicate, and morbid effects of the spirit" are for him ultimately merely *symptoms* of physiological processes (WP 899). In his view "the nihilistic movement is merely the expression of physiological *decadence*" (WP 38).

What does Nietzsche mean by the "physiological," which he tries to "draw forth" (D 542), not only from behind consciousness "as such" and its logical positings (BGE 3), but also from behind the moral (D 542; cf. GM I:17n) and aesthetic (GM III:9) valuations? Physiological processes are "releases of energy."[11] But this means power struggles of will-quanta. Physiology, rightly understood, is thus the theory of the will to power (BGE 13), just as is psychology, rightly understood, which amalgamates with the former into a "physio-psychology" (BGE 29). Thus, we can here refer back to the discussions in chapter 1.

Consciousness is, under such a physio-psychological aspect, still inadequately characterized as a weak late phenomenon. It is the "instrument" of a "many-headed and much divided master,"[12] "a means and tool by which not a subject but *a struggle wants to preserve itself*."[13] Quanta of will organize themselves into relatively independent units. Man is such an especially complex organization, which invents a consciousness for its service.[14]

Now the nature of this decadence, whose "logic" is nihilism (WP 43), can be clarified. It is a particular mode of physiological "releases of energy." The wills to power, previously held together in a unity, now strive to separate. Nietzsche describes this centripetal tendency as the "disintegration [*Disgregation*] of the instincts" (TI 9:35). The concept of *Disgregation* is already familiar to us. We have repeatedly come across the term and its problematic in the first two chapters. This problematic now needs closer analysis.

Our starting point will be Nietzsche's portrayal of literary decadence. The very style of a work of art can reveal "that life no longer dwells in the whole. The word becomes sovereign and leaps out of the sentence; the sentence reaches out and obscures the meaning of the page; the page gains life at the expense of the whole— the whole is no longer a whole." Something similar applies to all modes of manifestation of decadence. "The anarchy of the atoms" and "*Disgregation* of the will" go hand in hand in them. The leading will that previously organized the unity of the whole loses its power. Subordinate forces press for independence. Nietzsche finds these signs, for example, in the moral claim for freedom of the individual, as well as in its expansion to political theory with the demand for "equal rights for all" (CW 7).

Decadence, described as "*Disgregation*," is not a state but a process. To be sure, in it the dissolution of an organization is *intended*. But once this actually is completed, once a unity has disintegrated into a plurality without cohesion (which cohesion is possible only as a hierarchical structure), then we can no longer speak of decadence. This term can designate only the phases of the disintegration process of a whole, insofar as unity still remains despite all dissolution tendencies.

Therefore the question must be asked: What still holds together that which is in the process of disintegrating on the way to its actual disintegration? This is a specific process and not simply the mechanical disassembling of components. Nietzsche rules out a mechanical interpretation. Pressure and stress are "something unspeakably late, derivative, unprimeval." They already presuppose something "that *holds together* and *is able* to exert pressure and stress" (WP 622). This original thing is the "aggregate herd-condition of atoms"; in it "is precisely non-stress and yet power, not only of counter-striving, resistance, but rather mainly of arrangement, placement, attachment, transfering and coalescing force."[15] Mechanics is, however, oriented on the model of the persistent thing, which stems from logic inflated into metaphysics. Its concept of force remains an empty word as long as an inner will is not ascribed to it.[16]

The nihilistic disintegration process, too, is characterized by cohesion, and this cohesion too is established by an inner will. All cohesion presupposes the rule of one "drive," which subjugates a multiplicity of drives and forces them under itself. If the *Disgregation* of what was originally held together under such a rulership is to be carried out, that is possible only if the dominant "drive" gives the corresponding instruction. Otherwise the efficacy common to the subordinate drives to detach themselves from the union of the whole would be incomprehensible. "*Perishing*" thus takes the form of a "*self-destruction,* the instinctive selection of that which *must destroy*" (WP 55). The ruling will in such a whole must therefore be a *will to disintegration,* which strives for the end or non-existence of the unity it had organized. It is the will to the end (AC 9) or the will to nothingness or *for* nothingness (WP 401, cf. 55).

All drives subject to the will to nothingness promote disintegration. This common trait is, however, not uniform. Each drive has its "own law of development" that is determined by the conflict immanent within the whole. Each promotes the downfall in its particular way. The "rate of speed" of disintegration is different in each of them. Indeed, like every drive, the ruling will to nothingness arouses drives against itself among the drives ruled by it. If such a "counter-drive" is strong enough, it will seize the rulership for itself. Its function is, however, strangely discordant when it remains subject to the will to nothingness and nonetheless fights against it.

Nothing other than such discordant willing is expressed in the decadence phenomenon of *asceticism,* which Nietzsche investigates in the third essay of *On the Genealogy of Morals.* What concerns him there is the meaning of the *ascetic ideal:* "what it indicates; what lies hidden behind it, beneath it, in it; of what it is the provisional, indistinct expression, overlaid with question marks and misunderstandings" (GM III:23). This meaning becomes evident when Nietzsche analyzes the type of the ascetic priest: he finds on the ground of the ascetic ideal "a discord that *wants* to be discordant" (GM III:11).

Discord now emerges in full clarity in Nietzsche's arguments. On the one hand, life *denies itself* in ascetic practice. For asceticism serves only as a bridge to a completely different, indeed opposite kind of existence (GM III:11). For it employs force "to block up the wells of force" (11). An aversion to life is dominant here (28). On the other hand, the ascetic ideal is an "artifice for the *preservation* of life" (13). For even if life is to be merely a bridge, that bridge must be constructed and thus life must be maintained. The ascetic priest is, by the power of his desire "to be different, to be in a different place," chained to this life. Thus "this *denier* is among the greatest *conserving* and *yes-creating* forces of life" (13).

The ascetic simultaneously denies and affirms life. Naturally, it is not a matter of the simultaneity of a total No and a total Yes. His No and Yes are interwoven in a way that keeps in check the absolute claim of either side. The Yes restricts the No: in the ascetic ideal "the door is closed to any kind of suicidal nihilism" (GM III:28). And the No restricts the Yes: degenerating life that needs protection and healing (13) cannot be healed by ascetic practice (16). The ascetic priest, as a "nurse and physician" (14) does not fight "the real sickness" (17), he merely tries in his way to alleviate the suffering itself. The means he uses to treat the patients are: reducing the feeling of life to impede depressive affects from taking their full toll (17), distraction from suffering by mechanical activity (18), careful dosages of petty pleasures (18), orgies of feeling (19). The last means makes the patients even sicker afterwards (20, cf. 21). And even the prior ones merely alleviate the symptoms of the illness. Indeed, the ascetic priest, as "he stills the pain of the wound . . . at the same time infects the wound" (15). His practice, then, finally brings "fresh suffering with it, deeper, more inward, more poisonous, more life-destructive suffering" (28).

The possibilities and limits of a counter-drive dominated by the will to nothingness thus become clearly discernible. The ascetic priest is sick himself (GM III:15) yet must on the other hand still be healthy enough to be able to ward off immediate disintegration. His will must be strong enough to organize the still resistant vital instincts. In the struggle against depression, he strives for the formation of the herd (18). He fights "against anarchy and ever-threatening disintegration within the herd" (15). He seeks to vent *ressentiment*—this explosive material that threatens to blow up the herd—in such a way that it changes direction. This is done by shifting the cause of suffering into the sufferer himself (15). The result of all this, however, is merely that a chronic disease replaces a rapid death. The dominant will to nothingness still wins out at the core of the drive that is directed against it.[17] As long as it rules, one *must* "go forward, which is to say, step by step *further into decadence.* . . . One can retard this development and, through retardation, dam and gather up degeneration itself and make it more vehement and sudden: more one cannot do" (TI 9:43). Asceticism leads to such impediments and disturbances. These, in turn, prepare the way for explosions of *active nihilism,* which will be discussed below.

As for the root of the ascetic ideal, the will to nothingness must be examined in terms of what originally constituted it. And since Nietzsche traces back not only this ideal, but all manifestations and forms of decadence to it, his analysis is of decisive significance for the problem of nihilism. According to the foregoing reflections, nihilism can basically be nothing else but the will to nothingness, and in fact it is always so characterized by Nietzsche (GM II:21, 24; III:14).

First, it must be asked: How can nothingness be *willed* at all? How must the will be constituted so as to be directed toward nothingness? Again we can refer back to remarks in chapter 1. There is no mere will that would occur as something simple, simply given, as a characteristic or as pure potency. In such a conception "the 'whither?'" has been "subtracted" (WP 692). The "willing whither" means "willing an end," which includes willing "something" (WP 260).[18] As such a willing, it cannot *not will*. Therefore Nietzsche, in the context of his investigation of the ascetic ideal, characterizes it as "the basic fact of the human will" that the will needs a goal: "And it will rather *will nothingness* than *not* will" (GM III:1). Can the will at all intend nothingness? For even if we concede that nothingness could be "something" in the sense of being intendable, we must observe that, for Nietzsche, to want "something" means to want power.

In striving for nothingness, however, the will is carrying on its own "self-destruction" (WP 55). Can it, then, still be will to power? That is certainly Nietzsche's conviction. He does indeed write: "The will to nothingness has become master over the will to life, more precisely over the 'ascending instincts'" (WP 401, cf. 685). But the very formulation of this sentence (". . . has become master over . . .") makes it clear that the will to nothingness, in so doing, acts as will to power. And in his characterization of Christianity, Nietzsche expressly states that in it "the will to the end, the *nihilistic* will . . . wants power" (AC 9). The will to power must thus again and again be clearly distinguished from the will to life as understood by Schopenhauer. The will to life is "merely a special case" of the will to power (WP 692). Even this "process of decline" still stands "in the service of" the will to power (WP 675).

Even the will to nothingness is thus will to power. Its intention thereby merely becomes more incomprehensible. How can what wants power strive for nothingness? If Nietzsche were speaking of the will to power as a simple metaphysical basic principle that develops out of its own self and intensifies intrinsically, the assertion that there is a power-will to nothingness would be absurd. Nietzsche, however, starts with a multiplicity of wills to power engaged in conflict with one another and forming parties. In this struggle there are victors and vanquished. A victorious and dominant will is a strong will; a defeated and subjugated will is a weak will. Neither strength nor weakness belong to the wills as a property. They merely express the outcome of a struggle in which two wills have been engaged against one another. The victory of the stronger does not at first lead to the destruction but rather to the subjugation of the weaker.[19] It establishes a ranking order in which the two depend on each other; indeed, both are indispensable to one another.[20] Victory and rank are, however, never final; the struggle continues incessantly. In a reversal of the power relations, the subjugated will can become the dominant one, and the previously dominant will can be subjugated.

Of course, to speak of a conflict between a strong will and a weak will is a crude simplification of what is in truth a multiply gradated organization of will-quanta. It must always be remembered that "there is no will, and consequently neither a strong nor a weak will. The multitude and *Disgregation* of impulses and the lack of any systematic order among them result in a 'weak will'; their coordination under the hegemony of a single predominant impulse results in a 'strong will'" (WP 46). The simplifying way of speaking that Nietzsche employs again and again does not, however, impair his possibility to expound on the problematic of decadence and to make clear an essential concretization of an antithesis that determines his philosophical thinking. The simplification, must, however, not be carried so far that the multiplicity is traced back to one will to power. For then Nietzsche's basic idea is reversed. We can do justice to this problem only if we see at least "two 'wills to power' in conflict" (WP 401).[21]

Nothingness is intended by an initially defeated, weak will. This intention must be understood as a *reaction* to the strength of a victorious and at first dominant will. Thus the *ressentiment*-morality stems from a denial of the noble morality (AC 24). Although it may be "creative," it remains in its ground a *reversal* of values that is bound to what it reverses.[22]

The will to nothingness is a counter-will. The weak do not deny for the sake of denial as such. By their denial they want to conquer the strong and rule over them. For the stronger and weaker are the same in this: "They extend their power as far as they can."[23] For the purpose of domination, denial must act as a *condemnation*. The weak condemn the will to power in the values of the strong. But the condemnatory will is itself will to power. It can absolutely not be anything else, for basically all reality is will to power. Thus the only reality is condemned. How can that happen? Only by the decadent will to power *inventing* another reality from which point of view the condemnation can be made. The fictional world must appear with the claim to be the *true world*.

The *possibility* of this fiction is given in man's biological need, in the stream of becoming, to grasp the similar as the same and to fixate what moves. What is supposedly the same or constant can then be detached from becoming as something existing by itself. What is so detached, in truth "an apparent world," is constructed "out of contradiction to the actual world" (TI 3:6). Man "invents a world so as to be able to slander and bespatter this world: in reality he reaches every time for nothingness and construes nothingness as 'God,' as 'truth,' and in any case as judge and condemner of *this* state of being" (WP 461). Thus, as Nietzsche sees it, in the Christian concept of God "nothingness [is] deified, the will to nothingness sanctified" (AC 18).

In all this, the will to nothingness is a will to power that hides itself as such. In order to rule, it demands that the will to power that admits itself as such must abdicate. It acts as the absolute opposite of life in order to work against life within it. In reality it does not exit from life, for all opposites are *immanent in life*. We have in truth no situation "outside life," from which we could oppose it. Therefore "a condemnation of life by the living . . . is after all no more than a symptom of a certain kind of life" that is condemned to perish. The condemnation of life is a judgment made by condemned persons (TI 5:5).

That the condemning will is a will to power may have become clear, but the question arises: Can the fiction of a "true world," the self-orientation by something non-existent that this will performs, be equated with the will to self-destruction spoken of above? In both things, Nietzsche sees the will to nothingness at work. But whereas the latter instinctively seeks to destroy itself, the fiction established for the purpose of condemnation serves the self-preservation and power-instincts of the weak.

That the will to nothingness—in the sense of the will to self-destruction—has taken the upper hand may be all the less clear since Nietzsche himself shows that in "reality" the strong are weak and the weak are strong: "The strongest and most fortunate are weak when opposed by organized herd instincts, by the timidity of the weak, by the vast majority" (WP 685). Against Darwinism, which he once called "a philosophy for butcher boys"[24] compared with his own theory, he writes that selection did not take place in favor of the strong; rather, it marshaled up "the inevitable mastery of the mediocre, indeed even of the sub-mediocre types." Nature "is cruel toward her children of fortune, she spares and and protects and loves *les humbles*" (WP 685; cf. TI 9:14). Therefore Nietzsche must ask himself whether the "victory of the weak and mediocre" does not offer "perhaps a stronger guarantee of life, of the species" (WP 401), than the rule of the strong, who in ruinous struggles endanger not only themselves but also the very existence of the species (WP 864).

Everything suggests that this question must be answered in the affirmative. But is this not a grotesque reversal of what Nietzsche wanted to expound? Does not "life" condemn those who affirm it unreservedly? Does it not justify those who condemn it?

To counter such a supposed self-contradiction of Nietzsche's, we must refer back to what became evident in his analysis of the ascetic ideal. It was shown there that the weak remain weak even when they mobilize their still resistant vital forces against decline; all they can do is prolong the agony. Now it must be added that even their triumph over the strong, even their previous indispensableness for the preservation of the species must not hide the fact that they bring about their own self-destruction and hence the destruction of mankind. Their victory may be presented as a "slackening of tempo"; it may be "a self-defense against something even worse" (WP 401); nonetheless, the worst must happen at last, if they stay in power. They have preserved the "species" by redirecting the human aggressive instincts from outside to inside.[25] But the forces that formerly were exhausted in conflict are now dissipated. Finally they must dry up completely.

Thus neither the strong type nor the weak type seem able to prevent the downfall of mankind. But like the strength of the strong, according to Nietzsche, now the weakness of the strong, too, must in its necessity remain restricted to previous history, where chance prevailed.[26] Only a future "strong race," which will withdraw its power from chance by planning and discipline, will no longer surrender that power to the superior numbers of the weak. Such strong humans will stand in full agreement with "life," which in its genuine form is nothing other than the rule of ascendant wills to power over the descending wills to power.

As the will to the truly non-existent "second world," which guides the weak, is a disguised will to power in the only real world, it is also a disguised will to nothingness, in the radical sense of the word. "With your good and evil," Nietzsche shouts to the weak, "you have forfeited life and weakened your wills; and your valuation itself was the sign of the descending will that longs for death."[27] The longing can swing into action. Then the weak destroy so as to be destroyed. Self-destruction is the consequence of condemning life.[28] The process of wasting away that leads to self-destruction is the history of nihilism. It brings to light more and more what the *Ressentiment*-values really imply, at first without the knowledge of their representatives.

4

Nihilism and Christianity

The time has come when we have to pay *for having been* Christians *for two thousand years: we are losing the* center of gravity *by which we have lived.* —*Will to Power,* 30

The history of nihilism does not have *one* beginning. Nihilism is the expression of physiological decadence. Decadence appears in diverse cultures that have formed independently of one another. Wherever men or societies meet, so that a stronger organization of will rules over a weaker one, the conditions exist for decadence to arise. Consequently, "every fruitful and powerful movement has *also created* at the same time a nihilistic movement" (WP 112). Nihilism *won out* in Buddhism, in Socratic-Platonic philosophy, and in Christianity. That the "course of development" in India *and* Europe, despite their "complete independence" from one another, led to *essentially* the same results, is seen by Nietzsche as proof of the *logical* consistency that governs every nihilistic movement (GM III:27).[1] This *necessity,* which makes it seem possible to Nietzsche to narrate the European "history of the next two centuries" (WP 1), does not contradict his thesis of the *randomness* of all events that are not shaped by the creative force of the most powerful. His concept of randomness is conceived anti-teleologically. That events occur undeterred is not thereby contested.

Nietzsche pays special attention to the nihilism of his time. And it interests him mainly with regard to mankind's *future.* For its sake he looks back "as a sooth-sayer-bird spirit" (WP, Preface 3); what is to happen in the next centuries can be understood only by reflecting on one's origins.

He therefore searches the past again and again to detect the heralds of impending doom. In the process, he names those philosophers that the history of European (i.e., Western) nihilism ranks among its most important representatives. First there is Socrates, who was still "mostly healthy" (WP 432), but with whose appearance decadence made its entrance into Greek philosophy (WP 427, cf. 433). Socrates and Plato, who was seduced by him (WP 435, cf. BGE, Preface), are already "symptoms of decay . . . agents of the dissolution of Greece" (TI 2:2).

Starting with them, "philosophy has been dominated by morality" (WP 412).[2] In Nietzsche's view, Epicurus and Pyrrho represent two further "forms of Greek decadence" (WP 437).[3] Pyrrho is already labeled a nihilist (WP 437). "Stoic self-hardening" and "Platonic slander of the senses" prepare the ground for the nihilistic religion, Christianity (WP 427).

The series of those characterized by Nietzsche as decadents extends through the Christian thinkers of the Middle Ages all the way to modern times. It leads via the "self-animal-tormentor" Bacon (EH),[4] via Kant, the nihilist "with Christian dogmatic bowels" (AC 11), to Carlyle's "pessimism" (TI 9:1), to Comte, who "outchristianed Christianity" (D 132; cf. TI 9:4), to Spencer (TI 9:3, cf. WP 53), and to Schopenhauer's "nihilism" (WP 17), whose form is a tired, Romantic pessimism, as is also, among others, that of E. von Hartmann,[5] de Vigny, Dostoevsky, Leopardi, and Pascal.[6] Literary decadence, as Nietzsche sees it, is widespread in his time "from St. Petersburg to Paris, from Tolstoy to Wagner" (AC 7).[7]

Such a "list of names" must remain incomplete, simply because only the names that Nietzsche explicitly characterized as decadent are listed. This happens on various occasions. Nietzsche never wrote a coherent and detailed history of Western decadence.[8] And he was only seldom interested in subjecting the works or statements of such decadents to a detailed scrutiny—for instance, in the case of his dispute with Richard Wagner. He considers them mainly as representatives of the decline of mankind. And their effects on intellectual history are often more important to him than their own intentions. Socratism and Platonism concern him more than Socrates and Plato. A possible "wide influence" of Kant might appear "in the form of a gnawing and disintegrating skepticism and relativism" (UM 3:3),[9] which is an essential part of this thinker's profile.

The broad lines of intellectual history are what interests Nietzsche in connection with his discussions of nihilism. When he asks, for example, why it is "that from Plato on all philosophical architects in Europe built in vain," he finds "that all philosophers" succumbed "to the seduction of morality" and "that they apparently were aiming at certainty, at 'truth,' but in reality at what Kant had called '*majestic moral edifaces*'" (D, Preface 3).[10] But "all morality denies life." Therefore "the history of philosophy" is "a secret raging against the preconditions of life . . . against partisanship in favor of life." Nietzsche finally even suggests that there is historical evidence that "the philosophers" were "always decadent," always standing "in the service of nihilistic religions" (WP 461). From a physiological perspective, each of these religions is itself nothing else but "a systematic case history of sickness employing religious-moral nomenclature" (WP 152).

Nietzsche tries repeatedly to classify the history of the West—generally from

Socrates on—within the moral period of mankind[11] and thus to unmask it as a decadent movement. Then Platonism and Christianity draw very close together and melt into a unity. "The struggle against the Christian-ecclesiastical pressure for thousands of years" is for Nietzsche, then, nothing other than "the struggle against Plato," for "Christianity is Platonism for the 'people'" (BGE, Preface). Christianity adopted Platonism (WP 572); looking back, Nietzsche can then say ironically that Plato was "an antecedent Christian" (TI 10:2). For the sake of morality, Plato preferred "lies and fiction to truth," "the unreal to what is present," and he invented a "true world" beyond the solely given one, as did the Christians later. Since then the real is considered apparent and the apparent, real. Such a "reversal" is wrong (WP 572). It can be removed only by a second reversal. Nietzsche's own philosophy, which tries to do this, therefore is presented as an "inverted Platonism."[12]

The wrong turn that ultimately stems from the power-will of the weak is developed further in Christianity. Its history is classified by Nietzsche within the history of decadence. He thereby denies distinctiveness to Christianity. We have already seen that for him it is merely the logical extension of Judaism and flows into a Platonism, which it popularizes. Finally he understands it as a reservoir of all nihilistic tendencies. "As a European movement, the Christian movement has been from the very first a collective movement of the outcast and refuse elements of every kind," he writes in *Anti-Christ* (AC 51). It appears to him to be an "agglomeration of forms of morbidity growing together and seeking one another out" (WP 154).

In his efforts to fuse together the history of Christianity with the history of the Western decadence movement Nietzsche runs into difficulties when he turns his attention to Jesus of Nazareth. On the question of "the psychological type of the redeemer" (AC 29), he finds no characteristics of the *ressentiment* that constitutes the dominance-strivings of the weak. On the contrary, "everywhere that judgment was passed, he sided against the judges; he wanted to be the destroyer of morality."[13] In Jesus there is no trace of *ressentiment;* on the contrary, "the instinctive exclusion of all aversion, all enmity, all feeling for limitation and distancing in feeling" is one of the psychological roots of his teaching (AC 30).

Jesus' "good news" consists, accordingly, in the fact "that there are no more opposites" (AC 32). To live without contradictions means, then, to make no distinction between people, also not between me and you, and not to resist the one who opposes me, neither externally, nor internally (WP 163; cf. AC 33). Jesus demonstrated such non-resistance in his "bearing before the judges, before the guards, before the accusers and every kind of calumny and mockery"—in "his bearing on the cross." The practice of life alone mattered to him.[14] It is "what he bequeathed to mankind" (AC 35). The abolition of all opposites, on which his practice is grounded, into one's own inwardness (cf. WP 160) is already "bliss" (cf. WP 163). "The 'kingdom of heaven' is a condition of the heart—not something that comes 'upon the earth' or 'after death'" (AC 34); it is "an inward change in the individual" (WP 161). And "God" is then "the *evangelic practice*" (AC 33).[15]

Whoever, like the Jesus whom Nietzsche has in mind, dissolves in his interiority the opposites that are supposed to be the truly real, can as denier of reality still be merely decadent. Christianity, then, in its very origins is "a form of mortal hostility to reality as yet unsurpassed" (AC 27). Now Jesus' decadence, this most extreme denial of reality, opposes the decadence-instincts supported by Judaism. It is concretized as a "revolt against the Jewish church" (AC 27, cf. 33). And it has nothing in common with the continuation of the decadence-movement that refers to his name. For the Christian church, as Nietzsche repeatedly emphasizes, was "constructed . . . out of the antithesis to the Gospel" (AC 36). "'Christianity' has become something fundamentally different from what its founder did and wanted." It promoted "pessimism," whereas Jesus opposed it by preaching "the peace and the happiness of lambs" (WP 195). Only the falsification of the redeemer's life and teaching could hide the contradiction between Jesus' practice of non-contradictoriness and the power needs of Christian churches expressed in *ressentiment* (AC 39).[16]

In Nietzsche's view, Jesus' activity thus appears as a *break* in the history of decadence. Can Jesus, then, be a decadent at all?[17] Evidently only if he represents a decadence that remains foreign to the movement of decline that rejected him. In him a later phase of this movement could have been anticipated. What speaks for such a view on Nietzsche's part is that traces of Buddhism are detectable in his image of Jesus. For, according to Nietzsche, in Buddhism, decadence has been carried to a point not yet reached in the history of Christianity.[18] It is "a religion for *late* human beings" (AC 22); it has already left behind it what came to power in Christianity, namely "the self-deception of moral concepts" (AC 20).[19]

Jesus, too, stands beyond all morality. And like him the Buddhist rejects the "struggle against those who think differently" and resists "nothing more than it resists the feeling of revengefulness, of antipathy, of *ressentiment*" (AC 20, cf. WP 159). Both agree in seeking peace and reconciliation; and also in their practice, which is oriented completely to making people happy.[20] For both Jesus and Buddhism, *sin* is not a relevant concept (AC 20, 33; WP 160, 342). And as Nietzsche identifies the physio-psychological root of Jesus' personality—his "extreme capacity for suffering and irritation which no longer wants to be 'touched' at all because it feels every contact too deeply" (AC 30)—he also highlights as one of the two "physiological facts" on which Buddhism is based "an excessive excitability of sensibility which expresses itself as a refined capacity for pain" (AC 20).

Yet Nietzsche, particularly in *The Anti-Christ,* draws the difference between Buddhism and Christianity very sharply. His comparison is guided by polemic interests: Buddhism serves as a foil to highlight Christianity, which he condemns. When the two great nihilistic religions are contrasted, Nietzsche suggests to his reader, Buddhism without a doubt deserves the advantage. Admittedly, he has in mind mainly later Christianity. In *The Anti-Christ,* the original Christianity of Jesus is only indirectly drawn into the comparison and devalued compared with Buddhism, for instance, when he praises the latter's "realism" as expressed supposedly in Buddha's dietary regulations. Yet in his portrayal the contrast with Jesus' anti-realism seems to be something superficial compared with what they have in common.

On the other hand, Nietzsche does not want to blur the differences between Jesus and Buddha. He makes them clear by pointing out the particular conditions under which Buddhism originated. It is rooted in a centuries-old philosophical tradition. This gives rise to the second of its underlying physiological facts: "An over-intellectuality, a too great preoccupation with concepts and logical procedures under which the personal instinct has sustained harm to the advantage of the 'impersonal'" (AC 20). Original Christianity arose without such a tradition. Jesus therefore can only appear "as a Buddha on a soil very little like that of India," as Nietzsche once remarks (AC 31). With his death on the cross, "a new, an absolutely primary beginning of a Buddhist peace movement" is destroyed (AC 42).

As a "non-Indian Buddha," Jesus towers over his time. And as Buddhism is "later" than Christianity, Jesus, too, has bypassed its entire history until now. His *unfalsified* doctrine would first find its historical place in a *European Buddhism,* whose gradual rise Nietzsche believes to perceive in his own time. But he does not draw this plausible conclusion. Such an anticipation of the future would conflict with his view of historical continuity, which excludes the occurrence of events for which "the conditions" do not yet exist, although these may be of a "chance" nature. Now the appearance of Jesus, as Nietzsche interprets it, cannot be derived from the history of Judaism, at least not the essential part of it: the practice of non-opposition. Nietzsche can come to only one conclusion: this practice must be a constant possibility of man.

One can attempt to harmonize such a statement with the doctrine of the will to power, which dissolves everything supposedly permanent in the stream of becoming. This constant possibility of practicing non-opposition does not point to the suprahistorical, for that would be exempt from becoming. This possibility, indeed, constantly exists only because in the confrontations of wills to power oppositions constantly break out. That these oppositions can be canceled out by the practice of non-opposition presumes that they exist to begin with. *Which* oppositions are "abolished" in the various historical situations is not essentially significant for lived non-opposition, since for Nietzsche, contrary to its overt intentions, it can be nothing else but a form of the will to power—of the declining one, of course. It can be realized only in history, but then it is realizable at all times and everywhere.[21] Therefore, according to Nietzsche, "such a life" as Jesus lived is also "still possible today"; it can "even be necessary for certain people," in whom the described physio-psychological preconditions exist. It is in principle true: "Genuine, primitive Christianity will be possible at all times" (AC 39).

Reading *The Anti-Christ* one gets the impression that Nietzsche himself is not completely satisfied with the picture he draws of Jesus. Uncertainty remains at least on whether he did justice to the "psychology of the redeemer." He admits that he has read "few books with so many difficulties as the Gospels" (AC 28). To master these difficulties he calls for help from Dostoevsky, "the only psychologist from whom I had anything to learn" (TI 9:45). It seems to him that "that strange and sick world to which the Gospels introduce us" is a world out of "a Russian novel, in which refuse of society, neurosis and 'childlike' idiocy seem to make a rendezvous" (AC 31).[22] But since Jesus did not live in Russia of the late nineteenth century, Nietzsche finally is left with only regret "that no Dostoevsky lived in the neighborhood of this most interesting decadent, I mean someone who could feel the thrilling fascination of such a combination of the sublime, the sick and the childish." In his striving to understand the personality of Jesus, he once even ponders the idea whether Jesus was precisely not the uncontradictory person as he described him: could he not "in fact have been of a peculiar multiplicity and contradictoriness?" He rejects this idea immediately, but must admit: "Such a possibility cannot be entirely excluded" (AC 31).

Comparing later Christianity with the "Buddhistically interpreted" teachings of Jesus, Nietzsche discovers a sharp contrast between the two, as was pointed out above. Nietzsche sharpens the contrast by calling Jesus' lived non-opposition a unique event—contrary to his statements that the practice of original Christianity was and is possible at all times. This point is then formulated: "In reality there has been only one Christian, and he died on the cross" (AC 39). The new *ressentiment*-movement, which of course, more deeply understood, merely continues the old Jewish one, is set aflame precisely by Jesus' death. In view of the cross the disciples sought to identify Jesus' enemies and they discovered them to be the rulers of Judaism, whereas the redeemer, in his manner of dying, had triumphed over every feeling of enmity, indeed over all *ressentiment*. They had not understood him and now they tried to understand him by forging a new image of him. "The popular expectation of a Messiah came once more to the foreground; a historical moment appeared in view: the 'kingdom of God' is coming to sit in

judgment on its enemies." For Jesus this kingdom consisted in the non-opposition to be realized in every generation, but now it was shifted to the future "as a
last act, a promise."

From then on, Nietzsche continues, with contempt and bitterness toward the
Pharisees and theologians, *ressentiment* was inserted into "the type of the redeemer." Moreover, with the doctrine of his death as a sacrificial death and finally
with "the doctrine of the Resurrection" the entire concept of "blessedness," the
unique reality of the Gospel, "is juggled away—for the benefit of a state after
death!" (AC 40, 41). Since then "mankind falls on its knees before the opposite
of what was the origin, the meaning, the right of the Gospel." "In the concept
'Church' [is sanctified] precisely what the 'bearer of good tidings' regarded as
beneath him, behind him." Nietzsche seeks "in vain for a grander form of world-
historical irony" (AC 36).

In the very first Christian community, in Nietzsche's view, the evangelium [good
tidings] is changed into a "*dysangelium*" [bad tidings] (AC 39). "The most
unevangelic of feelings, *vengefulness,* again came to be uppermost" (AC 40) among
the first disciples. The actual history of Christianity then becomes, for Nietzsche,
the history of feelings of revenge that the weak feel toward the strong. To mention a few examples: Nietzsche points out passages from the Gospel of Mark
calling attention to the extreme punishments he expects from the "last judgment"
for those who oppose the believers (AC 45). St. Paul, through whom Judaism won
the decisive victory over original Christianity (AC 214), counts for him as "the
greatest of all apostles of revenge" (AC 45), as a "genius of hatred" (AC 42). In
St. Augustine he sees the triumph of "revenge against the spirit" (GS 359). He
cites Tertullian and Thomas Aquinas to show that, according to both, the sight
of the gruesome punishments of the damned will count among the blissful experiences in the Kingdom of God (GM I:15). And when the Renaissance, "in the
very seat of Christianity itself," had established the "opposing values, the *noble*
values" against the Christian ones (AC 61), at the very moment when Christianity "was vanquished" (EH),[23] Luther, driven by "vindictive instincts" (AC 61),[24]
restored the Church. Again it is "hatred against the higher human being" that
conveys impulses on Christianity (GS 358).[25] And logically, according to Nietzsche, God must still be a cruel ruler for Luther and also for Calvin (GM II:7):
for the Christian projects his instincts and desires into this fictional being he has
invented.

But now Christianity presents itself as a *religion of pity.* "More than that," however, Nietzsche believes he can say, it is "a religion of cruelty."[26] He seeks, moreover, to show that pity stems from the same hostility to the strong as does revenge. The practice that it produces aims to remove suffering. But precisely "the

discipline of great suffering" has created "all enhancements of man so far." "That tension of the soul in unhappiness" cultivates "strength" (BGE 225). To unbend such a "bent bow" is in truth what such practice aims for. What is behind it is not selflessness, but rather the power will of the weak. The familiarity of the pitier toward his neighbor (BGE 206) reveals a leveling tendency—in reality, it is an obtrusiveness (Z IV, "The Ugliest Man"). Christian pity wants to destroy the seeds out of which human greatness could grow. It seeks to keep man small. Therefore, it is typical of the Christian as his "reverse" side, to have "profound suspicion of all the joy of one's neighbor, of his joy in everything that he wants to do and can" (D 80). For that joy also proclaims the "strong type."[27]

Nietzsche's understanding of Christianity as a moral phenomenon is reflected in its emphasis on "the idea of punishment (which corresponds to that of 'reward')" (WP 141) as well as the idea of pity. But there is yet another idea that was "cultivated by morality" (WP 5) and "developed highly by Christianity" (WP, Outline, 2): the idea of *truthfulness*. It is now of special significance for Nietzsche's philosophizing. For, in its full development, as Nietzsche sees it, the history not only of Christianity but of the whole moral epoch of mankind comes to the end.

5

The Will to Truth and the Will to Power

By nature man is not made for knowing—
truthfulness *(and* metaphor*) have generated*
the tendency to truth. Thus a moral phenom-
enon, aesthetically generalized, generates the
intellectual drive. —Nachlaß, KGA X, 151

A question that would have to be asked in the aftermath of deliberations in the foregoing chapter is: To what extent does morality (always understood as *ressen-timent*-morality) stem from the demand for truthfulness? To what extent even is "the *sense for truth* . . . one of the highest and mightiest *efflorescences*" of the "*moral sense*"?[1]

The moral man is timid (BGE 197, 198). His "sense for truth" is really a "sense for security" (D 26). He feels insecure mainly in relation to other men together with whom he lives or whom he meets. Do the others perhaps understand themselves in terms of other value standards than his own? If so, dangers could arise for him. Suspicion of otherness, which Nietzsche detected at the very root of pity, is now supposed to provide the basis for the demand for truthfulness. For only when others express themselves as they think and feel can those dangers be countered.

Society is "the hearth of all morality" (HA:WS 40). The following applies to each of its members: "'You shall be knowable . . . otherwise you are dangerous: and if you are evil, the ability to dissimulate is the worst thing for the herd. . . . *Consequently* you must keep yourself knowable.'" Such self-knowledge presupposes "the *stability* of the person." For if the person recognizing believed he could change, then he would constantly be slipping away from himself. But if he makes himself *fixed* and expresses his fixated "inner nature by clear and constant signs," he stands fully under control of the herd (WP 277). "Mistrust," then, is "the source of truthfulness" (WP 278).[2] It requires that "one should denude oneself with every word one says" (WP 378).

Thus truth, insofar as it stems from truthfulness, appears "as a social need: by a metastasis it is later applied to everything, where it is not necessary."[3] The truth-fulness-impulse "becomes an innate tendency. From a practice for certain cases, it becomes a quality."[4] The "good man" who fixes himself on his truthfulness, finally believes in "the truth of all things. Not only of society, but of the world. Thus also in demonstrability [*Ergründbarkeit*]. For why should the world deceive him?"⁵ So that no other person may get the idea that he could fail to meet the demand for truthfulness—although this is possible, since his interior is inaccessible to others—it is projected into a judging God, to whom nothing remains hidden. What this God demands, he must himself be for the sake of the credibility of his demand: namely, the Truthful One. "God's veracity" is the basis for the idea "that things are, at bottom, ordered . . . morally" (WP 471). Truth, then, appears "as given, as revealed, as identical with the teaching of the priests: as the condition for all salvation and happiness in this life and the next" (WP 141). In all this, reality is surrounded with a world of appearance that is supposed to be considered the "true world."

But morality, by so consistently "demanding truth and honesty above all," has itself "put around its neck the noose with which it can, indeed must be strangled."⁶ In the course of history, "the concept of truthfulness that was understood ever more rigorously, the father confessor's refinement of the Christian conscience" is "sublimated into a scientific conscience, into intellectual cleanliness at any price" (GS 357). Truthfulness finally turns against its own origin. Self-knowledge leads to insight into the unfulfillableness of the moral norm. This then remains—in Kant as interpreted by Nietzsche—"suspended over actuality as a kind of beyond without ever falling down into it" (WP 331). At least, according to Kant, moral actions are "indemonstrable" (WP 786). Such a concession is itself a clear sign that morality is becoming more and more incredible. Subsequently reality too is more and more de-moralized.

> Looking at nature as if it were proof of the goodness and governance of a god; interpreting history in honor of some divine reason, as a continual testimony of a moral world order and ultimate moral purposes; interpreting one's own experiences as pious people have long enough interpreted theirs, as if everything were providential, a hint, designed and ordained for the sake of the salvation of one's soul—that is all over now, that has man's conscience against it, that is considered indecent and dishonest. (GS 357)

The next "consequence of the cultivation of 'truthfulness'—and thus itself a consequence of faith in morality" is then our insight "that we lack the least right to posit a beyond or an in-itself of things that might be 'divine' or morality incarnate" (WP 3). With morality "belief in the Christian God has become unbelievable." Nietzsche means nothing else but this when he speaks of the death of God as "the greatest recent event" (GS 343). After "a two-thousand year discipline for truth, in the end the lie in faith in God forbids itself" (GS 357). "The end of Christianity" is occurring "at the hands of its own morality," which Nietzsche considers undetachable from it (WP, Outline).

But it is not only *Christian* morality that is destroyed in this process. It is a matter of "the self-destruction of *the morality of ressentiment in general*" (WP 405),[7] of which Christianity is the particular historical concretion. "Morality itself, in the form of honesty, compels us to deny morality" (WP 404). Therefore one cannot "get along with a moralism without religious background" (WP 19). But morality is corroded by truthfulness even more deeply than it previously seemed. It does not stop by drawing the consequences from the unfulfillableness of the moral norms. It asks, beyond that, how such norms, to which nothing real corresponds, could take form. And it discovers the hidden "teleology," the "partial perspective" of morality (WP 5).

Morality's real interest proves to be absolutely not moral. It stands in the service of an instinct that is "fundamentally different" from the "conditions of virtue" (WP 284) that apparently comprise its goal. *Ressentiment*-morality is the expression of a will to power, although it indignantly opposes all will to power and condemns it as immoral. The will to power is itself a disguised power-will. Therefore "according to the valuation that evolved the antithesis 'moral' and 'immoral' in general, one has to say: *there are only immoral intentions and actions*" (WP 786). From such a point of view "morality itself" appears to be "a special case of immorality" (WP 401).[8]

However, the truthfulness cultivated by morality in the course of its radicalization cannot stop with the destruction of that to which it owes its impulses. In the end truthfulness must see through its own self. After having refined itself more and more in a history essentially determined by Christianity and "drawn one conclusion after the other, in the end it draws its strongest conclusion, its conclusion against itself; but this occurs when it asks the question; '*What is the meaning of all will to truth?*'" (GM III:27). Or, in a formulation typical of Nietzsche's thinking: "*What* in us really wants 'truth'?" (BGE 1).

We know the premises of the answer: The will to truth, in which truthfulness develops,[9] is rooted in the moral understanding of the world. This world-understanding was traced back to the power-will of the weak. But then the will to truth can itself be only "a tool" (WP 375) of *this* will to power. Now, however, the moral will *conceals* reality. It *deceives* by pretending to be the opposite of the power-will. It uses the will to truth to hide and deceive. When the will to truth seeks to emancipate itself, it recognizes that it arose from its opposite, the will to deception, and that, morally speaking, it served merely "to lie according to a fixed convention, to lie herd-like in a style obligatory for all."[10] "Truth" proves to be "a disguise for completely other feelings and drives."[11]

But even if emancipation were sufficiently achieved, if truthfulness detached itself from its origin by rejecting morality, it could still not abandon a more fundamental deception. For in self-reflection it becomes aware that it absolutely cannot forego fixating reality, even though reality is really in incessant "flux."[12] Thus what the will to truth seeks to grasp constantly escapes. Even when what is fixated is no longer superposed as the alleged true world of the permanent over the reality of becoming, degrading the latter to mere appearance, the original fixation still has the character of a "systematic falsification." It serves the "utilitarian purposes" of the human species (WP 584). Even if the eradicable errors can be removed, the ineradicable ones that are established with the human conditions of life as such still remain (WP 535).[13]

The will to truth, with the insight that its fixation is inadequate to reality, has penetrated through to its original nature. As was discussed in chapter 1, according to Nietzsche the falsification that is constitutive of this will to truth was inherited again and again from the lower organisms all the way to man. Fixating, then, does not first begin with human beings of the moral epoch. To be sure, that period is when the fixated first gets its meaning of something true, which finally leads to the assumption of metaphysical truths. From this initial situation, which truthfulness first caught sight of in the process of its refinement, Nietzsche then describes in broad strokes the genealogy of truth, or truthfulness, down to the then acquired insight as follows:

> To deceive oneself in a useful way; the means, the invention of formulas and signs by means of which we could reduce the confusing multiplicity to a purposive and manageable schema. But alas! now a *moral category* was brought into play: no creature wants to deceive itself, no creature may deceive—consequently there is only a will to truth. What is "truth"? The law of contradiction provided the schema: the true world, to which one seeks the way, cannot contradict itself, cannot change, cannot become, has no beginning and no end. This is . . . the essential fatality of error on earth: one believed one possessed a criterion of reality in the forms of reason—while in fact one possessed them in order to become master of reality, in order to *misunderstand* reality in a shrewd manner. . . . And behold: now the world became false, and precisely on account of the properties that *constitute its reality:* change, becoming, multiplicity, opposition, contradiction, war. (WP 584)

Nietzsche can speak of falsification and error from the standpoint now attained because he still applies the concept of truth in the traditional sense as *adaequatio.* Such "truth" is *not* truth because it *does not correspond* to reality, as it demands of itself. But the untruth of "truth," which must now be spoken of, applies solely to human truth as a fixation since it does not correspond to the real process. If the untruth of truth could be found only in the fact that it represented "*the kind of error* without which a certain species of life could not live" (WP 493), it would still remain truth insofar as it would be binding for all men, at every time and in every place. This would become evident in the fact that men in fixating would agree *not* with reality, but *with one another.*

Truth is occasionally described by Nietzsche as an expression of the general human need for *inertia.* This need is satisfied by those among the possible explanations of a state of affairs "which cause us the minimum of spiritual effort" (WP 279, cf. 537).[14] But is the repeatedly mentioned life-facilitating function of truths not the point of departure at least for a possible correspondence of human fixations? Though what one agrees about may be merely a fiction, it is common to all; thus it is possible, after all, to speak of truth.

But not even in this refuge of a general *human* truth does truthfulness, directed at itself, come to rest. For even if all men fixate to save energy, they still fixate something completely different about the same thing. This differentiality is rooted in the perspectivity of all cognition, which was pointed out above in our description of Nietzsche's genealogy of objectivity. "Every center of force—and not only man"—construes "all the rest of the world *from its own viewpoint*" (WP 636). And the "specific mode of reacting is the only mode of reacting" (WP 567). Perspectivism is necessary (ibid.): it is "the basic condition of all life" (BGE, Preface). For life is constituted by the conflict of variously perceiving power-wills. The world has no meaning for itself or behind itself; it has "countless meanings" (WP 481). If one disregards the perspectives and hence relativity, no world at all is left. There is nothing beyond "the totality" of the differently construing power-centers (WP 567).

Insight into perspectivity now destroys the idea that inner correspondence of human truths exists or is even possible. Two persons, for example, can ally themselves against a third. Their fundamental disagreement can remain hidden in such a common cause. They hide it from themselves, for each needs the other so as to impose his specific interest. What is needed for this is power, which is increased with each ally. "One is always wrong," Nietzsche writes, "but with two, truth begins" (GS 260). If the common opponent is removed, immediately the divergence of those who previously agreed becomes evident.[15]

The disagreement is not the result of one person's standing closer to the truth than the other. "Truth is not something that one person might possess and another not possess" (AC 53). Every perspective has its peculiar truth, which in view of the flowing reality cannot be truth in the purported sense[16] and which, in relation to the opposite interpretations, once again becomes untruth, beyond its basic "simplification and falsification" (WP 492) of flowing reality. For in any case the will to truth can give no general criterion that would permit one to prefer a particular perspective. Thus "the truthful person" ends up "comprehending that he always lies."[17] Nietzsche concludes: there are "many kinds of 'truths,' and consequently there is no truth" (WP 540). Hence "faith in truth itself has been abrogated" (GM III:24). At the end of its long journey it negates itself.[18]

Nihilism enters its decisive phase in the described process: in the perishing of Christianity from its own morality, in the "suicide of morality"[19] through the will to truth which it promotes—finally, in the self-destruction even of the will to truthfulness. For the reign of the will to nothingness is manifested in this process of dissolution. Even though for long stretches of the moral epoch it could remain hidden that nihilism was always at work in it, now it becomes clear that nihilism is the "ultimate logical conclusion of our great values and ideals."[20] The result is their *devaluation.*[21] And since Christianity received the moral values from the *ressentiment*-movement and promoted their downfall, "it is nihilistic in the most profound sense" (EH).[22] "Nihilist and Christian [*Nihilist und Christ*]: that rhymes, and does not merely rhyme . . ." (AC 58).[23] Nihilism was always implicit in the "Christian-moral" interpretation of reality (WP 1), but in the belief "that *there is no truth at all*" (WP 598), it reaches its extreme realization that "every considering-true is necessarily false." That is why Nietzsche calls this "insight" "the most extreme form of nihilism" (WP 15; cf. 13).

Here the movement of decadence[24] has reached the point at which it becomes clear that the will to truth developed in it is "a concealed will to death" (GS 344).[25] It has drawn out again one after another the values inserted into the world in the course of the moral epoch. After the will to truth, now reaching back still further, has freed itself from the conviction that it could grasp reality by fixating it, man has lost his power to interpret and to create fictions (WP 585). After "truth" has made the drastic shift to untruth and the incredibility of traditional morality has became evident, meaninglessness, a void of sense, becomes widespread. After the loss of "truth," "the aim is lacking; 'why' finds no answer" (WP 2). "The philosophical nihilist" comes to the conclusion "that all that happens is meaningless and in vain; and that there ought not to be anything meaningless and in vain."

When Nietzsche inquires into the extent of this "there ought not to be" (WP 36), the answer surely must be: *even the extreme nihilist measures reality by "truth," although he no longer believes in it.* Therefore, for example, "everything egoistic has come to disgust us (even though we realize the impossibility of the unegoistic)." The sphere in which he *lives* has by no means gained in value from the insight that it is the only one (WP 8). The extreme nihilist sees the existing world and "judges that it ought not to be, and of the world as it ought to be" he judges that "it does not exist" (WP 585). "Having reached this standpoint one grants the reality of becoming as the *only* reality, forbids oneself every kind of clandestine access to afterworlds and false divinities—but *cannot endure this world, though one does not want to deny it*" (WP 12). An "antagonism" (WP 5) develops out of this situation. In it, finally, the last secret longing for the already destroyed "truth" must either perish—or man himself, as he clings to it. Thus "future generations" could be placed before "the terrifying Either-Or": "'Either abolish your reverences,'" last of all even your reverence for the truth you no longer believe in, "'or—*yourselves!*'"

Whether the first alternative is nihilism is Nietzsche's own "question mark" (GS 346). The answer given here must still be postponed. The second alternative, however, the thought of doing away with oneself is, no doubt, nihilism. Here the will to nothingness is fulfilled. Various ways lead to its fulfillment. Whether the nihilist gradually perishes through an instinctive selection of things damaging to life (WP 55), whether he seeks to deny his will, in Schopenhauer's sense, for instance, or whether he proceeds to the "deed of nihilism, which is suicide" (WP 247), or whether he first directs his destructive will outwards, driven by the conviction that not only he himself, but "everything deserves to perish": this and other possibilities of nihilistic practice depend, according to Nietzsche, on the nihilist's power, on the strength or weakness of "his will."

Since nihilism itself ultimately stems from weakness of will, one can here, of course, always speak only of "relative strength." "It reaches its maximum . . . as a violent force of destruction, as *active nihilism*." But that the strength is missing "productively to once again set a goal, a why, a belief for oneself" is "a sign of insufficient strength." Nietzsche welcomes this active nihilism insofar as it will, through the *nihilistic catastrophe* (WP 64), put an end to passive nihilism, which is too weary to be able to attack (WP 23), and which crystallizes in his century as the culture of a second Buddhism, as was discussed in chapter 4.

Nietzsche places himself in the ranks of the active nihilists. He wants not only "to respect the fatality . . . that says to the weak: 'Perish!'" (WP 54), but to work for it himself. The strong, who stand beyond nihilism, should in general use nihilism—to fight against it. Thus "an ecstatic nihilism" can "under certain conditions be indispensable precisely to the philosopher—as a mighty pressure and hammer with which he breaks and removes the degenerate and decaying races to make way for a new order of life, or implant in that which is degenerate and deserves to die a longing for the end" (WP 1055). Nietzsche considers it necessary, for the sake of a "purifying great nihilism-movement" to encourage the weak to commit suicide (WP 247). Therefore he wants "to teach the idea that gives many the right to erase themselves—the great *cultivating* idea" (WP 1056).

This idea—namely, the eternal recurrence of the same—will be discussed in chapter 7. First, it is necessary to inquire in principle into that position "outside nihilism" that calls for nihilism to be abolished by destroying the weak. As opposed to active nihilism, here "saying No" and "doing No" is supposed to be derived from "a tremendous strength and tension of saying Yes" (WP 1020). But from the outset this Yes stands so little against nihilism that from the very first it stems from it. "Apparently, everything is decadence," he writes in one note. "One must guide the perishing so that it makes possible a new form of existence for the strong."[26] What Nietzsche expects is "a *counter-movement*" which "in some future or other" will replace "complete nihilism, but which presupposes it logically and psychologically; which can absolutely come only after and out of it." Nietzsche is, in his self-understanding "the first perfect nihilist of Europe who, however, has already lived through the whole of nihilism to the end, leaving it behind, outside himself" (WP, Preface).[27]

This shows clearly that he describes the most extreme type of nihilism in two incompatible forms: first, this extreme nihilism is the incurable disease of those weary of life, who are driven toward death, which "nihilism of the deed" must be "encouraged" (WP 247); secondly, this extreme nihilism is the logical and psychological precondition for the counter-movement. In the first instance, crude physiological ideas dominate: the "excision of the degenerating part" is demanded (EH).[28] In the second, Nietzsche has in mind a far-reaching history of the self-dissolution of morality, Christianity, and truth, which determines the present to such an extent that nihilism has become "a normal condition" (WP 23). In the first instance, self-dissolution is merely the expression of underlying physiological processes; in the second, it acquires a dynamics of its own. A consequence of the first viewpoint is that those affected by the nihilistic sickness are increasingly debilitated down to their inevitable end. The second one, on the other hand, shows that the possibilities of the counter-movement can grow the further nihilism advances, indeed out of its own history.

The extent to which the dynamics of the history of nihilism detaches itself from its physiological underpinnings, although Nietzsche often tries to press it back vigorously, always remains evident in his efforts to describe the overcoming of nihilism as its own most extreme consequence. The counter-movement, as we saw, follows logically and psychologically from complete nihilism. What previously had to be considered as such was the extreme nihilism that rejects reality as withdrawn from "truth." Because all "existence" is untrue, it has "no meaning: the pathos of 'in vain' is the nihilists' pathos." But Nietzsche continues, this is "at the same time, as pathos, an inconsistency on the part of the nihilists" (WP 585). Accordingly, putting this pathos to action, the condemnation to death, also is, "if you will, illogical" (WP 24).

To what extent is the extreme nihilist inconsistent and "illogical"? So far as, although he has lost belief in the "truth," he still measures reality by it. He would be consistent if he also gave up the standard of "truth." If the truthless "reality of becoming" is the only reality, such a nihilist no longer has a right to devaluate it, since the standpoint from which the devaluation takes place has itself already been destroyed.[29] He can no longer even say that there is no "truth," but only untruth. For then reality is still being thought in terms of "truth." With "truth" its opposite also is eliminated: untruth, falsehood, error, appearance. "We have abolished the real world: what world is left? the apparent world, perhaps? . . . But no! *with the real world we have also abolished the apparent one!*" This abolition was the removal of "the longest error" (TI 4). What remains is the real world. Measured by it the opposition truth/error itself proves to be an error. This means, however, that from now on the insight into the reality of becoming makes the claim to truth. Doesn't the self-destruction of truth thereby become merely apparent? Doesn't it still assert itself in its self-denial?

Actually all that has been denied is what previously was considered "truth." The old truth had to be given up in its most recent finding. But this self-surrender should lead to its transformation. Previously it had presented itself as that by which the real world is measured; now it submits to the real world as the only standard. By subordinating itself, it seeks to correspond with the reality of becoming. The new truth stands in contradiction to what was previously considered to be truth. "What I now call truth," the late Nietzsche writes, looking back on his former publications, "is something quite terrible and repulsive," for it gives all morally grounded truth a slap in the face. Therefore his truth must seek "to convince people . . . step by step to completely reverse their highest valuations."[30] The more or less hidden morality of the old truth is now the criterion for its untruth: "We refute an opinion by showing it to be dependent on morality, to be inspired by noble feelings" (WP 459).

The consequence of the self-surrender of "truth" consists in its self-transferal to reality, in which it is transformed into a new truth. This new truth makes its peculiar truth-claim by counterposing the "old" truth-error relation to itself as an error. Beyond this negative self-determination, it is supposed to preserve its trueness by corresponding to reality. Yet immediately difficulties arise, beginning with the very concept of correspondence. If we understand it in the sense of a likeness, we are still on the ground of the old truth. There is no truth "over" or "next to" the sole reality, however sublimely such an "over" or "next to" may be thought. When Heidegger characterizes Nietzsche's real truth as "accord [*Einstimmigkeit*] with the actual," that is, with becoming, he is trying by this choice of words to remove the possibility of this misunderstanding.[31] In the following reflections, the word "truth" is taken in a meaning that differs quite essentially from what Heidegger understands by it.[32]

What is accord here supposed to mean? As truth of becoming it, naturally, is "not a becoming conscious of something that is in itself firm and determined" (WP 551). Is it a mere awareness of the incessant flux? Or is the "stream as such" already the real? It is itself first constituted by the conflict of wills to power. The particular will to power in its reliance on opposing power-wills is the "truly" real. Accord with it is truth. Truth can, then, not at all be something "there, that might be found or discovered"; it is, rather, in attunement with the wills to power, "something that *must be created* and that gives a name to a process, or rather to a will to overcome that has in itself no end." Truth is, then, only "a word for the 'will to power'" (WP 551).

Now the will to power *exists* only as a particular one. It concretizes its peculiarity in the struggle against other particular power-wills. Truth as accord with the will to power could, therefore, itself only be particular, that is, perspective truth. To consider its own perspective true is indispensable for the will to power. "That a great deal of *belief* must be present; that judgments may be ventured; that doubt concerning all essential values is lacking—that is a precondition for every living thing and its life. Therefore, what is needed is that something must be held to be true" (WP 507). This holding to be true posits itself as absolute. Part of it is the negation of the perspective truths of the power-wills that oppose it, which thus become errors for it. A will to power's own truth is confirmed by overcoming others: the more power, the more truth. With this, we have finally found Nietzsche's "criterion of truth"; it consists "in the enhancement of the feeling of power" (WP 534).

We have not yet reached the end of his deliberations on the problem of truth. The positing of perspective truth is, as we have seen, a fixation of what is in flux due to the incessant shifts of the power-constellations. However, if the fixated is believed and the perspective absolutized, precisely the accord of this truth with the will to power is lost. For it can assert itself as power-will amid a constantly changing reality only if it too constantly changes. In order to preserve and enhance its power, it may not solidify into one of the previously acquired perspectives. Truth as belief in a particular power perspective thus once again becomes an error—this time not in relation to the truth-claim of the perspective truths opposite it, but rather in relation to the dominant will to truth itself, to which it falsely believes it submits in the aforementioned absolute-positing.[33]

A true accord with the will to power would, then, consist in assent to the ever-shifting perspectives it posits. Thus, the person who recognizes himself as will to power must believe in his particular valuation, but he also must give up this belief immediately when it no longer corresponds to the criterion of truth, namely the enhancement of the feeling of power. The new truth is supposed to achieve this twofold attitude, belief and simultaneous readiness to give up belief, by becoming the self-revealing and self-confirming of the constantly changing will to power. It would, then, be not only changing assent [*Zustimmung*], surrendering again and again to the varying perspectives and constantly re-solidifying, but simultaneously assenting to the changing itself. Each perspective is true, if only it serves power. In the truth that everything can be true, the human being can ultimately free himself from the millennia-old untruth of moral truth. The "rebound from 'God is truth' to the . . . faith 'All is false'" (WP, Outline, 2) is only the first step on the road to such a liberation. The negation of the old truth performed in it still needs the radical shift to the position of the new truth. The further consequence of the statement "Everything is false," or its negative expression "Nothing is true," consists in the insight: "Everything is permitted" (GM III:24)[34]—namely, insofar as "everything" (each particular perspective) can serve to enhance power.

However, the knowledge that everything is permitted can become independent. It can detach itself from its position of service to the demand for enhancement of power. Then such possibilities as are presented stand opposite others. None has a priority. Each one is paralyzed by the opposing ones. The belief in the truth of some particular perspective, a belief indispensable to life, is completely lost; hence, the consequence of the will to power's self-knowledge is merely that such a belief must not solidify as definitive. By absolutizing one perspective, the will to power is immobilized; by absolutizing "Everything is permitted," it loses any effective form.[35] In both cases, a self-damaging of the previously dominant power-will occurs and it will have to submit to a stronger will.

The latter absolutization always runs the danger of shifting into the former one—a danger to which Zarathustra alludes in the conversation with his shadow. The insight into the relativity of every truth has caused the shadow to lose its goal; the unbearableness of such a loss can pursue it into the "prison" of a narrow belief that again promises a goal and hence "new security" (Z IV).[36] Many new places of refuge present themselves after one has unlearned faith in "some superhuman authority." According to an old habit, "one then seeks *another* authority that can speak unconditionally and command goals and tasks. The authority of conscience now comes to the fore (the more emancipated one is from theology, the more imperativistic morality becomes) to compensate for the loss of a personal authority. Or the authority of reason. Or the social instinct (the herd). Or history with an immanent spirit and a goal within, so one can entrust oneself to it." In all these cases, one wants to "*get around the will,* the *willing* of a goal, the risk of positing a goal *for oneself;* one wants to rid oneself of responsibility (one would accept fatalism)" (WP 20).[37] In such a self-surrender to any old or new authority the will to power misunderstands itself, as much as the fixation of goallessness that stems from the detachment of the insight that everything is permitted.

Such a prohibitive characterization of the will to power that truly understands itself, or of the "new" truth defined as power, is, of course, not enough. It must also be asked how its positive concretion can be acquired. Before this is done, the essential stages should be reviewed again, from the origin of the traditional understanding of truth, to the need to overcome it, and to a new grounding of truth in Nietzsche's sense.

Herd-morality generates distrust of every kind of non-correspondence with it. Mistrust gives rise to the demand for truthfulness. This is the means to discover otherness in order to combat it effectively. In the course of its long history, the sublimation of truthfulness produces a truth-conscience that finally unmasks the immoral interest at the basis of previous morality. Morality thus is destroyed by what it had produced for its own consolidation. For the destructive force of truth is directed against its own self, too.

The extent of its influence is evidenced by the fact that its truthfulness affects not only morality, but also truth. The essence of "truth" can be grasped in an equalizing fixation. Such fixation is contained in the demand for moral truthfulness; its pillars are agreement with the "herd" and stability of the person amid changing events. Moreover, in many ways fixation is one of the conditions for the preservation of the living organism, man; it points back to something more primeval than the moral era of mankind.

The progressive self-inquiry of truth focuses on this fixation. It discovers that contrary to its purported intention it cannot achieve correspondence with reality. Reality is incessantly changing, and so the fixations are nothing more than fictions. In their use, there are indeed agreements among human beings. But these interhuman agreements do not mean that any tenable, subjectively universal basis of truth has been found. First, because, on closer examination, universal agreement occurs only within very narrow limits. Therefore it is impossible to eliminate the actual diversity of the specific world-perspectives within which the narrowly limited common ground takes on different meanings. Secondly, from a genealogical point of view, it must be noted, the agreements are nothing but accords made in order to facilitate life. They are something that has become and that cannot escape the possibility of further change, which necessarily would accompany any fundamental shift of the power relations. Even such interhuman accords are nothing fixed in the sense of the claim they make.

Intersubjective harmony is not "truly permanent agreement." Countless perspective truths are detectable behind it, each of them standing against all the rest. Measured by any one of them, the others become untruths; measured by every other one, the prerogative of the first is lost. Reflecting on the complex of relations of mutual negation, one sees that there are only untruths, no truth.

The self-scrutiny of truth thus leads to extreme nihilism. The belief that there is some "fixed," universally valid correspondence, a self-grounded truth, is seen through as an illusion. Now, "truth" is rejected, but even the rejection lays claim to what it rejects. It is rejected because it is not what it is supposed to be. Yet as what is supposed to be, it remains the standard for its own rejection.

Such a contradiction is the conclusion to which the truthful person is led by insight into "truth." If he remains bound to what was previously called truth, he must despair. If he has the strength to dismiss the "old" truth, he can forge ahead to what truth ultimately is: something terrible from the point of view of tradition: something new and hopeful for the person who has left tradition behind. The "new" truth has given up the demand for correspondence with reality as seen on its surface in favor of a harmonious assent to what actually exists. In its ground, the real is in manifold ways will to power. The "new" truth (which was always the only truth, but in the past was hidden) consists in being at one with the will to power.

Conversely, that truth ultimately reveals itself as will to power means that every will to power can reveal itself in its truth. The respective particularity of its perspective fixation can then be seen to have the character neither of universal validity nor of mere fiction. Nor does the fixation serve merely to facilitate life. Rather, it is primarily the way a power-will organizes the forces subject to it and seeks to overpower those not yet subjected. It does so by positing its perspective absolutely. Since the will is concerned with power, the fixation must not want to become definitive solidification; for the world, the totality of the power constellations, is engaged in continuous change. The will, wanting more and more power, must take this change into account by itself changing. This change, however, can happen only if the current truth-perspective is not posited absolutely and hence solidified.

Every will to power that sees through itself thus finds a peculiar contradictoriness in itself: it must be unrestrictedly convinced of the truth of its own current perspective, yet at the same time—in readiness for the need to change—it must refrain from this conviction. If one of the two modes of behavior overcomes the other, the result is either rigidity or the loss of self in the multiplicity of what could become real. The downfall becomes inevitable. The will to power is no longer "effective"; it is no longer truly will to power.

The "new" truth as accord with the will to power is therefore not assent to abstract change as such, in which the multiple entities are obscured. Nor is it only assent to any particular fixed perspective. Together with this, it should be assent to the concrete change of perspectives that serves the expansion of power.

At this point it must be asked how the will to power can be both at the same time absolutization and non-absolutization of its current perspective. Or, focusing on the problem of the "new" truth: can the prevailing truth, which pushes into untruth what does not subordinate itself to it, at the same time remain open to what is rejected?

The answer to this question will decide whether the will to power that understands itself in its truth will be able to overcome nihilism. Nietzsche's attempt to eliminate the contradictions arising within the dominant will to power took shape in his doctrines of the overman and the eternal recurrence of the same. We must now examine the tenability of these attempts.

6

The Way to the Overman

To rule? To impose my type on others?
Horrible! Is my happiness not precisely the
beholding of many others? Problem.
—*Nachlaß,* GA XII, p. 365

Chapter 1 of this book discussed in general terms the contradictoriness that guides Nietzsche's thinking and traced it back to its root, the conflict of wills to power. Chapter 2 reflected on their concrete occurrence in the history of mankind. The phenomena of decline thus brought to light were interpreted in the description of the will to nothingness, under which the *dissolution* of an organization into a multiplicity of antagonistic will-quanta occurs. The movement of decadence, which steers the dissolution in a peculiar direction, determines the history of Western nihilism, in which Christianity assumes particular significance. Moral demands and fictions of another reality function to *delay* disintegration [*Disgregation*] (chapters 3–4). Truthfulness, cultivated in Christianity, leads to the destruction of truth. This dissolves into a multiplicity of mutually opposing untruths. Such extreme nihilism can supposedly be overcome by a counter-movement stemming from this very nihilism. The strong power-will that uses a "new" truth is supposed to perform this overcoming. The question is whether it can do so, given its intrinsic contradictoriness. For it is required both to absolutize its particular perspective and to negate such an absolutization (chapter 5).

According to Jaspers,[1] Nietzsche, in forging his image of man, tries to overcome this contradiction. He names types of human enhancement by various titles; he speaks of the great man, of the mightiest, the wisest, the highest, the solitary, the complete, the rich, and the whole man. It is hard to differentiate the content of this and other nomenclature employed by Nietzsche. Many of the terms are used synonymously, or their meanings blend together when various texts are consulted. The same thing happens when one wants to capture the notion of 'degree of enhancement' that can be gathered from some of Nietzsche's statements.

Often characterizations under one of the terms bring out only one supposedly essential aspect of the higher man. But they all have in common that they are supposed to set him off from the lower man.[2] Nietzsche foresees two lines of development in the man of the future. "*One* movement is unconditional: the leveling of mankind, huge ant-like buildings, etc. The *other* movement, on the contrary, involves the sharpening of all oppositions and rifts, the elimination of equality, the creation of the super-powerful."[3] In contrast to the leveling tendencies of the "last man," the future great man will intensify the contradictions in the world. Nietzsche does not find what he is seeking in any of the prior realizations of greatness. Therefore he sketches possibilities of future powerful human existence that finally culminate in the *idea of the overman.*

Neither the multiplicity of names intended to suggest that there are *many forms* of ascendant humanity, nor the unity of the goal aspired to of producing the overman, can hide the fact that in Nietzsche's portrayals *two different tendencies* are locked in conflict, mirroring the incompatibility of their contradictory natures. This became evident in chapter 5, elaborating on the will to power that has seen its truth.[4]

Thus we find, on the one hand, portrayals according to which man's greatness consists in the absolutization of his perspective. "The most powerful man, the creator," imposes "his ideal *against* the ideals of other men and remakes them in his own image" (WP 1026). He is "*inventive*" in the quest for "*means* of communication" through which he can "immerse" himself "in great communities" (WP 964). But he always imposes himself.[5] "It is not enough to present a doctrine: one must also change people coercively so that they will accept it!—Zarathustra finally understands that." These are words from one of Nietzsche's notebooks.[6] The creative man would therefore have to "be the most evil"; and "terribleness is a part of greatness" (WP 1026).[7] "*Become hard,*" Zarathustra teaches, in order "to write on the will of millennia as on bronze" (Z III).[8] The great man must abolish what cannot be reshaped, not be made compatible with the ideal. He must "gain that tremendous *energy of greatness* in order to shape the man of the future through breeding and, on the other hand, the annihilation of millions of failures, and *not to perish* of the suffering one *creates,* though nothing like it has ever existed!" (WP 964).[9]

As a philosopher the great man is supposed to become a legislator, a commander, who says: "Thus it shall be!" (WP 972). "He who *determines* the values and directs the will of millennia by giving direction to the highest natures," is, accordingly, "*the highest man*" (WP 999). Such determination is at the same time an exclusion. In view of mutually contradictory instinct-systems of the modern era, "the rationale of education" requires "that at least one of these instinct-systems should be *paralyzed* beneath an iron pressure, so as to permit another one to come into force, become strong, become master" (TI 9:41). The "triumphant idea" that Nietzsche's own philosophy seeks to present will ultimately cause "all other modes of thought . . . to perish" (WP 1053).

The great man, who thus determines the horizon within which the ideals he has created find their range of development possibilities, allows nothing to arise that does not fit with himself. The great man can do this only if he shuts himself off from whatever is alien to him. Ignorance that is expressed in forgetting as a natural antidote to the historical sickness and against every excessive demand on his plastic powers must, then, be cultivated into the attitude of *wanting* not to know. The great man must have "the *will* to ignorance" that always implicitly underlies wanting to know. Knowledge of its indispensability first makes firm the great "dome of ignorance" under which he stands (WP 609). Such knowledge of the necessity of forgetting gives rise to effects contrary to the aforementioned natural forgetting: "Because we forget that valuation is always from a perspective, a single individual contains within him a vast confusion of contradictory valuations and *consequently of contradictory drives*" (WP 259). The forgetting of perspectivity makes room for what *should* be forgotten. "The wisdom that sets bounds even to knowledge" is, therefore, necessary (TI 1:5). Nietzsche regards as naive the assumption "that nothing could be disclosed by knowledge that was not salutary and useful to man" (D 424).

Nietzsche's references to the *danger of self-knowledge* belong in this context. "The relative ignorance" in which the regent in the "subject-unity" is kept "concerning individual activities and even disturbances within the communality . . . is among the conditions under which rule can be exercised." "The danger of the direct questioning of the subject *about* the subject and of all self-reflection of the spirit lies in this, that it could be useful and important for one's activity to interpret oneself *falsely*" (WP 492). The true-false antithesis alluded to here has its place in the realm of the "old" understanding of truth that Nietzsche recurrently takes as his point of departure. The criterion for the new understanding of "truth" consists in the enhancement of power. Nietzsche's demand can be understood by that criterion: "The knower avoids self-knowledge and leaves his roots buried in the ground."[10] For when the knower focuses on himself for the purpose of cognition, he must turn away from what can still be conquered. "The great egoism of our dominating will . . . requires that we shut our eyes to ourselves" (WP 426).

According to the foregoing account, what Nietzsche once confesses concerning himself applies to the great man: "Once and for all, there is a great deal I do *not* want to know" (TI 1:5). On the other hand, he also characterizes him, in contrast with the above remarks, as the one who withdraws from no possible knowledge—whether that object of knowledge is the "world" or the self. He should learn to see in various kinds of perspectives, with more and more eyes, omitting nothing ever known, including the most contradictory things, in order to prepare the "future objectivity."

Accordingly "the wisest man"—whose wisdom contrasts with the above-mentioned wisdom of *limiting* knowledge—would be the one "*richest in contradictions* who has, as it were, antennae for all types of men—as well as his great moments of *grand harmony*" (WP 259). "The great man" in this sense is "the bow with the great tension," which arises "from the presence of opposites and the feelings they occasion" (WP 967). This type sums up and synthesizes, whereas the former excludes and paralyzes. To him the domination of a single point of view over the multiplicity seems like fanaticism, although Nietzsche claims to find it only among the weak and decadent (GS 347).

But despite all differences, *both* types of greatness are concerned with power. But the man of the great synthesis, it would seem, must lose power and necessarily become all the more powerless, the more he absorbs mutually opposing ideas. Nietzsche indeed writes that "the sublime man" has "the greatest value . . . because an abundance of very difficult and rare things has been bred and preserved together through many generations." But that is precisely why he is also "terribly delicate and fragile" (WP 996). His "disintegration" becomes all the more probable, the greater the sum of ingredients he seeks to coordinate. "The richest and most complex forms—for the word 'higher type' means just this—perish more easily" (PW 684). Nietzsche can also speak this way. Can the "value" of this type be called the highest, if only "the quantum of power" is determinative of rank? (WP 858).

That the strongest men are weak compared with the more mediocre types was discussed in chapters 2 and 3. Of course, no distinction was yet made between the two concepts of strength used by Nietzsche. But this much was shown: in the course of time the men of action, the great relentless ones, were defeated by the more mediocre ones. They will ruin themselves again and again unless they can *produce* the "unfavorable conditions" they need in order to maintain their power. The planning of difficulties in life is supposed to serve to breed this type into ever mightier forms.

But when the strong themselves take charge of producing those conditions, they cannot remain relentless. They no longer can be interested in destroying those who oppose them, nor even in having other ways of thinking perish from their ideal. For the sake of their own strength, the relative strength of their opponents becomes essential. An ideal can become stronger only by repeatedly being challenged by other ideals. If it is elevated to the sole ideal, it loses the character of privilege, of priority it strives for. From this point of view it appears like a weakness to want to remake all humans in one's likeness. "Most idealists," who "at once propagandize for their ideal as if they could have no right to the ideal if *everyone* did not recognize it," are acting basically "out of terror of the herd" (WP 349).

The strong man, on the contrary, who has recognized the conditions for achieving and maintaining his strength, *should want resistance* and opposition. Nietzsche also occasionally understands his struggle against Christianity and morality under this aspect:

> I have declared war on the anemic Christian ideal (together with what is closely related to it) not with the aim of destroying it but only of putting an end to its *tyranny* and clearing the way for new ideals, for *more robust* ideals. . . . The *continuance* of the Christian ideal is one of the most desirable things there are—even for the sake of the ideals that want to stand beside it and perhaps above it—they must have opponents, strong opponents, if they are to become *strong*.—Thus we immoralists require the *power of morality:* our drive of self-preservation wants our opponents to retain their strength—it only wants to become master over them. (WP 361)[11]

To some extent the strong man, who is to be cultivated, also always takes into consideration the ideals opposed to his ideal and even calls them into existence:[12] they remain for him that from which he is separated by an unbridgeable chasm. To be aware of them cannot mean for him to recognize them. More precisely, only their *counter*-action is recognized because it is suited to preserve and intensify his own power—but not their specific contents.

With the man of the great synthesis things are different. He has the contradictions not outside but inside himself. His ability to assimilate them constitutes *his* peculiar strength.[13] In the power relationship to the herd this strength, to be sure, turns out to be a weakness. Thus he represents the *solitary* type that succumbs when it encounters "the instincts of the herd." His instruments of defense, his protective instincts, are from the beginning not sufficiently strong or certain. This type lacks the robustness of the relentless ones. For its preservation and development it needs precisely not the "unfavorable" conditions of constant struggle with the surrounding world, but compromise, such as is most likely found "in a democratic society," where "the coarser means of defense are no longer necessary and habits of order, honesty, justice, and trust are part of the usual conditions" (WP 887).

Nothing can be more harmful to this type than what Nietzsche elsewhere calls the means "by which *a stronger type maintains itself*": "To venture into states in which it is not permitted *not* to be a barbarian" (WP 921). He proves to be powerless against the herd and against masterful men. His impotence will grow to the extent that he "sums up" the contradictions in himself: the more multifarious these contradictions are and the more strongly they assert their particular claims, the more disunited and uncertain must the reactions of the "total person" become. The highest intensification of this trait in the "wisest man" would result in his inability to live.

It is not difficult to recognize in the portrayal of the two types of great man the two factors that are supposed to constitute the will to power persisting in its truth: the fixation of a perspective in exclusive opposition to other perspectives, and the opening up to the multiplicity of possible perspectives. Their incompatibility now seems to have been confirmed. The great man of whose breeding Nietzsche is thinking must—this is the outcome of the foregoing reflections—be *either* the strongest *or* the wisest. Each precludes the other in principle, that is, not merely due to previous history, which was determined by chance.

Increase of power is the criterion of man's true greatness. As described, this criterion can be fulfilled only by the first characterized type, the strongest man, who imposes *his* ideal upon the opposing ones. One becomes stronger, Nietzsche writes, "by clinging tenaciously to what one has decided" (WP 918). But the analysis of the truth-problem showed that this absolutization finally loses the very power it wants. Rigid insistence on *one* ideal—clinging to a certain perspective—must lead to a rigidity that can no longer take into account the incessant changes of the whole of reality through the struggle of "opposites." Even if the future strong man were to accomplish the relative recognition of the opposing ideals in the above-described sense for the sake of asserting power, he would be defeated as soon as one of the unforeseeable changes in the *global* constellation of wills to power, that is, in the entire world, required the establishment of a *new* ideal. Breeding the great man and planning conditions under which he can prosper, one must therefore promote both his ability to consolidate a leading ideal and the contrary ability to modify it or even to surrender it in favor of other ideals.

The great man's mobility required for this second objective will increase to the extent that he opens himself to the multiplicity of possible perspectives. The more perspectives are at his disposal, the more favorable are chances for maintaining and increasing his power. The two incompatible factors rely on each other. The strong man can only remain strong and become stronger if he becomes the wise man who not only has the multifarious contradictions outside himself but assimilates them into himself. And the wise man will be lost in the perspectival contradictions and suffer losses in form [*Kontur*] and strength, if he does not commit himself to the exclusive guidance of *one* ideal.

The two elements constituting the true will to power are supposed to be represented most outstandingly in the great man. But they stand in relation to one another. It is in the sense of intensifying their peculiarity that they exclude one another. This intensification is, however, supposed to be in the service of power. In view of this, it turns out that an element of the opposite type is always needed. Each must blend into its opposite if power is not to become powerless. Can a type be bred, or even thought, in which the contradiction of this dual relation can be abolished? Nietzsche once noted: "The *wise man* and the *animal* will draw closer and produce a new *type*."[14] But how could such an approximation be possible without reducing wisdom or animality, whereas the growth of *both* is supposed to be indispensable for the increase of power?

Nietzsche gives no convincing answer to this question. He has before his eyes the chaos of the multifarious man of his times, who is the cause of the unproductivity of the nineteenth century, the ruin of modern man. Therefore he calls for a violent, dominant race, for the "*barbarians* of the twentieth century" (WP 868). It is time for "iron men," such as have "never yet lived. Their immediate task is to make the personal ideal *prevail* and *become real*" (WP 908). The word "immediate" indicates the provisionalness of such behavior. Obviously this behavior is to be followed by another: readiness to accept other ideals.

But how that readiness can follow from this behavior remains incomprehensible. Whoever has imposed *his* ideal *against* others cannot open himself to the multiple contents of other ideals without giving up that prerogative. Such surrender would be self-surrender of the "iron man" in favor of the sublime. It can be understood not as a transition, but only as a qualitative leap; or rather—it cannot be understood. The attempt to bring the two elements of the will to power into a successive historical sequence in order to mediate between them is a failure. The fact remains that the great man is strong or wise. Only *alternation* of the two types of greatness could perhaps be made plausible in this way, but not their approximation, not to mention their amalgamation.

Nietzsche must, however, postulate this, if the truth of the will to power is to attain living reality in the great man and thereby overcome nihilism. A further objection is: if intensifying the peculiarity of the strong man and the wise man is mutually exclusive, perhaps that is only because they have not been carried forward to their most extreme possibilities. Man has become master of the earth because "in contrast with the animal" he has "cultivated an abundance of *contrary* drives and impulses within himself." In his intensification to the highest man he had "to have the greatest multiplicity of drives, in the relatively greatest strength that can be endured" (WP 966). But *at the same time* he had to be "a monster of energy, who demands a monster of a task" (WP 995).

The two extremes are to be united in that man in whom "the various forces are unhesitatingly harnessed for the attainment of one goal." He would be the truly

"great *synthetic* man" who has left the chaos of multifariousness behind (WP 883)—
and likewise the limited mentality of the barbarian. Synthesis then means, of
course, coercive subordination and reordering of all opposites acquired by hered-
ity or cognition under one dominant will.[15] Nonetheless, these contradictory elements must undergo their most extreme development. That is why the most
extreme strength is required to hold them together and make them productive.

Nietzsche must go beyond what man is and was with the idea of combining
the two extremes by way of their intensification. Of course, the strong men of
the past have repeatedly controlled "instincts that conflict powerfully." On this
point Nietzsche likes to cite as an example Shakespeare (behind whom he suspects Bacon) (WP 966, cf. 848). But they only accomplished—although they did
so excellently—what constitutes the peculiarity of every ascendant will to power:
to unite in oneself a plurality of will-quanta. The intensification of the opposites
and their greatest possible expansion was not within the scope of their intention;
they would not have been equal to such a task. Nietzsche, looking back in *Ecce
Homo,* writes that therefore even a Shakespeare "would be unable to breathe even
for a moment in this tremendous passion and height" that was expressed in *Thus
Spoke Zarathustra.* Zarathustra "has seen further, willed further, been *capable*
further than any other human being." He has "access to contraries." "In him all
opposites are blended into a new unity. The highest and the lowest energies of
human nature, the sweetest, most frivolous, and most terrible wells forth from
one fount with immortal assurance" (EH).[16] He wants to lose "no past of mankind, and to throw everything into the mold."[17]

From the height of his solitude Zarathustra teaches the overcoming of previous man. Looking down from there he has not yet seen "a great human being"
(Z IV).[18] "Whoever is the wisest among you is also a mere conflict and cross
between plant and ghost" (Z, Prologue, 3). But above all he looks still further
upward and forward. He proclaims the *overman,* who is supposed to be not only
the goal and meaning of human existence (7), but "the meaning of the earth"
(3). Zarathustra himself is not yet the overman. The "beauty of the overman" first
came to him "as a shadow" (Z II).[19]

The shadow delineates the silhouette of the overman. Perhaps indistinctly or
even distortedly, but in such a way that "some of the things" can be "guessed" as
to what he could be (WP 1000). Even the shadow presents an image. His profile
announces what man shall become. The image of the overman is not intended
as fiction. As the highest reality that can be realized he takes the place of the prior,
merely fictitious highest. "Only now is the mountain of man's future in labor.
God died: now we want—the overman to live" (Z IV).[20]

All prior images of man are supposed to be shattered by the image of the overman; that is what Zarathustra wants.[21] On the other hand, when he created the overman, he could not do without anything that man had acquired on his long journey.[22] What he smashes and what he preserves and accumulates are the same thing. It is smashed in its claim to independent validity; it is preserved as that which can serve the possibility of maintaining or expanding power. As accumulation it is to be directed toward the goal of having the overman establish himself.

The goal of the overman cannot be stated. Not because, as Heidegger writes, it belongs to the "essence of this human existence" that "every particular content-goal, every determinacy of this kind remains inessential and always only an occasional means." The superman represents "the essential indeterminacy of unconditional power," although Nietzsche did not "express it this way." Unconditional power is "pure overpowering as such, unconditional outdoing, being on top, and ability to command, the only and highest being."[23] The overman is "as the highest subject of perfected subjectivity the pure empowering of the will to power."[24] Indeterminacy of content is precisely where his "unconditional determinacy" resides.[25]

On the other hand, it must be pointed out that for Nietzsche there "can be no *sheer* overpowering, no sheer empowering of the will to power, because for him all willing is a willing-*something*." The overman indeed wants power "absolutely," that is, in unrestricted dominance. But he can achieve and exercise power only if he grasps it in its conditionalities. The thought of an absoluteness of power as such is an abstraction that is foreign to Nietzsche's thinking. Only from a goal with determinate content can the overman organize the multiplicity of goals of the subordinate wills to power that serve him as means. The overman cannot want power *as such;* if he intended it, he would become powerless in the concrete situation by striving for something empty. Of course, none of his actual goals can claim *constancy in domination.* If the overman is to remain the most powerful being, he must change his leading goals, because that is the only way for him to do justice to the process of changing reality. His goal is undeterminable, not because he has left behind him all contents as inessential. Rather, there cannot be only *one* goal for him, because in the flow of time the most varied contents can and must be considered the dominant goals. Not an exiting to lack of content, but rather the changing use of an overabundance of contents is the essence of the overman.

If the "greatest elevation of the consciousness of strength in man as he creates the overman" (WP 1060) could lead to the overman's image being transformed into reality, the will to power would have arrived at its truth. For this truth requires that the overman is to achieve *in one person* the intensification of the contradictions of all strivings to their extreme; their combination under the yoke of

one powerfully imposed ideal; and readiness to give up this ideal in favor of another, previously subjugated one, in accord with shifts of the power constellations in the entire unique world of becoming. Uniting all these factors, the overman would be revealed as the "type of supreme achievement" who could
effectively oppose nihilism (EH).[26] In him human existence would be trans-
figured.[27]

Insofar as *only the overman* can overcome nihilism, the destiny of humanity
depends upon the "*attainment of its highest type*" (WP 987).[28] In contrast with
the nihilist, who denies life, the overman will affirm life. The synthesizing overman's self-affirmation is true in the sense of the "new truth" only when he opens
up to the multiplicity of what is, without depriving himself of the possibility of
"creating." Just as the radical nihilist rejects reality totally, the overman's affirmative
openness must be equally total. His Yes must extend to the whole world, after
the nihilist has condemned this whole. If the overman's affirmation were only
partial, the nihilist would be right with regard to the excluded part. Since the
sole world comprises a seamless complex, a "half Yes" would be just as inconsistent as a "half No." Whoever says "Yes" to one fact must affirm all facts, if his
Yes is to be a *genuine* Yes. For the affirmed fact exists only *with* all others, *through*
all others.

The Yes to everything that *is* must consequently also be a Yes to everything that
was. Nietzsche notes as a "principle: *every* experience, traced back to its origin,
presupposes the world's entire past—to call *one* fact good means to affirm *all*! But
by approving all, one also approves all present and past affirmations and condemnations."[29] The overman must, then, affirm even the nihilistic condemnations
that he himself condemns. His saying "No" and even his *doing* No must stem
from an unrestricted Yes. Even Zarathustra, who says "'No' to an unheard-of
degree" to everything that was previously affirmed, is nevertheless "the opposite
of a No-saying spirit" (EH).[30]

The two contradictory factors emerge again in the overman's rejecting No and
preserving Yes. He sets his goal absolutely. He can do this only by rejecting the
claims of all other wills to power in order to subjugate or destroy them. Thus he
needs the *strength* of negative action. And at the same time he needs the *wisdom*
of positive discourse that allows those other wills to power in their multiple contradictions to attain the extreme degree, that is, the one most their own. By approving *all*, he abolishes the aforementioned absolute claim.

One gets the impression that Nietzsche, in his description of the highest man,
relentlessly harnesses that multiplicity under *one* goal, assigns primacy to *strength;*
but now one could think that with the affirmation of all affirmations and rejec-
tions he gives definite priority to *wisdom*. Pursuit of this difference would again

lead to two different types that could not be fitted together into the postulated unity of the overman.

Nietzsche's disparate statements quite often can be understood in terms of what he envisages at the moment as the obstacle to overcome. When he is concerned with portraying the overman in relation to the chaotic man of modernity he accentuates the power that combines opposites coercively. When he stresses the affirmation of all things, he has in mind not only negation, which culminates in total denial of the world by nihilism, but also the denial of *this* denial as performed in the violent subjugation of the multifarious under *one* ideal that prevents other strivings from developing their own most peculiar desires. The latter denial receives its right from an affirmation expressed in the domination by *one* goal. But the absolutization of this goal must, in its limitation that is inadequate to reality, be abolished in favor of the affirmation that recognizes *all things,* in which the determinate Yes is only one among countless many to which it seeks to expand.

Once again we see referral of the two factors of the will to power to one another, and again Nietzsche cannot show plausibly that this can lead to their blending *in a single form.*[31] Looking at himself, at his own actuality, he notes that what is supposed to become a unity disintegrates. "To preserve myself I have my protective instincts of contempt, disgust, indifference, etc. They impel me to solitude; but in solitude, where I feel that everything is necessarily interconnected, every being is divine."[32] Driven back and forth between world denial and world deification he finds no solid footing. He fails to affirm life in the dual meaning of the negating Yes to the restricted individuality and of the Yes to all that was and is. Thus he is left only with "the look to the overman" who will be able to affirm this life. "I have tried to affirm it myself—alas!"[33]

Never yet has there been an overman (Z II).[34] The combination of conflicting elements that is supposed to follow from intensification to the extreme must be expected from the future. The two currents striving in opposite directions within what has become visible until now are supposed to flow together in what is invisible so far. Thus it can be said with Jaspers that *faith* is involved in Nietzsche's idea of the overman.[35] But not in the sense that Jaspers means: that this faith primarily "creates the idea of the overman." Nor is it based on Nietzsche's "drive," understood purely existentially, "that allows him to find no foothold anywhere in any finite sphere" and leads his thought to "higher and higher abstraction," which movement in the end even requires the abolition of such a faith[36] because the indefiniteness of the Whither can mean "nothing for a living person."[37] These statements merely show the limitedness of Jasper's existentialist thinking. Whatever falls outside the framework of this familiar way of thinking is condemned to insignificance or, at best, is used as a "failure" to confirm one's own point of departure.[38]

For Nietzsche does not wind up in empty abstraction when he carries the image of man to the extreme. His problem, rather, is the concrete abundance that he must fit into it. The most extreme form of being human finally becomes unthinkable because the multiplicity of contradictions that must be assimilated cannot be integrated in one person of superior power. The conflict between wisdom and power remains unsolved in the highest man. Nietzsche must, however, cling to the possibility of a solution, since only it warrants that the will to power can attain its truth and overcome nihilism. Because the philosophical proof of this possibility does not succeed,[39] it can be kept open only as an *object of faith*.[40] In the end nothing remains except stubborn hope: "But some day, in a stronger age than this decaying, self-doubting present, he must yet come to us, the *redeeming man* of great love and contempt. . . . This man of the future . . . this antichrist and anti-nihilist, this victor over God and nothingness—*he must come one day* . . ." (GM II:24).

7

The Two Types of Overman and the Doctrine of Eternal Recurrence

---

*The desire to experience all things again
eternally. . . . —Nachlaß, XII, p. 427*

Two opposite conclusions can be drawn from the unrestricted Yes whereby the overman is to profess his ideal—and himself. First, such unrestrictedness can mean that he must tolerate no counter-ideals. Wherever they appear, he must subject them to his own ideal or seek to destroy them. Secondly, the Yes should extend not merely to the leading goal-idea and what it subsumes. Here unrestrictedness means expansion of the Yes to all that is and was. Self-affirmation in this sense does not require negation, but quite the contrary, the recognition of the independent claims of other ideals. This approval and that rejection are, however, mutually exclusive.

Nietzsche cannot admit such mutual exclusion without destroying the previously demonstrated foundations of his philosophy. His "belief" is that if the two conclusions are pushed to their extremes, they will not lead apart, but rather will converge into one. That such a unification could be realized in the overman, could not be made plausible in the previous reflections. To be sure, one more of Nietzsche's fundamental ideas still needs to be considered: his doctrine of the eternal recurrence of the same, "of the unconditional and infinitely repeated circular course of all things."[1]

The introduction of this idea into our deliberations seems, however, to increase even more the difficulties of an investigation seeking to understand the contradictions in Nietzsche's philosophy in light of his philosophy of contradictions. For discussion of the problem inherent in Nietzsche's works has repeatedly been re-ignited precisely by the question of the relationship between the doctrines of the overman and of eternal recurrence.[2] Oskar Ewald cited the most evident contradiction between the two doctrines: the idea of the overman includes "the infinite unrestricted possibility of development which implicitly entails the presupposition of an unlimited time during which it can be performed," that is, "the concept of an infinite length of time"; the idea of recurrence, on the contrary, "requires as *conditio sine qua non* the direct opposite, the concept of a completed infinity."[3]

Subsequent Nietzsche-interpretations display numerous attempts to eliminate the contradiction. Frequently the doctrine of eternal recurrence is reduced to its ethical meaning, or it is left merely with the character of a symbol. Alfred Baeumler makes it easiest for himself by regarding it "as the expression of a highly personal experience" that is "of no consequence" to Nietzsche's "system," for "if taken seriously" it would "shatter the coherence of the philosophy of the will to power."[4] Karl Löwith, among others, interpreted it mainly cosmologically. His interpretation wants to trace back Nietzsche's many contradictions, to which no essential significance is given,[5] to the *basic contradiction* mentioned in our Introduction, "consisting in the fact that Nietzsche repeats the ancient view of the being of the world at the apex of modernity, and thus repeats Greek cosmology on the ground of a post-Christian anthropology of willing."[6] Löwith's interpretation is, then, ultimately oriented on the history of Western thought.

Heidegger, in sharpest contrast with Baeumler's assertion, interpreted the doctrine of eternal recurrence in terms of the history of metaphysics. For him the theories of eternal recurrence and the will to power expressed the same thought. They are fundamental determinations of being as a whole, and as such they make it possible, "in the perspective of metaphysics and with the help of its distinctions," to draw a line to "the identity" of both.[7]

These examples may suffice to document the many efforts to deal with the contradictions we have been analyzing. The following remarks are based on none of the interpretations mentioned, though perhaps occasional reference to one or the other may be made, especially to individual statements by Heidegger. A presupposition of what follows is the contradictoriness of the wills to power that are given concrete formulation in Nietzsche's statements on the overman. Is it possible to find access from there to the idea of eternal recurrence?

The figure of Zarathustra points to the interconnection of the two doctrines: he proclaims both the overman and eternal recurrence. Nietzsche notes that "once the prospect of generating the overman is given—the great horrible moment when Zarathustra proclaims the doctrine of eternal recurrence!—which now first becomes *endurable,* for himself *for the first time*!"[8] From such formulations one may try to derive a merely extrinsic relation of the two doctrines; but in Nietzsche's posthumous notes, on the contrary, suggestions are found that the doctrine of eternal recurrence can be adequately *understood* only if the overman has been seen in his possibilities. Thus Zarathustra is said to forget himself and to teach "the eternal return *from the standpoint of the overman,*"[9] and he tells the secret that everything returns "out of the happiness of the overman."[10]

Chapter 6 described two ultimately incompatible types of the overman. Which type is impelled to announce the secret of the eternal recurrence? The following pages will show that both the *strong man,* restricting himself to his own ideal, and the *wise man,* assimilating the multiplicity of ideals, find the criterion for their overmanship in the eternal return, although in different meanings. The question, then, will be whether the differences can be eliminated or at least so complemented as to remove the incompatibilities to which the discussions of the will to power and the superman have led.

First, distinctions must be made. As an initial characterization, it can be said that the doctrine of eternal recurrence becomes for the strong man, who tries relentlessly to impose his ideal, a touchstone both for his own vital strength and for the strength of those who hold different ideals. Here the doctrine exercises selective functions. What counts are the effects; its "content" loses importance. For the relentless person, even if he has succeeded in imposing his views and finds in the doctrine of eternal recurrence the possibility to consolidate his power insofar as it must return again and again, the idea still retains the character mainly of means to an end.

Although the doctrine of eternal recurrence cannot be derived from the peculiarity of the violent overman—not even if it totally defines his self-understanding and his understanding of the world—it does, on the contrary, follow logically from the radical self-understanding of the synthesizing wise man. The following pages will therefore focus on the wise man, insofar as he enhances his possibilities to transcend the human. The synthesizing overman understands himself—as does also the violent man—as relying on what stands opposite him. He knows that he owes himself to what he condemns; indeed, that he owes himself to everything that ever has been. For the sole world comprises the total complex of a play of forces in which necessity rules. The past contains the conditions for the present and the future. The Yes that such an overman says to his goal must therefore also be a Yes to everything that ever was.

The extension of this Yes becomes evident in the characterization of the "wisest man," who sums up and synthesizes the various things that protrude from the past into the present. It found its extreme expression in Zarathustra's claim to lose *no* part of mankind and to cast *everything* into the mold. Finally it was shown that it is part of the synthesizing overman's consistency to affirm *without exception* all that ever was. Only such an expanded Yes is a genuine Yes.

Now there are different degrees of *intensity* of affirmation. The merely declamatory Yes is only an apparent affirmation. There is less Yes in concession than in recognition; and in turn less in recognition than in "reconciliation" (Z II).[11] And less in this than in consent [*Einverständnis*]. Consent can in turn be heightened to *identification* with what is affirmed. Finally, what is affirmed can become *what dominates and leads all action and thought.* Only such a Yes is a Yes willed with ultimate urgency and hence a genuine Yes.

In Chapter 6, the overman's Yes was characterized as a genuine Yes insofar as it extends to the whole of reality. Now it turns out that the extension of the affirming will as such cannot yet constitute the overman's full truthfulness. This can be spoken of only when the most extreme, that is, the highest degree of intensity of affirmative will exists. But such intensity must not be restricted to the overman's self, to his goals and the effective means to achieve them. Since everything that ever was is the precondition for what the overman is and can become, the highest intensity of willing himself includes the highest intensity of willing everything past. To approve one fact actually means to affirm all facts, as Nietzsche says. But what is required of the synthesizing overman is an urgency of the Yes that leaves every form of approval behind. He is supposed not merely to approve. Nor is he supposed "merely to perceive the necessity of those sides of existence hitherto denied, but their desirability." And this desirability is not supposed to be legitimated "in relation to the sides hitherto affirmed (perhaps as their complement or precondition), but for their own sake."

These statements of Nietzsche's in a posthumous aphorism, entitled *"My New Way to the Yes,"* aim to validate the "more powerful, more fruitful, truer sides of existence, in which its will finds clearer expression." This happens in the passage through an "experimental philosophy," that "anticipates experimentally even the possibilities of the most fundamental nihilism." This passage is to lead "to the opposite," hence the privileging of the powerful sides of existence that are willed for their own sake (WP 1041). But it is also inherent in such a revaluation that not only it is wanted with all urgency. It is a matter of "attain[ing] a height and a bird's eye view, so one grasps how everything actually happens as it ought to happen: how every kind of 'imperfection' and the suffering to which it gives rise are part of the *highest desirability"* (WP 1004). What first seemed worthy of approval as having to be co-willed as a precondition, becomes for the overman something he wills as such with most extreme intensity. In this way fundamental nihilism can cross over to a Yes "to the world as it is, without subtraction, exception, or selection" (WP 1041). Such a Yes combines widest extension and highest intensity.

Nietzsche seeks to express this intensity, for example, by speaking of an *ecstatic affirmation.* As an affirmative will, Yes-saying becomes the process of *sanctification. All* of life, even its "most terrible and questionable qualities" (WP 1050), is supposed to be sanctified. But how can affirmative will become sanctification? By having affirmative will become a *wanting back.* To want back "the same things, the same logic and illogic in their intermeshing" means to truly will everything.

This willing must not be restricted to the wish for a single or multiple repetition. For then the intensity of the Yes has not reached its peak. The overman's genuine Yes is perfected only in the will that everything that is and was return again an infinite number of times. Thus "the idea of eternal recurrence" is revealed to be the "highest formula of affirmation that is at all attainable" (EH).[12] It constitutes "the ideal of the most high-spirited, alive, and world-affirming human being who has not only come to terms and learned to get along with what was and is, but who wants to have what was and is repeated into all eternity, shouting insatiably *da capo*—not only to himself but to the whole play and spectacle" (BGE 56).[13]

The overman's Yes, it turns out, springs with inner necessity out of the "desire"[14] for the eternal recurrence. Thus, there can be no question of an incompatibility of Nietzsche's two doctrines. The exposing—drawing upon evolutionary ideas—of an alleged contradiction between the two theories fails to see that the superhuman in Nietzsche's sense does not require an unlimited progression that loses itself in a bad infinity, but the gathering together of everything that was and is. The surpassing of prior humanity is not a progression to ever new things that leaves others behind. What is "new" compared with former figures of the great synthesizing men of the past is the highest intensification of the most extreme extension. But only what does not fade away into the contentless future of an endless upward development can be intensely willed.

In this context, attention must be called to the fact that this intensification is supposed to give "weight to inner life."[15] That human life needs "a center of gravity" is a thought repeatedly voiced by Nietzsche.[16] In the history of the Western world, Christianity was for a long time "the *center of gravity* by virtue of which we lived." Now, however, after the self-destruction of Christian truth, we have for some time not known which way to turn (WP 30).

We need a *new* center of gravity.[17] As opposed to the Christian center of gravity, it shall be the *true* center of gravity. Since St. Paul "the center of gravity of life" was shifted not into life, but into the "'beyond'—into *nothingness*" (AC 42). And now what was taken away from life must be given back to it. Life can acquire true weight only in life. The task, then, consists in desiring the whole of life in the actual performance of life. If this whole consists purely in the intermeshing of particular wills to power, then each will to power must, at every moment of its action and passion, want itself as it is. That is how it acquires weight. A center of gravity in life is gained by the will to power presented in the synthesizing overman, when he wants himself not only in his transitory existence, but rather when he wants himself back again. But this center of gravity is hardly thinkable in its priority when he wants himself again and again *as he is* in all the most varied moments of his existence.

Nietzsche therefore calls the idea of eternal recurrence "the greatest weight" (GS 341). Indeed, the first published mention of the idea, in the form of an experimental thought, is so characterized in its heading, in Book IV of *The Gay Science*. The greatest weight is placed on human actions when the question is asked of "each and every thing" and answered affirmatively: "Do you desire this once more and innumerable times more?" Whoever *assimilates*[18] this "thought of thoughts," whoever becomes "well disposed" to himself, and hence to life, "so as to *crave nothing more fervently* than this ultimate eternal confirmation and seal" (GS 341), grows beyond prior humanity.

Thus the overman and the desire for eternal recurrence belong together as the most extreme expressions of Nietzsche's philosophical thinking. They are mutually required. The utmost that is achieved in the idea of recurrence overcomes both the nihilistic religions, in which man formerly thought he could find his center of gravity, and the resulting weightlessness of no-longer-knowing which way to turn. The new center of gravity should become the new religion. The affirmation that constitutes it becomes sanctification, as was seen above. As the greatest weight, the thought of eternal recurrence will be nothing other than the "religion of religions."[19] This means that this "religion" is unsurpassable. The unsurpassableness requires a long period of preparation for it to reveal itself completely in its unsurpassableness.[20] "Let us beware," Nietzsche writes "of teaching such a doctrine as a sudden religion! It must seep in slowly, entire generations must build at it and become productive—so that it will become a large tree that shades all future humanity. What are the few millennia in which Christianity has maintained itself! For the mightiest thought, many millennia are necessary—for a long, long time, it must be small and powerless!"[21]

Before Nietzsche's questions and probing thoughts are followed to the history that the doctrine of eternal recurrence will face, some attention must be paid to the paradox that this radical proponent of atheism in the end proclaims a new religion. Nietzsche tries to clarify his doctrine with regard to its relation with or its contrast to prior religions. He also sees it—as will be shown—as a religion that takes up elements of earlier religions and so makes the claim to be *the religion of religions*. But precisely as the overtowering religion, it is ultimately supposed to escape comparison with other forms of religion.

Two possible misunderstandings that can be made when eternal recurrence is presented as a religion will be discussed briefly in this context. The first misunderstanding is to understand this doctrine solely as a religion. This would reduce it again to one religion among others. Nietzsche's "thought of thoughts" could then appear to be, for example, a particular form of pantheism, or "a lame historical reminiscence of classical doctrines about the cyclical course of world events," or a mere renewal of an even more ancient burden that allowed the history of Eastern antiquity "to become bogged down in fatalism." Heidegger is well aware of such possibilities of misunderstanding.[22] He opposes decisively any interpretations that could seek "to snatch the thought of return from philosophy and turn it over to religion."

Nietzsche redefines "the essence of religion in his own terms"; we must not classify his doctrine "among the various religious sects or customary forms of religiosity."[23] In the context of these remarks, Heidegger seeks to trace Nietzsche's understanding of the new religion to his understanding of belief,[24] and, finally, belief as a taking to be true, to Nietzsche's understanding of truth. However, Heidegger does not present a detailed portrayal of the relation: religion—belief—truth.[25] For in his line of argument on this topic he is concerned mainly with preventing the thought of return from being earmarked as a "religious" thought in the sense of ostracizing it from Nietzsche's thinking.[26]

Nonetheless, one must not miss the significance of the fact that Nietzsche in elaborating his thinking speaks of the doctrine of eternal recurrence *as a religion*. An investigation into the concept of *belief* as used by Nietzsche can lead to essential insights on the "religion of religions." However, it runs the risk of not giving sufficient account to the claim that Nietzsche raises by such a designation. What *belief in eternal recurrence* is supposed to mean could be made clearer by understanding this doctrine as a religion than by his statements on belief, defined as meaning "taking to be true."

The second misunderstanding would consist in removing the peculiarly religious character that Nietzsche conveys on the doctrine of eternal recurrence. When in *Twilight of the Idols* he describes the attitude of no-longer-denying represented by the free spirit as a belief grounded on the fact that "in the totality, everything is redeemed and affirmed," this points to a mode of believing that is legitimated by *the religion of eternal return* and can be made adequately understandable only in terms of that doctrine as a faith. "Such a faith is the highest of all possible faiths," Nietzsche writes. "I have baptized it with the name *Dionysos*" (TI 9:49).

Thus Nietzsche's statements on the nature of religion must be discussed again. In the present book, this can of course mean only inquiry into the fundamental, often repeated possibilities of understanding this thinker.

In Nietzsche's so-called enlightenment phase his conviction is often stated decisively that "religion" has been "annihilated by our mode of thinking" (HA I:34). Such a statement claims validity not only with regard to theistic religiosity. "Never again," Nietzsche writes in *Human, All Too Human,* will there be "a life and culture bounded by a religiously determined horizon" (HA I:234). And looking back over the history of religions, he says in the further context of a dispute with Schopenhauer: "A religion has never yet either directly or indirectly, either as dogma or as parable, contained a truth." "The alleged truths of every religion were and are born out of 'fear' and 'need'" (HA I:110).

To track down the real basis of religious sentiment and unmask religious "truth" as falsehood, Nietzsche calls for a "chemistry" of religious ideas and of the moral and aesthetic conceptions, which he usually discussed in the same context in this phase. He asks—and the question is not merely rhetorical: "What if this chemistry concluded with the discovery that in this field too the most magnificent colors were obtained from base, indeed despised materials?" (HA I:1). Feelings of this sort may be felt as a unity: "In truth, however, they are rivers with a hundred tributaries and sources. Here too, as so often, the unity of the word is no guarantee of the unity of the thing" (HA I:14).

Religion is supposed to have been formed of "base materials." Again we see Nietzsche apply that genealogical procedure mentioned in chapter 1: he seeks to derive a state of affairs from its opposite.

Although in such a way of thinking the sphere of religion loses its independence, and hence the significance it claimed, Nietzsche even in his early writings avoids the simplicity of mere condemnation. Religion may be destroyed "today," but it "has had its time." And Nietzsche often looks back with thinly concealed longing to that time when what has now been unmasked as false by "scientific thinking" was still considered true. "Many very good things can never thrive again because it was only out of it [religious feeling] they could grow" (HA I:234). The "man of today," who becomes aware of his condition, "sighs for the man who will lead him back to his lost love, whether she be called religion or metaphysics." Nietzsche shakes off such temptations again and again: "In such moments his [i.e., the man of today's] intellectual probity is put to the test" (HA I:153).

But Nietzsche's nostalgic looking back leads him to even more far-reaching considerations. In such reflections, religious feeling seems to him to be a perhaps necessary "exercise" and "prelude" for something future (GS 300). And he goes far beyond such an acceptation when he grasps such feeling as something that continues, and *should* continue, to be vitally active. In such considerations, the genealogy of religion that makes use of natural scientific conceptions, for example, by reducing the religious to "chemical elements," is finally complemented or even replaced by a *historical* conception.

First, attention should be paid to Nietzsche's positive valuation of the religious "prelude." In *Human, All Too Human* there is a call for an apotheosis of cognition that provides man with "a ladder with a hundred rungs":

The age in which with regret you feel yourself thrown counts you happy on account of this good fortune; it calls to you to participate in experiences that men of a later age will perhaps have to forego. Do not underestimate the value of having been religious; discover all the reasons by virtue of which you still had a genuine access to art. Can you not, precisely with aid of these experiences, follow with greater understanding tremendous stretches of the paths taken by earlier mankind: is it not on precisely *this* soil, which you sometimes find so displeasing, the soil of unclear thinking, that many of the most splendid fruits of more ancient cultures grew up? One must have loved religion and art like mother and nurse—otherwise one cannot grow wise. (HA I:292)

And in *The Gay Science* Nietzsche writes that all religion "could have been the strange means to make it possible for a few single individuals to enjoy the whole self-sufficiency of a god and his whole power of self-redemption. Indeed—one might ask—would man ever have learned without that religious training and prehistory to experience a hunger and thirst for *himself,* and to find satisfaction and fullness in *himself*?" (GS 300). To be sure, in such a valuation Nietzsche is speaking from a vantage point that has "outgrown" the traditional type of religion: if one remains under its spell, one does not understand it (HA I:292).

All the more attention should be paid to Nietzsche's statements in his "enlightenment phase," in which religion appears not merely as the school through which man must pass in order to find himself. According to such statements, religious sentiment has also given rise to something distinctive that should not be lost even in the future, despite all other efforts detectable elsewhere in Nietzsche to elaborate on scientific man as the progressive development of the artistic and religious type. One has given up religion, he says in *Human, All Too Human,* "but not the enhancement of feelings and exaltations one has acquired from it." The question arises how the "wealth of feeling" that religion and art have accumulated can find fulfillment in scientific man. The "intensity implanted" by both still demands "satisfaction" (HA I:222).[27]

In *The Gay Science* (Book V) Nietzsche later reaches the insight that even science stems from a faith. Under the title "How We, Too, Are Still Pious," he states that even "the discipline of the scientific spirit . . . would not permit oneself any more convictions," and instead must settle for hypotheses, although one single conviction is presupposed. It is the conviction that nothing is needed more than scientific truth. It rises above all other convictions. Nietzsche investigates this conviction and it reveals itself to him as the will not to deceive, including not even oneself. As was shown in chapter 5, he interprets such not-wanting-to-deceive as a moral phenomenon stemming from *ressentiment.* Morality, however, lives and acts together with the fiction of an other, transcendent world. It can, then, be said "that it is still a *metaphysical faith* upon which our faith in science rests" (GS 344), even though this faith in science may think it has abandoned the moral-religious way of thinking intrinsic to it, and even though it may oppose traditional religiosity.

The progress from religious to scientific man asserted in Nietzsche's earlier publications thus proves to be an occurrence that only plays on the surface of reality. Scientific knowledge no longer stands opposite the untruth of transcendental faith. It is not even a matter of two modes of essentially different kinds of belief. The quest for scientific truth and traditional religion are equally rooted in the soil of *Ressentiment*-morality; the one no less than the other.

Grounded in morality, the will to truth is a declining will to power, and ultimately a will to death. It is the same metaphysical faith stemming from a weakened will to power that appears in such fundamentally different forms. The attempt to overcome religion by means of *science* ultimately turns into shadow-boxing. Is there, then, any other way to break out of this spell of *Ressentiment*-determined thinking? The possibility of breaking out is decisive for overcoming nihilism: unless the religious is *not necessarily* a mode of expression of decadence. Much speaks for such non-necessity. Religion, and art, which is based on it—according to Nietzsche's "enlightenment phase"—have caused a wealth of feelings to grow and have implanted "the intensity and multifariousness of the joy in life" (HA I:222) to such an extent that these kind of "astonishing effects of the religious feeling" (HA I:234) cannot be interpreted exclusively as a *degeneration* of man (WP 48), at least not in all their forms.

The later Nietzsche therefore sees himself compelled again and again to trace the astonishingness of religion down to its foundations. And he discovers the "origin of religion" in the "extreme feelings of power" that man experiences in himself. Carried along and overpowered by them, man understands them as something of which he is not the master. He manages to grasp them as something foreign to his person and located outside it, whereas in reality they are a part of himself. Nietzsche, in his effort to explain the "formation of God" psychologically, finally cannot settle for understanding the fixation of a "second world" *solely* as a means used by the weak in the struggle for power against the strong men who dominate them (WP 135). The positing of something "foreign" resulting from such self-experience or from the experience of exceptional conditions in other persons—among those Nietzsche names are the epileptic, the "great criminal," the person agitated by the passions of love or hatred—also occurs "among intelligent, strong, and vigorous races." Among them, too, it can serve "for inventing extra-human powers." "A condition is made concrete in a person: and when it overtakes us is asserted to be effected by that person."

It must be kept in mind that it is precisely "conditions of power" that impute to man the feeling "of *not* being the cause, of *not* being responsible for them—they come without being willed, consequently we are not their originator." Such a conclusion is naive, but it is drawn not only by the weak, such as, for example, Christians "of today," who attribute "hope, repose, the feeling of 'redemption,' back to psychological inspiration by God." Here Nietzsche finds only the expression of vital weakness. But while the Christian separates "his person into a mean and weak fiction which he calls man, and another which he calls God (Redeemer, Savior)," the stronger human of former ages unconsciously invented cruel and relentless deities in whom his own cruelty and relentlessness were expressed.

Such naiveté, which does not see through the process of god-formation stemming out of the self, reveals the relative weakness even of the stronger men (WP 135, 136). Nietzsche can now write: "In itself religion has nothing to do with morality," although "both descendants of the Jewish religion are *essentially* moralistic religions" (WP 146). But even religion in the premoral age, as conceived by Nietzsche, was determined by the projection of inner states into a merely imagined reality. Astonishing strength may have been manifested in such naive religious behavior of men, but they did not attribute it to themselves as *their* strength. Of course, the relative strength expressed in such religiosity, as will be shown, can lead to an affirmation of the natural that is contrary to the Christian denial of this very nature. Generally, it is true of previous religious modes of behavior that "man has not dared to credit *himself* with all his strong and surprising impulses—he has conceived them as 'passive,' as 'suffered,' as things imposed upon him: religion is the product of a doubt concerning the unity of the person, an alteration of the personality: insofar as everything great and strong in man has been conceived as superhuman and external, man has belittled himself" (WP 136).

The abolition of such self-belittling, which Nietzsche demands, can, accordingly, be achieved only by the overcoming of the supposedly superhuman through the anticipated reality of the overman. This may occur in intermediary stages when "step by step man takes possession of his exalted and proud states, takes possession of his acts and works" (WP 137). Indeed, owing to self-belittlment, Nietzsche says, a long time may be necessary, as will be discussed below. But when man no longer distances his amazingly strong side from himself, when he no longer considers his self pitifully weak, will he not himself become the "god" whom he previously placed over himself as an alien power? (WP 135). Nietzsche's thinking, in fact, claims to be laying the groundwork to abolish the human god-formation by the deification of man. "The 'I love God'—the only old form of religious life—is transformed into the love of *my ideal,* and has become creative:—

sheer god-men."[28] But is the doctrine of eternal return that stems from the self-understanding of the divine overman, then, elevated to true religion?

If so, a new contradiction emerges. On one side are the modes of expression of the previous will to power. Their scale extends from naive religious dualism to the still religiously grounded basic conviction of the indispensability of scientific truth. On the other side is the constantly heightened will to power of actual religiosity proper that sanctifies life in ecstatic affirmation. The latter is supposed to belong to the future, together with the "decline of European theism." Nietzsche ascertains that in the nineteenth century "the religious instinct is indeed in the process of growing powerfully" (BGE 53). As an atheist—more precisely an anti-theist—he even wants to support "the religions and moralities of the herd instinct": "For these prepare a type of man that must one day fall into our hands, that must desire our hands" (WP 132).

Along with all the common features of prior forms of religion, the fundamental difference among them for Nietzsche must not be overlooked. Religions of the declining will to power—according to Nietzsche's view of history—follow after a more primordial rule of the mightier. In the premoral epochs characterized by the latter, Nietzsche finds a religion that affirms life and differs fundamentally from any religiosity based on morality. Accordingly he contrasts "*two types*": *Dionysos* and *The Crucified*. When it is said that "the typically *religious* man" is "a *decadent* form," this excludes the *pagan* type, Nietzsche writes. "Is the pagan cult not a form of thanksgiving and affirmation of life? Must its highest representative not be an apology for and a deification of life? The type of a well-constituted and ecstatically overflowing spirit! The type of a spirit that takes into itself and *redeems* the contradictions and questionable aspects of existence!" (WP 1053).

Such a religion assimilates the contradictions into the whole of the unique reality and thus sanctifies life. "The richest in fullness of life, the Dionysian god and man can allow himself not only the right of the terrible and the questionable, but even the terrible deed and every luxury of destruction, dissolution, denial—in him the evil, senseless and ugly seem permitted, as it were, as they are permitted in nature—as a result of an excess of generating, restoring forces—which can turn any desert into a sumptuously fertile land."[29]

In the pagan religions of the past, the affirmation of life is originally naive. Self-deception, to which people were subjected even in them by assigning their own strong conditions to imagined deities, showed their inability to understand themselves in their truth. The "second innocence" that Nietzsche expects in the future can therefore not mean a return to former cults. But it must accept and assimilate what began in them and also what developed during the moral epoch.

What consolidated the rule of the weak in these epochs must not simply be denied. For the sublimation of the will to truth in this epoch is the precondition that ultimately makes that self-deception of naive religion impossible.

After these comments, it will not be surprising that Nietzsche's discussion of the history that the doctrine of eternal recurrence will undergo as the religion of religions is occasionally oriented by what he regards as having been especially effective in the history of religion. He notes: "Even if circular repetition is merely a probability or a possibility, even *the thought of a possibility* can move and transform us, not only feelings and particular expectations! How the *possibility* of eternal damnation has worked!"[30] The conviction of infinite repetition appears to be a grace—of course, without a giver of grace—for Nietzsche writes: "If the thought of the eternal return of all things does not overwhelm you, there is no blame: and there is no merit if it does." This statement is directed, of course, against the Christian sense of guilt,[31] as Nietzsche generally emphasizes the contrast between the highest of all possible faiths that *he* has "baptized" under the name of *Dionysos* (TI 9:49), and dualistic religion.

Even here the contrast remains an opposition and not something mutually exclusive. Every culture must indeed perish if it takes the alleged Beyond to be more important than this world (e.g., Alexandrian culture, which despite all "pleasure in the knowledge of this world," did not "give *this* world, *this* life supreme importance"),[32] but the soil is thus prepared on which a new and more powerful culture can grow. "The *dwarfing* of man must for a long time count as the only goal; because a broad foundation has first to be created so that a *stronger* type of man can stand on it. (To what extent every strengthened type of man hitherto has stood upon a level of the lower—)" (WP 890). The support of the "herd religions" is supposed to speed up the soil-formation.

Nietzsche notes that in his time the religious need is growing simultaneously with Christianity's loss of credibility. He is convinced that the more theism is "supported," the more clearly its untenability becomes evident. The next consequence is awareness of the *transitoriness* of human existence. Belief in eternity is declining. "Secularization" takes on the meaning of striving after pleasure here and now. Man seeks his own "welfare" and an easy life. The result is socialism: "The *transitory individuals* want to conquer their happiness through socialization; they have no reason to *wait,* like persons with eternal souls and eternal becoming and future improvement."[33]

Nietzsche counters such a lack of "center of gravity" with his doctrine of the eternal recurrence of every moment. It stands in contrast both to religious dualism and to its mere destruction: "Let us imprint the likeness of eternity on *our* life! This thought contains more than all religions which taught men to despise this life as transitory and to look toward an indeterminate *other* life."[34] After the fall of the false religion that long prevailed, true religion shall, in a new meaning, regain the eternal that had been lost in disbelief. Yet despite all opposition to Christian belief in eternity, Nietzsche in the last analysis agrees with Christianity in opposing every shallow atheism. There is evidence for this in a statement of Nietzsche's such as: "Whoever does not believe thinks of his life as *fleeting*."[35]

But this should not mislead one to assume anything in common as to ultimate intention. When he wrote that sentence, Nietzsche had only the doctrine of eternal recurrence in mind. He wants to leave the transitory living creatures in their transitoriness; he believes that this sets him off clearly from Christianity. The sentence before the last quoted one reads: "This doctrine is gentle toward those who do not believe in it, it has no hell and no threats." Of course, Nietzsche is convinced that those who live transitorily cannot endure their existence. In the end the following is true of them: "Whoever can be destroyed by the statement 'There is no salvation,' should die out."[36] The idea of eternal return is presented, then, as a doctrine from which mankind perishes, "*except for those who can endure it.*"[37] There is no longer any escape. The God of Christianity is dead; those who believe that this death destroys all religion can really no longer bear their existence. Nietzsche, then, believes that his doctrine will be "more and more" victorious in future history—"and those who do not believe in it will, according to their nature, finally *die out.*"

The religions of decadence, along with their mere negations, are without strength. Nietzsche extracts from both the elements of "truthfulness" that he believes are made one-sided in them *and hence falsified,* and he combines them within the horizon of his new religion. Eternity is, in his theory, no longer self-resting transcendence; the transitory is no longer the merely past. Eternity becomes unending repetition of that which passes away. "From the moment this thought is there, every color changes and there is another *history.*"[38]

Nietzsche inquires into such a change from many angles. But in pondering the course this doctrine of eternal recurrence is supposed to take, many questions arise. Nietzsche's Zarathustra names a few. "Fear of the effects of the theory: the best natures may perhaps perish from it? The worst will accept it?" Is the thought of thoughts not perhaps an easy reassurance for the person who is frightened by his past? In fact Nietzsche does believe that the doctrine will "at first smile at the rabble who are cold and without much inner hardship. The crudest vital drive is the first to give its assent. *A great truth wins over the highest men last of all: this is the affliction of the truthful.*"[39]

The transformation that "the mightiest thought" is to accomplish on the way to this goal[40] must be investigated further. Let us start with Nietzsche's fear that the "best natures" could perish from it. Because they—in contrast with the "lesser, less sensitive natures"—experience the burdensomeness of their existence much more strongly, the doctrine of eternal recurrence must crush them; it is "apparently the means to exterminate them." Of course, the adverb "apparently" must be noted. Only those "more noble" ones who have already been incurably afflicted by the disease of life-denial will not be able to bear the doctrine.[41] They are more or less aware of their nihilism; their distrust of traditional valuation finally is heightened "to the question: 'Are not all values lures that draw out the comedy without bringing it closer to a solution?'" For them "duration 'in vain,' without end or aim" must be "the most *paralyzing* idea, particularly when one understands that one is being fooled and yet has lost the power not to be fooled." If such duration is even thought under the aspect of eternal recurrence "without any finale of nothingness" to put an end to this phantasmagoria, these decadent noble ones would lose their last shred of hope. To them the doctrine of eternal return appears "in its most terrible form." Nietzsche writes: "This is the most extreme form of nihilism: the nothing (the 'meaningless') eternally!" (WP 55).

The various types of decadents whom Nietzsche sees as the main representatives of contemporary pessimism do not get the thought of duration as eternal recurrence that drives them to the most extreme despair from their own understanding of the world and of themselves. It must be paraded before their eyes most vividly by the stronger ones. "The *unhealthiest* kind of man in Europe (in all classes)" will then "experience the belief in the eternal recurrence as a *curse,* struck by which one no longer shrinks from any action." Active nihilism that seeks to "extinguish everything" will become rampant (WP 55).

To bring about such movements is the task Nietzsche assigns to the *violent* overmen. In their hands, the doctrine of eternal recurrence becomes a weapon, a hammer. They claim it as the "*cultivating* idea." Their confrontation with the doctrine of eternal recurrence reveals who is too weak "for a new order of life." Whoever cannot bear it is "condemned." Whoever, on the contrary, finds it to be the "greatest benefit" is "chosen to rule" (WP 1053, 1055). Nietzsche, then, puts this theory in the service of "strength," indeed of "barbarism." As a "selective principle" it not only confirms those capable of life in their claim to power, but at the same time it excludes the weaker ones (WP 1058).

The violent men who are assigned their specific historical task, however, differ so essentially from the wise ones that it remains incomprehensible how the two types, who raise themselves to the superhuman level and are expected to coalesce in such extreme elevation, can be thought of as compatible. The problems that emerged in chapter 6 arise again, indeed even more sharply, in connection with the thought of eternal recurrence. How shall the one who selects and rejects, breeds and destroys, possibly be the same as the one who unconditionally affirms everything that is, was, and will be, without condemning anything? How can the overman who is driven to the thought of desiring again and again in the same way with all intensity the most variegated things—including what is contrary to his own ideal—how can he use this thought as a weapon for the goal of eliminating what his ideal condemns? The latter mode of behavior does not merely lag behind the first; it is fundamentally different. Each of the two types of overman must with his consistent self-realization destroy what is peculiar to the other. Their incompatibility is as glaring as before.

The effort to construe a transition between the two types in the form of a historical sequence also fails. It is impossible to speak of the wise man emerging from the violent one without assuming an incomprehensible qualitative leap. Moreover the violent one would be left behind as a mere preliminary stage of the overman perfected in the Yes to everything; he would not himself be a genuine overman.

A further objection to the assertion of incompatibility would be that in it the esoteric aspect of the doctrine of eternal return is separated from its social aspect and played off against it. It is one thing to portray the process of most extreme intensification of self-willing that must determine the overman's inner development; it is another to speak of the history of the effects that will be caused by the thought of eternal return when the same overman uses it as a means of exclusion. The interior and exterior would be distinctly separated, whereas it would have to be a matter of seeing them as two sides of one intrinsically unitary thing.

Now Nietzsche, in his sketches for the "last part" of *Thus Spoke Zarathustra,* does speak of the great "synthesis of the creating, loving, destroying one."[42] But, in such a synthesis, to understand the element of love as the esoteric aspect and destruction as the exoteric aspect is impossible because this would relegate unrestricted affirmation to an "inconsequential interiority," a view that certainly runs contrary to Nietzsche's intentions. For we have shown that this affirmation stems precisely from a self-understanding of the overman, who knows that he is exposed to the actual conflict of wills to power and can deal with the contradictions of reality so as to take this reality upon himself as the only reality. This philosophy leaves no room for a distinction into "interior" and "exterior," into self-reference and world-reference. "We laugh as soon as we encounter the juxtaposition of 'man *and* world,' separated by the sublime presumption of the little word 'and'!" (GS 346).

The point of departure must be the unity that is given before all foreground or apparent separations into "interior" *and* "exterior," subject *and* object, man *and* world, and so on. This unity can be designated—taking some license in its use—by Heidegger's concept of *being-in-the-world.* It makes it possible to designate the connection of a *Who* with the *How* of allowing an encounter with being in the whole world. When we speak here of being-in-the-world, no more is meant than the actual "existential" context. The existential-ontological meaning of being-in-the-world, as elaborated by Heidegger in *Being and Time,* because of his totally different method, lies completely outside Nietzsche's way of seeing things, which alone concerns us. But leaving aside any attempt at a fundamental ontology, it can still be said: *the Yes to eternal recurrence is the being-in-the-world of the overman.* He (the *Who*) understands himself as belonging to the multiplicity of "existing" wills to power in their antagonism (the still modifiable *How*), which makes up the whole of the world, whose eternal recurrence he desires.

At first we are still exposed to Nietzsche's claim to think love and destruction as combined in the overman's activity. Yet, according to the foregoing line of reasoning, even what is destroyed must be loved most intensely (cf. Z III).[43] The question must therefore be asked again, whether under the aspect of the eternal recurrence of the same the condemnation and destruction of the weak can be combined with their unrestricted affirmation.

Nietzsche remains silent on this point. But we can think through the conclusions that are derivable from his doctrine. It can, then, be said that the destroyer can remain the lover if he knows that the destruction is not final. "Eternally recurs the man of whom you are weary, the small man" (Z III).[44] Zarathustra is supposed to overcome the disgust that comes over him with this insight. For the synthesis of destruction and love, which the overman (whose advent Zarathustra merely prepares) is supposed to represent, the one to be destroyed could be the ever *coming* one, whose return is desired. For the "great man" needs the "little man" as his opposite. The will for the "little man" to perish would then be one with the will for his return.

In fact, each action can be called neither destroying nor loving. What returns again and again is not destroyed. What is apparently destroyed is only put "out of play" for the further course of the respective period. And what is wanted as opposite merely for the sake of opposition is not loved, that is, not affirmed most intensely, as is demanded of the overman. From such a perspective, creative activity [*das Schaffen*] seems like throwing a boomerang. Thrown away, it returns to its starting point, making it possible to be thrown again. The absurdity that Nietzsche tries to overcome with its help so as to amalgamate the loving overman with the condemning and destroying one in a single figure is back again.

We cannot, then, avoid assuming a dichotomous truth of the overman's being-in-the-world. Or rather, each of the two types of overman can be characterized by a different "most extreme re-willing" (as to what is willed), although in this, too, both are concerned with power. The respectively different "re-willing" determines "how" all other beings, including the overman himself, are understood. The overman's last "re-willing," which has been imposed coercively, is the securing of his own power. This is ultimately "guaranteed" by the conviction that the acquired fullness of power will return eternally. And at the same time the doctrine of eternal recurrence serves him as a weapon with which to fight weaker men's claims to rule. While the strong man tries to destroy what does not submit to his claim to rule, the overman of the all-comprehensive synthesis opens himself longingly even to what is opposed to his own ideal. His "most extreme re-willing" consists in the acceptance of all that was, is, and will be, which at the same time is supposed to be the *liberation* of the most diverse things in their own interest. The synthesizing overman submits to the circularity of all that happens.

But it is not only with regard to the attempt to "mediate" between destruction and love in the overman that *no unitary meaning* can be found in the thought of eternal recurrence. If the thought is taken by itself, detached from the context of meaning in which it belongs for the "wise" man, the loving, synthesizing overman, it still turns out to be ambiguous. As discussed above, Nietzsche tries to master this ambiguity by understanding the possible meanings of the thought as elements of a historical process that, from a very broad perspective, also is supposed to have determined the fate of all previous great thoughts. The doctrine of eternal recurrence, as we have seen, appeals first to "the rabble," then it destroys the more noble ones who are too weak for it, before it finally is accepted by the best natures. But the discussion of the sequence of its reception did not consider that there will at all times be mediocre and sub-mediocre types toward whom the overman will have to stand in essential opposition. This was also recalled in the comments on the activity that supposedly can destroy and love in one operation.

This means that after the "turning point of history,"[45] when the thought of eternal recurrence has been accepted as true, very different receptions of the doctrine will be played out simultaneously. Again and again, from then on, lower types will find assurance in the doctrine, namely, when they have led and are leading a comfortable life. Others will be satisfied with the idea that not only pain and suffering return, but also the joys that have been granted to them. Those whose lives have entailed mainly sorrow will be horrified to see themselves exposed to the thought that their sufferings will have to be repeated countless times—if they do not have the strength to affirm even the horrible. Others will sink into fatalistic indifference. Sublime natures, such as the pessimists, must, out of insight into the shallowness of everything one can wish for, fall into despair when hope of the end of their existence is taken away. Active nihilists will turn their desperation outward. They will be driven to acts of destruction that must remain senseless because they keep destroying the "same thing" over and over, without ever being able to put an end to it—or to *themselves,* as is their secret desire (WP 55).[46] But the doctrine can also increase "good will" toward life by replacing the false, transcendentally oriented belief in immortality.[47] Whoever seeks to draw something higher from it will have to face the task of learning to endure true immortality.[48]

Such a differentiation of the simultaneous effects of the doctrine of eternal recurrence falls absolutely within Nietzsche's field of vision. For it is supposed to serve both as the touchstone for the strong man's strength and to arouse in the weak ones the wish for self-extinction. But the doctrine cannot achieve the second of these objectives, at least not with regard to all types of lesser human beings. That the same thing returns again and again will under some circumstances be no less pleasing to the little egoist than to the great lover.[49]

Clearly, then, the doctrine of eternal recurrence, understood in the sense of the "old" understanding of truth, can offer meaning, indeed justification, for the most varied kinds of things. This means, in turn, that understood thus externally, it does not have a clear and distinct meaning. Because it can mean the most opposite things to various men, it has no meaning in itself. As a generally valid "truth" it is devoid of meaning.[50]

In Part III of *Zarathustra,* Nietzsche gave expression to such absence of meaning in the form that is typical of that book. In the section "On the Vision and the Riddle," Zarathustra tells his companion, the dwarf, of the eternity of the cycle. The dwarf merely mumbles "contemptuously" as if it were an ordinary platitude: "All that is straight lies. . . . All truth is crooked; time itself is a circle." Zarathustra is angry with "lamefoot" because of the thoughtless matter-of-factness with which he speaks of the thought of eternal recurrence: "You spirit of gravity! . . . do not make things too easy for yourself!" (Z III).[51]

In a later section of the book, "The Convalescent," we find Zarathustra still trying to "crow awake" his most abysmal thought, which behaves like a sleepy worm. After he has been struggling with the thought for seven days, his animals speak to him. They speak joyfully of the "ring of being" that encompasses everything that is, was, and will be. Although Zarathustra likes to listen to their "chatter," he knows that they do not do justice to the thought. The animals do not understand its deep seriousness; they do not know the pains with which the assimilation of the doctrine of eternal recurrence must come about. "And you," Zarathustra shouts to them, "have you already made a hurdy-gurdy of this? But now I lie here . . . still sick from my own redemption. *And you watched all this?*" (Z III).[52]

Heidegger rightly points out that "the speeches of the dwarf and of the animals" show a "fatal resemblance." The essence of the doctrine of eternal recurrence is no less missed in the "hurdy-gurdy" song of the band-organ than in the contemptuous mumblings of the dwarf, who understands it as a banal platitude.[53]

Referring back to something mentioned above, it can be said that the thought is understood only superficially whenever it takes on the character of a generally valid statement in the sense of the "old" truth. This is true even when, as in Zarathustra, it is not expressly reported as theory. In such generality, the thought can mean anything possible; therefore it means nothing definite. It becomes essential, that is, true in Nietzsche's sense, only when it is not viewed from the outside, but assimilated. Zarathustra, too, struggles to assimilate it, in Part III of Nietzsche's book. In one of his notes from the year 1883, Nietzsche mentions some reflections that occurred to Zarathustra in fear of the consequences of his doctrine. Zarathustra finds "assurance" in the conviction that *the effects cannot be foreseen!* But the fundamental uneasiness provoked by that thought cannot be dismissed: "Perhaps it is not *true:*—may others struggle with it!"[54]

This note does not express any doubt on Nietzsche's part concerning the doctrine of eternal recurrence. The last-quoted sentence merely marks one phase within Zarathustra's "development," which—as the context shows—is to be described in Part III of the book.[55]

Thus Zarathustra's question of the truth of the doctrine still moves within the "old" understanding of truth. For us the question thus seems to be superfluous because—according to the line of thought in chapter 5 above—for Nietzsche truth has found its new criterion in the ascending will to power. Of course, this view opened up an inconsistency. In the "new truth" one perspective is absolutized; but this absolutization at the same time requires its own relativizing abolition in order to do justice to the constantly changing constellations in the whole world by new absolutizations, which in turn must be posited absolutely as well as relativized. The inconsistency was carried over into the problem of the path to the overman, whereby it was shown that one then could speak only of two kinds of overman, who turned out to be fundamentally different as regards what the doctrine of eternal recurrence means for them. It is impossible to go beyond such different meanings. For the essence of truth is fulfilled in them, as Nietzsche thinks.

This would therefore prohibit any inquiry into the truth of the doctrine of eternal recurrence in an "objective" manner detachable from the designs of the perspicacious wills to power. For such "objectivity" would be a relapse into the old, vanquished concept of truth. Despite the fundamental difference between the Nietzsche-interpretation presented here and Heidegger's we must agree with him when he writes: "If . . . the doctrine of return is sundered and removed as a 'theory,' is observed as a compilation of assertions, then the resulting product is like a deracinated root, torn from the soil and chopped from the trunk, so that it is no longer a root that roots—no longer a doctrine that serves as a fundamental teaching, but merely an eccentricity."[56]

We would, therefore, no longer have to tarry at such an eccentricity—if Nietzsche did not impose it on us and if this imposition had not found an echo in Nietzsche criticism. Nietzsche tried to ground his theory in a rather large number of notes printed mainly in volumes XII and XVI of the *Gesamtausgabe*. Oskar Becker investigated this in a 1936 essay by the title "Nietzsche's Proofs for his Theory of Eternal Recurrence." He complains that, in contrast with a few French interpreters (Andler, Abel Rey), discussions in Germany, as a result of the particularly pronounced division between the natural sciences and the human and social sciences, did not treat seriously the "purely theoretical side of the matter."[57] Becker's publication in 1936 was surely what Heidegger was primarily referring to in the lecture he gave just one year later on the "Eternal Recurrence of the Same":

> And so the proofs are taken in earnest. Commentators show—by mathematical exertions, no less—that his proofs are not so bad, apart from a few "mistakes." Indeed, Nietzsche anticipated several lines of thought in contemporary physics—and what could be more important for a real contemporary man than his science! This apparently more material and more affirmative stance with respect to Nietzsche's "proofs" is, however, every bit as dubious as its opposite; it is immaterial, inasmuch as it does not and cannot confront "the matter" that comes into question here. For both the rejection and the acceptance of these proofs hold fast to the common identical presupposition that here it is a matter of proofs after the manner of the "natural sciences." This preconception is the genuine error. It precludes all understanding from the outset because it makes all correct questioning impossible.[58]

Becker remarks critically that occasionally some even doubted "whether Nietzsche himself took his theory quite seriously. However, evidence to the contrary was the well-known biographical fact that in 1881 Nietzsche had planned to study mathematics and physics for ten years in order to ground his doctrine scientifically."[59] Becker even goes so far as to say that only the objective theoretical demonstrability of the doctrine of eternal return may decide about its ethical or religious significance.[60] But he is also compelled to refer to the view of Nietzsche, established several times above, that Nietzsche's doctrine of the will to power conflicts with his claim to natural scientific truth and with physical "subjection to natural law[s]."[61]

Again we come upon a contradiction in Nietzsche's philosophy. If his attempt at mathematical and natural scientific proofs is taken seriously, fundamental questions arise: How can something that can claim truth only as embodied ever be made "conclusive" by such proofs? Or do his proofs have merely the character of discourse for public consumption? Taking into account the scientifically oriented spirit of the times, does he want to lead to the thought of eternal return in an initially unsuitable form in order to promote the process of a gradual approximation to the "new truth"? Evidence against this is that his sketches on the proofs of the doctrine are found in the unpublished notes that obviously served for Nietzsche's self-understanding about his thought of thoughts. Or does Nietzsche simply succumb to that "old truth" that he had already left behind?

Admittedly, Nietzsche's lines of argument relate to essential insights that are constitutive of his philosophizing. Whether the definitions he uses in his proofs for force, finitude, infinity, sameness, recurrence, becoming, space, time, chaos, and necessity, as originally conceived, have anything to do with natural science, is very doubtful, as Heidegger says. For natural science presupposes such definitions, namely "as elements that remain eternally barred from their realm of inquiry and their manner of demonstration."[62]

On the other hand, Nietzsche occasionally also refers to natural scientific principles of the modern era. For example, he writes: "The law of the conservation of energy demands *eternal recurrence*" (WP 1063). Therefore, we have no other choice but to investigate his lines of argument. However slight their significance may be for his thought of eternal return, even if they prove to be wrong, one cannot disregard Nietzsche's reflections on this subject. Four tasks, then, must be accomplished. *First,* the proofs must be made visible with regard to the theoretical presuppositions supporting them. *Second,* the cogency of the proofs must be examined in the sense of mathematical, natural scientific truth. *Third,* the question will arise whether the presuppositions of the proofs are consistent with the presuppositions of Nietzsche's thinking otherwise, which led to the doctrine of eternal recurrence. And *fourth,* the significance of Nietzsche's arguments for the whole of his philosophy will have to be studied.

Concerning the *first* task, it must be said that Nietzsche's writings, in which the doctrine is given a theoretical grounding, are not composed as a unity. Different proof attempts must be gathered from various writings. Becker did this in his noteworthy monograph. Of course, it turns out that Becker's differentiations tear apart the structure of Nietzsche's trains of thought, which is a unified structure despite its diverse points of departure. Nonetheless, in the following passages we use Becker's description as a starting point, because it brings out sharply the limits of a theoretical proof of the doctrine of eternal return. The discussion of Becker's views will occasionally have other tasks in mind, also, for example, to show that Nietzsche's own view of the probative force of mathematical formulas comes into play.

What must be proven is: "Everything has existed countless times, insofar as the total situation of all forces always recurs."

A. The *first proof* discovered by Becker starts with the fact that Nietzsche denies the existence of a God who acts arbitrarily.[63] The "circular process of the cosmos" stands in fundamental "opposition to all previous theistic" views.[64] If the assumption of an arbitrary divine creative force is "not true," then there is no longer any possibility to assume that the amount of force in the world is constantly increasing.

Becker remarks on this point that Nietzsche "overlooks that—as the decimal fraction development of an irrational number such as the square root of 2 or pi shows—non-periodic developments running to infinity are possible, unreeling according to a previously determined regular rule without divine creative arbitrariness."[65] Of course, Becker's counter-argument does not consider Nietzsche's reservations concerning mathematics' claim to truth, which reached the point of its critical rejection. Thus Nietzsche writes: "When mathematics is applied . . . reality is first *arranged* and *simplified* (falsified—)."[66] For it is—like mechanics—a form of "applied logic."[67] In mathematics, as in applied logic, "reality does not appear at all, not even as a problem; just as little as does the question what value a system of conventional signs such as constitutes logic can possibly possess" (TI 3:3).

The inadequacy of Becker's argument against Nietzsche stems from the fact that he does not take into account Nietzsche's critique of science. But this suggestion does not restore the force of the "first proof." Becker is right that the proof is "too indefinite to be evaluated objectively."[68] To put it more sharply: to remain on the level of proof, first the non-existence of a creative agency [*Instanz*] that contributes ever new forces would have to be demonstrated for that proof to claim validity. But this non-existence can neither be proven nor refuted. Even Nietzsche's genealogy of theism, indeed, does not have the character of a formal proof required here.

B. The second proof starts from the finiteness of cosmic space. This finiteness permits only a finite number of force situations in discrete multiplicity. Consequently "merely a *finite number of possible combinations* of these elements that determine a particular state of the world, i.e., only a *finite number of possible states of the world*" is thinkable. Add to this finding the assumption that each particular state of the world determines the next one unequivocally, then the eternal recurrence of the same is "absolutely necessary. For after exhausting all possible states of the world, one of them must necessarily come back. But since this one has a single unequivocally determined successor, and it in turn likewise, the states of the world run their course in fixed sequence until the first repeated one is repeated for a second time, and so on, for all eternity."[69] Nietzsche has stated his view on this most clearly as follows:

> If the world *may* be thought of as a definite quantity of force and as a certain definite number of centers of force—and every other representation remains indefinite and therefore *useless*—it follows that, in the great dice game of existence, it must pass through a calculable number of combinations. In infinite time, every possible combination would at some time or another be realized; more: it would be realized an infinite number of times. And since between every combination and its next recurrence all other combinations would have to take place, and each of these combinations conditions the entire sequence of combinations in the same series, a circular movement of absolutely identical series is thus demonstrated; the world as a circular movement that has already repeated itself infinitely often and plays its game *in infinitum.* (WP 1066)

It is striking that Nietzsche presents the presuppositions of his argument in hypothetical form (if . . . it "may be thought"), and linguistically continues in the form of a potential subjunctive. Becker characterizes the logic of Nietzsche's argument as "faultless"; he questions merely the extent to which the "questions of finiteness have really been stated by Nietzsche."[70] Since he finds that Nietzsche teaches the finite sum of all force, finite space, a discrete scale of force, a determinate number of force levels, the existence of an unequivocal causal connection, and finally also, though only indirectly, the discreteness of space and time, he sees "that Nietzsche on all essential points gives a complete enumeration of the presuppositions for his line of argument; under these presuppositions his proof of eternal return is absolutely clear and cogent." Of course, the question is "whether these assumptions are accurate in the real world"; the decision on this is "a matter of comprehensive physical investigations"; and therefore the second proof remains a "mere program."[71] The indispensable assumption of the infinity of time, named by Nietzsche, is not expressly discussed by Becker in this context. Becker reserves its discussion for the third proof.

Nietzsche's talk of the great dice game of existence seems to Becker to be merely a variant of the second proof.[72] But Nietzsche's fundamental thought of the conflict of wills to power is more adequately developed in it than the assumption of "unequivocal causality," which Becker regards as "otherwise" constitutive for Nietzsche's proof attempts.[73] For what Nietzsche presents "as a counter-hypothesis to the circular process" is conceivable: namely,

> that the origin of the world would be a lawless game . . . so that all our mechanical laws would not be eternal, but have become among countless different mechanical

laws, left over from them, or having prevailed in certain parts of the world but not in others?—It seems that we need *randomness,* a real lawlessness, only an ability to become lawful, a primeval stupidity, which itself is not valid for mechanics? The *origin of qualities* presupposes the origin of quantities, and these in turn could arise according to a thousand kinds of mechanics.

At the end of this note, after deliberations that we need not go into here, Nietzsche asks several questions:

> Could different things result from "force"? Randomly? Could the regularity [*Gesetzmäßigkeit*] which we see be deceiving us? And not be a primary law? Could the variety of qualities even in our world be a result of the absolute origination of random qualities? Except that it no longer occurs in our corner of the world? Or have adopted a *rule* which we call *cause and effect* without being that (a *randomness that has become the rule,* for example oxygen and hydrogen chemically)??? Could this "rule" just be a longer *mood?*———[74]

Becker, referring, for example, to Aphorism 1062 of *The Will to Power,* seeks to show that, according to Nietzsche, the thought of an arbitrary deviation from eternal recurrence in the world reveals an attachment to traditional religious models of thought. In fact, Nietzsche writes in the cited passage: "It is still the old religious way of thinking and desiring, a kind of longing to believe that *in some way* the world is after all like the old, beloved, infinite, boundlessly creative God—that in some way 'the old God still lives.'" On this point, Nietzsche recalls Spinoza.

But Becker is less concerned with this. He dismisses the thought of the possible quest to avoid recurrence in the world and turns to the idea that the processes in the world are not causal but are ruled by the "law of chance." World condition A would under certain conditions not be followed immediately "by a very determinate world condition B," but perhaps by B* or B**. But that would not militate against the ultimate return of A. After all, "given a finite number of conditions, A, B, and C" would recur again and again, according to the laws of probability. Becker seeks, among other things with the help of Aphorism 22 in *Beyond Good and Evil,* to document his thesis that Nietzsche advocated "a pure force mechanics without any constraints by rigid bonds." However he fails to consider the important final sentence of that text.[75]

Because of its far-reaching and fundamental significance, the entire aphorism will be cited here:

> Forgive me as an old philologist who cannot desist from the malice of putting his finger on bad modes of interpretation: but "nature's conformity to law," of which you physicists talk so proudly, as though—why, it exists only owing to your inter-

pretation and bad "philology." It is no matter of fact, no "text," but rather only a
naively humanitarian emendation and perversion of meaning, with which you make
abundant concessions to the democratic instincts of the modern soul! "Everywhere
equality before the law; nature is no different in that respect, no better off than we
are"—a fine instance of ulterior motivation, in which the plebeian antagonism to
everything privileged and autocratic as well as a second and more refined atheism
are disguised once more. "*Ni Dieu, ni maître*"—that is what you, too, want; and
therefore "cheers for the law of nature!"—is it not so? But as said above, that is interpretation, not text; and somebody might come along who, with opposite intentions and modes of interpretation, could read out of the same "nature," and with
regard to the same phenomena, rather the tyrannically inconsiderate and relentless
enforcement of claims of power—an interpreter who would picture the unexceptional and unconditional aspects of all "will to power" so vividly that almost every
word, even the word "tyranny" itself would eventually seem unsuitable, or a weakening and attenuating metaphor—being too human—but he might, nevertheless,
end by asserting the same about this word as you do, namely, that it has a "necessary" and "calculable" course, *not* because laws obtain in it, but because they are
absolutely *lacking*, and every power draws its ultimate consequences at every moment. Supposing that this also is only interpretation—and you will be eager enough
to make this objection?—well, so much the better. (BGE 22)

The aphorism first states that even natural scientific "matters of fact," "nature's
conformity to laws" must be conceived as a human emendation, indeed a "perversion of meaning." If we take this statement seriously, then we must judge
Schlechta's opinion, which is already cautious, even more cautiously, when he says
that according to Nietzsche strictly scientific inquiry is "as a result of a generally
binding method the inquiry that—in its true nature—is least dependent on falsifying 'interests' of the subject." Schlechta "intentionally" uses the formulation
"least," since with regard to complete independence Nietzsche "all his life had
the most interesting doubts."[76] The assertion of a relatively lesser emendation of
the real in the natural sciences is applicable, in our view, only to his "enlightenment phase," but not, as Schlechta claims, to Nietzsche's later works and notes.
When Nietzsche in the above-cited aphorism characterizes the term "tyrant" as
"too human" for interpreting the backgrounds of natural scientific falsification,
that does not go against what we are saying. For he is concerned only with seeing at work in all that happens (including the non-human) the conflict of wills
to power, a conflict that can be expressed only inadequately by excessively anthropological terms (such as "tyranny").

But back to Becker's view. The fact that according to Nietzsche there are no
natural laws, that "every power at every moment seeks its ultimate consequence,"

leads him to the conclusion that "this probability—physics and—mechanics" in no way contradicts "eternal recurrence," but practically *requires* it.[77]

One could let this pass if Nietzsche did not close the aphorism with the sentence: "Supposing that this also is only interpretation—and you will be eager enough to make this objection?—well, so much the better." In this sentence, the fundamental, constantly changing perspectivism of the "new truth" is given full validity. Nietzsche thereby goes even beyond what Becker calls the "law of chance." Certainly, the "new truth" has displayed itself to us in its irrevocable fragmentariness [*Zwiespältigkeit*]. But precisely it must be taken into account, insofar as any positing (even that of a probability-physics and a force-mechanics) must give up its absolute claim *at the same time* as it posits it. Becker, who remains oriented by the "old truth," clings solely to the absolute positing. That is why the last sentence of the aphorism does not fit into his conception and he omits it. For it raises the possibility of capitulation.

C. What Becker distills out of Nietzsche's notes will get its essential concretization in the third proof he examines. This will be "the decisive one . . . for the contemporary objective judge."[78] What is decisive is that in it Nietzsche proves the unending circularity of time. This proof is supposed to be "objectively independent of the first and second proofs." That it "often appears interwoven with the other two in the texts" makes it seem "doubtful" to Becker "whether Nietzsche was fully clear about the meaning of precisely this proof."[79] Becker does not want to believe that what is portrayed in the first two proofs serves the purpose of securing the third proof against possible objections—which he also raises, though only in passing. This securing function makes it clear that Nietzsche tries to intermesh together what Becker separates.

If we continue to follow Becker's line of argument, we find that he attributes special probative force to the third proof "under the presupposition of the 'systematic whole'" of Nietzsche's philosophy. More than of the second argument, it is supposedly true of the third that it "can hardly be refuted."[80]

In his statements to prove the infinity of time, which necessarily is subject to circularity, Becker reaches back to ancient philosophy. He shows how in fact "regression to infinity" and "progression from infinity" have again and again been separated, contrary to reality. He discusses, on the one hand, ideas from Empedocles and Plato, and on the other hand, those of Parmenides and Aristotle, and draws upon the first antinomy of Kant's *Critique of Pure Reason* and its denial by Schopenhauer, and he also cites natural-scientific discussions from the nineteenth century (Eugen Dühring, Johannes G. Vogt). A critical analysis of Becker's ideas on this topic, concise as they are—though, perhaps for that very reason, not unproblematic—is impossible here because of our exclusive focus on Nietzsche's thinking.

We must limit ourselves to examining Becker's views insofar as they seek to prove that Nietzsche's doctrine of eternal return is theoretically "hardly" contestable. For it overcomes the above-cited separations. Becker cites passages in Nietzsche that thematicize the *progressus ex infinito*.[81] Thus Nietzsche states that one need only go backwards in time to discover that the world can have neither a goal nor an unintended final state, because otherwise one or the other would necessarily already have been reached (cf. esp. WP 1062).

Becker finds the presumption of an infinite process intolerable, if it is conceived as progress to ever new things. On the other hand, he considers infinite progression to be incontestable in the formulation given it by Kant. Since Becker can assent neither to the *transcendental* solution of the problem[82] nor to the assumption of a transcendence-related, rationally incomprehensible change,[83] there remains only the necessity to "posit the infinite way of the world as strictly periodic."[84]

We can now undertake the second task arising from the question of Nietzsche's attempt at a theoretical proof. Becker's argument is based on presuppositions that he finds in Nietzsche but does not sufficiently problematize. Now his line of argument culminating in proof C must be investigated to see if it is scientifically tenable. Yet we must impose essential restrictions upon ourselves. Considering that Becker is convinced that the assumption of the infinity of time is well-grounded, it suffices for our question to develop the extreme counter-position. This consists in expanding the second thermodynamic principle to a theory of the finiteness of the world process. According to that principle there can be in the world only a limited stock of events, which finally will have been completely used up. That theory has found its most popular representative in recent times in C. F. von Weizsäcker, whose lectures on *The History of Nature* from the year 1946 will be cited here.[85]

Although in the following pages we will have to digress from Nietzsche's statements, our point of departure remains one of the notes we have alluded to, which states that the principle of the conservation of energy requires eternal recurrence. This principle is the First Law of Thermodynamics, from which the above-characterized Second Law can be derived. Nietzsche, too, knew the Second Law.[86]

The First Law of Thermodynamics states that the quantity of energy within a closed system is subject to no change. The Second Law states that the forms of energy within such a system do change. Thus the transformation of kinetic energy into heat, and vice versa the change of heat into kinetic energy, is always taking place. But the generation of heat is to a certain extent not reversible. The resulting heat-energy is no longer operative. With regard to its quantity one speaks of *entropy*. Weizsäcker formulates the Second Law as follows: "The entropy of a closed system can increase or remain constant, but it cannot be reduced. It remains constant only as long as no other forms of energy are transformed into heat; otherwise it increases." Weizsäcker continues: "Since practically every natural process produces heat, though often in very small quantities, every process is strictly speaking irreversible. Every pendulum-swing is extinguished, and even the movement of planets around the sun undergoes a weak braking action through interstellar gas. No process, then, is repeated exactly. Nature is a one-time process. The final state would be that all movements come to rest and all heat differentials are equalized. This state has been called 'heat death.'"[87]

Accordingly, two opposite theories have been derived from the principle of the conservation of energy: the doctrine of eternal recurrence of the same and the doctrine of the end of all movement in "heat death." Both are disputed. We cannot make it so easy for ourselves by playing off the second against the first and thus rejecting Nietzsche's attempt at a theoretical grounding of eternal recurrence, as Gast did.[88] But light can be cast on each of the two theories by the other. This will show the weaknesses and strengths of each. The following remarks will be limited to this topic.

Starting from a "now" point in time, the "heat-death" theory can, to a certain extent, be thought in a forward direction. It forms a self-consistent explanation of future events that ends with the ultimate extinction of all events. Its particular strong cogency consists in demonstrating this progression. Its weakness is shown when one *goes back* from "now" toward the beginning of time. Weizsäcker concludes "that not only does an end await events in heat-death, but also that they must have had a beginning in time. And it is just as conceivable that events began suddenly, as that they have grown slowly out of an unending eventless time, just as heat-death is generally attained asymptomatically. I will leave open to what extent it makes sense to apply the concept of time to an uneventful interval."[89] At any rate, according to this theory we now find uneventfulness described no longer merely as the "future" facing us, but also as the condition *prior* to all events.

Both possibilities that Weizsäcker offers to explain the origin of events out of uneventfulness, this sudden appearance or their gradual development, are unsatisfactory. If these two explanations are taken seriously, then the thought is not far afield that the future heat-death need not have the character of definitiveness. For it is conceivable that after a future uneventful period a new beginning of events could follow. Difficulties arising for proponents of the heat-death theory from the question of the beginning of events as soon as they try to think through the regressus into the past were already seen in the nineteenth century.

Nietzsche, too, took note of these difficulties, for example, when J. G. Vogt's book *Energy: A Real Monistic World View* appeared in 1878. Becker expressly calls attention to Nietzsche's reading of this book. At the end of a note Nietzsche refers to page 90 of Vogt's book.[90] Vogt's remarks are indeed "quite dilettantish," as Becker rightly comments. However in the passage cited by Nietzsche he does propose, among other things, the argument that the advocates of the "entropy-theory" cannot show "how the compelling factors that conditioned the present unequal distribution of heat and the phenomena of movement came into the world."[91]

Even if the heat-death theorists bracket out the question of how the beginning came about, indeed even if they deny a beginning to the aperiodically conceived course of the world, they cannot escape the enigma. Becker therefore still sees "in the form of an asymptomatic approximation to a uniform and dead final state: dissipation of all energy ('heat-death'), eradiation of all matter, scattering of the 'expanding universe' into completely unconnected parts (when the expansion speed exceeds the speed of light)" the only "precise idea of an aperiodic unending process" that has become visible in the history of human thought. But, he says, the idea fails when, in connection with such unending processes, one also thinks an unending temporal past. Nothing could explain "how the endless time that has gone by would not have sufficed to attain the minimal point of entropy an infinite time ago (calculated back from now). Even less could one picture the 'beginning' of the process, which by definition is supposed to be without beginning, and whose beginning nonetheless in turn would have to exist, since everything that was as such had an actual existence!—Unsolvable difficulties that disappear only with the assumption of periodicity!"[92]

If the way *from now back into the past* is where one cannot follow the proponents of the heat-death theory, it is the way *from now into the future* that makes acceptance of the theory of eternal return impossible. Even Becker's modulated reasoning that culminates in his third proof (C, above) is vulnerable to the objection presented by Simmel to Nietzsche's proof of an eternal recurrence. He offers a counter-proof:

only for the simplest case of a system consisting only of three elements. Imagine three wheels of equal size that rotate on a common axis. A dot is marked on each of them, in such a way that at one particular moment these three dots will lie in a straight line designated by a string stretched above the wheels. Now spin the wheels, so that the second wheel spins twice as fast as the first one. Then the two dots marked on them will be located together under the string only when the first wheel has made one rotation and the second two; then again after the second full rotation of the first wheel and the fourth rotation of the second wheel; in short, the initial situation of these two wheels will take place exclusively after n complete rotations of the first wheel and 2n rotations of the second wheel. Now give the third wheel a rotation speed of 1/pi of the first wheel. If the first wheel thus has completed 1, 2, 3, . . . , n rotations, then the third has spun, 1/pi, 2/pi, 3/pi, . . . , n/pi times. According to the nature of the number pi, none of these fractions can be a whole number. This means that the third wheel will never have completed a whole number of rotations when the first wheel has completed a whole number.

Now, since the simultaneous location of the dot marked on the first wheel and on the second wheel under the string can come, as was described above, only when the first wheel has made a complete rotation, the designated point on the third wheel can never cross the string at the same moment as these dots on the two other wheels are located under it. This means that the location of the three points with which the movement started cannot return in all eternity. Thus if there are three movements anywhere in the world corresponding to the speed ratio of these three wheels, the combinations between them can never return to their original form. Finiteness in the number of elements, then, even if their movements have an unending time available does not necessarily result in the situation of any given moment ever being repeated unchanged.—Naturally the situation *could* also be different. The world movements could be so arranged that they run through an ever repeated circle of combinations. But the mere possibility sketched above is sufficient to demolish the alleged *proof* of the eternal recurrence of the same as an illusion.[93]

We have recounted Simmel's counter-proof at some length. The preconditions for the correctness of his thought experiment cannot be elaborated here any more than those ultimately supporting Becker's third proof or the Second Law of Thermodynamics. This would require reflection going far beyond the framework of the present book. However, it is essential for our plan to retain the "direction of proof" that determines Simmel's argument. It has its strength in the *progressus ex nunc*. It indicates where the weakness of a theoretical grounding of the doctrine of eternal return is located. The *progressus ex nunc* is, on the contrary, the strength of the heat-death doctrine and related theories. Its weakness in turn lies in the *regressus ex nunc:* until an incomprehensible beginning or into infinity. The latter *regressus,* in turn, is the point of departure for proving the doctrine of eternal return and gives strength to its argument. The purpose, with regard to the attempted proofs under discussion was to show that where the *progressus ex nunc* is attributed its theory-forming function, the past cannot be adequately interpreted; where the *regressus ex nunc* gains decisive significance, the future following the now cannot be interpreted without contradiction in the intended sense on the level of a demonstrative procedure. Such is the fate of efforts to give Nietzsche's doctrine of eternal recurrence a theoretical grounding.

Attempting to solve our third task, we return to Nietzsche's philosophy of contradictions after having detached his doctrine of eternal return from it and considered it by itself. For Becker did not base his arguments on the foundation of the systematic whole of Nietzsche's thinking, as he believed.[94] To accomplish this, at least a discussion of Nietzsche's critique of the "old" truth concept would have been necessary.

In contrast, in the first part of this chapter we explained the doctrine of eternal return as the conclusion reached by the synthesizing overman in his "new" understanding of truth. It was a matter of showing how this overman must will himself with ultimate intensity and extreme extension in connection with the sole reality. This gave rise to the thought of eternal recurrence in its meaning as constitutive of the overman's being-in-the-world. One misses the point if, as has often happened, one speaks only of the *ethical* meaning of this thought and removes it from its scientific content. In the end, however, a fissure also opened up here in our attempt to think through Nietzsche's statements on the doctrine of eternal recurrence. This became evident when Nietzsche's efforts to prove the theory were confronted with the unrestricted affirmation of eternal recurrence, which affirmation left all proof behind as belonging to the "old truth."

If we continue to take Nietzsche's arguments seriously, the question arises whether—despite all the "scientific inadequacies" discussed above—they do not conflict at least with the presuppositions of his own thinking. That is the case, as the two following representations will show.

A. Let us recall that Nietzsche's characterization of the will to power as the ultimate given must not be understood as if we thereby came upon something simple, ultimately unchangeable. From the first, multiple wills to power are always found in conflict with one another: hence, there is no numerical ultimate to be reached. In such conflict one will to power can become two, just as vice versa two can become one. In any case, the "number" of beings is itself in flux. Nor may Nietzsche accept any limit on the divisibility of wills to power, otherwise he would fall back to positions he precisely wants to overcome. But with the presupposition of a potentially unlimited splitting of the wills to power, the demonstrability of the statement that all that was, is, and will be returns can no longer be maintained. It is, indeed, not impossible that under the given presupposition disgregations and aggregate conditions of wills to power may recur again and again in the same constellation. But Nietzsche himself has eliminated the *necessity* of such an assumption as a consequence of his theory of the unlimited divisibility of the wills to power.[95]

B. But the doctrine of eternal recurrence contradicts not only the doctrine of the will to power as the theory of the ultimate that can be reached, which is not a numerical ultimate. It also contradicts Nietzsche's reflection on the breeding of the super-powerful, that is, his statements with regard to the highest development of the will to power. In them Nietzsche tries to show how the rule of the strong over the mediocre and the weak must be definitively consolidated by the production of unfavorable conditions. Bringing about difficult living conditions, which remain essentially the same, is supposed to prevent the future great men from decimating one another in ebullient power struggles, or on the other hand from weakening through lack of opposition. If the planning of such conditions is neglected, then the mediocre or weak finally retake power. To preserve their own domination, the future strong men must therefore preserve or even promote the relative strength of their opponents. If breeding and planning succeed, the highest man can develop fully. Then he can have "the greatest multiplicity of drives, in the relatively greatest strength that can be endured" (WP 966).

But this possibility of a definitive rule of the strong men intensified into the overman is lost if everything that was always recurs. Here what is "hard to bear" is not that the small and pitiful proves to be finally unconquerable, but rather that the overmen, despite breeding and planning, must lose their power again and again if eternal recurrence as the extreme form of the "new truth" is to maintain its correctness. Breeding and planning may delay the downfall of the strong men longer than could be possible under the "accidental conditions" of previous history. But even this can involve only a relative prolongation of their rule. Under this aspect, every distinction in principle between the history of chance and planned history falls by the wayside. "The 'ape' ideal could at any time be ahead of mankind—as goal," Nietzsche writes. Certainly, such a "retrogression and decline will produce its ideals: and one will always believe to be progressing!"[96] But Nietzsche's own ideals are surely lost in any such "progress."

Now this aspect—the inevitable decline of the overman—certainly does not take into account the full truth of the doctrine of eternal return. For the overman, too, will always recur again, although he will also perish again and again. But the inevitability of his downfall does not release one from the demand that one should realize the highest. After all, only the achievement of the highest within a cycle *justifies* its recurrence as a whole. Nietzsche, then, can will the perishing— for the sake of the recurrence. He writes: "One must want to perish in order to be able to emerge again—from one day to the next. Transformation through a hundred souls—that is your life, your fate! And then finally: to want this whole series once again!"[97]

Mention of the "series" is revealing. Nietzsche thinks the circle of all events from the point of view of a series that runs toward something; the series obtains its justification through the circle that brings everything back. This points to the last contradiction of Nietzsche's philosophical thinking that stems from his philosophy of contradictions. Two things are expected of the overman: he is supposed to want at the same time his highest development in the series and his perishing in the cycle.

Once again, then, it is necessary to spell out the contradictions that concerned us, starting with the portrayal of his ambivalent truth of the will to power to the elaboration of the two basic types of superman. Will Nietzsche finally succeed in abolishing these contradictions, after all, in the doctrine of eternal return?

The difficulties of this problem become clearer when we inquire with Nietzsche about the center of all that happens. If this is interpreted as a pure circling, there is no center. One can also say, as the animals say to Zarathustra, that the center, then, is "everywhere" (Z III).[98] Even for the synthesizing overman—despite all fundamental differences about the animals' opinion—every moment is center.[99] But if the center of that series of events that must be run off before everything begins again is sought, then the assimilation of the doctrine of eternal recurrence by the overman, who is perfected thereby, occupies this place.[100] Thus Zarathustra announces the "*Great Noon,*" when the higher man becomes master (Z IV).[101] "In every ring of human existence at all there is always an hour when the mightiest thought, that of the eternal recurrence of all things occurs first to one, then to many, then to all—each time it is for mankind the noon hour."[102]

Occasionally it seems as if Nietzsche wanted to give up this meaning of the center of history in favor of periodic flux. Thus he notes: "On heroic greatness as the only state of those preparing the way (striving for absolute perishing as means to endure oneself). We must not long for a [final] condition, but rather we must want to become *periodic beings*—just like existence."[103] On the other hand the great shapers should prepare the end of the previous history of chance through the power of their creative will; they should give history a goal. That would be "the great noon," the hour "when man stands in the middle of his way between beast and overman and celebrates his way to the evening as his highest hope." *This* way to evening leads to the "going under" of man, but it is at the same time the transition to the "new morning" on which the overman begins to live (Z I).[104]

The center of what happens can, accordingly, mean several things: first it can be thought as the attained peak of one period (series) of human history; secondly, as the noontime at which man first catches sight of the overman; thirdly, every event in the circulation can become the center. In the first two cases, the infinite repetition of the series of events is the vantage point; only in the third case does the circularity dominate over every attainable state within the series.

Insofar as the eternal recurrence appears as both the goal of history and as what absorbs all history into itself, one can find, as does Löwith, that with the thought on the one hand "a new purpose [*Wozu*] of human existence" is given "beyond itself," and on the other "also the exact opposite: an equally selfless and aimless circling of the natural world in itself, also encompassing human life."[105] "The problem of the doctrine of eternal return" is "the unity of this conflict between the human will and the aimless circling of the world."[106] But Nietzsche's fundamental contradiction is not between the doctrines of the overman and eternal recurrence, as Löwith believes. For, as was shown in this chapter, the doctrine of eternal return can be understood as the synthesizing overman's Yes to the world. Nietzsche's fundamental contradiction breaks forth in his conception of the will to power, as was shown in chapter 5. It leads to the separation of the characteristics of the overman, which ultimately can be located only in two opposite types. Their division is also not bridged in Nietzsche's explanations of the doctrine of eternal recurrence.

Thus the fundamental inconsistency must not be placed in the wrong place, as Löwith does. When Löwith then speaks in greater detail about the conflict between the cosmic and the anthropological meaning of the doctrine of eternal recurrence "so that one becomes the nonsense [*Widersinn*] of the other,"[107] he is moving like other Nietzsche-interpreters on a level on which the antithesis between the worldly "truth" of the doctrine and a practical postulate can be erected.[108] He quotes Nietzsche's statement: "My doctrine says: to live in such a way that you must wish to live again is the task—you will in any case!"[109] For Löwith this dash designates "in reality a breach in his thought!"[110] But if the eternal return is to announce the "new truth" that Nietzsche has to announce, then the statement must be understood from its second part. This truth means that beyond all wishing, eternal return constitutes the being-in-the-world of the highest man. The task spoken of in the first part of the sentence then names what must be striven for when one sets out on the path whose destination is the insuperable "knowledge" that is expressed in the Yes to all that is, was, and will be. The supposed break is then a *transition*. But, of course, Nietzsche has already taken on the challenge expressed before the dash [in the passage under consideration] by the truth that everything recurs.

This truth does not have a merely cosmic sense; it is supposed, more originally, to express the unity of the overman's being in the world. Cosmology and ethics can, in the light of this unity, be only derivative determinations. Nietzsche, to be sure, often obscured his original intention, for example, by his proofs.

This brings the *fourth* task we have posed for ourselves into the field of view: the question of the significance of his proofs for the doctrine of eternal recurrence. This can be formulated briefly. When Nietzsche asserts that the world would already have had to reach a final state if such a thing were possible at all and seeks to buttress his theory with the arguments cited above in our discussion of Becker, this statement must not be taken in isolation. In such a context he does say: "This is the sole certainty we have in our hands to serve as corrective to a great host of world hypotheses possible in themselves" (WP 1066). But the overman's Yes, which he says to himself and to the world in a most extensive *and* intensive manner, lies prior to and first grounds this certainty (questionable as a *theory*) in the sense of the "old truth." Any *explanation* of eternal recurrence—including Nietzsche's own—comes too late to reach the agreement required from the overman's being-in-the-world in the sense of the "new truth."

We should concede only prohibitive character to Nietzsche's resorting to the "old truth," although surely it must be doubted whether he himself understood it so. For is it not all too understandable that he brings the doctrine of eternal recurrence into play versus the other "world-hypotheses"? Thus, in the context of the last cited note he opposed William Thomson, who drew from mechanism the conclusion of a final state. He cannot allow the "old truth," whose expression he found present in the natural science of his time, to stand as *truth*. In order to oppose it, he enters its own territory. Then he himself succumbs to the "old truth." This happens, however, in the expectation that this "old truth" will prove untenable in its hypotheses that oppose the eternal recurrence. In order to demonstrate such untenableness, he presents the doctrine of eternal recurrence itself as a theory, thereby not merely curtailing but even reversing the true meaning of the doctrine.

We explained above that the establishment of the opposition between a cosmic and an anthropological or ethical meaning of the doctrine of eternal recurrence remains inadequate. The two determinations must be taken back to the unity of the overman's being-in-the-world.

However, this unity is given an inconsistent portrayal by Nietzsche, as was made clear in the discussion of the *center* of all events. Is the overman to become a periodic being for whom every moment is the center of events, or does he represent the peak of a developmental series that is supposed to be repeated? Does the series have primacy over the cycle, or does the cycle swallow up the series?

Such questions evoke once again the problem of the two types of overman with regard to their incompatible being-in-the-world. The *synthesizing* overman affirms everything that was, is, and will be, including himself, *to the same extent*. In his affirmation, he submits to the course of events. He wants everything again, just as it already has been countless times, not only for his own sake, but for the sake of all things. Even the thought of eternal recurrence as represented in this overman does not leap out of the closed cycle so represented. Nietzsche writes: "It has all come again: Sirius and the spider, and your thoughts in this hour and this your thought that everything comes again." The note at the end of which this sentence stands begins characteristically with the demand: "Let us beware of believing that the universe [*das All*] has a tendency to attain certain *forms,* that it wants to become more beautiful, more perfect, and more complicated!"[111]

The *dominating overman,* on the contrary, wants to see himself as the peak of a series. His goal is to expand his rule, and he affirms his opponents only to that end. What counts for him is the moment of self-realization: for its sake he approves what was and is. Thus Nietzsche does justice to *this* type when he writes: "Immortal is the moment when I generated recurrence. For the sake of this moment I *endure* recurrence."[112] Of course, eternal recurrence has a different meaning for the ruler type than for the wise man. It can be asked, finally, whether powerful rulers must want it at all, apart from its being a useful weapon in the struggle with the weak: for, in Nietzsche's conviction, the rulers can create the conditions to preserve their dominance.

But with eternal recurrence, this dominance not only can be preserved but *fixated* once and for all. And this means with the complete *sameness* of the course of the periods: "There *is* no 'second time.'"[113] For what will be is already decided prior to all becoming. Clearly, here the series determines the cycle. In this interpretation of the thought of eternal recurrence Nietzsche can even teach "deliverance from the eternal stream": "The stream constantly flows back into itself, and again and again you step into the same stream as the same ones."[114] It is true of the dominant overmen: "To *impose* upon becoming the character of being—that is the supreme will to power. . . . *That everything recurs is the closest approximation of a world of becoming to a world of being*" (WP 617).

Its constancy and becoming reach this closest approximation in Nietzsche's doctrine of recurrence. But even what tends to fuse together in it still remains separate in the end. Finally we still find two antithetical possibilities, which can be expressed as follows: Either infinity seeks to absorb the finite, or infinity has no other function than the definitive fixation of the finite.

This difference is most clearly evidenced in relation to the different ways of being-in-the-world of the two types of overman. In both cases this being-in-the-world is constituted by saying Yes to everything that is, was, or will be. But in each case this Yes has a different meaning. One type is concerned with dissolving in the stream of becoming, desiring oneself and everything else unrestrictedly again and again. He is the mighty one insofar as he corresponds to change and in such correspondence goes beyond any fixable particularity of willing. The other seeks to fixate his dominance in the will to return for all times. In such a fixation, the eternalization of his dominance, he becomes the mighty one. Although both types of overman want recurrence, they want something different in and by it. But since the recurrence *is* only as a thought and a doctrine, its meaning remains insurmountably split into a duality. While the contradictions in Nietzsche's lines of thought seem to be overcome, in the end they break open again in a fissure that we come upon repeatedly in all his essential statements.

8
Nietzsche's "Doctrine" of the Will to Power

When Nietzsche writes that the world is the will to power and nothing besides, he seems by this clear statement to be giving us a key to understanding his thinking, such as philosophical interpreters are accustomed to using. He names the ground of being and defines being as a whole in terms of it; his thinking is metaphysics in the sense we are familiar with from the long history of Western philosophy. To understand this thinking, then, does not in principle place us before new problems. Although Nietzsche explicitly opposes metaphysics, we can quickly become convinced that he speaks of this only in the sense of a two-worlds theory. If we disregard such a narrowing of the term, Nietzsche's claim that his philosophy is not a metaphysics is surely unsustainable. Nietzsche, it could be said, merely extends the chain of metaphysical interpretations of the world by one more link.

Heidegger attributes a special significance to Nietzsche's philosophy within the history of metaphysics. He interprets Nietzsche's philosophy as the *completion* of Western philosophy, insofar as the *inversion* of metaphysics performed in it supposedly exhausts its essential possibilities. But even more occurs in Nietzsche's thinking: the *destruction* of metaphysics by its own resources. It can be shown that in Nietzsche's philosophy precisely as the highest peak of the "metaphysics of subjectivity" this subjectivity plunges into the bottomless pit. The metaphysical "will to the will," in the form of the will to power that sees itself as itself, becomes *willed* will that no longer refers back to *one* willing entity, a single will, but rather merely to the *complex* of willing that interrogates itself concerning its ultimate actual givenness and withdraws into the undeterminable. Nietzsche certainly remains a metaphysician. He certainly restores metaphysics; for example, when he sees the doctrine of eternal return as the closest approximation of becoming to being. But it seems more essential to me that, behind the facades that he constantly re-erects, metaphysics collapses under his incessant questioning. The complete significance of this process could be interpreted adequately only within the framework of a far-reaching discussion in which metaphysics was thematized on its many levels.

I would like to remark that although my Nietzsche-interpretation differs radically from Heidegger's I do not therefore disagree with Heidegger's effort to "overcome metaphysics." Rather, the need to do this—as well as the need for an "other beginning" prepared by Heidegger—seems to me to follow far more drastically from Nietzsche's thinking than was evident from previous interpretations.

This discussion focuses on the question of the will to power. It will try to move completely within the horizon of Nietzsche's philosophy. It will show what a complex set of problems lies behind such an apparently simple statement as that the world is the will to power and nothing besides.[1] We wish to penetrate step by step into this set of problems. Because of its complexity it seems advisable first to cite some of Nietzsche's typical statements about what he means by "will to power." These quotations are intended to give a first access to what will then be explained.[2]

1. Preliminary Characterization of the Will to Power

Will to power is not a special case of willing. A will "in itself" or "as such" is a mere abstraction: actually no such thing exists. All willing is, according to Nietzsche, a willing-something. What is essentially posited in all willing is: power. The will to power seeks to rule and incessantly to expand its domain of power. The expansion of power occurs in processes of overpowering. Thus wanting power is not just a "'desiring,' striving, demanding." It entails the "*affect of commanding*" (WP 668).[3] Command and execution belong together in the unity of the will to power. Thus "a quantum of power . . . is designated by the effect it produces and that which it resists" (WP 634).

Nietzsche finds the will to power at work everywhere. It can be most clearly "shown that every living thing does everything it can *not* to preserve itself, but to become *more*" (WP 688). But even in the inorganic realm the will to power is the only active agent. Nietzsche distances himself from Schopenhauer's "will to life" as the basic form of will: "Life is merely a *special case* of the will to power— it is quite arbitrary to assert that everything strives to enter into this form of will to power" (WP 692).

Not only in what rules and extends its domination does the will to power manifest itself, but also in what is dominated and subjected. Even the "relation of the obedient to the ruler" must be understood "as a counter-striving" in this sense.[4] Man too is—in whatsoever mode of behavior—fundamentally will to power. Nietzsche traces all our intellectual and psychological activities to our *"valuations,"* which correspond to our drives and the conditions for their existence. A note from the *Nachlaß* then adds: "Our drives are reducible to the *will to power*. The will to power is the ultimate fact we arrive at."[5] This makes it clear that for Nietzsche "the innermost essence of being is will to power" (WP 693).

These first statements on the theme of the will to power are based on Nietzsche's *Nachlaß*. The question is whether such a foundation is legitimate. Would it not be better on such an important question to rely only—or at least primarily—on works published by Nietzsche himself? What is the situation with the philosophical reliability of the published *Nachlaß*? What philosophical weight do the sketches not published by Nietzsche have compared with the works he authorized?

2. On the *Nachlaß*-Problem

The greatest part of Nietzsche's unpublished notes, insofar as they are directly relevant, were made available to Nietzsche-discussion in the so-called *Groß-Oktav-Ausgabe*. However, the complete *Nachlaß* will be presented only when the *Kritische Gesamtausgabe* published by G. Colli and M. Montinari is completed. But even after the volumes published so far, it can be said that Nietzsche-scholarship will find itself in a new situation in many respects because of material first made known in them.

It cannot yet be said whether the still unpublished texts will bring essential new insights in answer to the fundamental questions of the will to power. I doubt it, not least of all because of the particular attention paid to it by the earlier publishers. Thus in 1901 an anthology limited to 483 aphorisms and in 1906 another one containing 1067 of Nietzsche's posthumous notes were published. Their editors oriented themselves by one of the numerous plans drafted by Nietzsche for a future work that was never completed. By basing their project on Nietzsche's outline of March 17, 1887, and following Nietzsche's very general arrangement, they assembled texts that are in many regards of disparate kinds and only in part—though in considerable part—contribute to clarifying what he means by "will to power." It is true, moreover, that the selections and systematic arrangement, of the aphorisms are more than questionable, not to mention the sloppy editorship in details. In addition, other volumes of the *Nachlaß* in the *Groß-Oktav-Ausgabe* contain significant material on Nietzsche's conception of the will to power. But that the *problem* of the will to power came to public awareness, both in the sense of sound philosophical inquiry and in a bad, slogan-like use, is attributable mainly to the fact that with the 1906 edition a book with the title *The*

Will to Power appeared and became influential, a book that was said to be Nietzsche's masterpiece.

It is inaccurate to speak of such a masterpiece of Nietzsche's. But it is also wrong to disregard the aphorisms and fragments published in this compilation and in the other volumes of the *Groß-Oktav-Ausgabe* as *mere Nachlaß*. A distinction must be made between "genuine *Nachlaß*," on the one hand, and paraphrasing excerpts that Nietzsche made, as well as "preliminary drafts" for material he published himself, on the other. Here the new critical edition will open essential insights. But even in the relation between earlier drafts and later texts revised for publication, Nietzsche's case is different from that of other authors. Nietzsche not only held back many of his insights; he also expressed many of them in his writings only in a disguised, allusive way or else in a hypothetical form.

Reference to the peculiar significance of Nietzsche's *Nachlaß* loses its strangeness when we hear that Nietzsche understood himself as the most hidden of all persons.[6] In *Beyond Good and Evil* he even writes that one does not love one's knowledge enough as soon as one communicates it (BGE 160). And in a posthumous note from 1887 he writes: "I no longer respect the reader: how could I write for readers? . . . But I take notes only for myself."[7] What Nietzsche held back takes on particular weight from such statements. There are, then, solid reasons for Martin Heidegger's view that "Nietzsche's real philosophy" did not receive "its final formulation and its publication in book form, neither in the decade of 1879–89 nor in the previous years. What Nietzsche himself published was 'always foreground.' Nietzsche's real philosophy was left behind as posthumous legacy" (*Nachlaß*).[8]

3. Schlechta's View of the Significance of the *Nachlaß*

The opposite pole to the valuation of Nietzsche's *Nachlaß* exemplified by Heidegger's especially striking statement is Karl Schlechta's conviction that Nietzsche had "expressed himself with complete clarity, beyond any misunderstanding, in the works he published himself or clearly intended for publication. As far as a genuine possibility of understanding, nothing essential remains to be desired." One must seek to understand Nietzsche only in what he has published.[9] Schlechta published a highly respected edition of Nietzsche's works in three volumes that has since been used by quite a few authors as the only textual basis for their interpretation. But this edition is not restricted to Nietzsche's publications, as might be expected from its editor's above-cited view. Rather, in volume III, along with other texts, Schlechta included *Nachlaß*-passages that had been collated in the 1906 edition of *The Will to Power*.

This shows Schlechta's inconsistency. But the "historical weight" attributed to Nietzsche's alleged masterpiece in scholarly literature seemed to him to justify a new and complete edition of the texts compiled in *The Will to Power*. Schlechta's approach, however, was to dissolve the systematic compilation made by the earlier editors and instead seek to produce a strictly *chronological arrangement* of the aphorisms it contained. He did not succeed in this enterprise; nor could he, since the original manuscripts were not at his disposal.

The merit of Schlechta's edition consists mostly in his having destroyed the legend of a masterpiece in the public consciousness once and for all. But that he published only those texts already selected by the editors of the 1906 compilation had the disastrous effect that the users of his edition saw only this part of the *Nachlaß,* which accordingly again gained particular substantive salience compared with the parts of the *Nachlaß* not published by Schlechta. Yet Schlechta had rightly pointed out that it was really quite inexplicable why the editors of *The Will to Power* had not included in their collection of aphorisms those notes that can be found in volumes XIII and XIV as "additional *Nachlaß.*" The same criticism can be made against Schlechta: if he took the effort to present a chronological sequence of the *Nachlaß* edition, why not include the "additional" *Nachlaß* in chronological order?[10] Didn't Schlechta actually—though contrary to his own intention—promote a higher valuation of the sketches that had been published in *The Will to Power*?[11]

4. Nietzsche on the Will to Power in His Published Works

Schlechta's low estimation of the philosophical relevance of Nietzsche's published *Nachlaß* led to a controversy that also involved the substantive problem of the will to power. Karl Löwith accused Schlechta of having spread a new Nietzsche-legend, namely "that the will to power did not exist as a most broad-based and wide-ranging problem posed and thought through by Nietzsche."[12] In his answer,[13] Schlechta stated that of course he did not deny "that Nietzsche in his published works often addressed the will to power as a fundamental characteristic of life," as when he had Zarathustra say: "Wherever I found a living thing, I found will to power." But where Nietzsche tried "to analyze and precision this idea of his" he achieved no "demonstrable *result.*"

This judgment of Schlechta's is untenable. Nietzsche's authorized works do not offer a sufficient basis for understanding the will to power. The profundity of what he seeks to name by this phrase can be seen only by drawing upon the *Nachlaß.* Yet Schlechta claims that the *Nachlaß* published in the *Groß-Oktav-Ausgabe* has nothing new to offer that Nietzsche has not said in his published works. Thus

Schlechta becomes absolutely convinced that the idea of the will to power cannot be sustained. Although in Nietzsche's books often only "foreground ideas" are found concerning the will to power, the fact remains that more can be gathered from them to clarify this problem than Schlechta is willing to recognize.

Let us here discuss only what Schlechta himself states. In his reply to Löwith he presents "two samples" from Nietzsche's works that he considers to be representative of the problem under discussion. They are—as Schlechta wants to show—not only incompatible with one another; each of the two statements is, moreover, problematic in itself. In the following pages I will subject the two samples to a more precise scrutiny. I too consider the cited texts to be representative of Nietzsche's published works.

Schlechta's "first sample" is Aphorism 36 from *Beyond Good and Evil*. Nietzsche here presents his idea of the will to power in the context of a series of reflections clad in the form of hypotheses. They need not be cited here in detail since the interpreter Schlechta is concerned only with their hypothetical character, which is expressed by such turns of phrase as "suppose that," "one must venture the hypothesis . . . ," "assuming, finally, that one would succeed," and the like. Nietzsche concludes his remarks with the reflection: "then one would have gained the right to determine *all* efficient force univocally as—*will to power*. The world viewed from inside, the world defined and determined according to its 'intelligible character'—it would be 'will to power' and nothing else" (BGE 36).

Schlechta finds remarkable the caution with which Nietzsche expresses himself in this his first published discussion of the problem of the will to power. That Nietzsche chooses the subjunctive; the world *would be* "will to power" and nothing else, leads Schlechta to write: "That does not sound very confident for a thought that is supposed to hold up."

Two arguments can be made against Schlechta's view:

A. In the cited aphorism Nietzsche is not speaking only hypothetically. After he has written, "Suppose, finally, we succeeded in explaining our entire instinctive life as the development and ramification of *one* basic form of will," he adds the parenthetical remark: "namely the will to power, as my proposition has it." Eckhard Heftrich rightly comments: "The definite assertion of the parenthetical remark, however, restricts the hypothetical formulation of the aphorism; indeed it encloses it completely in brackets. Thus the content of the parentheses becomes the solution, the basic principle ('*my* proposition')."[14] By inserting that remark, Nietzsche actually goes beyond the reflections presented in the aphorism as questionable assumptions and names his fundamental conviction. Surely there is no trace of lack of confidence here.

B. This aphorism from *Beyond Good and Evil* is located in Part II, subtitled

"The Free Spirit." The free spirits are supposed to be the new "philosophers of the dangerous 'maybe' in every sense" (BGE 2), as Nietzsche writes earlier in Part I of his book. He recommends to them their "masks and subtlety," *so that* they will be mistaken for what they are not. This is how they will show their style (BGE 25). As a note on the writings of his middle creative period states, Nietzsche is concerned with gaining "access to understanding a yet higher and more difficult type than even [the] type of the free spirit: no other way leads to an understanding."[15] If the thought-experiments presented in Aphorism 36 of *Beyond Good and Evil* are considered under this aspect, one will have to agree with Alfred Baeumler's critique of Schlechta. Baeumler writes that it is wrong to interpret "a stylistic means as an objective distancing on the main point."[16]

In a closing remark on Schlechta's first "sample" I will refer to a posthumous note of Nietzsche's that will be dealt with more closely below (WP 1067). It comes from the year 1885 and belongs to the materials he considered while writing *Beyond Good and Evil*. At the end of this note, Nietzsche expressed himself similarly on the world as will to power. What interests us in the present context is only the interesting difference between the two texts[17] consisting in the fact that in the text written earlier Nietzsche speaks not hypothetically but with unambiguous decisiveness: ". . . do you want a *name* for this world? A *solution* for all its riddles? a *light* for you, too, you best-concealed, strongest, most intrepid, most midnightly men?—*This world is the will to power—and nothing besides!*" (WP 1067). It will have to be shown below with what unshakable conviction Nietzsche thinks world-reality in terms of his fundamental thought of the will to power. If it is a matter of elaborating Nietzsche's ultimate "insights" and not of the problem of the questioning attitude of the "free spirits," then here—as in other cases for other reasons—the *Nachlaß*-text, which is an "earlier stage" deserves interpretive priority over the published version.

Examining Schlechta's second "sample," we fall deeper into the difficulties one encounters when inquiring into the will to power. From the first text one could conclude that Nietzsche was seeking a metaphysical "basic principle" to which all "efficient forces" could be traced back; the second passage Schlechta cites refers to a different structure of the will to power. It is Aphorism 12 of the second treatise of *On the Genealogy of Morals* (GM II:12), only a few passages of which he considers. In his opinion, this text is "at least as conclusive" for the untenableness of Nietzsche's idea as the previously cited one. Nietzsche here opposed the prevalent taste of the time "which would rather be reconciled even to the absolute fortuitousness, even the mechanistic senselessness of all events than to the theory that in all events a *will to power* is operating." Schlechta finds that the two positions rejected by Nietzsche, "progress toward a goal" and "mechanistic senselessness" are only "verbal counterpositions" versus Nietzsche's "genuine" understanding of the world that consists in "a world of absolute randomness."

Now for Nietzsche there are two kinds of "chance," just as there are two kinds of "necessity," depending on whether he uses these words in the sense of "mechanistic conceptualization" or in connection with his own interpretation of the will to power. When Schlechta states that Nietzsche obtains his concept of force "from the arsenal of positivistic natural science," he does not take seriously enough what Nietzsche says in the last part of the aphorism about the modern development of the "strictest, apparently most objective sciences." They fail to see through "the democratic idiosyncrasy" that opposes everything that dominates, the contemporary physiology, the essence of life, its will to power. "Thus one overlooks the essential priority of the spontaneous, aggressive, expansive, form-giving forces that give new interpretations." *The* will to power is here imagined by Nietzsche as a plurality of forces.

Precisely this annoys Schlechta; striving to develop the thought of multiplicity, he clearly overdraws it. He stresses that Nietzsche speaks of "processes of overpowering that are independent of one another." Schlechta comments: "If the processes of overpowering actually are independent of one another, then every intermediary meaning is nonsense." By the "intermediary meaning" he obviously is referring to the will to power. However, he quotes incompletely and in a way that distorts Nietzsche's meaning. Let us complete the formulation Schlechta extracted from Aphorism 12 at least to the extent necessary to understand the text. Nietzsche writes: "The evolution of a thing, a custom, an organ is . . . a succession of more or less profound, more or less mutually independent processes of subduing." These are more or less independent of one another. Their independence is thus restricted. Even processes of overpowering that have "more" independence of one another are still not *completely* independent of one another, as Schlechta interprets them. That Nietzsche, who elsewhere so emphasizes the relation of all things to all things, speaks in this context of independence is because here he is polemicizing against every causally or teleologically oriented determination of sequences of events. Compared with such determinations the overpowering processes of the wills to power, which in reality constitute all "evolutions," are more or less independent of one another.

Nonetheless, Schlechta's two "samples" have led us to two apparently incompatible possibilities of interpreting the will to power. Has Nietzsche actually not "thought through" the problem of the will to power sufficiently? For either the will to power is the principle that grounds the world, or the world is the ungrounded, unprincipled co-occurrence of events, in which at every moment "one will to power has become master over something less mighty," as is said in the cited aphorism.

5. On Interpreting the Will to Power as a Metaphysical Principle

The prevalent view in Nietzsche-interpretations is that the will to power is to be understood as the metaphysical grounding. Even if the understanding of the will to power as "distinctly" metaphysical will in Schopenhauer's sense is rejected— namely as "a self-grounded, substantial and transcendent principle of reality"— one can still insist that Nietzsche "in the last analysis does think the many concrete wills to power as manifestations of a unitary principle that determines all reality," as W. Weischedel does.[18] Despite all other differences, his interpretation is related to that of Jaspers, who states that Nietzsche substantializes real being into the will to power within a reality conceived as transcendent, in the world of "pure immanence."[19] Under quite a different aegis, Heidegger's point of departure, too, is from a self-preserving, self-overpowering uniqueness of the will to power. The "enhancement character" of the will, as interpreted by Nietzsche stems from its self-overpowering. And W. Schulz, in agreement with Heidegger's interpretation, asserted that what the will opposes is "no longer anything external, but rather always only itself." It always overcomes only itself in an eternally imposing self-abolition.[20] These allusions will have to suffice.

That Nietzsche, especially in the *Nachlaß*, very frequently speaks of *the* will to power, seems to support interpretations of this kind. And when, as has been mentioned, he writes of "*the* will to power and nothing besides," apparently this debars any view in which reality as understood by Nietzsche is *not* seen as a metaphysically grounded unity. That the same note states that the world is "a monster of energy . . . at the same time one and many," does not exclude a metaphysical interpretation in this sense. Nonetheless at the beginning of this definition of Nietzsche's I wish to develop a different understanding of the will to power and the world. I believe it portrays more accurately what Nietzsche is aiming at.[21]

The world is one and many. The world is will to power. This suggests that the will to power, too, is one and many. Assume that the will is one. How, then, can this being-one be understood? Zarathustra rejects the One as a theological or metaphysical grounding. "Evil" is what he calls "all this teaching of the one" (Z II).[22] Anyway, oneness is for Nietzsche by no means simple. "Whatever is real, whatever is true, is neither one, nor even reducible to one" (WP 536). What does unity then mean for Nietzsche? He answers: "All unity is unity only as *organiza-*

tion and cooperation: just as a human community is a unity" (WP 561). This compels us to reflect on the oneness of the will to power, too, under this aspect. The many comes to the foreground. Only a multiplicity can be organized into a unity. The organized many must entail "power quanta" if the one world is nothing else but the will to power. Now I can refer to what was stated about Schlechta's "second sample."

The will to power is the multiplicity of forces locked in struggle with one another. *Force* in Nietzsche's sense can be called a unity only in the sense of organization. The world is indeed "a firm, iron magnitude of force"; it is "a certain quantum of force" (WP 1067, 638). But this quantum is given only in the opposition of quanta. Gilles Deleuze rightly observes: "Every force is . . . essentially related to another force. The being of force is plural; it would be literally absurd to think of force in the singular."[23] But if forces are nothing else but the "will to power," Heidegger's assertion that the will to power is "never the willing of an individual, real being," but rather "always essential will"[24] is untenable.

The world Nietzsche is speaking of reveals itself as a play and counterplay of forces, or respectively, *wills to power.* If we recall first that the accumulations of power quanta are constantly increasing or decreasing, then we can speak only of continually changing unities, but not of the one unity. Unity is always only organization under the short-term reign of dominant wills to power. Nietzsche further radicalizes his view by his remark that every such unity means "one" only as a "domination-structure," but is "not one" (WP 561).[25] There *is* nothing that is "one." Then the will, too, is not "one." The unity of domination-structures, in which a multitude of power-quanta are joined together, has no reality.

On the other hand, Nietzsche says, as we have seen: there *is* unity as a unity of organization. Does Nietzsche not contradict himself here? If we believe in "'reason' in language" we must answer this question affirmatively. But, for Nietzsche the reason of language is "a deceptive old woman." Nothing has previously "had a more naive convincing power," he writes in the same context, "than the error of being, as it was formulated, for example, by the Eleatics: it has every word for it, every sentence we speak for it" (TI 3:5). Nietzsche is convinced that language deceives us, if we take the word at its word, that is, if we stop at it and do not let ourselves be directed by it to the states of affairs that do not appear in it. Because Nietzsche speaks so referentially he can both say "is" and at the same time deny reality to the "is."[26]

Of course, it must be asked in what sense there is no being. "Being," according to Nietzsche, is "an empty fiction." That he believes he can attribute this statement to Heraclitus (TI 3:2), shows, as does his reference to the Eleatics, what "restriction of being," to cite Heidegger,[27] is constitutive of Nietzsche's understanding of being: being is contrasted with becoming and derived from it as "delusion."[28] "Being," as the opposite of becoming, is considered to be constant. The idea of constancy, however, is compatible with the thought of multiplicity. Nietzsche remarks: "Even the opponents of the Eleatics were still subject to the seductive influence of their concept of being: Democritus, among others, when he invented his *atom* . . ." (TI 3:5).

Nietzsche does not succumb to such a seduction. If there is no being in the sense of something constant, then there also are no atoms. Not only the oneness of an organized domination-structure has no such "being," but even the multiplicity that "interplays" in such a structure "is" not, insofar as it is thought of as composed of solid units. The multiplicity of power quanta must therefore be understood not as a plurality of quantitatively irreducible ultimate givens, not as a plurality of indivisible "monads."[29] Power-shifts within the unstable organizations allow one power quantum to become two or two to become one. If we use numbers in a fixating and conclusive sense, it must be said that the "number" of beings always remains in flux. There is no "individual," there is no ultimate indivisible quantum of power, that we can reach. Nietzsche claims to think "radically" for having discovered "the 'smallest world' as what is everywhere decisive."[30] This smallest thing can, as actual, never be an ultimate. It is, as "world," always a structure that is constituted by "power-quanta whose essence consists in exercising power on all other power-quanta."[31]

A power-structure "is" not one, it *means* one. What does "mean" here mean? In *Beyond Good and Evil,* Nietzsche writes that willing seems to him mainly as "something *complicated,* something that is a unity only as a word" (BGE 19). We have already heard that language dangles unities before our eyes. But meaning is of a more original nature than speech. Speech is a mode of expression of the power-will.[32] It seals what previously had already been interpreted *as something.* All interpretation stems from the power-structures' striving for power. These arrange what they wish to overcome, or perhaps to assimilate, or against which they wish to defend themselves. Arrangement is always a falsifying equalization and fixation. What is made equal or fixed is prepared for encroachment or else for the defensive stance of a power-will. Nietzsche writes: "If I remove all the relationships, all the 'properties,' all the 'activities' of a thing, the thing does *not* remain over; because thingness has only been *invented* by us owing to the requirements of logic, thus with the aim of facilitating communication" (WP 558).

For the interpreter, the thing means oneness, although in reality what he has before him is only a multiplicity. But the interpreter, too, is nothing other than a multiplicity "with uncertain boundaries."[33] We are a multiplicity that "*has imagined itself a unity,*" Nietzsche notes.[34] Consciousness, the intellect, serves as a means by which "I" deceived "myself" about "myself."[35] There must be a quantity of consciousness and will in any complicated organic being, but "our uppermost consciousness usually keeps the others closed."[36] The domination-structure that I am presents itself *as one* to *itself* through this consciousness: through "simplifying and making overseeable, i.e., falsifying." In this way the apparently simple acts of will become possible.[37]

All this must have made it clear that Nietzsche always has actual multiplicities of will to power in mind, which always "mean one" in the sense of simplicity or stability, but in truth are complex, incessantly changing structures without constancy, in which a conflict of power-quanta organized in manifold gradations is played out. By what right, however, can Nietzsche then repeatedly speak of "*the* will to power" as if it were not given in the characterized multiplicity, as if it were actually one? As if *the* will to power as something simple grounded the world?[38]

6. "Will to Power" in the Singular

Nietzsche uses the phrase "will to power" in the singular in three ways. In the first of them the will to power refers to the totality of the real. As we have seen, the world is the will to power, and nothing besides. The whole in its multiplicity is designated by the name "the will to power." What does the use of the singular here refer to? Nietzsche expresses by it that the will to power is the *sole quality* that can be detected, no matter what one examines. But we must refrain from substantializing quality in any way, however sublime. Quality does not exist as something self-subsisting, not as a subject or quasi-subject, also not as the one, whose "productions" then are the complex structures with relative duration, as Heidegger states.[39] The sole quality is rather always already given in such quantitative particularizations, otherwise it could not be *this* quality. For every will to power relies on the conflict with other power-wills in order to be able to *be* will to power. The quality, "will to power," is not a real unity; this unity exists neither in any way for itself, nor is it ever the "ground of being." There is a "real" unity only as organization and interplay of power-quanta.

When Nietzsche speaks of will to power as the only "quality," he often leaves out the article. This makes it especially clear that the power-will is not a principle or a metaphysical entity. This also is the case with two of Nietzsche's formulations that are often cited to push his philosophy into a metaphysical pattern into which it does not fit. In *Beyond Good and Evil,* in connection with his critique of Schopenhauer, he speaks of a "world, whose essence is will to power" (BGE 186); and in the *Nachlaß* (as cited above) he says that "the innermost essence of being" is "will to power." Now, whether Nietzsche writes "the will to power" or "will to power" he always means the sole quality, of course apart from the cases in which by the term "*the* will to power" he is emphasizing *one* power-will in its determinate constitution.

As for the second meaning of Nietzsche's "singular way of speaking," since the will to power is the sole property of the real, Nietzsche can use the singular also in regard to general determinations by which the multifarious is assembled into areas or that have some other comprehensible meaning. Let us cite, for example, the draft of a plan for the spring of 1888 that has the title: "*Will to Power: Morphology.*" In this note Nietzsche lists a series of topics:

> *Will to power* as "nature"
>   as life
>   as society
>   as will to truth
>   as religion
>   as art
>   as morality
>   as mankind.[40]

We cannot discuss here the individual items nor the sequence in which they are grouped together.[41] Starting from this note it should be clarified how (the) will to power must not be understood. It is not an underlying foundation of the world that produces life or externalizes itself as art or realizes itself as mankind. Rather the "formations" listed by Nietzsche are *in their essence* "will to power." To make this essence visible in the various "fields" is the task of a "morphology of the 'will to power,'" which is mentioned in another of Nietzsche's plans from the first half of the year 1888.[42] This is the case especially when the will to power remains hidden in certain modes of expression (not products!). We may cite a part of the outline from another plan of Nietzsche's from the same year with the title: "The Will to Power. Attempt at a Revaluation of all Values." It shows how the will to power must be understood, for example, as morality and religion:

> II. *The false values*
>   1. morality as false
>   2. religion as false
>   3. metaphysics as false
>   4. modern ideas as false
> III. *The criterion of truth*
>   1. the will to power.[43]

Morality and religion, in their traditional forms, which still shape the age, are *essentially* will to power, even if this essence appears in a reversal. The criterion for "false" and "true" can be found where the will to power is undisguised as will to power. It is revealed "in the enhancement of the feeling of power" (WP 534).[44]

But going a step further, the general formations and determinations are not only "false" insofar as they combine particular contents into a unity. They are already "false" because of their *generality*. This is true at least when "existence" is attributed to the universal. Even *the* will to power, thought of as the universal and highest principle, does not have existence. Actually it exists as the sole quality only in power-quanta, or else as a being only in irreducibly variegated actual being, or else again as essence only in the abundance of conflicting "existences."[45] "The 'highest concepts,' that is to say the most general, the emptiest concepts"— we read in *Twilight of the Idols*—"comprise the last fumes of evaporating reality" (TI 3:4). Such a universal is only fumes; reality consists in the ever determinate total play of actions and reactions that are guided within complex structures of power-centers (WP 567).

This is the point of departure, where one must begin. One of the "idiosyncrasies of the philosophers," however, is "to confuse the last and the first. They put what comes at the end (i.e., the highest and most general concepts)—unfortunately, for it should not come at all—at the beginning, as the beginning." Basing oneself on reason (insofar as it does not take into account the historical sense and think through what the senses attest), one stops at the "monstrosities and not-yet sciences,": that is, "metaphysics, theology, psychology, epistemology." Or in "formal science, semiology; such as logic and that applied logic, mathematics." Nietzsche says of those disciplines that operate in various determinations that are general in form or content: "Reality does not occur at all in them" (TI 3:4, cf. 3).

Nietzsche speaks of unreality and "falseness" even concerning those "general determinations" (in the present discussion we must stay with this unspecific term) that—as really dispensable—do not come at the end but have become indispensable for human existence: "Change, mutation, becoming in general were formerly taken as proof of appearance. . . . Today, on the contrary, we see ourselves as it were entangled in error, *necessitated* to error to precisely the extent that our prejudice in favor of reason compels us to posit unity, identity, duration, substance, cause, materiality, being; however sure we may be on the basis of strict reckoning, that error is to be found here" (TI 3:5). Here too the "false" is a transformation of the true nature of the will to power. This true nature can, however, be shown in everything transformed, indeed even as the condition for the possibility and necessity of such a transformation. This is made clear in another of Nietzsche's notes, which lists:

"End and means"
"cause and effect"
"subject and object"
"action and passion"
"thing-in-itself and appearance"
[All] as interpretations (not as facts) and to what extent perhaps *necessary* interpretations? (as required for "preservation")—all in the sense of a will to power. (WP 589)

If one regards something as purpose or as means to an end, one does not have a state of facts in mind, one undertakes an interpretation. Even when a will to power necessitates such an interpretation, what is interpreted does not thereby attain the dignity of being real.[46]

In the last-cited text Nietzsche speaks of a will to power. This takes us to the problematic third meaning that the singular has for him. A will to power is a particular will to power different from others. The cited note obviously refers to *man* as a will to power. Will to power here does not mean only the essence of reality as such, but a real entity in its reality. Often, especially in brief notes of the *Nachlaß*, it cannot be distinguished clearly whether Nietzsche means this entity or the essence of reality. Quite frequently in his remarks he shifts from one meaning to the other. I will cite an example of this from a text that deals, among other things, with the previously mentioned question of the way an "end" is given. Nietzsche writes "that all purposes, aims, meaning are only modes of expression and metamorphoses of a will that is inherent in all events: the will to power . . . [and] that the most universal and basic instinct in all doing and willing has for this reason remained the least known and most hidden, because *in praxi* we always follow its commandments, because we *are* this commandment" (WP 675).

The transition is easy to detect here. Until the last comma in the cited passage he is speaking of the universal essence of the will to power. When in closing he says that we ourselves are the will to power "as commandment," Nietzsche has in mind *existing "beings"* as the will to power. In this sense, of course, not only man, but every organized unity of power-quanta is a will to power. Thus Nietzsche noted: "—greater complexity, sharp differentiation, the contiguity of developed organs and functions, with the disappearance of the intermediate members—if that is perfection, then there is a will to power in the organic process by virtue of which *dominant shaping, commanding* forces continually extend the bounds of their power and continually simplify it within those bounds: the imperative *grows*" (WP 644).

If Nietzsche speaks thus of a will to power, then by the singular expression he presupposes the plural as given. This also applies, of course, to the statements in which he combines "will to power" with a possessive pronoun. Thus each nation, for example, is characterized by *its particular* will to power. Zarathustra says that a tablet of goods hangs over every people as the tablet of its overcomings; it is "the voice of their will to power" (Z I).[47] In a *Nachlaß* note, Nietzsche writes that a nation that still believes in itself honors "the conditions that place it on top" by projecting its feeling of power into its god. This god represents "the aggressive and power-hungry soul of a nation, its *will to power*."[48] We must not be led astray by the possessive pronoun: the nations do not "possess" their different power-wills in addition to something else that would still be peculiarly theirs. They are determinate wills to power—and nothing besides.

This applies to everything to which Nietzsche attributes reality. Every "specific entity" is what it is only as "its" will to power. In a discussion of contemporary natural science, Nietzsche states "that every specific body strives to become master over all space and to extend its force (—its will to power): and to thrust back all that resists its extension. But it continually encounters similar efforts on the part of other bodies and ends by coming to an arrangement ('union') with those of them that are sufficiently related to it:—*thus they conspire together for power.* And the process goes on . . ." (WP 636). A will to power in this sense is a particular organization of power-quanta in opposition to other wills to power. The particularization is intrinsically always a pushing back of resistances; it makes possible overpowering as well as submission, incorporation, and compromise relative to something else that is particularized. Separating and separate action and reaction relate to something else that separates itself; this is how everything happens.

Nietzsche writes that we cannot "imagine any change which does not have a will to power." And so that we will not think that he is speaking here of the "sole" will to power, we must read on: "We do not know how to explain a change except as the encroachment of one power upon another power" (WP 689). If one will to power establishes dominion over a lesser power, then the latter operates "as a function of the greater power" (WP 552).

To speak of one will to power submitting to another one is, of course, a simplification. That *a* will to power always is a hierarchically structured combination of many particular power-wills was described in especially vivid terms in Nietzsche's remarks on the human body.[49] "One cannot admire sufficiently," he writes, "how such a tremendous combination of living beings, each dependent and subordinate and yet in a certain sense in turn commanding and acting on its own will, can live as a whole, grow, and exist for a time."[50] Again we are referred from the "one" to the "many," which are internally organized and unstable units without a permanent core of being. "Even those smallest living creatures that constitute our body . . . are not considered by us to be soul-atoms, rather as something growing, struggling, multiplying, and dying off again: thus their number is constantly changing." To make completely clear the grounding reality of multiplicity for everything that "claims to mean" a unity, Nietzsche inserted parentheses in the quoted sentence. He speaks of "those smallest living creatures that constitute our body (more accurately: whose coordination is the best simile for what we call 'body')."[51]

What Nietzsche often calls a will to power is the actual conflict and cooperation of many wills to power likewise organized into unities. And each will, in its turn, is inserted into the conflict and cooperation of a more comprehensive power-will. Thus, for example, a human being is a power-quantum that organizes in itself countless power-quanta. Moreover, in contrast to and in union with other human beings, the individual human belongs to more comprehensive "organisms."

The question then arises as to the nature of the outermost organization, the furthest expanded will to power. As "the *last organisms,* whose formation we see," Nietzsche mentions: nations, states, societies.[52] In contrast with the general formations and determinations, which are merely modes of expression, interpretations, "effects," or "signs" (GM II:12) of the will to power, these are the *real domination-structures.* Since in them as existing organisms, the essence of the will to power is given in actual existence, these ultimate and highest organisms can "be used for instruction concerning the first organisms."[53] For a retro-translation of the false universal into the true particular is not necessary. The essence of particularization in the mode of organization as it is constitutive of all power-wills, can more easily be elaborated for macro-organisms than for the "smaller units."

Though for human forms of organization the three mentioned structures may be the "ultimate ones," the question remains whether *reality as a whole,* the world, is an organized reality. If the answer to this question were affirmative, then the possibility of the existence of *the* will to power as ground of reality would have to be reexamined.

We started with two of Nietzsche's assertions: the world is one and many; the world is will to power, and nothing besides. Then we speculated that the will to power, too, is one and many. The result of our reflections up to this point is: there exists only a multiplicity of wills to power. *The* will to power is an essential determination. Actual unity is ascribable to a will to power only as a cooperation *in opposition to other power-wills.* The following section will treat of Nietzsche's first statement: the world is one and many.

7. The Many Worlds and the One World

In this sentence "world" means that which is called the "universe of being" or "being as a whole." This is not the only meaning of world in Nietzsche's philosophy. He writes: "The whole of the organic world is the interweaving of beings surrounded by imagined little worlds as they project their force, their desires, their habits in experiences outside themselves as their *outside world.*"[54] The world accordingly is, first, a whole: the world of the organic. When in the same note we read "that there is no inorganic world," we can take "world" as world of the organic to mean the whole of reality. Second, the note speaks of the imagined little worlds of particular beings. It can readily be supposed that such fictions do not carry much weight. Only the aforementioned "concept of world" seems to be essential. But when we hear that the whole contained in it consists of the interweaving of beings with their "little worlds" we are again led from the comprehensive term to these particulars. And if we recall that Nietzsche calls the "smallest world" everywhere decisive, it is surely sensible to develop the question of Nietzsche's understanding of the world from this decisive point.

Talk of little and littlest worlds arises from the pluralism of Nietzsche's will to power. "Every center of force adopts a *perspective* toward the entire remainder" of the forces to which it relates, "i.e., its own particular *valuation,* mode of action and mode of resistance" (WP 567). In each case, such a perspectively evaluative action and reaction constitutes "a world." To the objection that in this way one always reached only apparent worlds, Nietzsche replies: "As if a world would still remain over after one deducted the perspective! By doing that one would deduct *relativity*!" Relativity, however, is an essential part of the conflicting, organizing wills to power. Thus, as a consequence of irremovable perspectivity "each being different from us" lives "in a different world from the one we live in" (WP 565). If only perspective worlds can be spoken of, then the problem of their alleged apparentness is solved. Nietzsche asks: "Isn't the world for us merely a combination of relations under one standard?" The next sentence contains the affirmative answer: "As soon as this arbitrary standard is missing, our world *dissolves*!"[55] If there is no "absolute standard," then "no shadow of *right* remains . . . to speak of appearance" (WP 567).

The development of the world-problematic seems to lead to the same outcome as the discussion of the will to power. We were led from the singular to the plural. If we take seriously Nietzsche's statements on perspectivity, it seems incomprehensible by what right he can speak of the world. Must we not draw the conclusion: what exists is not *the* world, but only worlds? But Nietzsche repeatedly uses the expression "the world" in the sense of reality as a whole. At the beginning of this section we cited an example in which he reflects on the relationship of the many little worlds to the world as a whole. We must therefore seek to clarify this relationship.

It must be kept in mind that we cannot bracket out our perspectivity in order to be left with only *the* world. "The world, apart from our condition of living in it . . . does not exist as world 'in itself'" (WP 568). Assuming that *the* world exists as the whole of reality, then we can turn what the cited sentence states into the positive. Our particular life-conditions and hence our perspectives would belong to this world, just as the perceptively determined actions and reactions of all individual beings belong to it.

When Nietzsche says that the "world" is "only a word for the total interplay of these actions" (WP 567), this means that he conceives the world as a "world of forces."[56] Every force develops its own world. But each such own world does not lead to a capsuling off from the worlds of other forces. For each force (i.e., each will to power) relates to the other forces in opposition or accommodation. The world "under some circumstances . . . has a *differing aspect* from every vantage point." But as the aggregate of all forces it is the "material" for all particular world-designs. The world does not result from the sums of the perspective worlds: for they are "in every case quite *incongruent*" (WP 568). Even the "interweaving" mentioned above does not produce a coherent unity of the particular worlds. But the world is indeed the sum of beings that fabricate worlds, the sum of the forces that actually exist.

According to Nietzsche, the sum of forces is limited. "The standard of all energy is *determinate,* not 'infinite.'"[57] He calls the world "a firm, iron magnitude of force that does not grow bigger or smaller, that does not expend itself but only transforms itself; a whole of unalterable size, a household without expenses or losses, but likewise without increase or income" (WP 1067). Nietzsche accepts more than a limit to the possible number of *power situations.* In so doing, he contradicts himself: infinite divisibility of forces, which excludes any thought of a quasi-substantiality of wills to power, leaves room for the thought of infinitely many power-combinations. But he must also assume a limit to the *power-dispositions,* if his doctrine of the eternal return of the same is to have cosmological validity. As grounds for the limitation he notes: "Endlessly new becoming is a contradiction; it would presuppose an endlessly *growing* force. But *from what* should it grow! *On what* would it feed, feed to excess!"[58] This argument is convincing with regard to the unchangeableness of the quantity of force: the assumption of an endlessly growing total force is absurd. But, contrary to Nietzsche's view, endlessly changing combinations of force are by no means excluded within a constant quantity of force if the force-quanta are infinitely divisible.

Our question about the world centers on the problem of the will to power. It is essential for it that Nietzsche adds, in this foundation-laying connection, that the idea that the universe is an organism contradicts the *essence of the organic*.[59] The world as a whole is no more a living being than it is an organization in any other sense. Now, we have seen that unity is unity only as organization. Nietzsche, therefore, cannot speak of the universe as *the unitary world*. Significantly in a later note he rejects the possibility that the world is the "universe" as a unity: "It seems important to me to get rid of the all, of unity." Even more significant is the reason he gives for this. Such a unity would require "some force or other, something unconditional. One could not avoid regarding it as the highest court of appeal and baptizing it 'God'" (GS 109). To constitute the unity of the all would require an original grounder to organize the *total multiplicity*. One would succumb to the metaphysical prejudice Nietzsche opposes. So he demands: "One must shatter the all; unlearn respect for the all; take what we have given to the unknown [and] the whole and give it back to what is nearest, what is ours" (WP 331).[60] Nietzsche thus expressly rejects the thought that *the* world could be rooted in *the* will to power as in an actually existing ground of being.

The world is not an all as a unity, if all unity is organization. For there is no grounding force organizing it into a whole. To speak of a world has, then, for Nietzsche, only the meaning that he assumes a limited quantity of force that is constantly in process of change. Limited quantities of force are also involved when Nietzsche speaks of the organic world, the inorganic world, and so on, in a particular realm. Such "worlds" do not exist by themselves; nor are they organized unities. They involve divisions, in the last analysis, for heuristic reasons.

"The world is *chaos*," as Nietzsche says:[61] a lawless aggregation and *Disgregation* of forces. Since the world is not an *organized* whole, there is also not the will to power as its metaphysical constitutive principle. There exist only multiplicities of wills to power; *the* will to power does not exist.

8. "The" Wills to Power in "the" World

The most important thing has already been said about what characterizes a will to power. The following paragraphs will describe being in its particularity as power-will in the world.

All beings are understood by Nietzsche as structures of domination, as hierarchically organized power-quanta. Man too is, as we have seen, such a composite. "What man wants, what every smallest part of a living organism wants, is an increase of power" (WP 702). Every "drive" in him is itself a will to power. Each one is "a kind of lust to rule; each one has its perspective that it would like to compel all other drives to accept as norm" (WP 481). Drives combine together in order to carry out their opposition to other drive-complexes. The conflicts of the drives lead to incessant shifts in the power-constellations: "Every drive also arouses a counterdrive."[62] As in every existing thing, in man too "all events, all motion, all becoming" must be interpreted "as a determination of degree and relations of force, as a *struggle*" (WP 552). In this sense, Nietzsche described the ego as a "plurality of person-like forces, of which now some, now others are in the foreground and look at the others as a subject does at an influential and determining outside world." Domination within the drive-complexes changes: "The subject point leaps around."[63] This must in no way be understood as a stable entity. It is inaccurate to posit behind the multiplicity of our affects "a unity: it suffices to grasp it as a regentship."[64]

What purportedly applies to man is for Nietzsche also true of every living thing: "In the organic 'realm of reality' there is nothing else but complex combinations of power-quanta, a multiplicity of conflicting beings,"[65] each of which in its particular perspectivity struggles in concert with other quanta or against them for domination within relative unities. Under this aspect even a protoplasm seems "like a *multiplicity of chemical forces*"[66] to which unity is ascribed only insofar as the multiplicity presents itself as a self-protective league. From man down to the protoplasm, the living thing, because of the multiplicity of perspectives operating in it, perceives what it encounters in multiple ways. What it encounters is under some circumstances only temporarily opposed to it. An organism can assimilate what was originally foreign to it, for incorporation is a basic way the will to power operates.

In any case, the power-will needs what resists it. "The will to power can manifest itself only *against resistances;* therefore it seeks that which resists it—this is the primeval tendency of the protoplasm when it extends pseudopodia and feels about. Appropriation and incorporation are above all a desire to overwhelm, a forming, a shaping and reshaping, until at length, that which has been overwhelmed has entirely gone over into the power domain of the aggressor and has increased the same.—If this incorporation is not successful, then the form probably falls to pieces; and the *duality* appears as a consequence of the will to power: in order not to let go what has been conquered, the will to power divides itself into two wills" (WP 656, cf. 702).[67] "The self-dividing protoplasm, ½ + ½ = not 1, but rather = 2," Nietzsche notes.[68]

If the world is the will to power and nothing besides, then the processes in the inorganic "realm of reality" must also be interpreted as power-struggles. Nietzsche repeatedly brings up this interpretation in connection with his critique of mechanistic thinking. We have already seen that he opposes mechanism with his "theory of a power-will operating in all events" in our discussion of Schlechta's "second test." We cannot here go into Nietzsche's critique to the required extent but must restrict ourselves to a few suggestions that clarify how he criticizes mechanism from the vantage point of his own theory.

"Mechanism" reduces the world "to the superficial" in order to make it "comprehensible." It is "really only an art of schematization and abbreviation, a mastering of multiplicity by an art of expression—not 'understanding,' but a designation for the purpose of *communication*."[69] Mechanistic thinking "imagines" the world "so as to be calculable." It invents "causal unities . . . 'things,' (atoms), whose effect remains constant." As our false subject-concept as a fixed I-unity is transferred to the "atom-concept" and the "thing-concept," so our pretended "subjectivity" hides behind the mechanistic concept of motion and the concept of "activity (separation of being into cause and effect)."

Mechanics has not only this psychological prejudice as its presupposition, but also the prejudice that the "language of our senses" foists upon us—especially in the concept of motion. The mechanistic interpretation of the world has "our *eye*, our *psychology* still in it" (WP 635).[70] What that concretely implies can be explained by the concept of "cause." A particularly revealing *Nachlaß* note of Nietzsche's, from which we can cite only a few passages, says:

> Psychologically considered, we derive the entire concept from the subjective conviction that we are causes, namely that the arm moves. . . . We separate ourselves, the doers, from the deed; and we make use of this pattern everywhere—we seek a doer for every event. . . . We search for things in order to explain why something has changed. Even the *atom* is this kind of superadded "thing" and "primitive subject." . . . At length we grasp that things—consequently, atoms too—effect nothing: because they *do not exist at all*—that the concept of causality is completely useless. . . . *There are neither causes nor effects.* Linguistically we do not know how to rid ourselves of them. But that does not matter. If I think of the *muscle* apart from its "effects" I negate it. (WP 551)

We must eliminate all "additions" of our erroneous subjective conviction to arrive at what is concealed in the mechanistic understanding of reality. We then find "dynamic quanta in a relation of tension to all other dynamic quanta: their essence consists in their relation to all other quanta, in their 'effect' upon the same" (WP 635). Even for the inorganic "realm of reality," the proposition holds true "that all driving force is will to power." There is no other force. Precisely the acting and reacting activity, the enhancement and diminution of forces, are not grasped as such "in our science"; that which needs to be considered remains hidden behind the cause-effect schema (WP 688).[71]

In order to show the consequences to which Nietzsche is driven in elaborating his doctrine of the will to power, two additional problems will be discussed here: *perception* in the "inorganic realm" and *necessity* in all events. We will start with the problem of necessity.

A. First a question: doesn't the universal applicability of "natural laws" indicate an original constancy in all events governed by their formulas? Nietzsche replies: "The unalterable sequence of certain phenomena demonstrates no 'law,' but a power relationship between two or more forces. To say 'but this relation itself remains constant' is to say no more than 'one and the same force cannot also be another force'" (WP 631). "I beware of speaking of chemical '*laws*.' . . . They are a question of the absolute establishment of power relationships: the stronger becomes master of the weaker, insofar as the latter cannot assert its degree of independence" (WP 630). This necessity expressed in laws is replaced by Nietzsche with the necessity with which the struggles of the power-quanta proceed. If it is true "that a certain force cannot be other than this certain force," that means that it can release itself upon a quantum of resistant force "only according to the measure of its strength." And this in turn means: "Event and necessary event is a *tautology*" (WP 639). Necessity, of which mechanistic theory also speaks, seems to remain in force, even though Nietzsche interprets it differently.

That this is not so becomes clear from Nietzsche's striving to contest the validity-claim of natural laws in two respects (without casting doubt on their applicability, indeed usefulness). First, he opposes the conviction that natural laws have timeless validity; secondly, he rejects the view that events are comprehended fundamentally in these laws.

Nietzsche writes: "We cannot assert an eternal validity of any 'law of nature'; we cannot assert of any chemical quality its eternal permanence; we are not *fine-tuned* enough to see the presumable *absolute flow of events:* anything *permanent* is there only by virtue of our crude organs which summarize and deposit on the surface that which absolutely does not exist *in that way.*"[72] Of chemical "qualities"[73] he says elsewhere that they flow and change,

> . . . though the time-span may be enormous for the current formula of a compound to be successfully refuted. Meanwhile the formulas are true: for they are crude; for what is 9 parts oxygen to 11 parts hydrogen! This 9 to 11 ratio is totally impossible to achieve precisely; there is always an error of implementation, consequently a certain range within which the experiment succeeds. But eternal change, the eternal flux of all things, also falls within that range; at no moment is oxygen exactly as before, but rather it is always something new: even though this novelty is too fine for all mea-

surements, indeed the entire development of all novelties as long as the human race
has existed is perhaps not yet great enough to refute the formula.[74]

The mechanistic interpretation of reality, led by the deceptive prejudices of language, the senses, and "psychology," does not take note of the fundamental changes
of the smallest and finest sort. It simplifies by fixating stable unities between which
it constructs compounds. Remaining on a coarse level, based on such compounds,
it establishes laws to which it ascribes inevitable necessity. But such necessity is
not truly inevitable; it is not necessity at all. Constant change is inherent in the
smallest and finest entities. Nothing remains what it is at any point in time. Its
changes sometimes exceed that "certain range" required for a law, a formula to be
applicable. Beyond the "false necessity" of mechanism, Nietzsche seeks "true necessity." It consists in the fact that every power-quantum at every moment can
draw only one particular consequence in its relation to other power-quanta.

B. Inorganic "beings," too, are will to power. A power-will seeks, for example,
to overpower another power-will. Overpowering requires an ever-specific way of
"knowing" what is to be overpowered. No will to power is a "blind will." Therefore Nietzsche is forced to concede a "knowledge,"[75] a *perception also for the
inorg[anic] world.*" We find scanty allusions to this in some *Nachlaß*-notes. He
tries to characterize such perception as distinguished from perception in the organic world. He goes so far as to say that "in the chemical world, the sharpest
perception of differences of force" prevails. Compared to that, even a protoplasm,
as a multiplicity of chemical forces, has "an uncertain and indefinite total perception of a foreign object." Uncertainty and indefiniteness stem from the fact
that many forces are "beings in conflict with one another" and their conflicts are
still carried out even when the protoplasm "feels itself opposite the outside world."
The sharpness of perception that supposedly characterizes chemical forces as such
lies in their certainty and definiteness. These can be given only in "fixed perceptions," which Nietzsche actually ascribes to the inorganic. Insofar as fixedness in
the sense of constancy is the criterion of the traditional truth-concept, he can
say of perception within the inorganic world: "there truth prevails!"[76]

I believe that in these and other notes one can sense Nietzsche's scarcely hidden longing for that "truth" whose destruction is one of the main objectives of
his philosophy. This longing also resonates when he notes that the "inorganic
world" behind organic life is "the highest and most worthy of reverence." No
"error, perspective limitation" exists there. Everything organic represents "a specialization." In all specialization the loss "consists manifestly in the loss of sharpness and fixedness of perceptions." The lack of these qualities then reflects the
"perspective limitedness" Nietzsche speaks of.[77] "All feeling and imagining and

thought" must "originally have been one," he says in another note. "This *unity* must be present in the inorganic: for the organic already *begins* with separation."[78] "Everything organic differs from the inorganic insofar as it . . . never is identical with itself, in its processes."[79] The inorganic, then, is what is self-identical. Here Nietzsche himself projects identity into "what is most worthy of reverence," whereas everywhere else he unmasks it as mere projection.

We must not place all too much weight on this inconsistency of Nietzsche's, which is found only in scanty allusions. Nietzsche's broadly developed basic thought is that there is no unity in the sense of constancy. Unity always is unity as an organization of conflicting and cooperating power-quanta. Thus the given "relations first constitute beings" (WP 625). But this must always be kept in mind: "That a thing is indissoluble into a sum of relations is no proof *against* its reality."[80] This, of course, also applies to the "smallest" inorganic unities.

Let us return to Nietzsche's statement about the inorganic world: that "truth" prevails there! In the same note he states that "appearance" begins with the organic world. Now we can draw on Nietzsche's critique of the traditional pair of contraries: truth versus appearance. For the present context we will merely indicate its result. Nietzsche, by always starting from perspectival overpowering, transforms every "truth" into "appearance" and every "appearance" into "truth." In the end the antithesis dissolves. All knowledge, all perception proves to be "adjustment" of something in the service of some dominant will to power.

The adjustments have the form of fixations of something that in reality is constantly changing. These adjustment fixations involve resistant forces both in the perspectives of the inorganic (to which at most a relative "fixedness" can be granted)[81] and in the perceptions "by many eyes" that Nietzsche discovers in the organic world. All being fixates, and it does so with necessity. Fixation is a basic trait of the will to power. But the doer and the object of fixation are continually changing. If a fixating power-quantum wants to remain dominant it must continually re-fixate the changing dominated force in ever new ways (for it too is continually changing and thus its perspective too changes). The perception of all wills to power can be formally described as the interrelation of events that cannot be grasped as events but mutually fixate themselves, only to let every fixation go again and again—paying tribute to the events.

Starting with Nietzsche's statements on perception in the inorganic world, we have described fixation as a property of *all* wills to power. Looking back at the "realms of reality" that we have examined according to Nietzsche's statements, it can be said that everywhere we find the same basic situation: processes of aggregation and disgregation of wills to power. The question remains whether in view of this state of affairs one can correctly speak of "realms." What meaning does

Nietzsche's distinction between the organic and the inorganic world have? We must definitely not assume a qualitative difference between such realms. Protoplasm, as a synthesis of chemical forces, is not something essentially different from the chemical forces themselves.

That Nietzsche draws no boundaries between these "worlds" is shown when, in the described problematic manner, he speaks of the particularity of "inorganic perception." He also speaks of the "transition from the world of the inorganic to that of the organic."[82] If he once speaks of the organic as a specialization of the inorganic and another time states that there is no inorganic world (as was mentioned above), the contradiction here is only apparent. In the first case he is thinking "genealogically."[83] In the second case he is opposing mechanistic thought: what rules in the inorganic world is not pressure and stress; in it, too, there is a conflict of "organisms," in the same sense as nation, state, society are also organisms. We must, then, distinguish in Nietzsche a narrow and a broad sense of organism. It hardly need be mentioned after the above remarks that we must not assume that the "organic world" as a "realm of reality" is encompassed by the organic world of reality as a whole. The world is not an organic world, but a world of "organisms": the chaos of constantly changing power-organizations.

9. Will to Power as Interpretation

We have surveyed Nietzsche's interpretation of reality. There are many such interpretations. Does Nietzsche's philosophy merely increase their number, as we asked at the beginning of this treatise? Or does it have any advantage over the others? Here we are not concerned with any advantage of Nietzsche's thinking over any others. What interests us is Nietzsche's self-understanding. He himself claims superiority over other world-interpretations. Examining his thinking in terms of this claim, we come upon the problem of the justifiability of his "doctrine of the will to power."

We will start with Aphorism 22 in *Beyond Good and Evil.* There Nietzsche points out the inadequacy of the mechanistic world-interpretation. We are familiar with his arguments and we have discussed or at least mentioned them based on other aphorisms and fragments in which they are more extensively described. It is essential for the current topic that he accuses "the physicists" of "bad philology." "Nature's conformity to law" is "not a matter of fact," not a "text," but "interpretation." He opposes their interpretation with his own:

> Somebody might come along who, with opposite intentions and modes of interpretation, could read out of the same nature, and with regard to the same phenomena, rather the tyrannically inconsiderate and relentless enforcement of claims of power—

an interpreter who would picture the unexceptional and unconditional aspects of all "will to power" so vividly that almost every word, even the word "tyranny" would eventually seem unsuitable, or a weakening and attenuating metaphor—being too human—but he might, nonetheless, end by asserting the same about this world as you do, namely, that it has a "necessary" and "calculable" course, *not* because laws obtain in it, but because they are absolutely *lacking,* and every power draws its ultimate consequences at every moment.

Nietzsche then adds to this statement the following remark: "Supposing that this also is only interpretation and you will be eager enough to make this objection—well, so much the better."

The physicists' possible objection is not only tolerated, it is openly welcomed. Like the mechanistic theory, the will-to-power theory, too, is "only" interpretation. Do we not, then, have one interpretation opposite another? Should not the same truth-claim, then, be accorded to both? Yet Nietzsche writes that if the physicists raised that objection, "so much the better." In what sense "better"; and better *for whom?*

The objection plays right into the hands of Nietzsche's interpretation. In "*also . . . only*" it contains the admission that the thesis of nature's conformity to law is interpretation. If that is admitted, however, one is on the plane where *interpreting as such* must be inquired into. Whoever says that one thing or another is interpretation must allow room for the question as to what interpretation is. Interpretation turns out itself to need interpretation.

Nietzsche claims to have interpreted interpretation appropriately. Jaspers finds in Nietzsche "the theory of all world reality as one of merely being interpreted, of world-knowledge as always an *interpretation,*" which theory was acquired "from a transformation of Kantian critical philosophy."[84] "The unending movement of interpreting seems to come to a kind of perfection in the *self-comprehension* of this interpreting: in the *interpretation of interpretations.*"[85] Nietzsche's interpretation knows that "all knowledge is interpreting"; it takes "this knowledge into its own interpretation by the thought that the will to power itself is the infinitely varied driving force of interpretation at work everywhere." "Nietzsche's interpretation is in fact an interpretation of interpretations and hence for him miles apart from all earlier, comparatively naive interpretations that did not have the self-consciousness of their interpreting."[86]

Despite all of the problems with Jaspers's Nietzsche-interpretation, in whose context these statements belong,[87] this is seen correctly: for Nietzsche all knowledge is interpretation; all knowledge of this knowledge is interpretation of interpretation. After our remarks above we can also say: the interpretations in their multifariousness are interpretations of power-wills; *that they are this* is likewise interpretation. What this says more precisely and what consequences follow from this will be explained in the following pages.

First, we must contemplate the breadth of Nietzsche's concept of interpretation. All wills to power interpret. Thus, for example, even the perspective perceptions of the inorganic are interpretations. And not only all perceptions, all cognitions and all "knowledge" are interpretations, but also all actions and developments, indeed all events.[88] For example, "when an organ is formed" *that* is "*an interpretation.*" "The will to power *interprets.*" That means in every case: "It defines limits, determines degrees, variations of power. Mere variations of power could not feel themselves to be such: there must be present something that wants to grow, and interprets the value of whatever else wants to grow. . . . In fact, *interpretation is itself a means of becoming master of something.*" Nietzsche adds: "The organic process presupposes continual interpretation" (WP 643).

The mode of expression chosen here by Nietzsche is open to a misunderstanding. One could think that will to power (whether understood as *a* will to power or as *the* will to power misinterpreted as *ens metaphysicum*) is a subject of which the interpreting could be predicated, and which in its turn would constitute the prior precondition for processes. We must not succumb to the seduction of grammar and separate what belongs inseparably together. Thus a different note states: "one must not ask: '*who* then interprets?'" The question is out of place "because interpreting itself . . . has existence" (WP 556); it is "fiction" "to posit an interpreter behind the interpretation" (WP 481). The interpreting does not have "existence . . . as a 'being'" in the sense of constancy, but "as a *process, a becoming*" (WP 556). If at the end of the previous section we characterized the perception of power-wills as a relation of mutually determining events to one another, it can be said under the aspect we are looking at now that power-wills face one another as constantly changing interpretations. All this makes it clear that Nietzsche can affirm against positivism: "There are no facts, only interpretations" (WP 481).

Still moving within Nietzsche's familiar trains of thought we can now count on it that every interpretation is *perspectival.* Nietzsche, who liked to use the philological relation of text and interpretation to explain fundamental relations of reality,[89] writes that the same text allows for countless interpretations.[90] When we think of the infinite divisibility of the perspective power-quanta, we cannot be surprised to read in *The Gay Science:* "The world has become 'infinite' for us all over again, inasmuch as we cannot reject the possibility that it may include infinite interpretations" (GS 374).

The perspectivity of every interpretation now becomes a problem that finally strikes back at Nietzsche's own philosophical project, if we reflect that among the countless interpretations of a text there is "no 'right' interpretation."[91] We have no right to assume an "absolute cognition": "The perspective, illusory character is part of existence."[92] Then every world-interpretation, too, is only perspective, illusory interpretation, the mechanistic one no less than one that understands world events as the chaos of cooperating and conflicting wills to power. The world understood as a sum of forces would accordingly be *one* perspective world-interpretation among countless others. In view of the fundamental relativity of all world interpretation what could be said in favor of the "truth" of Nietzsche's interpretation?

Nietzsche himself has given us a criterion for what he understands by truth. It is based on power-enhancement. The "unending interpretability of the world" is subject to this criterion. "Every interpretation" thus supposedly turns out to be "a symptom of growth or decline" (WP 600). If an interpretation serves power-enhancement, then it is, in this sense, truer than those that merely preserve life, make it bearable, refine it, or else separate the sick and cause them to die off.[93] Let us first measure by this criterion mechanistic philosophy, which Nietzsche repeatedly grasps as the essential contemporary counterpart to his own philosophy.[94]

We have let Nietzsche show us[95] in what sense the mechanistic way of thinking is only a "foreground-philosophy. More importantly still, it is *false*. It schematizes, abbreviates, selects "designations" for the sake of general understandability. It invents constant unities, constant effects, laws. It imagines the world for the purpose of calculability. The "common sign language . . . for the purpose of easier calculability" facilitates the *domination of nature*.[96]

Here we are taken aback. If the mechanistic perspective makes such domination real, so that moreover it constantly grows, then it may be "false" since it cannot see events in their "real course." But is it not, according to Nietzsche's criterion of truth, "more true" than all earlier world interpretations, since it has enhanced and continues to enhance man's power as none before ever did? Hence we can understand that Nietzsche occasionally speaks with approval of this world-interpretation. He considers it "not as the most proven world view, but as the one that requires the greatest stringency and discipline and most casts aside all sentimentality." Nietzsche even accords it a selective function with words that remind us of the "effect" that his doctrine of eternal return is supposed to evoke.[97] The mechanistic idea is "at the same time a test for physical and psychic well-being: misbegotten, weak-willed races perish from it."[98]

Although the mechanistic world-interpretation may be "one of the *most stupid*," indeed though it may even be heralded as "the principle of the greatest possible stupidity" (GS 373; WP 618), that is no argument against its power-enhancing "truth." Although it may be a matter of a surface-perspective, it remains "marvelous that for our needs (machines, bridges, etc.) the assumptions of mechanics suffice." And though it may be a matter of "very great needs" and "the 'little errors' may not come into consideration,"[99] with this interpretation we rule over nature, so that it is irrelevant whether the interpretation is stupid, crude, and defective.

Yet it does not appear certain that the insight that the world exists only in an infinity of perspective interpretations of wills to power serves to enhance the power-willing—quite apart from a question to be discussed below as to how such an insight on all-pervasive perspectivism can be possible. If the mechanistic interpretation is *false* in the sense of the discovery of what really happens and *true* in the sense of Nietzsche's own understanding of truth, then it could be that the interpretation of the world as a multiplicity of wills to power is "true" in the sense that had to be denied to the mechanistic world-view, but still *wrong* in the sense of the truth-criterion of power-enhancement. Is it not likely that the insight into the relativity of our interpretations cripples our striving for power, while *ignorance* of relativity lets our desire for power develop unconstrainedly and hence successfully?

Nietzsche himself quite often refers to the necessity of ignorance or even self-delusion for the preservation and power-enhancement of that organization that man is. Our "subject-unity," in which we must think there are "regents at the head of a community," requires "the relative *ignorance* in which the regent is kept concerning individual activities and even disturbances within the community" as "conditions under which rule can be exercised." We should acquire a high esteem "also for not-knowing, for seeing things on a broad scale, simplification and falsification, perspectivity." It is so especially for our mind "that it could be useful and important for its activity to interpret itself *falsely*" (WP 492). The "psychology of the future" must be aware that "the great egoism of our dominant will" requires of us "that we shut our eyes to ourselves" (WP 426).

It must now be shown how Nietzsche in the end manages to reverse the valuation of mechanistic theory and the theory of power-wills, measured by the standard of his understanding of truth. For in mechanism the laws of nature are the real masters; and we are supposed to understand ourselves as their subjects. That something always happens thus and thus is here interpreted as if a creature always acted thus and thus as a result of obedience to a law or a law-giver, while it would be free to act otherwise were it not for the "law." "But precisely this thus-and-not-otherwise might be inherent in the creature, which might behave thus and thus *not* in response to a law but because it is constituted thus and thus" (WP 632). "It is mythology to think that forces here obey a law, so that, as a consequence of their obedience, we have the same phenomenon each time" (WP 629).

Nietzsche, who, as is known, smells "slave-morality" behind all spiritual appearances of Western history—and not only this one—finds it at last also behind the mechanistic interpretation of the world: "I beware of speaking of chemical '*laws*': that savors of morality. In truth everywhere the stronger becomes master of the weaker," since there is no "respect for 'laws'" (WP 630). But whoever sees himself as necessarily obedient to laws suffers losses of this respect itself.

Nietzsche, on the contrary, wants to give "a new interpretation . . . to future philosophers as masters of the earth."[100] Now, precisely radical perspectivism seemed to lead one who wills into embarrassment. His own interpretation is relative; thus he seems, as the one who knows this, to be able to think only refractedly and to act with weakened conviction. But that is the case, as Nietzsche tries to show, only if one does not think perspectivity through and accept it down to its last consequence. All interpretations are perspective; there is no absolute standard by which one could check which is "more right" and which "less right"; the only criterion for the truth of an interpretation of reality consists in whether and to what extent it can impose itself against other interpretations. Every interpretation has as much right as it has power.

The insight into the perspectivity of all interpretations, to which Nietzsche's "doctrine of the will to power" leads, can consequently procure for the powerful the "good conscience" to unconditionally implement their "ideals." Only the "ideals" of other power-wills, belonging to other perspectives, stand opposed to their willing. No values are pre-given that are binding on them. For such a binding would presuppose a fixed world-transcendent or world-immanent authority. What has authority, however, is always only the dominant power-will. Thus the strong must finally also break with the belief that they are subject to natural laws by subjecting them to the truth-criterion of power-enhancement. Let us regard this from the perspective of one of Nietzsche's fundamental thoughts: "The moral God" (WP 55) has been "overcome." But his "shadow" is still visible. It still has to be "vanquished" (GS 108). Even the mechanistic world-interpretation still stands under this "shadow." The "moral connotation" that still clings to its natural laws betrays it.

The interpretation of future powerful men, which posits new values, can also only be perspective. A factor in this is that it delimits and selects. For the sake of its own coherence there is much that it does not become cognizant of. Ignorance takes on constitutive significance for interpreting, it must even become *willful* ignorance. *Forgetting* too is essential for the powerful man's interpretation—as for every interpretation. *Knowledge of perspectivity itself,* however, should not be "forgotten." For this knowledge frees one for unrestricted overpowering.

If the future philosophers are to become lords of the world, their interpretation must, on the other hand, have the necessary "breadth of content." It must interpret reality in its totality as well as in its particulars in order not to lag be-hind the already existing global interpretations and thus be defeated. It must unmask the other world views as interpretations that can only misunderstand themselves because they do not understand themselves at all as interpretations or at least do not see through the essence of interpreting. This does not prevent them from using another interpretation as an instrument insofar as it serves to enhance power, as is the case with mechanism with regard to domination of nature. It thus does not grasp this world view as true in the sense of its own claim to validity.

If Nietzsche's philosophy of the will to power claims to speak the truth about reality, still it does not end up in contradiction to the truth-criterion stemming from this philosophy itself. In its own terms it is the only coherent world view. We are caught in a circle. Such circularity is inherent in all understanding. Nietz-sche knows this very well; his thinking is guided by this knowledge: "Ultimately, man finds in things nothing but what he himself has imported into them: the finding is called science, the importing—art, religion, love, pride. Even if this is a piece of childishness, one should carry on with both and be well-disposed to-ward both—some should find, others—we others!—should import!" (WP 606).

This, of course, does not mean that some only find what others have only imported. Importing and finding again belong together in the specific unity of interpretation. Nietzsche, however, accentuates the importing as decisive. What he calls for is an importing that creates new values. Rediscovery, then, is not only a renewed awareness of the importing but also the finding of what has been in-serted into everything interpreted, the expansion of the imported to the under-standing of all reality. Doesn't Nietzsche's philosophy, which wants to encourage future philosophers to create new valuations, itself merely deploy in perspective interpretation what it originally "imported"? Doesn't his own particular perspec-tive speak in everything he writes? Doesn't the relativity he asserts of all interpre-tations recoil back upon his own interpretation?

In the following paragraphs we will try to cast light on the circularity of Nietz-sche's thinking. As with all understanding, it is a matter of "entering the circle in the right way," to use a phrase of Heidegger's.[101] We have shown that Nietzsche can ground his philosophy's claim to be the true world-interpretation upon the truth-criterion that stems from this philosophy itself. According to this criterion, an interpretation must impose itself against the other world views. For only thus can its strength and power be displayed. If we inquire further into what the strength and power of an interpretation mean, we are drawn deeper into the circle. They cannot simply be read off by "success," for instance, in prior history. For Nietzsche the millennia in which domination by the morally determined world-conception has lasted are not an expression of its strength but a sign of weakness. The desire for power is here precisely not released as the *true* will to power.

Nietzsche's own interpretation of strength in the sense of relentless ability to overpower must be made the basis if we want to trace his philosophy's claim to be true because it is stronger than all other world-interpretations. And again the circle closes when Nietzsche accepts a "pre-moral period of mankind" that encompasses prehistoric time, and is followed by the moral period. Here we find an interpretation of human "history" that is intended to ground the necessity of future strength in a post-moral age upon a return to what supposedly existed in the beginning. This strength would then be *true* strength.

Jaspers writes that Nietzsche "thinks in a circle that seems to be abolished but breaks forth again."[102] The circle cannot be abolished. If we look on it as only a formal structure, then the particularity and radicalness of Nietzsche's interpretation remain hidden. If we move into it, they can be made visible. It must be shown that Nietzsche not only understands all world-interpretation essentially as constituted by the will to power, but that he also reflects on the consequences resulting from the self-understanding of his philosophy as interpretation. His philosophy of the will to power cannot have a merely contemplative nature. It is itself the expression of the will to power. It wants future value-creators to understand themselves as *wills to power.* "You yourselves are this will to power—and nothing besides!" he calls out to men. That is a rallying cry. It means: "Understand at last what you really are! God is dead, now go on and fight his shadow! The tablets of values that you have till now hanged over yourselves have no validity! No longer allow yourself to be determined by these values, determine the values yourself! Reevaluate the old values; create new values out of your self-understanding as will to power!"

Nietzsche too is concerned not merely with "reinterpreting" the world, but rather with changing it. He has indeed understood that all change is interpretation and all interpretation is change. Even the moral period of mankind is characterized by a succession of ever new world-interpretations. But the fundamental change has not yet occurred. One must not merely reflect on its necessity, one must call for it. Nietzsche's understanding of reality as the will to power makes him a *herald.* In *Thus Spoke Zarathustra* his philosophy does not decline to mere "literature." Zarathustra is the mouthpiece of his proclamation. Since his call echoes away unheard, Nietzsche sees himself cast back upon his task of showing the invalidity of the still dominant moral world-interpretations. Since this too goes relatively unheard, the arguments he makes in his last creative years become ever cruder, his self-portrayal ever more exaggerated, the tones he strikes up ever shriller. By all this he calls out: "Listen to me at last!"

We must, however, not regard Nietzsche's philosophy only under the aspect of proclamation and challenge, important as this is for understanding his works, especially from *Zarathustra* on. In developing his interpretation he see himself compelled to investigate the thought-presuppositions implicit in it. Only in reflecting on them can his philosophy fulfill its claim to present a *grounding* interpretation of reality as a whole. Let us begin with the question: To what extent can Nietzsche claim that his interpretation of interpretative reality accurately capture its interpretative character?

Once again the focus is on the perspective nature of all interpreting. In Book V of *The Gay Science,* Nietzsche expresses himself on this:

> How far the perspective character of existence extends, or indeed whether existence has any other character than this; . . . whether, on the other hand, all existence is not essentially actively engaged in *interpretation*—that cannot be decided even by the most industrious and most scrupulously conscientious analysis and self-examination of the intellect; for in the course of this analysis the human intellect cannot avoid seeing itself in its own perspectives, and *only* in these. We cannot look around our own corner: it is a hopeless curiosity that wants to know what other kinds of intellects and perspectives there *might* be; for example, whether some beings might be able to experience time backward, or alternatively forward and backward (which would involve another direction of life and another concept of cause and effect). (GS 374)

Nietzsche's line of argument is quite convincing. "We" are beings who interpret from a perspective; of course, our intellect cannot fathom whether all other beings also interpret. The assumption of other perspective beings says nothing about the particular character of their perspectives. We can perceive only under our own perspective; even if we want to perceive our perceiving, we remain under our perspective. The cited text speaks of the intellect's self-examination. Nietzsche has frequently stressed its impossibility.[103] But why should it be true of the intellect that it cannot see around the corner? For all interpreting, even when not restricted to the intellect, is perspective. But then the critical reservations that Nietzsche here cites for our knowledge of "other existences" are justified. This, in turn, surely means that, in the light of the critical self-reflection of interpreting, Nietzsche's statements on the conflict of perspectively interpreting wills to power as *mundane reality as such* prove to be a mere construct.

Had Nietzsche not yet performed this self-reflection, had he forgotten it again after performing it, when he speaks of perspective perception in the organic and inorganic "realms"? This can surely not seriously be considered. Is Jaspers right when he states that Nietzsche "did everything in his power . . . to open up and keep what is possible," but closed it again "in the end by absolutizing" the will to power; so that the "metaphysics of the will to power," elaborated "in absolutely all appearances," is "of a kind with earlier dogmatic metaphysics"?[104] Jaspers misunderstands Nietzsche when he ascribes such dogmatism to him. His argument is also intrinsically unsatisfactory. What could have caused Nietzsche "in the end" to close up again, since opening and keeping open was his objective?

An answer presents itself from the presuppositions elaborated in the present inquiry. If Nietzsche's philosophy too is a quest for power that seeks to enable the future strong men to assume power, then all particular interpretations as well as the interpretation of reality as a whole must be put in the service of this task. If men are shown that everywhere in the world there are power-struggles of will-quanta in which the stronger ones take the upper hand, and nothing besides, then in view of the absolute universality of the "law" that every power at every moment draws its consequence, the strong men must lose all their "inhibitions" stemming from their being rooted in a tradition, and exercise their power relentlessly in positing new values. The interpretation of the world as "will to power" would, then, under the self-critical examination of this interpretation, be only a *fiction*. Yet in terms of Nietzsche's own truth-criterion it would still be *truth*.

However, it can immediately be argued against this understanding of Nietzsche's world-interpretation that Nietzsche, in the doctrine of the will to power, would be asking too little of the strong men, of whom he asks the utmost with the doctrine of eternal return. Why should they not be required to see through the fiction *as fiction*? This would be all the more understandable since Nietzsche himself has called attention to the perspective "limitation" of all interpreting. If the future powerful men—precisely for the sake of power, as the strongest—are supposed at the same time to be the wisest,[105] then the fictional character of the interpretation of the whole reality must not remain hidden from them. For with regard to the dogmatism of their interpretation of overall reality, a dogmatism that follows from their own presuppositions, they would have to "feel" less wise, and hence weaker.

We can escape this dilemma by moving further into the circle and examining Nietzsche's interpretation of what possibilities of interpretation it concedes to man and by what it determines them. This question has, it will be shown, only apparently been answered when we cited Aphorism 374 of *The Gay Science*. The remark immediately after the quoted passages takes seriously the possibility that the world contains infinite interpretations. Indeed the title of the aphorism reads: "Our new 'infinite.'" We can gather from this what weight, despite all critical objections, the idea has for Nietzsche that there may also be non-human existence that interprets. But the critical objections are not thereby completely eliminated. We are taken a step further by a *Nachlaß*-note from the year 1886 or 1887.[106] Nietzsche there opposes the "modesty of philosophical skepticism or . . . religious resignation," which say that the essence of things is unknown or only partly unknown. It is truly immodesty insofar as it claims knowledge that the distinction between an "essence of things" and an "apparent world" is right.

> To be able to draw such a distinction, one would have to think of our intellect with a contradictory character: on the one hand, equipped for perspective seeing, as is needed so that precisely beings of this kind can preserve themselves in existence; on the other, with a faculty of comprehending just this perspective seeing as perspective, the appearance as appearance. That is to say, equipped with a belief in "reality" as if it were the only thing and yet also with insight into this belief, namely that it is only a perspective limitation as regards true reality. A belief looked at with this insight, however, is no longer belief; it is dissolved as belief. In short, we must not think our intellect so contradictorily that it is a belief and simultaneously a knowledge of this belief as belief.

At the end of this meditation Nietzsche calls for the abolition of the concepts "thing in itself" and "appearance." Their opposition is just as "untenable" as the "older one of 'matter and spirit.'"

The untenable opposition "thing in itself/appearance" stems from a way of thinking that inserts a contradiction into our intellect. The contradiction makes clear the untenableness of the construing of that opposition. Yet Nietzsche "for once" does not use "contradiction as the ultimate truth-criterion for his assertions," as Jaspers remarks in his interpretation of the cited note.[107] The "principle of contradiction" is for Nietzsche a crude and falsifying adjustment that obfuscates the real antithetical character of existence. But he must consider contractions that lead to the abolition of *his own truth-criterion* to be unacceptable. Actual exercise of power cannot be both possible and impossible.[108]

Our intellect, too, stands in the service of exercising power; it is, as we have seen, an organ that the many power-wills that we are have made for themselves. If, as the instrument of these power-wills, it is to constitute the "belief in reality," then as such an instrument it cannot at the same time be destined to negate this belief by understanding it as perspective fiction. This means that even here in the case under discussion not the avoidance of contradiction in the formal-logic sense is the criterion of truth—as little as Nietzsche's statement that an instrument could not judge its own validity as an instrument can be regarded as a "logical argument"—but rather the actual impossibility for the same organ of power-willing to be assigned mutually abolishing functions.

The question how it could happen that the intellect learned to misunderstand itself as described here could be answered by Nietzsche only in the broad context of a genealogy of human self-understanding. We cannot go into such a portrayal here. The problem that Nietzsche, with regard to the intellect as a determinate organ, can master in terms of his presuppositions comes at us again, however, with regard to *interpreting*. Certainly, we can say after the remarks above that the self-understanding of an interpretation as interpretation does not have to be directed against the power-willing, but rather precisely can and should set it free. Interpreting as a whole is not restricted to particular functions as is the intellect. Yet some questions cannot be rejected: How is it possible that perspective interpreting can understand itself as such interpreting? What right can Nietzsche validly claim for his contention that *his* interpretation is more than a merely human perspective, more than even just the particular perspective of the philosopher Nietzsche?

To answer this question in terms of Nietzsche's own interpretation, we must start with the point that for him man is "not only a single individual but one particular line of the total living organic world" (WP 678). This presupposition makes it completely clear why the "analysis and self-examination of the intellect" is capable of discerning neither anything about the rightness of our knowledge nor anything sufficient about the intellect itself: in it not even man, but only one of his "tools" is torn from the flux of becoming, taken by itself, isolated and examined by itself for its validity. Nietzsche accordingly wants to "translate man back into nature," to remain "deaf to the siren songs of old metaphysical bird catchers who have been piping at him all too long, 'you are more, you are higher, you are of a different origin!'" (BGE 230).

Man's origin lies in nature, and he is not "more" in any qualitative sense, but surely in a quantitative one. The total organic world lives on in him. And insofar as every organic thing is a synthesis of inorganic forces, the inorganic also "lives" in him.[109] What is oldest, "firmly embodied" in him, is locked in conflict with newer elements. Man contains multiplicity in himself and he interprets it. And he could not have taken it into himself, he could not be the interpreter that he is, if what he has taken up were not itself of an interpretative kind. From this presupposition Nietzsche can go one step further: that man endures "proves that a species of interpretation (even though accretions are still being added) has also endured, that the system of interpretation has not changed" (WP 678).[110]

This is the key to answering the two questions we asked. Nietzsche can interpret the multifarious reality, natural being, as multifarious interpreting, because man himself is an interpreting being and can be this only because what flows together in him as inorganic and organic being itself already interprets. As a synthesis and multiplicity of interpretations, man can become aware of his perspective interpreting, insofar as "the center of gravity shifts" and the perspectivity alters from each new point. He has knowledge of this shifting because he, like everything organic, gathers experiences, and is equipped with memory.[111] The possibility of interpreting interpretation thus stems from the changing of interpretations. Neither is a special faculty needed for this, nor is the perspectivity of interpreting abandoned.

Nietzsche once summed up his thinking as follows:

> That the *value of the world* lies in our interpretation (—that other interpretations than merely human ones are perhaps somewhere possible—); that previous interpretations have been perspective valuations by virtue of which we can survive in life, i.e., in the will to power, for the growth of power; that every *elevation of man* brings with it the overcoming of narrower interpretations; that every strengthening and increase of power opens up new perspectives and means believing in new horizons—this idea permeates my writings. (WP 616)

We will limit ourselves to bringing out two points, drawing upon this self-description. A. Increase of power means the gaining of new perspectives (because further power-quanta have been incorporated) and hence broadening of the interpretations. This in turn characterizes the elevation of man. Vice versa, it holds true that "the plurality of interpretations is a sign of strength" (WP 600). The converse is true, of course, only when the many interpretations can be organized into a unity and do not result in disgregations, as Nietzsche especially stresses for the "modern" age.

B. Nietzsche's interpretation of the interpretations does not understand itself as absolute philosophy. Although his thought is filled with the conviction that everything is interpretation, this does not exclude there being other interpretations that have not entered into human reality. For man is "only" the total living organic world in "one particular line." Thus the possibility is kept open that future men, "over-men," by assimilating interpretations inaccessible to us present-day men, could yet expand their understanding of reality compared with those now living. "Among a higher kind of creatures, knowledge, too, will acquire new forms that are not yet needed" (WP 615). Nietzsche's interpretation includes the possibility, indeed the necessity of its own expression and hence modification as one of its essential aspects.

After we have moved in many ways in the circle of Nietzsche's interpretation, let us in conclusion once again deal with the question of the *who* of his interpretation. We have seen that this question is impermissible insofar as there is not first something that then interprets. The interpreting itself exists. To understand Nietzsche's perspectivism as subjectivism is therefore wrong. "'Everything is subjective,' you say; but even this is *interpretation*," Nietzsche writes, rejecting such talk (WP 481). In a longer note from the year 1884 he says:

> The thought . . . emerges in me—from where? through what? I don't know that. It comes independently of my will, generally surrounded and darkened by a crowd of

feelings, desires, aversions, also by other thoughts. . . . One draws it out of this crowd, cleans it, sets it on its feet . . . : *who* does all that—I don't know and am surely more an observer in this than an originator of the process . . . so that in all thinking a plurality of persons seems to be participants—: all this is not at all easy to observe; we are basically schooled for the reverse, namely while thinking not to think of thinking. The origin of a thought remains hidden; the probability is great that it is only the symptom of a much more comprehensive state; in the fact that precisely it comes and not another, that it comes precisely with this greater or lesser clarity, at times sure and commanding, at times weak and needing support . . . : in all this something or other of our total condition expresses itself in signs.[112]

What the "psychologist" Nietzsche writes here as a self-observer—he who otherwise so decisively rejects self-observation, or at least warns against it—makes clear the eventful character of interpretations. As interpretation, man is will to power, certainly. But this will to power is the continually changing organization of power-wills, which are internally organized power-wills. The "*more comprehensive*" the power-organizations become, the more independent the organizing forces are from the organized ones. For in the end it is their shifting constellations of power that decide who will rule. Man is so complex an organization of power that he can no longer find out what motivates him "deep down." He is interpretation, but he is interpreted. He is will to power, but—as "will of man"—a powerless will to power as regards his self-constitution (cf. D 120).[113] To have this insight means to affirm without restriction what is seen into as ultimately true. "Amor fati" is the last word of the philosophy of the will to power. But this word, too, could be "addressed" to itself only out of its own abysmal depth.[114]

Nothing would be more wrong and inaccurate concerning Nietzsche's interpretation than after all to have *the* will to power emerge as a *deus ex machina,* if not as the one metaphysical subject, yet as a fundamental event. For Nietzsche there are complexes of events, but there is not one fundamental event. There is no single entity, there are always pluralities, coalescing and separating. Nietzsche's philosophy excludes as irrelevant to actual events the question of the ground of being in the sense of traditional metaphysics.

9

The Organism as Inner Struggle: Wilhelm Roux's Influence on Nietzsche

Preliminary Remark: On Nietzsche's Natural-Scientific Studies

Reminiscing on his "philologist's existence" in Basel, Nietzsche writes in *Ecce Homo* that in the end he was "utterly emaciated, utterly starved: my knowledge simply failed to include *realities,* and my 'idealities' were not worth a damn. A truly burning thirst took hold of me: henceforth I really pursued nothing more than physiology, medicine, and natural sciences—and I did not return even to properly historical studies until my *task* compelled me to, imperiously" (EH).[1] Even if we relativize this statement of Nietzsche's in view of the particular character of his "autobiography," its "core of truth" still remains indisputable.[2] The great number of natural-scientific books he bought or borrowed is evidence enough of his efforts to understand states of affairs for which his education had not prepared him.

This is a fundamental problem. One can ask with K. Schlechta whether Nietzsche ever "seriously" studied natural science. Schlechta's answer is that the insights that Nietzsche acquired sufficed in any case for him to see through the "nihilistic traits" of scientific thinking, as Dostoevsky and Kierkegaard also had done.[3] Such a comparison, despite its general accuracy, is inadequate not only because it does not take account of Nietzsche's very extensive (though disparate) studies, for which we find no equivalence on the part of the other two thinkers. The comparison also fails to see the intensity with which Nietzsche immersed himself in contemporary scientific questions. He was constantly aware that the sciences had to be taken *critically,* that the path of his philosophical thinking had to lead through them.

It is therefore also taking things too lightly to state, as B. Steverding does, that Nietzsche's natural-scientific ideas stemmed "not from an intensive study of the natural sciences," but were "essentially the fruit of the general 'scientific worldview' prevalent in the second half of the last century."[4]

Nietzsche's thinking did develop in the medium of this "general knowledge" and in many respects it did not extend beyond such generalities. On the other hand, he immersed himself deeply in specialized investigations, seized upon their findings, and made them productive for his philosophizing. Recourse to his reading and utilization of such works is indispensable for an understanding not only of his statements on natural philosophy. His scientific studies show through especially in questions of "psychology," "morality," and "metaphysics"—just as vice versa he refers from these disciplines back to science.[5]

Objections can be raised against Nietzsche's procedure of transporting many things from problematic and objective contexts in particular fields to "completely different fields." But the objections strike only the surface and remain inadequate, unless one keeps in mind the idea that all "events"—even of the most different kind—have a similar structure—an idea that guides Nietzsche's methodology. The fundamental structures of events are, according to Nietzsche, mostly concealed: in different ways depending on the particular nature of the respective reality. The reciprocal application of insights from one area of reality to another is supposed to make more transparent what is going on beneath the surface.

Insofar as Nietzsche's study of scientific books focuses mainly on elaborating fundamental structures, the specific technical importance of the research he studies is secondary. Often it even lies beyond his grasp because of his lack of specialized training.[6] Nonetheless he retains his ability to recognize the prejudices from which those researches take their point of departure.[7] Nietzsche does not settle for merely detecting this; he works his way thoughtfully through them and seeks to get *behind them* to the fundamental structuring factors.

This intention will become clear in the following remarks tracing the influence that the first book by Wilhelm Roux, the founder of "evolutionary mechanics," had on Nietzsche.

Nietzsche's Roux Readings

In a note on Darwinism written in 1886–87, Nietzsche objects to the overestimation of the influence of "external conditions" in the formation of organs; Darwin had, he says, carried it to the point of "nonsense." Nietzsche's objection to this is that "the essential thing in the life-process is precisely the tremendous shaping power, creating form from within, which *uses, exploits* the 'external circumstances.'"[8] That form is created from within is a basic motif of Nietzsche's thinking. It is found in his early writings and can be followed until the elaboration of the motor-centers as will to power in the late works.[9] This force from within applies to the most varied modes and gradations of organization: in the second

Untimely Meditation it appears as man's *plastic strength,* which produces a closed horizon versus the plurality of historical traditions, assimilating and reshaping the past and the foreign or else expelling them through forgetting (HL);[10] in 1885 Nietzsche even traces the physical concept of force back to a creative interior.[11]

In the polemics against Darwin's overestimation of the external, Nietzsche brings into play the inner dynamics of the organic: "The individual itself as struggle of the parts (for food, space, etc.): its development associated with a *victory, hegemony* of individual parts, with a *stunting* or 'reduction to organs' of other parts." The origin of an organ cannot be explained by the "utility" that it offers to the individuals in the struggle for existence: "For the longest time during which a quality is being formed, it does not preserve the individual and does not benefit him, least of all in the struggle with external conditions and enemies."[12]

Nietzsche's line of argument is based mainly on a work by the anatomist Wilhelm Roux. The very title of this book already suggest this: *Der Kampf der Theile im Organismus. Ein Beitrag zur Vervollständigung der mechanischen Zweckmäßigkeitslehre* [*The Struggle of the Parts in the Organism. A Contribution to Complement the Mechanical Theory of Purposefulness*]. Roux's book was published in 1881. It was in Nietzsche's library; he probably acquired it soon after its publication. In any case a first utilization of Roux's research shows up in the notes from the spring–fall of 1881. From this time on Nietzsche uses specific terms of Roux's, in part with slight modifications, to describe organic processes. Thus he speaks of "self-regulation," "excessive replacement" ["*überreichlichem Ersatz*"], and "vital stimulus."[13]

Nietzsche re-read Roux's book in the spring–summer of 1883. The greater number of concepts, summaries, and comments found in KGW VII 1, compared with 1881 is evidence of his intensified Roux studies.[14] In 1884 Nietzsche then made critical remarks about Roux's basic concepts.[15] His critique flows from his reduction of all organic processes to will to power. Yet it must be said that Nietzsche's understanding of the organism as a plurality of conflicting wills to power was prepared by his reading of Roux. That even later he still referred directly to Roux can be seen from his critique of Darwin, which we cited initially.

The following remarks will focus exclusively on Roux's influence; this could give the impression that Nietzsche's readings of other relevant scientific books remained without decisive influence on him. Yet, for Nietzsche's reception and for his multidimensional critique of Darwinism, a whole series of books to which he had access would have to be mentioned; here a wide field is open for research.[16] As can be shown from his 1881 notes, Nietzsche, at the time of his first reading of Roux, also read J. R. Mayer's book *Die organische Bewegung in ihrem Zusammenhang mit dem Stoffwechsel* [*Organic Movement in its Connection with Metabo-*

lism, 1845], along with other works by that author, and he also drew on M. Foster's *Lehrbuch der Physiologie* [*Textbook on Physiology,* 1881], in pursuit of his physiological studies.[17] But his notes from that year show that Roux's book especially stimulated him to a deeper understanding of physiological processes.[18]

Phenomenalism and Science

In order to estimate the impact even his first study of Roux necessarily had on Nietzsche, we will begin our remarks on this topic by describing briefly how and with what results Nietzsche treated the interior of human individuals in *Daybreak* and in the contemporaneous notes of 1880–81.[19] Nietzsche's statements reveal above all the influence of A. Spir and F. A. Lange, an influence that lasted even in later years. He writes: "We have expended so much labor on learning that external things are not as they appear to us to be—very well! the case is the same with the inner world!" (D 116). Our "fathoming of inner processes and drives" is hampered by language's inadequate capacity for differentiation and the resulting imprecision in observation and thinking. "*We are none of us* that which we appear to be in accordance with the states for which alone we have consciousness and words" (D 115).

Nietzsche alludes again and again to the fact that the internal sphere of the "subject" is unknown. At least nothing remains "more incomplete than his image of the totality of drives" that constitute man's being (D 119). What we become aware of in preparing an action as a struggle of motives is an illusory foreground for the real process. What goes on in the background or, better, in the underground, is for us "something completely invisible and unconscious." Perhaps the real struggle is going on: unconscious habits, incalculable physical aspects, scarcely fathomable feelings for others, suddenly arising emotions, this and much more acting on one another. In any case this struggle remains hidden, "and likewise the victory as victory; for though I certainly learn what I finally *do,* I do not learn what motive has actually proved victorious" (D 129).

Accordingly "our moral judgments and evaluations too are only images and fantasies based on a physiological process unknown to us, a kind of acquired language for designating certain nervous stimuli" (D 119). But not only "morality" stands "in the service of physiological functions";[20] "All our so-called consciousness is a more or less fantastic commentary on an unknown, perhaps unknowable, but felt text" (D 129). The underlying physiological reality is felt; this shows its incontestable actuality. What is felt can be interpreted more or less fantastically, thus suggesting a gradation with regard to the adequacy of the interpretations. The natural-scientific "commentary" on the unknown physiological processes is, for Nietzsche, apparently less fantastic than the restriction to mere self-experience. This is shown initially when he describes the conjectured real inner struggle in mechanistic terms as "a battling to and fro, a rising and falling of the scales" (D 129). But even science cannot remove the hiddenness of the physiological process. If a corporal process, e.g., chewing, is grasped "with greater scientific precision" we find "a great number of bodily movements." But we can "grasp their process only in symbols (of touch, hearing, seeing of colors) and in single segments and moments. The 'essence' of this process remains just as alien to us as its continual course." Nietzsche writes this in the spring of 1881.[21]

Despite all his openness to natural-scientific research, at first epistemological and language-critical skepticism[22] were dominant when Nietzsche began reading Roux's book a short time later. "Now *struggle* has been discovered everywhere and one speaks of a struggle of the cells, tissues, organs, organisms," he writes in one of the first notes referring to Roux. That even the anatomist could speak of struggle, victory, dominance, resistance, and the like necessarily impressed Nietzsche. But on the other hand he immediately asks whether it is permissible to transfer such terms of our affective self-experience to the unknown. Is it not only a matter of "intellectual interpretations where the intellect knows absolutely nothing, but *believes* it knows everything?"[23] Yet in the very next notes he transports the "characteristics of the lowest living being into our 'reason'" in order to show that moral drives arise thereby.[24] Under the impression of Roux's analyses he makes a new reversal: precisely reason can be kept within its limits by the findings of anatomical and physiological research. Philosophical reason, in particular, is "*without knowledge* . . . something totally foolish." Nietzsche opposes the "presumption of reason" even to be the center of bodily processes with a formulation taken word for word from Roux's book: "The centralization is not at all so complete" (HA I:11).[25]

Such clues show that Nietzsche is pushed by Roux in the direction of recognizing scientific research. Such "positivism," to be sure, faces a language-critical reservation: "Our natural science is now on the way to clarifying the smallest processes through our acquired affect-feelings, in short to creating a *way of speaking* for those processes: very well! But it remains a *picture-language* [*Bilderrede*]."[26]

This reservation of Nietzsche's is not meant as a rejection. We must not think that he expected more technical accuracy from a formalized or even mathematical scientific language than from a "picture-language." Mathematics and logic are based, rather, "on presuppositions to which nothing in the real world corresponds," since, for example they invent identities (HA I:11). That human knowledge, even in the natural sciences, necessarily is locked within a picture-language is one of Nietzsche's early convictions. The question is what kind of imagery deserves priority. A note from the year 1872 reads: "Darwinism is right in pictorial thinking too; the stronger image consumes the weaker one."[27] Thus a struggle takes place also between the various picture-languages. A scientific picture-language that starts with the image of struggle must be conceded the advantage over others. For struggle is such an "elementary phenomenon" that to speak of it points back beyond our "acquired affect-feelings," to more original dimensions; for, as has been shown, "learning" too is a struggle.

These remarks are not meant to solve the language-philosophical problems[28] with which Nietzsche continued to struggle even later, as we shall see. They are meant merely to show that Nietzsche's initial reservations about Roux's imagery diminish and give way to the unbiased acceptance of his scientific knowledge. Yet Nietzsche at first finds that Roux's description of the physiological contexts leads to an "image" of human life that differs essentially from our idea determined by affective experiences.

In autumn of 1881, after his first study of Roux, we therefore hear a completely different tone in Nietzsche's notes than in spring of the same year: "How cold and strange the worlds discovered by science seem to us till now! How different, for example, is the body as we experience, see, feel, fear, admire it and the 'body' as the anatomist teaches it to us!" What science shows is indeed a "*totally alien*" world. But this alienness is no longer the unknowable. It is rather "a just discovered *new* world, the greatest contradiction to our feeling!" The expectation Nietzsche now sets on science becomes evident, when he continues: "And yet gradually 'truth' is supposed to concatenate in our dream and—we should eventually *dream more truly!*"[29] This note is remarkable. We *dream:* phenomenalism, as always, is predominant. We can dream *more truly:* science's new discoveries resolve hidden secrets. We *should* eventually dream more truly: thus a task is assigned for the future. The cited fragment is a good example for Schlechta's suggestion that it remains an open question how Nietzsche's general skepticism, including toward scientific truth, can be harmonized with his positivistic confidence.[30]

Nietzsche's turn toward science, renewed in 1881, needs greater clarification with respect to its goal. What he is interested in is not knowledge as such, but rather its significance for human existence. This can be seen from his remark about the scientist, which he adds to his note about "true dreams": "It is a completely new situation—it too has its devotion, it too can be understood heroically: although no one has yet done it." The scientific men work "in a realm closed off from their feeling." "For them science is mainly something stern, cold, sober—no heart-moving outlook, no daring, no standing alone against demons and gods. Science is of no concern to them—that gives them the *capacity for it*! If they were fearful or had any sense for the monstrous—they would keep their hands off."[31] Naturally, Nietzsche, in the course of his creative work, took varying stances toward the monstrous. Here he accepts the challenge. The nihilistic consequences of science, which he first spoke of in 1870,[32] are replaced by the idea of a long-term change of human existence especially by adapting physiological knowledge. At present, so he writes in 1881, "the old physiological *errors* have spontaneous force. . . . For a long, long time we will be able to use the new knowledge only as stimuli—to discharge spontaneous forces."[33] In so doing "one can give meaning to the closest little fleeting thing by understanding it as the root of habits."[34]

This is the result of Nietzsche's first reading of Roux. It is typical of his attitude toward knowledge that he immediately transports the anatomist's research findings to aspects of the human shaping of life. In the second note dealing with Roux's definitions, he writes: "Men living alone, if they do not perish, develop into societies; a number of fields of labor are developed, and there is likewise a great deal of struggle of the drives for food, space and time. Self-regulation is not present all of a sudden. Indeed, on the whole man is a being that necessarily perishes because it has not yet developed it. We all die too young of a thousand mistakes and ignorance of practice."[35]

But beyond such anthropological applications, in later years Roux takes on essential significance for Nietzsche's philosophical understanding of the organic. The following treatment of Roux will make this clear.

Nietzsche's Acceptance of Roux's Fundamental Ideas (1881–83)

Nietzsche could not know that the new information he found in Roux's book heralded a new scientific discipline. Roux, a disciple of C. Gegenbaur, E. Haeckel, and R. Virchow, is the founder of experimental and causal-morphological research in evolution, to which he gave the name "evolutionary mechanics" in 1884.[36] Its later world-wide dissemination will not be described here, nor its significance in the history of science for the current state of evolutionary physiology, which stemmed from it. What matters for us is that Roux as early as his 1881 book, which he had in part presented the year before as his inaugural dissertation, elaborated fundamental determinations and explanations that also guided his later investigations. Before Roux, anatomy had limited itself basically to describing and comparing organic forms. How questionable Roux's experimental and causal-analytical methodology seemed to contemporary descriptive anatomy can be seen from a remark made to him by one of his teachers after *The Struggle of the Parts* appeared: "Never again write such a philosophical book, otherwise you will never become a Full Professor of Anatomy." Even "the striving for causal knowledge of the shapes of living creatures was . . . branded with such criticism," Roux remarks in his autobiography.[37]

We now turn to Roux's book. In describing his aim and his basic ideas we at the same time examine Nietzsche's reception of Roux both in the 1881 notes and in the 1883 notes. Roux wants to complement the theory of evolution, since its principle of natural selection is unsuitable for explaining the "finer inner purposefulness of animal organisms."[38] For example, the characteristics of the blood-vessel walls showing variegated and complex differentiations cannot be explained by the fact that they, as variations occurring randomly at first, could have been bred in the struggle for existence.[39] Unless one wants to fall back into "teleology" and hence into the metaphysical dualism that Darwin had "happily" eliminated,[40] one must start with the assumption of an internal self-regulation and self-differentiation by processes of functional adaptation. What this means can be clarified by the example just cited. The evolution of the blood vessels is pressed in a particular direction by the circulating blood. Thus one organ acts on the other.[41] More precisely, such action proves to be a mutual conflict of parts of the organism, which Roux describes at variously differentiated stages of organization.

No doubt Roux derives his concept of struggle from Darwin, even though he uses it to explain inner processes of breeding.[42] But he goes back to Heraclitus and Empedocles to describe how early it was known that permanent and purposefully organized unities grow precisely out of the struggle of antithetical forces. Nietzsche includes these historical references in his first reflection on Roux.[43] Roux sees them as evidence that in principle the philosophical solution to "the problem of evolution" was found in early Greek thought but then "completely lost" and had "to be rediscovered all over again by the laborious way of empirical scientific detailed research."[44]

It is important that Roux understands struggle as a mechanical process. We will describe this process very briefly based on his portrayal of the struggle of the smallest process-unit, the molecular cell-components, in the period of growth.[45] That particle that can assimilate more rapidly in metabolism and hence regenerate more rapidly will develop more strongly in size than its neighboring particle that shows less affinity. The first particle will "thus take away space" from the second one. When this process is repeated, the second one is pressed further back and if this process lasts for a longer time it will "finally disappear." As in the struggle for space, likewise in the struggle for food—when there is a food-shortage—those particles will win out whose speed of regeneration is greater. Finally, if assimilation exceeds consumption in the process unit, so that "over-compensation for the consumed," that is, growth, begins, while the other cell-particles do not assimilate as much, then such a unity will gain hegemony in the cell. Finally, Roux names direct conflict as the third mode of conflict in the cell. In it newly appearing qualities win out over old ones by destroying and assimilating them. Roux stresses especially strongly the struggle for space. "Where everything bound in a spatial unity is adjacent and pressing at once, the struggle must be greater than the struggle of individuals among one another."

In the year 1883 Nietzsche wrote synopses of the processes described by Roux.[46] One aspect from which Roux starts was especially important to him. Nietzsche noted: "The struggle for food and space takes place in the cell as soon as there is inequality in the components."[47] Shortly before, we find a reference to Roux's fundamental statement that the inequality of the parts is the basis for the struggle;[48] from it, Roux states in the cited passage, "*the struggle follows by itself as a result of growth*" and indeed "simply because of metabolism."[49] In 1881 Nietzsche had extracted from Roux: "Difference is prevalent in the smallest things, spermatozoa eggs—equality is a great delusion."[50] The difference of the parts points to their "relative independence." That this independence can be shown "even in the highest organisms"[51] found its full expression in Nietzsche's later understanding of the body as a plurality of living beings. In the proof of independence cited by Nietzsche, Roux bases himself on a publication by his teacher, R. Virchow, in which the transplantability of cells had been described.[52]

How Roux elaborates on struggle as the constitutive principle of the formation processes on the levels of the cells, tissues, and organs cannot be treated in detail here. Nietzsche, in his 1883 reading, registers exactly where in Roux the internal struggle points beyond the pure selection character. This happens in the struggles of the tissues. Struggle here becomes "a *regulating* principle," the "principle of the functional self-regulation of the most purposeful size-ratios."[53] Roux's idea of organic self-regulation without pre-given purposefulness is incorporated into Nietzsche's interpretation of corporeality.

The cited references to Roux must suffice to clarify his particular understanding of organic processes.[54] As opposed to inorganic processes, the life-process bears "the cause of its preservation within itself." Even in *assimilation,* the appropriation and transformation of "foreign" material, a certain self-production of the organic is performed, whereas in the inorganic realm anything similar is found only in the flame. On the contrary, *overcompensation for consumption* (Nietzsche's expression for this is: "excessive replacement" [*überreichliche Ersatz*]) is proper only to organic beings. It determines growth and makes life's specific achievements possible. Finally, the *durability* of life-processes is guaranteed by this self-regulation, which to a certain extent establishes the economic balance in an organism. The functional harmony in a whole, which the concept of self-regulation expresses, also stems, according to Roux, from the breeding struggle of the parts: their "usefulness for the whole is not at all intended by the parts. The parts live merely for their own preservation." That only those qualities of the parts that serve for the durability of a whole have been preserved is attributed by Roux to "external" selection in the Darwinistic sense.[55]

This shows that Roux's investigation does not seek to reduce "the significance of Darwin's and Wallace's principle of the struggle of individuals for the origin of multifariousness and for adaptation to external conditions." What he explains by internal struggle are those inner purposes that cannot be derived from the struggle of individuals. The struggle of the parts carries on a pre-selection for the "struggle for existence": "The relation between the two kinds of struggle" is "such that of the generally vital and most strongly reacting substances, or more correctly processes, bred by the struggle of the parts, generally the struggle of the individuals for existence selects those special ones that are also suitable for survival in this second struggle too."[56]

In Nietzsche's 1883 notes on Roux, the significance of the "second struggle" declines. He notes passages in which Roux emphasizes the inadequacy of Darwinian derivations. We find, for example, a reference to Roux's explanation of the possibility of the transition of animals from water to land[57] as having been able "to occur only through the simultaneous formation of thousands, indeed millions, of purposeful individual qualities." This simultaneity can be explained, according to Roux, only by the principle of functional self-formation, but not by Darwin's principle of selection, which permits only successive formation of purposeful qualities. Nietzsche apparently finds here documentation for his view of the priority of an inner principle [*Von-Innen-Her*] compared with an outer one. On another occasion Nietzsche cites a passage from Roux discussing the one-sidedness of the Darwinian mode of explanation: "Until now all the good qualities of an organism have been derived solely from the struggle for existence between individuals!"[58] Finally, Nietzsche discusses Roux's description of processes in which the stimulus becomes vitally necessary. He writes on that: "These are the *highest processes*." And he quotes Roux: "All this happens *without* the struggle of individuals."[59]

We must go into more detail on the problem of stimulus-effect, since it becomes particularly important for Nietzsche's understanding of organic processes. Roux is essentially concerned with treating adequately the effect of functional stimuli. These stimuli influence the struggle to some extent from the outside. They act on the parts in many ways: primarily trophically, that is, increasing nutrition, but also differentiating and shaping. Roux distinguishes two periods in the life of the parts. In the first phase the parts develop, differentiate, and increase in size; in the second phase, growth, in certain cases even the complete replacement of what has been used up, takes place only under the effect of stimuli.[60] Thus a complete dependence of the life-processes on the stimuli can arise. Roux then speaks of an *"indispensable vital stimulus."*[61]

But dependence does not abolish the self-formation of the parts. Nietzsche characteristically emphasizes this aspect in particular and transfers it to the relation of man to his environment: "The active quantitative and qualitative *food-selection* of the cells which determine the whole evolution is matched by the fact that man too *selects* the events and stimuli, hence behaves actively, among all the things that press upon him by chance—and thus *defends* himself against much. Roux, p. 149."[62] Such transferals are often found in Nietzsche's 1883 Roux notes.[63] Again and again physiological data are "applied morally" by him.[64] Thus he remarks on the "influence of stimuli on quicker assimilation—in morality: increase of power where an abundance of *subtlest violations* occurs and the need for *appropriation* is therefore intensified."[65] Here too Nietzsche stresses activity in the processing of stimuli. He does so even more emphatically when he writes: "My task: to place the good drives so that they become hungry and have to activate themselves."[66] No doubt he is here alluding to Roux's statement: "The enduring processes must be hungry."[67]

In his reflections on the problem of morality, he once also takes up the "second struggle" in Roux's sense and argues "Darwinistically": "*Selection in the struggle of the individuals* will choose for lasting preservation those qualities that prove useful for *entire individuals.* Thus many kinds of morality must arise—the struggle of their bearers and victory brings to *lasting preservation* that kind of morality that is useful and vitally indispensable for the mightiest men."[68] In later notes Nietzsche will stress that natural selection in Darwin's sense does not connect the "best morality" with the "higher individuals," as he considers possible in the cited note. But though in 1883 he calls the "struggle of the various moralities" the "means of their formation,"[69] we also find at the same time the more radical—because it undermines morality—"practical consequence," which he draws during his second reading of Roux: "Transformation of characters. Breeding instead of moralizing. To exert direct action upon the organism instead of the indirect one of ethical discipline. A different corporeality then creates for itself a *different* soul and morals. Thus a *reversal*!"[70] In 1881, as we saw, physiology is supposed to be put in the service of a fundamental transformation of human existence.

Mechanistic and Teleological Explanations of Nature

In 1884 Nietzsche was preoccupied with fundamental ideas of Roux's in a different general respect. He was concerned with the methodological question of the accuracy and effectiveness of the mechanistic and teleological explanations of nature. He seeks to show the inadequacy of both types of explanation, while at the same time ascribing essential advantages to the mechanistic derivation over the teleological one. He counts among his "presuppositions": "no final 'causes.' Even in human actions the intention does *not at all* explain the action."[71] He notes with approval the "victory of the anti-teleological mechanistic way of thinking as *regulative hypothesis,* 1) because science is possible only with it; 2) because it presupposes the least and must under all circumstances first be tried out."[72] Once he even expresses the "suspicion that all qualities of the organic world itself are *underivable* by us from mechanical causes, because we ourselves first projected anti-mechanical processes into them: we first inserted the underivable."[73] On the other hand he remarks also that "all our mechanical laws . . . *come from us,* not from things! We construe 'things' according to them."[74] The mechanistic explanation serves "'calculability' for practical purposes,"[75] but it thus gives up "ultimately any understanding."[76]

The reduction of organic processes to pressure and stress, which in turn cannot be explained, according to a note from 1885, does homage to "the principle of the greatest possible stupidity."[77] Accordingly, as early as 1884 Nietzsche writes: "The ideal is to construct the most complicated of all machine-beings that arises through the *most stupid* of all possible methods."[78] The mechanistic way of thinking is stupid insofar as it leaves out of consideration "the spiritual," which seems to be "the essence of the organic."[79] Nietzsche finds "the spiritual" in the selection of what is more important, more useful, more urgent"; it consists in *estimation* even in the will of the lowest organisms.[80] At the same time he also is opposed to the spiritual as a teleological principle: "Until now both explanations of organic life have not succeeded; neither that based on mechanics, *nor that based on the spirit.*" Nietzsche underscores particularly the latter. But he has no objection to drawing on both methods for the purpose of symbolic explanation.[81]

With such ambiguous positions Nietzsche is striving to find a third way to explain the organic, running in a certain way between the two above-described ways. The distinctions he makes often give the impression that he is criticizing each of the two methods from the other's standpoint. This can be shown from his statements on *self-regulation* in the spring of 1884. First, self-regulation indicates to him—in contrast with the meaning Roux gives it—that the "machine-character" is totally *absent* "in everything organic." In the organs' relation to one another, "all *virtues* must be practiced—obedience, industriousness, helpfulness, alertness."[82] One could conclude from this that he is contesting the mechanistic standpoint from the teleological one. But at the same time as Nietzsche praises "the method of the mechanistic world-view . . . as for the time being by far the *most honest,*"[83] he also states that it too is practically crawling with "teleological interpretations." Among these he lists the determination of self-regulation, which of course cannot be "dispensed with" for the moment. But to read this as meaning that Nietzsche is siding with the mechanistic solution to the problem would also lead us astray. The mechanistic way of thinking deserves priority over the teleological one, for its own honesty requires it to free itself of teleological "remnants."

That Nietzsche has mainly Roux in mind in this context can be seen from the fact that he considers "the interpretation of hunger as aiming at 'substitution,' or even 'excessive replacement'" to be "a deep and dangerous misunderstanding" of teleological origin.[84] In a note from the summer or fall of the same year Nietzsche opposes the "teleological coloration" of Roux's "excessive replacement" and criticizes his understanding of self-regulation.[85] The next statement then mentions the will to power for the first time "in the functions of the organic."[86] From then on Nietzsche's own interpretation of the struggle within the organism, which had been in preparation for a long time, is elaborated in detail.

But before going into this interpretation, we will take a brief look at Roux's terminology, which Nietzsche characterized as teleological. We will cite the later discussion of the principles of evolutionary mechanics, although Nietzsche could not yet have known it. But we are objectively justified insofar as Roux kept the essential terms developed in his 1881 book, and their meanings, all the way to his last publications, although in the course of his further research he made considerable additions and differentiations.[87] We cannot go into greater detail here about the fundamental change Roux had undergone on the question of the inheritability of acquired qualities, when in 1895 he undertook a revision of *The Struggle of the Parts*. This leads to our portrayal's highlighting very strongly the autogenetic perspective, which is emphasized anyway, over the phylogenetic one.[88]

Before our digression, let us remark that Roux did not attach the notion of *purposeful spontaneity* to the expression "self-regulation." By the prefix "self-" he wished merely to stress the causal-mechanical determination of the processes within the organism.[89] He did ask himself the question whether "non-mechanistic events of whatever conceivable kind participated" in "the harmonious cooperation to promote durability" of processes in the living being.[90] He denied this especially sharply in his dispute with Hans Driesch.

Driesch, in continuing Roux's embryological experiments, had arrived at other results than Roux and finally drawn opposite conclusions. In 1887 Roux, after killing off one of the two segmenting cells of a frog's egg, had observed the development of the living cells into a half-embryo and interpreted this process causally as self-differentiation. Driesch's similar experiments on the cells of sea urchin eggs (1891) led to the development of a whole (though smaller) organism. Based on this and other experiments, Driesch finally became convinced that a purposeful agent must underlie such formative processes.[91] Roux regarded Driesch's teleological mode of derivation as mere metaphysics that forsakes exact causal explanation.[92] Of course, as late as 1923 he had to concede that his doctrine of self-differentiation was "still misunderstood even after almost forty years," and was being understood as a "mode of action" and not as a "causal principle."[93] At any rate the ambiguity of his concepts, which Nietzsche already sensed, did not draw Roux away from his mechanistic mode of explanation; living creatures remain for him "machines for self-preservation, self-reproduction and self-regulation."[94]

Nietzsche's understanding of self-regulation stands out sharply from the contrary positions cited in this digression. He finds that this concept presupposes "the ability to rule over a commonalty," which can be grounded neither mechanically nor teleologically. "The evolution of the organic is not attached to nutrition," he now notes in obvious polemics against Roux's stress on the effect of trophic stimuli. It is rather "commanding and being able to command" that directs the "self-regulation."[95] The concept of domination used by Roux is stripped of its mechanical character by the complementary concept "commanding."

Command, Release of Power, Stimulus

During the years 1884 and 1885, Nietzsche elaborated ever more subtly what he means by "commanding." Commanding must be understood as a *willing*.[96] The will as command is characterized as "tense, clear, with only one thing in mind, an innermost conviction of superiority, certainty that it will be obeyed." Nietzsche speaks of the "commander's feeling of superiority" over those who obey. The (illusory) experience of "freedom of the will" is represented in the feeling: "*I* am free, *he* must *obey*."[97] The physiological "ranking of the organs and drives," the "difference between *lower* and *higher* functions can be explained by the dependence of those who obey on those who command."[98]

Rankings result from struggles that can be followed down to the simplest organic processes. Nietzsche wants to comprehend such processes more originally than the natural scientists of his day. So he notes in 1884: "If two organic beings collide, if there is *only* struggle for life or food: what? There must be struggle for its own sake."[99] The living thing wants "to *release* its power" in the corresponding processes;[100] in its releases of power it is concerned with power, and nothing besides.[101] This basic thought, expressed again and again by Nietzsche in the following years, can be exemplified by two notes from the fall of 1887 and the spring of 1888. The "simplest case" is discussed in them, namely that "of primitive nutrition: The protoplasm stretches out its pseudopodia seeking something that resists it—not from hunger but from will to power." "The will to power can express itself only against obstacles; it seeks what resists it—this is the original evidence of protoplasm,"[102] which intrinsically is a "plurality of conflicting beings."[103]

Starting from this tendency we describe the way an organic will expands its power. In its *releases of power,* what it wants is "to become *stronger.*" It can do this only in the struggle with something that resists it, which it must seek.[104] What underlies such seeking is a *perception* of its opposite, which has formed in the course of gradual developments, whereby "every smallest cell is now the heir of the entire organic past."[105] In the spring of 1884 Nietzsche states that he presupposes "memory and a kind of spirit in every organic thing,"[106] which we alluded to at the beginning of this chapter.[107] If a will to power has sought out one opposed to it, then it strives to *overpower* it. "Appropriation and assimilation" take place—in case the overpowering succeeds—as a "forming, building up and transforming until finally the one overpowered has fallen completely into the attacker's power and increased it."[108] What has been overpowered can, with some remodeling, be put into service by the overpowerer. This results in an order of rank in the complex organic formations that leads to processes of self-regulation representing a "continuation of the struggle" between the commanders and the obedient.[109]

Roux had understood the inner struggle as a causal-mechanical event and thus explained both the way the parts act upon one another and the necessity of the course of processes in the organism. Nietzsche admits that the mechanistic theory can describe the processes for the purpose of calculability, but claims that explanation in the sense of understanding lies beyond its possibilities. But does Nietzsche's reduction of the "mechanistic" course of events to struggles of wills lead any further? First, it must be established that this reduction does not remove the character of necessity from the sequence of events. "To happen and to happen necessarily is a tautology," Nietzsche writes. For "a particular force can simply not be anything else . . . than precisely this particular force"; it does not release itself upon "a quantum of power-resistance otherwise than as is appropriate to its strength."[110] The force releases of a living being are, as a *will,* always also a *must:* "Both words weigh the same to me!" he says in a note already cited above from 1884.[111] However, one simply must not reason from such a *must* to "*laws of nature*";[112] "the alleged 'natural laws' are nothing but formulas for the 'power relations.'"[113] "There is no law; every power draws its last consequence at every moment."[114]

Nietzsche traces all events back to "an encroachment of power over other power."[115] We have described this encroachment in its course but this still does not explain how will can act upon will. If, according to Nietzsche, there is "absolutely no other causality than that of will upon will,"[116] this implies that it must be of a different kind than the way of acting graspable by mechanistic thought. In *Beyond Good and Evil* Nietzsche calls for a *reversal*. He asks whether the "given" of our human "world of desires and passions" is not sufficient to "understand also the so-called mechanistic (or 'material') world" (BGE 36).[117] Do we perhaps not find in the outside world the "same realities" as in ourself? We must, Nietzsche writes in 1885, "use the analogy of man to the end": this applies to physics as well as to biology.[118] In 1881 Nietzsche made the reservation toward Roux that the latter used the "language" of our affects to portray the smallest biological processes; but now it seems to him thoroughly proper to use our affective language to explain *all* events. He justifies this procedure in *Beyond Good and Evil* with the idea of economy of methods: one must try to get by with one single kind of causality. If his way of explaining things proved correct, then one acquired the right "to unmistakably define *all* active power as 'will to power'" (BGE 36, cf. 12).

To understand the peculiar nature of the action of will on will, we should thus start from man. Nietzsche describes man as "a *plurality of 'wills to power'*: each with its plurality of means of expression and forms."[119] The many are locked in struggle; their action in common "is produced by commanding and obeying." But in what way does a command that is obeyed take effect? That in the command "a higher, stronger individual commands" and proclaims "*his* feeling as the *law* for others"[120] is no more of an answer than the statement that the stronger will directs the weaker one.[121]

Nietzsche's efforts to find a tenable answer are shown in a note from spring 1884. He approaches the problem via the word of command that is transmitted from one man to another. He discovers that the command understood as will acts "*not* as word, *not* as sound, but rather as what is hidden *behind* the sound." "Something is transmitted" by the command. If this transmission is ascribed to some "vibrations" or other, "the real process again" is hidden.[122] But what does the real process consist in, since it originally is supposed to occur "soundlessly" between the power-wills within the human organism? Not much later we find Nietzsche's suggestion that the will does not move, does not overcome resistances without their cooperation,[123] it is apprehended as a stimulus "on whose initiative the movement begins."[124] Accordingly, one should speak "not of causes of willing but rather of stimuli of willing."[125]

The stimulus as command is, then, for Nietzsche not a particular *kind of cause* along with others, as it was for Schopenhauer. With the help of this concept, rather, he describes the way the will to power acts as such. For that reason his understanding of stimuli cannot be restricted to physiological usage. Nietzsche rejects the reduction of stimuli to physical or chemical processes. On the contrary, he reduces these processes to stimuli. Here, too, he remains oriented by the "language of our affects."

These characteristics of the concept of stimulus make it prove usable for Nietzsche's view of concerted action. (1) The stimulus excites, and this excitement itself is already a release of power. (2) As excitement the stimulus is an *incitement*. It evokes the reception of the stimulus.[126] (3) The reception of the stimulus is a *counter-movement*. A self-activity of the stimulus-receptor underlies it, and under some circumstances it includes a *selection* of stimuli from among those offered.

We alluded to Nietzsche's stress on activity in the processing of stimuli in our discussion of his Roux studies from the year 1883. This activity must now be inserted into the opposition of commanding and obeying, and indeed on both sides.[127] "The commanding of other subjects" (we must understand as a subject also every inner power-will in the organism) leads to "these others then changing." "The only power there is"[128] consists in this two-sided process. The incitement emanating from the commander leads those who obey to undergo a change in themselves *on their own initiative.* By this explanation of the will's action Nietzsche carries his idea of the spontaneity of the inner initiative to the extreme. The subjugated element can exercise the dictated function only if it undertakes it on its own.

Nietzsche's resorting to the stimulus event to explain the way the will to power works must not be misunderstood in the sense of reducing the will to a *mere* stimulus. What he intends, on the contrary, is to capture the stimulation of willing in its full concentration. The concrete willing always includes feeling and thinking along with the affect of commanding. This is also true of the counter-stimuli that stem from those who obey: in them too is found the aforementioned triad, which is truly a unity.[129] "Here it is presupposed," he writes in 1884, "that all organic structures participate in thinking, feeling, willing."[130]

The Body as a Command Structure

In the last section of this portrayal we turn to the development of Nietzsche's understanding of the whole body as a command-structure, starting with his 1881 notes.

After his first reading of Roux, Nietzsche at first developed a very simple pattern of the organic functional whole: "Whoever has the strength to reduce others to a function, dominates their continual struggles. Those subjugated in turn also have their subordinates—their preservation is to a certain extent a condition for the life of the whole." The idea of a differentiated stimulus-reception, even connected with thought, on the part of the subjugated is still excluded at this time; obedience is understood solely as "coercion." "If all wanted to stand at their posts with 'reason' and not continually display so much strength and hostility as they need to *live*—then the driving force of the whole would be *missing*."[131]

In a later note of 1881 the idea of rulership is linked with the "feeling of power." The unilateralness of the formative processes, which run from "above" to "below," even undergoes a strengthening: "The feeling of power first conquering, then ruling (organizing)—it regulates what has been overpowered for *its* preservation and moreover it *preserves what has itself been overpowered*. Even the function has arisen from the feeling of power in the struggle with yet weaker forces. The function is maintained by overpowering and ruling over yet lower functions—*and it is supported in this by the higher power*!"[132]

In the First Part of *Thus Spoke Zarathustra* (1883) it is said of the human body that it is "a plurality with one meaning [*Sinn*], a war and a peace, a herd and a shepherd." This may still be compatible with Nietzsche's prior statements, although the language coinages of Zarathustra, delivered with poetic pathos as they are, tend to obscure rather than clarify the fundamental philosophical issues. However, when in the same context the body is apotheosized as "a great reason," if such a way of speaking is not taken metaphorically, then Nietzsche's prior understanding of corporeality has undergone a drastic change (Z I).[133]

The change becomes evident in the later fragments of the *Nachlaß*. Thus in a note written in the summer or fall of 1884 it is said that physiology gives only "a hint of the marvelous commerce" that goes on within the human plurality. The "subordination and coordination of the parts into a whole" presupposes "struggle and victory." Nietzsche, like Roux, still finds in the self-affirmation of the individual beings at the same time the *involuntary* (not explicitly intended) affirmation of the whole.[134] But at the same time he is also already pushing ahead to a more differentiated view of the dependent relationship of the obedient forces on the ones that command. To carry out even the most definite command in the organism requires "a great number of individuals . . . who all must be in a certain condition": they must "understand" the order "and also their special task in it."[135] Beyond this, as early as 1884, Nietzsche suggests that a weakened counter-drive can "as impulse" give "the *stimulus* for the activity of the main drive."[136]

In the 1885 notes Nietzsche increasingly highlights the relative independence of the obedient. At first he says only: "So that obedience can be perfect, the individual organ has a great deal of freedom."[137] Later he states that in man "in finer cases . . . the role" between rulers and servants has "to change temporarily and the one who commands occasionally obeys."[138] Nietzsche had already stressed that obedience always is also a *resistance* depending on the strength that is left for it.[139] Now it is characterized as a *counter-striving* that indicates that "one's own power is not at all surrendered." Commanding then appears as "an admission that the opponent's absolute power is not vanquished."[140]

The whole human body, however, later is represented as "a tremendous assembly of living beings, each one dependent and subjected and yet in a certain sense in its turn commanding and acting by its own will." In this "magnificent combination of the most varied life," of the "arrangement and disposition of higher and lower activities,"[141] we then find a "dependence of the rulers on those who are ruled" that goes beyond this earlier asserted mere subjugation. Ranking now also involves "a division of labor as empowerment of the individual and the whole."[142] The service of *all* the "living beings" now is geared primarily to the *whole* body. Thus the body indeed seems to be a great reason.

The problem this raises for Nietzsche's thinking emerges in the question of rulership in this "domination structure." Zarathustra in speaking of one shepherd of the herd can easily be misleading. No "absolute monarch" stands at the top of the "body's social structure";[143] rather the "main center of gravity" is "something changeable."[144] In 1881 Nietzsche had adopted Roux's thesis of the imperfect centralization in the organism to polemicize against the claim of an allegedly *centrally regulated* reason;[145] but now in 1885 he stresses the perfection that arises from the change of ruling centers. The cooperation of the living beings in the body is no more derivable from reason than from the so-called nerve- and brain-apparatus. This mechanistic concept obscures the "delicate bonding and mediation system" that makes the "synthesis" man possible.

Since this making-possible should not be understood teleologically, for example, as "'divinely' constructed,"[146] Nietzsche in late summer 1885 sees himself again moved to accept *fundamentally determinative* commanders who regulate the whole body, including the change of assignments and centers of gravity and the shifting arrangement and service. He asks whether the "coordination and struggle" of "our" plurality might be based on "a kind of *aristocracy* of cells." "Certainly of equals who are accustomed to ruling together and know how to command," he adds, thus rejecting the idea of one shepherd or ruler.[147] In *On the Genealogy of Morals* the formative strength and the "dominant role of the highest functionaries" in the organism are stressed over the "second rank" activities, which develop in inner processes of adaptation (GM II:12).[148]

By attributing the cooperation of the many living beings in the organism to the original spontaneity of such supreme masters, Nietzsche escapes teleology as the ultimate ground for "the great reason of the body." Yet it can be said that his description of bodily functions is practically crawling with teleological interpretations—to use his criticism of "mechanics" against himself. For example, in 1884 he states that "all *preservation-tendencies*" presuppose "a visualization of the whole," including its "goals, dangers and advancement," and if this visualization involves that "the lower, obedient beings . . . to a certain extent" must also be able to imagine the task of the higher ones,[149] in such a perspective we can find more than mere "*purposefulness,*" for this does not imply that any goal was "intended."[150] In any case the "thousandfold obedience" that the many living intellects summon up within the bodily abode is "not a blind, still less a mechanical, but rather a selective, clever, considerate, even resisting obedience," as Nietzsche states in 1885.[151]

The description of this and other "purposeful activities" in the organism[152] requires a cautious appraisal. In a long note in early 1884 Nietzsche once assumed "that a purposefulness rules events on the smallest level" and he weighed the possibility that it "could be ascribable" to "*tremendously much higher and more comprehensive intellects* than the one we are conscious of. But he does not take up again the hypothesis of such an originally guiding purposefulness "in the action of nature."[153] By 1885 he has long since overcome this "teleological temptation." Even when he rejects a mechanistic understanding of obedience, as we have seen, he still agrees with the mechanistic mode of explanation insofar as for him, too, all purposeful formations stem from the unpurposeful. Like Roux, Nietzsche starts with selective processes that are carried out in the form of inner struggles. But since he understands the parts of the organism as will to power, their "movements cannot be conditioned from outside, cannot be caused," as he notes in 1888. He needs inner "movement-initiatives and -centers, from which the will reaches around itself."[154] Unlike Darwin, Roux allowed room for an inner struggle, but by analyzing causally-mechanically he still remained on the "outside." The formative strength acting from within and the way it works remained hidden from him.

We must keep this fundamental difference in mind when Nietzsche in his 1886–87 note "*Against Darwinism,*" cited above, writes in apparent agreement with Roux "that the *new* forms shaped from within are not formed for a purpose, but that in the struggle of the parts a new form will not stand for long without relation to a partial benefit, and will then *in its use* take ever more complete shape."[155] The orders arising from power struggles look "similar to a purposeful design," but it is always a matter only of "the appearance of an order of means and end."[156] This applies also to "that delicate bonding and mediation system," through which "a lightning-fast communication" of all "higher and lower beings" in the body is created, "indeed through sheer living mediators."

This is no more a teleological matter than it is "a mechanistic problem."[157] The teleological mode of expression is for Nietzsche a temporarily indispensable means of portrayal, and nothing else.[158] To highlight the specific nature of his interpretation of "organic self-regulation," he says in 1885 that it is "a *moral* problem that is posed here."[159] Morality must here, as is said in *Beyond Good and Evil,* be understood as the doctrine of the relations of domination "under which the phenomenon 'life' comes about." Accordingly, he considers the body to be "a social structure of many souls" (BGE 12, 19), that is, living intellects.

In 1883 Nietzsche was still applying mechanistic physiology to the problems of morality; now, on the contrary, morality serves to explain physiological processes. But the concept "morality" is taken so broadly that it transcends the sphere of human desires and passions that—according to the above-cited statements from *Beyond Good and Evil*—are supposed to be the "model" for all events. The "imagery" of the body as a social structure points to the supra-individual realm of social organization—like other above-mentioned terms, for example, "commonalty" and "aristocracy."

But with such language Nietzsche is not using a different "model." The social formations, too, are for him organisms. Therefore, as early as 1881 he could plan to use "the *last organisms* whose formation we see"—and by these he means "nations, states, societies"—"for instruction about the first organisms."[160] In the same year he detects the imperfections of those last organisms although he compares them with the simplest ones.[161] But that *all* beings have the character of organization, and thus of a domination structure with basically similar structuring, remains beyond question for him until the end of his creative life. The transposal of inner structures of one form of organization to another is a methodical procedure he practices again and again, but we cannot here go into detail about the problematicalness of this.[162]

In conclusion we wish to show one more consequence of Nietzsche's understanding of the body as a plurality of wills to power. He calls "the *wanting-to-become-stronger* of every power center" "the only reality." In terms of this basic tendency, "self-preservation,"[163] and hence also self-regulation and durability (to name the terms by which Nietzsche for a time oriented himself) are only secondary phenomena. "Preservation is only a *consequence* of the original releases of force," he wrote as early as summer 1884.[164] In the notes from spring of the same year, shortly before his first critique of Roux and before the first derivation of organic processes from the will to power, the principle of self-preservation was still dominant.[165] In 1885 Nietzsche then defines "life" as "a lasting form of a *process of strength-determinations,* in which the various contenders in their turn grow unequally."[166] In spring 1888, finally, he says "the rich and living want victory, overcoming opponents, a streaming out of the feeling of power over broader realms than before: all healthy functions have this need—and the whole organism . . . is a complex of systems struggling for growth of the feeling of power."

I intentionally cited this passage from Aphorism 703 of the compilation *The Will to Power* in order only now to add the completion of the text that was first published in KGW VII 3, p. 154. For Nietzsche restricts the above-mentioned organic growth of power to the time "until the age of puberty." The editors of *The Will to Power* must have seen this as a restriction at least subject to misunderstanding, otherwise it can hardly be explained why they omitted it. Here we add the factual question: What is the situation of the body's expansion of power *after* puberty?

Nietzsche's answer to this question consists in allusions to the phenomenon of *procreation*. In 1886–87 he calls "procreating" the real *achievement* of the individual and hence his "highest interest"; he understands procreation as the "*highest expression of power*" from "the center of the whole individual."[167] As such it is, to be sure, on the other hand de-externalization: the entire body—as a separate and distinct domination structure—surrenders power in favor of the origination of a new body. This renunciation of power by virtue of power, however, stands in contradiction to Nietzsche's fundamental understanding of the conflicting wills to power. It would be more consistent with that view for procreating to be characterized, as he did in 1885–86, as "disintegration setting in through the impotence of the ruling cells to organize what they have appropriated"—as distinguished from nutrition as "the consequence of the insatiable appropriation" of the will to power.[168] Nietzsche adds to this portrayal of procreation in a later note: "Where a will does not suffice to organize all that has been appropriated, a *counterwill* becomes effective and undertakes detachment, a new organizational center after a struggle with the original will."[169]

Such statements are admittedly overlayered by a basic thought of Nietzsche's that is not readily compatible with them: namely, that, as he wrote in *Daybreak*, "by means of procreation a still more victorious life" can be prepared (D 150). "O my brothers," Zarathustra later says, "I consecrate and direct you to a new nobility: you shall become for me procreators and breeders and sowers of the future" (Z III:12).[170] Nietzsche's talk of the forming of a higher body, of the rise of the organic to yet higher levels, and finally of the overcoming of man tends to gain consistency, rather, in an episodic fragment from the winter of 1883–84, in which he presupposes a hidden natural teleology. This speculative hypothesis remains, however, without effect in Nietzsche's philosophy. To understand it or to critically assess the idea that he repeatedly adopts from early on through his later works—namely the idea of the *conscious breeding* of great individuals who are supposed to make the crowd their "instrument"[171]—would require an examination of other presuppositions of Nietzsche's thinking that would go beyond the framework of the present reflections.

Notes

Introduction

1. For example, some negative statements on the Greeks, whom Nietzsche esteemed so highly, refer to the time from Socrates on. "The pre-Socratic world remains inviolable for him," writes Karl Jaspers, *Nietzsche,* p. 239. See also note 28, below.

2. Thus, according to Walter Bröcker, in "Nietzsche und der europäische Nihilismus," p. 166, Nietzsche's anti-Semitic remarks are really motivated against Christianity, and his philo-Semitic ones against Germany. That, of course, falls short of the truth. More primarily, namely with regard to Nietzsche's theory of the will to power, Ludwig Klages (*Die psychologischen Errungenschaften Nietzsches,* pp. 152f.) understands Nietzsche's ambivalent valuation of the Jews more originally, namely in regard to his theory of the will to power: Nietzsche sees in them "the people of the mightiest and most successful priesthood there ever was." He admires their deep and strong will to power, their wisdom and genius; he opposes this will to power, insofar as it is ultimately aimed against life.

3. Cf. Martin Heidegger's comments on the apparent contradictoriness in Nietzsche's interpretation of the "dead": *Nietzsche* I:341–43.

4. Richard H. Grützmacher, *Nietzsche,* p. 143.

5. Alois Riehl, *Friedrich Nietzsche,* p. 25.

6. Wilhelm Windelband, *Lehrbuch der Geschichte der Philosophie,* pp. 577ff.

7. Paul Deussen, *Erinnerungen an Friedrich Nietzsche,* p. 100.

8. Karl Löwith called attention to this misuse in *Von Hegel zu Nietzsche,* p. 211. In the same passage Löwith gives a series of examples of the obvious and irresoluble contradictions in Nietzsche's works.

9. *Nietzsche als Philosoph,* p. 69.

10. Ibid., pp. 6f.

11. Ibid., p. 69.

12. "Zur Einführung," p. xxiii.

13. *Nietzsche, der Philosophy und Politiker,* pp. 79ff.

14. *Schopenhauer und Nietzsche,* p. ix.

15. *Die Zerstörung der Vernunft*, pp. 316f.

16. Jaspers, *Nietzsche*, p. 154.

17. Heidegger, *Nietzsche* I:78f.

18. *Nachlaß*, GA XII, p. 224.

19. "Why I Am So Wise," 2.

20. *Friedrich Nietzsche in seinen Werken*, p. 33.

21. Ibid., p. 23. Andreas-Salomé states, among other things, that Nietzsche's alleged "self-idolization" was rooted in the fact that he was a "dividual" [*sic*]: split into two essential natures, he related to one of them as to a higher being (ibid., pp. 34–39). That the other one had to be subjugated was expressed in his view of the struggle between master and slave morality. It was "no more than a magnified illustration of what goes on in the highest individual person, the cruel psychic process by which he must split into victim god and sacrificial animal. Here Nietzsche was describing the contradictoriness of his own ego" (ibid., pp. 196f.).

22. *Nietzsche, Versuch einer Mythologie*, p. 10.

23. Ibid., p. 15. Cf. also pp. 41, 52, 135, 196, 203, 213, 308.

24. Ibid., p. 8.

25. *Geist und Leben*, p. 85.

26. Ibid., p. 121.

27. Ibid., pp. 97f.

28. *Nachlaß*, XI, p. 135.

29. Ibid., p. 391.

30. "Epilogue."

31. *Nietzsches Philosophie der ewigen Wiederkehr des Gleichen*, pp. 13f.

32. *Nietzsches Philosophie*, pp. 173–76.

Chapter 1: Apparent Contradictions and Real Contraditions of the Will to Power

1. "If you want to become a person of standing you must hold your shadow too in honor" (HA II:81). Cf. also the preliminary sketch, in *Nachlaß*, 1878, KGW, IV/3, p. 369: "If one wants to have one's own embodied personality, one must not resist also to have a shadow." Against the adherents of socialist theories, Nietzsche writes: "If you would do away with firm opposition and differences in rank, you will also abolish all strong love, lofty attitudes, and the feeling of individuality" (WP 936).

2. On the reproach of biologism against Nietzsche, cf. Heidegger, *Nietzsche* vI:615ff.

3. "All knowledge that advances us is *an equating of what is not the same* but similar, i.e., it is essentially illogical. We obtain a concept only in this way and then act as if the concept 'man' were something actual, whereas it was formed by us only by abandoning all individual features" (*Nachlaß*, X, p. 171).

4. *Nachlaß*, XII, p. 28.

5. Cf. *Nachlaß*, XIII., pp. 21ff.

6. "Prior to logic, which operates everywhere with comparisons, equalization, assimi-

lation must have prevailed: and it continues to prevail, and logical thinking is itself a continual means of assimilation, of *wanting* to see identical cases" (*Nachlaß*, XIII, p. 236). Concept-formation and sensory perception collaborate in this. The latter, too, is determined by the compulsion to equate. Its "simplification, coarsening, emphasizing, and elaborating" are "supported by reason" (WP 521).

7. *Nachlaß*, XIII, p. 88.

8. Ibid., IX, p. 187.

9. Ibid., XII, p. 101. Cf. also WP 37: "Opposites suit a plebeian age because easier to comprehend."

10. A note from the time when *The Gay Science* was being written (1881–82), however, *reverses* this relation: "First belief in the persistence and sameness outside us arises—and only later, after a tremendous training in what is *outside us,* do we grasp *ourselves* as something *persistent* and *self-identical,* as something unconditional" (*Nachlaß*, XII, p. 45.)

11. *Nachlaß*, XIII, p. 59.

12. Ibid., XII, p. 45.

13. Ibid., XI, p. 235

14. Ibid., XIII, p. 62, cf. pp. 258f.

15. "All events, all motion, all becoming, as a determination of degrees and relations of force, as a *struggle* . . ." (WP 552).

16. *Nachlaß*, XI, p. 283.

17. Ibid., XII, p. 7.

18. Ibid., XI, p. 283.

19. Ibid., XIII, p. 70.

20. Ibid., XIV, p. 32.

21. The influence of A. Spir and G. Teichmüller on Nietzsche's thinking was of great significance for the development of this polemic—and not only for it. Cf. on this topic, K.-H. Dickopp, *Nietzsches Kritik des Ich-denke.* The first to call attention to the importance of Teichmüller for Nietzsche's philosophical development was H. Nohl ("Eine historische Quelle zu Nietzsches Perspektivismus: G. Teichmüller, *Die wirkliche und die scheinbare Welt*").

22. *Nachlaß*, XIV, p. 37.

23. Ibid., p. 419.

24. "Although we constantly need to make use of the language and habits of reason, still the appearance of constant self-contradiction does not militate against the justification of our doubt (namely in comprehending)" (*Nachlaß*, XIII, p. 52).

25. *Nachlaß*, IX, p. 264.

26. "Linguistic means of expression are useless for expressing 'becoming'" (WP 715).

27. "On Truth and Lying in an Extra-Moral Sense." Nietzsche continues in the cited passage: "As certainly as one leaf is never completely identical with any other one, so certainly has the concept 'leaf' been formed by arbitrarily disregarding these individual differences, by forgetting the distinctions, and now this gives rise to the idea that besides leaves there is in nature something that is 'leaf,' as it were a prototype, after which all leaves

were woven, sketched, traced off, colored, curled and painted, but by unskillful hands, so that no particular specimen turned out correctly and reliably as a faithful copy of the prototype. We call a person 'honest'; we ask: why did he act so honestly today? Our answer usually is: because of his honesty. Honesty! That means again: the leaf is the cause of leaves. For we know nothing of an essential quality that would be called 'honesty,' but we do know of individualized, and hence dissimilar actions which we equate by discarding the dissimilar and now characterize as honest actions; finally we formulate from them a *qualitas occulta* by the name of 'honesty.'"

28. *Nachlaß,* XIII, p. 254.

29. Ibid., p. 81.

30. Ibid., X, p. 151.

31. "A quality exists *for us,* i.e., is measured by us. If we remove the measure, what is then left of any quality!" (*Nachlaß,* X, p. 152).

32. *Nachlaß,* XIII, p. 133. Of course, Nietzsche does not mean that willing can be *without an end.* Rather, the following is true: "'Willing': means willing an end" (WP 260). Its difference from a concept of will marked by the idea of entelechy becomes especially clear in a note aimed against Hegel's teleologically determined idea of history. In this context he writes: "That my life has no purpose is clear from the accidentalness of my origin: *that I can set a purpose for myself is another matter.* But a state is not a purpose; rather, only we give it this purpose or that one" (*Nachlaß,* X, p. 275).

33. *Nachlaß,* XI, p. 161.

34. Schopenhauer, *Die Welt als Wille und Vorstellung,* vol. 1, 2, §17 (*Werke,* ed. A. Hübscher, vol. 2, p. 119).

35. Cf. *Nachlaß,* XII, p. 267.

36. Ibid., XIII, p. 262; cf. also p. 265.

37. Ibid., p. 254.

38. Ibid., XII, p. 156.

39. Ibid., XIII, p. 249.

40. Ibid., pp. 247f.

41. Such a "self-experience" is supposed to be fundamentally different from self-observation in which a "subject" seeks to obtain a view of his "subjectivity"—from that "self-reflection of the spirit" (WP 492) in which the intellect deceives itself about itself. It reaches beyond the phenomenalism of the latter to the real inner facts. "Guided by the body, we get to know man as a multiplicity of living creatures, partly struggling with one another, partly adjusted and subordinated to one another, which in approving their individual being involuntarily approve the whole" (*Nachlaß,* XIII, p. 169). In the starting point from the body "we gain the correct idea of our subject unity, namely as regents at the head of a community (not as 'souls' or 'life forces'), also of the dependence of these regents upon the ruled and of an order of rank and division of labor as the conditions that make possible the whole and its parts" (WP 492).

42. *Nachlaß,* XIII, p. 250.

43. Ibid., p. 249.

44. Ibid.

45. Ibid., p. 239. On the prejudice of separating the organic and the inorganic, cf. *Nachlaß*, XIII, p. 81 and WP 637. On the spirituality of each will-quantum, cf. *Nachlaß*, XIII, pp. 227, 227f., 232, and WP 462.

46. *Anhang* to *WzM*, XVI, p. 415; cf. *Nachlaß*, XIV, p. 327.

47. *Nachlaß*, XIV, p. 418.

48. Ibid., p. 420.

49. *Vorträge über Nietzsche. Versuch einer Wiedergabe seiner Gedanken*, p. 42, cf. p. 45.

50. This can be gathered from a previously unknown letter of Gast to E. Holzer, dated January 26, 1910, of which M. Montinari cites excerpts in the Appendix of vol. VIII/2 of the KGW (p. 475).

51. Italics added. Since the excerpt from the letter cited in the previous note goes beyond deciphering mishaps and describes Elisabeth Förster-Nietzsche's misuse of the sentence, it will be quoted here in full: ". . . on the chapter of 'Frau Förster's Sense of Truth,' I must tell you one of the examples that come to my mind and make me laugh—what sorts of things must one share responsibility for as a former archivist, things that one can never be responsible for as an honest person. In 1904, when we were printing Vol. II of the biography [meaning E. Förster-Nietzsche, *Das Leben Friedrich Nietzsches*, II/2, Leipzig, 1904], Nietzsche's letter, in which he praises our then 29–year old Kaiser for negative statements about anti-Semites and the *Kreuzzeitung*, also was included. Now, you know how much Frau Förster is burning to interest the Kaiser in Nietzsche and if possible to get him to make a positive statement about Nietzsche's tendency. What does she do for that purpose? (Please pick up Vol. II of the biography.) She inserts a sentence that is not in the letter at all, which is dated from the end (not the beginning) of October 1888:—she writes on p. 890, line 9 from the bottom, the sentence '*The will to power as principle surely would be understandable to him* (the Kaiser)!' You will remember from where this sentence is taken—from sketches for the preface to *The Will to Power*, which is printed in Vol. XIV, p. 420. The handwritten text of this sketch (written on the inner oil-cloth cover of Notebook W IX) is one of the most difficult tasks in deciphering Nietzsche. Before me, the Horneffers had already tried their hand at it; but their deciphered text displayed more gaps than words. But precisely this sentence was the only thing they had completely deciphered. Such prior work is often more of a hindrance than a help to the next person who works at it. Enough: I, as the final decipherer of the text, failed to see at the time that the Horneffer's deciphering of the preface-sketch, '*The will to power as principle would already (schon) be understandable to them* [the Germans],' can absolutely not be right. And when I took up Notebook W IX in April of last year, my suspicion was confirmed that it had to read without question '*difficult*' (schwer) to 'understand' rather than 'surely understandable.' Isn't it a very good joke that if Frau Förster wanted to be exact, she would now have to have printed "'the will to power as principle would be hard for him (the Kaiser) to understand'?!"

Gast apparently did not know that Frau Förster-Nietzsche had smuggled not only one sentence into the letter allegedly addressed to her by Nietzsche. Nietzsche had not written this letter at all. Like many other letters, it is a forgery by Nietzsche's sister. Cf. K. Schlechta's "Philologischer Nachbericht" to his three-volume edition of Nietzsche's works, III:1410ff.; also KGW, VIII/2, p. 475.

52. *Nachlaß,* XIV, p. 420.

53. Ibid., XIII, p. 245.

54. Ibid., p. 70.

55. Cf. also ibid., XIII, p. 274.

56. *Nietzsche* I:,72; Eng.: I:60f.

57. Ibid. II:103.

58. Ibid. I:73; Eng.: I:61.

59. Ibid. II:103

60. Ibid. II:36.

61. Ibid. I:73; Eng.: I:61.

62. Ibid. I:77; I:64.

63. Ibid. I:73; Eng.: I:61.

64. Ibid. I:78.

65. Ibid. I:76f.

66. See note 32, above.

67. *Nietzsche* I:73.

68. [The dictionary meaning of *Punktation* is "treaty agreement." Walter Kaufmann translates it thus and explains in a footnote that the "meaning is unclear but the point perhaps is that the will is not a single entity but more like a constantly shifting federation or alliance of drives." *Trans.*]

69. Nietzsche's perspectivism does not contradict his theory of the continual flux of all events. We must think of "the whole of the organic world" as "a stringing together of creatures with fictional little worlds around them" (*Nachlaß,* XIII, p. 80).

70. *Nachlaß,* XIV, p. 325; cf. WP 656, and *Nachlaß,* XIII, p. 259, XIV, p. 37.

71. In a "Lecture on the Pre-Platonics," which Nietzsche delivered several times in the 1870s, in his portrayal of Heraclitus made current by digressions into contemporary science he says: "Nature is just as unending inwardly as toward the outside: we now reach down to the cell and to parts of the cell: but there is absolutely no limit where one could say, here is the last point inward; becoming never ceases down to the infinitely small" (XIX, p. 176). A. Anders points out that Nietzsche here is departing from K. E. von Baer's train of thought, which he was following in a digression, and giving room to his own reflections (K. Schlechta and A. Anders, *Fr. Nietzsche. Von den verborgenen Anfängen seines Philosophierens,* pp. 66f.).

72. Thus the regent within an organization is also dependent on his subjects: WP 492; cf. *Nachlaß,* XIII, pp. 243f.

Chapter 2: The Problem of Contradictions in Nietzsche's
        Philosophy of History

1. *Nachlaß,* XIII, p. 321.

2. The components always exist only in what they constitute; they are fully comprised in it. They do not form a first reality, which then creates a second one for itself. Nietzsche, then, does not let the two-world metaphysics in by the back door after he has thrown it out of the house of his philosophy.

3. *Nachlaß*, XIV, p. 203.

4. Ibid., X, p. 406.

5. Ibid., XII, p. 367.

6. Ibid., X, p. 352.

7. They are untimely only insofar as they say what the time does not want to hear about itself, although it is "about time." Nietzsche, later looking back to them, sees himself as "the most modern of the moderns" (*Nachlaß*, XIV, p. 373). In 1875 and 1876, Nietzsche still intended to continue the series of *Untimely Meditations* for years. On his projected programs, cf. *Nachlaß*, X, pp. 473ff., and also the fragments KGW, IV/1, pp. 85f. and 128 (edited by F. Koegel), as well as the still unedited fragment 16 [12] KGW, IV/2, p. 386.

8. This gave E. Rohde "the impression that some items and passages had *been polished only for himself*, and then, without being completely recast, had simply been inserted into the whole." So he writes in a letter to Nietzsche dated March 24, 1874 (Ges. Br. II, p. 452). Nietzsche did not respond to this criticism.

9. What K. Schlechta writes in *Nietzsches Verhältnis zur Historie* should be noted: "The time when the *Untimely Meditations* were conceived and composed (1872–1875) is especially rich in ambiguous ideas, ambivalent thoughts, notes that would yet be repressed. Some things that would come to light only later are already contained in the notebooks; indeed, in the *Untimely Meditations* themselves the fluctuating and iridescent passages keep increasing . . ." (*Der Fall Nietzsche*, p. 56). Thus, even before publication of the second *Untimely Meditation*—especially before the essay "On Truth and Lying in an Extra-Moral Sense," which Nietzsche never published—thoughts are formulated that go far beyond what found expression in *On the Uses and Disadvantages of History for Life* (cf. K. Schlechta and A. Anders, *Fr. Nietzsche*, pp. 10–20, 48). Attempts to study Nietzsche's development chronologically face very unusual difficulties from peculiar discrepancies between written sketches and notes that were in part included in later publications and what was published at the time of such writings.

10. Here Nietzsche undertakes only a first and tentative step in the direction of a historical understanding of the modern excess of historical sense, when he derives this from the medieval "*memento mori*" (HL 8). A generalized remark from the year 1873 states: "*How science* could become what it now is can be clarified only from the development of religion" (*Nachlaß*, X, p. 185).

11. To what extent this work is based on personal experiences can be seen from the foreword: "I have striven to depict a feeling by which I am constantly tortured; I revenge myself upon it by handing it over to the public. . . . And it may partly exonerate me when I give an assurance that the experiences which evoked those tormenting feelings were mostly my own and that I have drawn on the experiences of others only for purposes of comparison; and further, that it is only to the extent that I am a pupil of earlier times,

especially the Hellenic, that though a child of the present time I was able to acquire such untimely experiences" (HL, "Foreword").

12. [Hollingdale's translation omits the word *Ueberschwemmung* = flood, deluge.— *Trans.*].

13. In the *Nachlaß* to *Untimely Meditations* is found the note: "The number of historical works appearing each year! Added to which almost all of archeology belongs there! And moreover in almost all sciences just about the preponderant mass of works is historical, except for mathematics and individual disciplines in medicine and the natural sciences" (*Nachlaß* X, pp. 271f.).

14. Nietzsche's critique of *scientific knowledge in general,* expressed early in his works, has numerous points of departure. It would require a separate treatise. The following remarks will mention only a few aspects that acquired essential relevancy for his critique of *historical science.* Nietzsche's belief that historical science is the root cause of the disorganized spirit of the times has earned him repeated criticism, which will be treated here because of its fundamental significance. K. Hillebrand was the first to express it ("Ueber historisches Wissen und historischen Sinn," 1892): "Nietzsche speaks as if the entire German nation had enjoyed an academic education and had suffocated in historical knowledge" (p. 316). It is "a basic error" of Nietzsche's and of related minds "that they still consider Germany to be a huge university and believe that each German is an Associate or Full Professor of History and Philology. If they ever went to Hamburg or Chemnitz, they would soon enough find too many 'unhistorical' Germans and if they looked a little into the professional activities of German civilian officials and military officers, they would soon become convinced that the 'hypertrophied virtue' of historiography does not prevent them from acting swiftly, surely, and opportunely" (p. 306). Hillebrand believes that the majority of educated persons, who according to him alone deserve the name of nation (p. 323), are interested only in "the direction that the writer finds in historical development or inserts into it, or even allows to be imposed on him by his readers." Of course, "the citizens or officers who have worked their way through the works of those scholars, or have absorbed either the after-effect or selections of such works, are relatively unconcerned" with "study of the sources," which "the authors are so proud of" (p. 307). But all this is not at all the problem that Nietzsche has in mind. Precisely because the educated persons are interested only in *direction,* they necessarily face a chaos of contradictory valuations resulting from the diverse, historically mediated positions of modern historians. The fundamental difference between Nietzsche and his critics consists in the fact that he perceives the extreme consequence of historicism, namely historical relativism, while it remains hidden from them. It may have seemed to Hillebrand that in 1875, when his critique first appeared, the nationalistic and anti-Catholic spirit, pervasive since the 1820s, still determined the general understanding of history (cf. p. 307). But Nietzsche sensed the symptoms of disintegration that were and are today still spreading behind this and other facades. Nor were they limited to "the educated." Their uncertainty is projected in all directions. Thus Nietzsche sees that the people's "unity of feeling" is being lost; "the people falls asunder into the cultured with a miseducated and misled subjectivity . . . and

the uncultured with an inaccessible subjectivity." Since "the instinct of the nation" is disturbed, it no longer comes out to meet the great productive spirits (HL 4). "Culture without a people," Nietzsche notes during an enumeration of "factors of contemporary culture" in the year 1873 (*Nachlaß*, X, p. 253). Beyond this, Nietzsche also considers in *Untimely Meditations* the effects of the general dissemination of the "theories of sovereign becoming" (theories "of the fluidity of all concepts, types and species, of the lack of any cardinal distinction between man and animal"), i.e., ultimately of the loss of faith in any suprahistorical powers. If these theories are "thrust upon the people for another generation with the rage for instruction that has now become normal, no one should be surprised if the people perishes of petty egoism, falls apart, and ceases to be a people; in its place systems of individual egoism, brotherhoods for the rapacious exploitation of the non-brothers, and similar creations of utilitarian vulgarity may perhaps appear in the arena of the future" (HL 9).

15. The dominant position of science allows an "unselective urge for knowledge" to prevail. It is then, Nietzsche notes, "like the unselective sexual drive—a sign of *crudeness!*" (*Nachlaß*, X, p. 111).

16. *Nachlaß*, X, p. 155.

17. Historical knowledge is "purely luxurious; it does not elevate contemporary culture at all" (*Nachlaß* X, p. 154).

18. "Through isolation, some series of concepts can become so vehement that they draw the strength of all other drives to themselves. For example, the cognitive impulse" (*Nachlaß*, X, p. 174).

19. *Nachlaß*, X, p. 416.

20. Ibid., p. 255.

21. Ibid., p. 268.

22. *Nachlaß*, 1875, KGW, IV/1, p. 117.

23. Ibid., X, p. 154.

24. In 1862, Nietzsche even asked himself: "Is man perhaps not merely the evolution of the stone via the medium plant, animal?" (BAW, II, p. 56). He ascribes the antithesis "organic—inorganic" to the "world of appearances" (*Nachlaß*, XIV, p. 36). If, however, the organic exists, then it cannot have had an origin (*Nachlaß*, XIII, p. 232, XIV, p. 35): it must be eternal. Besides the *elimination* of the difference between inorganic and organic, we also find attempts to work out the *difference* between them (*Nachlaß*, XIII, p. 231) or to describe the *transition* from one to the other (*Nachlaß*, XIII, p. 227). In all three cases Nietzsche's basic thesis of the seamless unity of the reality of becoming remains untouched.

25. *Nachlaß*, X, p. 481.

26. Occasionally, for the Nietzsche of the *Untimely Meditations,* this illusion becomes the truth, and the "truth of becoming" becomes the illusion. A note from the year 1874 may serve as illustration: "Does not every culture want to withdraw the individual human from the pushing, shoving, and crushing of the historical stream and to let him understand that he is not only a historically limited being, but also an absolutely extrahistorical, unending being, with whom all existence began and will cease? I cannot be-

lieve that this is the human being who with dismal industriousness creeps, learns, calculates, politicizes, reads books, bears children, and lies down to die—that is surely only an insect larva, something contemptible and transitory, and totally superficial. To live in this way means only to have a bad dream. Now the philosopher and the artist shout to the dreamer a few words taken from the waking world: will they awaken the restless sleeper? Rarely enough: usually he hears in these words nothing that would disturb his dream, he weaves them in and increases the unclarity and the crowding of his life" (*Nachlaß*, X, pp. 320f.). Schopenhauer's influence here surfaces powerfully once again.

27. His statements on this subject are indebted, down to individual formulations, to his reading of #153 of Schopenhauer's *Parerga und Paralipomena,* vol. 2 (WW, ed. A. Hübscher, vol. 6). Schopenhauer writes, for instance, of the animal that it knows only an "extremely short tether" of fear and hope (p. 314); in Nietzsche, the herd is "fettered to the moment and its pleasure or displeasure" (HL 1) [*literally:* tied with the short rope of its pleasure or displeasure to the peg of the moment.—*Trans.*]. On the next page Schopenhauer speaks of the "complete containment in the present" (p. 315); in Nietzsche, the animal is "contained in the present, like a number without any awkward fraction" (HL 1).

28. *Nachlaß,* X, p. 255.

29. Jakob Burckhardt named the three antitheses at the end of his letter, dated Feb. 25, 1874, in which he thanked Nietzsche for sending him a copy of the second *Untimely Meditation* and spoke of the "antagonism between historical knowledge and ability (here: between the fatal aspect of historiography and life's claim) or existence (here: between becoming and being) and in turn between the enormous accumulation of knowledge in general and the material impulses of the time" (here: disgregation and the need for organization). Cited from E. Salin, *J. Burckhardt und Nietzsche,* p. 208. On the interpretation of the Burckhardt letter, cf. ibid. pp. 113f.; cf. also K. Schlechta, *Nietzsches Verhältnis zur Historie,* pp. 62ff.

30. *Nachlaß,* X, p. 164.

31. Ibid., p. 268.

32. Ibid., p. 272. "Knowledge of the higher and better," Nietzsche writes, can become "so powerful that one no longer has the courage at all even to be able to do the lesser. This is the greatest danger of history" (*Nachlaß,* X, p. 279).

33. Lack of authority is one of the characteristics of the modern era: *Nachlaß,* XIV, p. 203.

34. *Nachlaß,* XI, p. 196.

35. "To a eunuch one woman is like another, simply a woman, woman in herself, the eternally unapproachable—and it is thus a matter of indifference what they do so long as history itself is kept nice and 'objective,' bearing in mind that those who want to keep it so are ever incapable of making history themselves" (HL 5).

36. Cf. *Nachlaß* XIV, p. 207.

37. In *On the Uses and Disadvantages of History for Life,* Nietzsche trusts in the healing instincts of youth. In order to employ history again someday *"in the service of the life"* he

has learned to live, a struggle is needed against dry scholarship, which has been elevated as an ideal in "the *historical education of modern man*" (HL 10) but in reality *ruins* him for life. The Greeks are held up as model. Threatened by the "danger of being overwhelmed by what was past and foreign, they gradually learned *to organize chaos* by . . . thinking back . . . to their real needs, and letting their pseudo-needs die out" (HL 10). The youth of his own time needed abstinence from history, indeed "indifference and reserve . . . even towards much that is good" that was handed down by tradition; "up to the point at which they will be sufficiently healthy again" to employ the past *under the domination* of life. (HL 10).

38. Cf. W. Müller-Lauter, "Metaphysik und Wissenschaft in Nietzsches Aufklärungs-philosophie," pp. 156ff.

39. In a self-critical reminiscence from the years 1881 to 1883, Nietzsche writes: "Behind my *first period* grins the face of *Jesuitism,* I mean the conscious adherence to illusion and compulsory incorporation of the same as the *basis of culture*" (*Nachlaß,* XII, p. 212).

40. *Nachlaß,* X, p. 352.

41. Ibid., XII, pp. 216f. Two other "series of ancestors" whom Nietzsche names: "My predecessors, Heraclitus, Empedocles, Spinoza, Goethe" (*Nachlaß,* XIV, p. 263). "When I speak of Plato, Pascal, Spinoza and Goethe, I know that their blood flows in my veins" (*Nachlaß,* XII, p. 217).

42. Those who translated books in past times, Nietzsche writes in *The Gay Science,* really transposed them into the present age. Are they not right when they seem to ask us: "Should we not make new for ouselves what is old and find ourselves in it? Should we not have the right to breathe our own soul into this dead body?" (GS 83). Finally he is convinced that "historical knowledge is only *re-experiencing*" (*Nachlaß,* IX, p. 264). "A fact, a work is eloquent in a new way for every age and every *new* type of man. History always enunciates *new truths*" (WP 974). Such re-experiencing is, like all cognition, always also a "falsification" (*Nachlaß,* XIV, p. 134). So there is "no 'objective history'": the appropriation of history always occurs "under the guidance of the impulses and drives" (*Nachlaß,* XIV, p. 314), which must be interpreted from the perspective of present life.

43. As early as 1872, Nietzsche wrote that "enormous artistic forces are necessary against iconic history and against natural science" (*Nachlaß,* X, p. 114). While the horizons are always changing in the latter two, the work of art *simplifies,* concentrates "under one law," as a later note states (*Nachlaß,* XIV, p. 134).

44. *Nachlaß,* X, p. 252.

45. The points of departure for such reservations are diverse. Let us mention here only: historicizing *egalitarianism:* Nietzsche speaks of the effrontry of those who use the historical sense (*Nachlaß,* XIV, p. 182). Behind it he sees "an offensive scepticism toward the difference of rank between one person and another," to which even the dead are subjected (ibid., p. 189); *lack of ideals:* the historical sense is "a proof of mistrust toward one's own ideal, or lack thereof" (*Nachlaß,* XII, p. 136; cf. XIV, p. 213). "By seeking to know how everything *came to be,*" one flees from "ideal-formation and improvement" (*Nachlaß,* XIV, p. 189); *loss of unity:* the historical sense, scattering in the multifarious, seems to be "a sign

of *weakness* and *lack of unity*" (ibid., p. 207); *loss of good taste:* the historical sense opens understanding for so many other things, for almost all, that it dulls the look for the noble, the intrinsically perfect (BGE 224).

46. Preface of 1886, p. 1.

47. *Nachlaß,* 1878, KGW, IV/3, p. 351.

48. It is presented expressly against Plato (*Nachlaß,* XIV, p. 207), Leibniz, Kant (*Nachlaß,* XIII, p. 10), and the English moral philosophers (GM I:2).

49. Cf. also AC 4, p. 126: "The European of today is of far less value than the European of the Renaissance."

50. *Nachlaß,* XIII, p. 321.

51. The fighters "*against history,*" that is to say, against "the blind power of the actual," receive the young Nietzsche's highest esteem (HL 8). The greatest among them form a republic of geniuses, in Schopenhauer's sense. One misunderstands their effectiveness if one believes that this republic of geniuses is completely absorbed by the process of history. Those great men live beyond time "contemporaneously" (HL 9); history is here nothing else but the conditions that make possible the timeless conversation between the high intellects.

52. Cf. *Nachlaß,* XIII, p. 322: "The first insight is that hitherto there was no plan, neither for human beings nor for a people."

53. "The very crudest accidents were the most commanding on the whole—and they still are" (*Nachlaß,* XIII, p. 322).

54. Cf. *Nachlaß,* X, p. 402: "Whoever does not grasp how brutal and meaningless history is will also not understand the urge to make history meaningful." In efforts to prove its rationality, Nietzsche sees at work the "born theologians," who falsify reality (*Nachlaß,* 1875, KGW IV/1, p. 152).

55. EH, "Why I Am a Destiny," 9, p. 333.

56. *Nachlaß,* XIII, p. 78. In a critical remark on Hegel's philosophy of history, Nietzsche writes: "every story must have its purpose, hence also the history of a people, the history of the world. This means: we demand stories only with purposes. But we do not *demand* any stories of the world process, because we consider it a hoax to speak of that. That my life has no purpose is clear from the very accidentalness of my origin: *that I can set a purpose for myself is something else.* But a state has no purpose: rather we merely give it this purpose or that" (*Nachlaß,* X, p. 275).

57. *Nachlaß,* XIII, p. 284.

58. Insofar as a religious-transcendentally determined meaning was ascribed to previous history, "a *lie* was called truth." Nietzsche in *Ecce Homo* sees his fate as "to stand in opposition to the mendaciousness of millennia." Although he can now exclaim: "I contradict as has never been contradicted before," he immediately adds that he is "nonetheless the opposite of a No-saying spirit" (EH, "Why I Am a Destiny," 1).

59. Although G. Häuptner, in his critique of the second *Untimely Meditation,* points out that historical culture in the sense of historical science could not be blamed for the diminution of the shaping power of life, as Nietzsche claimed, but rather that the shap-

ing power must already have declined for such a thing as historical culture to emerge; still attention must be called to the fact that the later Nietzsche drew from this the same conclusion as Häuptner demands: that historical culture could be only "a symptom of the degeneration of life, not however the cause of its degeneration" (*Die Geschichtsansicht des jungen Nietzsche,* p. 95n).

60. In *On the Genealogy of Morals,* not only "all modern history writing" is described as a *symptom* of declining life (GM III:24), but modern science in general (GM III:25).

61. *Nachlaß,* XI, p. 356.

62. Ibid., XII, p. 238.

63. Ibid., X, p. 483.

64. Therefore Nietzsche foretells the utimate disintegration of the monstrous state that he assumes will arise in the future. It will swallow up the big state that will have previously swallowed up the small state. The monstrous state will have to burst apart, "because in the end it will be lacking the belt to encompass its body: the hostility of neighbors. The splitting apart into atomistic state-structures is the furthest perspective of European politics that is yet visible" (*Nachlaß,* XI, p. 139).

65. *Values* are, for Nietzsche, "the results of certain perspectives of utility, designed to maintain and increase human constructs of domination" (WP 12, p. 14).

66. *Nachlaß,* XIII, p. 327.

67. The above-depicted threefold division of history is also discussed by Karl Reinhardt in *Nietzsche und die Geschichte,* p. 298. Reinhard writes: "The simple affirmation and denial that speak from his [i.e., Nietzsche's] youthful works, his *Untimely Meditations,* his approval of the great pasts, above all the Greeks, and the disapproval of his own 'time' give rise—the more he feels called to be the destroyer and creator of new values—to a threefold pattern. The parts of this pattern are: 1. prehistoric time; 2. historical time; 3. the present. Indeed, the present either as the end of what came before, or as the beginning of a different kind of future (for the two are basically the same). The pattern is thus really very simple: formerly—then—now." However, Reinhardt thus formulated the three phases in such a way that the forward-running time suggests the idea of progress, which is based on it and which Nietzsche's later philosophy of history precisely opposes. The leveling to this pattern by no means does justice to Nietzsche's awareness of the problem, as will yet be shown. That, for Nietzsche, the future that must be planned by the powerful is at the same time (though admittedly not in a clearly defined manner) supposed to be a return to a former stage, while preserving on a new and higher plane what was gained in the course of the first revaluation, recalls rather, Hegel's way of thinking. But one must not allow oneself to be misled into wanting to find in Nietzsche "only a bad Hegelian construction of history, whose results are already established prior to investigation," as A. Riehl does (*Fr. Nietzsche. Der Künstler und der Denker,* p. 114). Nietzsche, rather, is compelled by his own questions to wonder about the future of mankind in his own particular way.

68. In the concept of the *extra-moral* Nietzsche denies only the prevalent "herd animal morality . . . beside which, before which, and after which many other types, above all *higher* moralities, are, or ought to be, possible" (BGE 202).

69. "With all the tensions of the past three hundred years, for example, we have not yet reattained the man of the Renaissance, and the man of the Renaissance, in turn, is inferior to the man of antiquity" (WP 881). The tendency to call for such a return aims, as the context shows, for anti-morality or pre-morality.

70. A more thorough analysis would have to show to what extent as a consequence of Nietzsche's thinking "the objective is only a false concept of a genus and an antithesis *within* the subjective?" (WP 560).

71. *Nachlaß,* XIII, p. 69.

72. Cf. *Nachlaß,* XII, pp. 13f.: "The task is to *see things as they are*! The means: to be able to see out of a hundred eyes, out of *many* persons! It was a wrong way to stress the impersonal and to label seeing out of the neighbor's eye as moral. To see *many* neighbors and out of *many* eyes and out of sheerly personal eyes—is the right way. The 'impersonal' is only the *weakened* personal, dull." However, Nietzsche adds that such impersonality "here and there can also be useful." Since, as described above, the second and longest phase of objectivity is characterized by the weakening of subjectivity, it must, for Nietzsche, represent a confirmation of his genealogy of objectivity, that hitherto "the *branches* of knowledge where *weak* personalities are useful have been elaborated *best*." He names *mathematics* as an example.

73. K. Schlechta is right when he writes: "Nietzsche on the whole—until about the year 1875—denied 'history writing,' especially extreme history writing, 'historicism,' because it is an expression of a nihilistic impulse; he approved it from approximately 1876 on, because it leads to nihilism, to that final condition which Nietzsche saw ever more clearly as the indispensable precondition for *his* new beginning" (*Nietzsches Verhältnis zur Historie,* p. 60, cf. p. 54).

74. *Nachlaß,* XIII, pp. 34f., cf. XIV, p. 102.

75. Two examples for Nietzsche's idea of the unity of antitheses in *one* person have already been presented here (this problem will be discussed in chapter 6). "Formerly, the clergyman and the 'free thinker' were opponents: now, a kind of rebirth of the two in one person is possible" (*Nachlaß,* 1876, KGW, IV/2, p. 391, cf. p. 400). "I imagine future thinkers in whom European and American unrest is combined with Asiatic contemplation inherited in a hundred ways: such a combination finds a solution to the world-riddle" (*Nachlaß,* 1876, KGW, IV/2, p. 402).

76. *Nachlaß,* XIV, pp. 44f.

77. Ibid., XI, p. 246.

78. *Anhang* to *WzM,* XVI, 417.

79. *Nachlaß,* XI, p. 277.

80. At the time of writing *Daybreak,* Nietzsche noted: "Certainly the world would be infinitely farther along, if the human intellect could have been in charge instead of chance; it would also have saved billions of years" (*Nachlaß,* XI, p. 175).

81. Its dissolution is in the end part and parcel of the genealogy of morality. But this leads, as Nietzsche noted in the first half of the 1880s, "in its practical consequence to the

atomistic individual and then even to the breakdown of the individual into majorities"
(*Nachlaß*, XII, p. 358).

82. See note 45, above.

Chapter 3: Nihilism as Will to Nothingness

1. We cannot go into details here on the history of this concept. Some hints, however, should be given. In France this history goes back to the French Revolution, where the word "*nihiliste*" was used to designate an attitude of political or religious indifference. The philosophical use of the term is first found in F. H. Jacobi, who in his *Sendschreiben an Fichte* (1799) labels his idealism as nihilism. From then on the term plays a role in various philosophical and political disputes. Its application to the movement of French socialism in the nineteenth century and to the "left Hegelians" (who are the heirs to the reproach of nihilism that had first been leveled against the idealist philosophies of Fichte, Schelling, and Hegel) determined the use of the word in the social and political struggles in Russia. From there it radiated back to the central European language area, so blurring the ongoing history of the term that I. Turgenev, in his *Literatur- und Lebenserinnerungen* (German edition of 1892, p. 105) cound state that he had invented the word, an error that was repeated after him until our time (e.g., by G. Benn, *Nach dem Nihilismus*, 1932, GW I, 1959, pp. 156f., and by A. Stender-Petersen, *Geschichte der russischen Literatur*, II, 1957, p. 251). Turgenev, however, was not even the first to use the word in Russia; quite a few authors used it there before him.

2. The spiritual relationship between Nietzsche and Dostoevsky has frequently been brought out since the turn of the century, especially in France, occasioned above all by the translation of D. S. Mereshkovski's book on Tolstoy and Dostoevsky (1903). A. Suarès, A. Gide, and L. Shestov have taken up this theme. On this topic cf. H. F. Minssen: "Die französische Kritik und Dostoevski." E. Benz discussed Dostoevsky's influence on Nietzsche in *Nietzsches Ideen zur Geschichte des Christentums*, pp. 83–93, with consideration of the works of Minnssen and Ch. Andler. Benz published an expanded and partly revised version of his book under the title *Nietzsches Ideen zur Geschichte des Christentums und der Kirche* in the year 1956. He also cites works of Shestov and Tshizhevski on the Nietzsche-Dostoevsky problem (p. 92). This problem is quite as inadequately treated in both versions of his book as in the two authors he cites. The extent of Dostoevsky's influence on Nietzsche had to remain unknown in any case, as long as there was incomplete knowledge of Nietzsche's reading of Dostoevsky. Only recently have G. Colli and M. Montinari, in Volume VIII/2 of the KGW (pp. 383–95), published the excerpts that Nietzsche copied from the French translation of Dostoevsky's novel *Les Possédés*. Only by taking into consideration Nietzsche's knowledge of *The Demons* can one do justice to his understanding of Dostoevsky, and moreover of Russian nihilism.

3. Cf. M. Montinari, *Das Leben Friedrich Nietzsches in den Jahren 1875–1979*. Chronik, in: KGW, IV/4, p. 27. I additionally owe M. Montinari important references to sources inaccessible to me about Nietzsche's reading of these two Russian authors. Unfortunately

they do not provide information as to whether Nietzsche read Turgenev's novels *Fathers and Sons* (1862) and *New Land* (1872), in which that author uses the term "nihilism." But I consider it highly probable.

4. F. Würzbach states this in vol. XIX of the *Musarion-Ausgabe*, p. 432. Cf. however O. Weiß, in GA, XVI, pp. 515f.

5. Ch. Andler, *Nietzsche, sa vie et sa pensée*, 6 vols., 1920ff., III:418, 424.

6. The first volume appeared in 1883; the second, in 1885. H. Platz, "Nietzsche und Bourget," pp. 177–86, cannot confirm Ch. Andler's assumption that Nietzsche read not only the second, but also the first volume of Bourget's *Essais* (p. 181). But there is no doubt about it. Among other authors, Bertram (*Nietzsche*, p. 231) called attention to the fact that Nietzsche's description of literary decadence is "a paraphrase of sentences" from Bourget's first volume. Proof that Nietzsche read this volume is found in a still unpublished fragment in a notebook from Summer 1887, which information I owe to M. Montinari: "*Style* of *decadence* in Wagner: the individual turn of phrase becomes *sovereign*, subordination and adjustment become accidental" (Bourget, p. 25).

7. *Essais* I, 1887, pp. 13ff. As an example of the "universal nausea before the inadequacies of this world," Bourget names "the murderous rage of the St. Petersburg conspirators, Schopenhauer's books, the furious arsenies of the Commune, and the implacable misanthropy of the naturalist novelists."

8. Ibid., p. 15.

9. Nietzsche writes thus about Bourget in EH, "Why I Am So Clever," 3.

10. *Nachlaß*, XIV, p. 339.

11. Ibid., XIII, p. 263.

12. Ibid., p. 257.

13. Ibid., p. 71, cf. pp. 164f.

14. Here we must forego a further investigation of Nietzsche's understanding of consciousness.

15. *Nachlaß*, XII, pp. 72f.

16. Cf. WP 619.

17. As an example of how one can simplify the *antitheticalness of the real*, which Nietzsche is trying to show, into the *absurdity of his philosophical thinking*, L. Klages's statements on the "priestly will to power" can be cited: "If it were not the Christian in Nietzsche who with his doctrine of the will to power is addressing confessors of the will to power, namely, Christians, even his sparkling dialectics and incomparable art of description would hardly have sufficed to hide the self-contradiction even where it emerges very openly from within to the outside. The will to life is supposed to be life; life, the will to power. Now precisely the priest proclaims the most stubborn, relentless will to power that never fails even under the most difficult conditions, . . . becomes master over warriers, kings, over all mankind: then he would most clearly be the mode of appearance of *life* that is most worthy of respect. But he supposedly represents the power will of a sickness, indeed a power will of weakness and a will to nothingness. Is one to believe that anyone except Nietz-

sche himself . . . fails to notice the complete vacuity of such turns of phrase?" (*Die psychologischen Errungenschaften Nietzsches*, p. 196).

18. See chapter 1, note 32.

19. "First conquering the feeling of power, then mastering (organizing) it—it regulates what has been overcome for its preservation and *thus it preserves what has been overcome itself*" (*Nachlaß*, XII, p. 106).

20. *Nachlaß*, XIII, p. 170.

21. The cited passage does not speak of *one* "will to power" engaged in a "struggle with itself" and thereby doubled, as E. Biser, says, interpreting it as a "principle" (*Gott ist tot*, pp. 169ff.).

22. E. Fink finds in Nietzsche's writings after *Zarathustra* an ambiguity in the use of the terms *life* and *will to power*. Thus Nietzsche speaks of power "brilliantly . . . in the sense of ontological universality and then again in the sense of the ontological model" (*Nietzsches Philosophie*, p. 128). Fink accordingly distinguishes between the "transcendental value-plan of existence" and "a 'contentual,' 'material' interpretation of life" in Nietzsche. The transition from the one to the other is, for Fink, "perhaps the most disputable point in Nietzsche's philosophy." This disputableness also crept into his dual understanding of the will to power. The will to power was, firstly, "the basic tendency in the movement of all finite being," expressing itself, for example, as much in the heroic-tragic valuation as in Christian morality. "So understood, *everything* is will to power." Secondly, it was given a particular content and meaning, such as that of the heroic mode of thinking. Nietzsche did not succeed in overcoming such ambiguity. The estimation according to strength and weakness was nothing but a valuation of Nietzsche's, which represented only one possibility of *life's valuating activity of life*, of the "great player." Fink asks whether from the standpoint of the universal as the "ultimate gambler," and "player," "all values are not of equal rank"? "Are they not all equally forms in which life tries its hand for a period of time?" (p. 122). The ontological dimension of life or of the will to power, prior to anything ontic, is a construction of Fink's. Nietzsche not only does not need the presupposition of such a universal; it contradicts his thinking, as was shown above. The ambiguity that Fink discovers in Nietzsche was inserted into the philosopher he is interpreting by Fink himself.

23. *Nachlaß*, XII, p. 273.

24. *Nachlaß*, 1875, KGW, IV/1, p. 335.

25. But the species did not preserve itself through them. In truth "there is no species"—in the sense of such an active subject—"but solely sheerly diverse individual beings." There is also no "nature," which "wants to 'preserve the species,'" but rather only the fact that "many similar beings with similar conditions of existence" more easily preserve themselves "than abnormal beings" (*Nachlaß*, XII, p. 73).

26. See chapter 2, note 54.

27. *Nachlaß*, XII, p. 262.

28. A logical consequence of Nietzsche's thinking is that even the act of suicide is the expression of a power-will: in his self-extinction the suicidal person wants to triumph over life.

Chapter 4: Nihilism and Christianity

1. [Walter Kaufmann here translates *innere Folgerichtigkeit* as "inner consequences."— Trans.]. Nietzsche, in his *Philosophy in the Tragic Age of the Greeks,* disagrees with the view that the Greeks in truth had "merely imported" the essentials of their philosophical thinking from the Orient (*Nachlaß,* X, pp. 12f.).

2. Cf. *Nachlaß,* XIII, p. 103.

3. On Epicurus, cf. AC 30.

4. "Why I Am So Clever."

5. *Nachlaß,* XIII, pp. 17f.

6. Ibid., XIV, p. 244.

7. Nietzsche wrote to Gast on November 10, 1887: "Volume II of the *Journal des Goncourt* has come out; the most interesting novelty. It deals with the years 1862–65; in it the famous '*diners chez Magny*' are most vividly described, those dinners which brought together twice per month the then most intellectual and sceptical band of Paris personalities (Saint-Beuve, Flaubert, Théophile Gautier, Taine, Renan, the Goncourts, Schérer, Gavarni, occasionally Turgenev, etc.). Exasperated pessimism, cynicism, nihilism, alternating with boisterousness and good humor; I myself would not fit badly in there—I know these gentlemen by heart, so much so that I'm actually sick and tired of them. One has to be more radical; actually they all are missing the main thing—'*la force*'" (Ges. Br., IV, pp. 337f.). That Nietzsche does not exempt himself when he speaks of the contemporary nihilists is shown in a letter written six months earlier (May 23, 1887) to E. Rohde, in which he says: "Moreover Taine was the only one for many long years who wrote me a warm and sympathetic word about my writings: so that meanwhile I consider him and Burckhardt to be my only readers. We must rely completely on one another, we three complete nihilists; although I myself, as you perhaps sense, still do not despair of finding a way out and the hole through which one gets to 'something'" (Ges. Br., II, p. 582).

8. Nonetheless, Nietzsche's individual interpretations on this topic stand in one context. This cannot be dealt with in detail here. As far as the constitutive basic trait in modern philosophy from Descartes to Schopenhauer is concerned, let me refer to the instructive remarks by G.-G. Grau in *Christlicher Glaube und intellektuelle Redlichkeit,* pp. 33–81. Decadence seems there to be the philosophical self-dissolution of Protestant Christianity.

9. *Schopenhauer as Educator,* 3. The next passage reads: "only in the most active spirits who have never been able to exist in a state of doubt would there appear instead that undermining and despair of all truth such as Heinrich von Kleist for example experienced as the effect of the Kantian philosophy."

10. "But in the entire history of philosophy there is no intellectual integrity—only 'love of the good'" (WP 460).

11. If one consults the fragment written by Nietzsche in the spring of 1873, *Philosophy in the Tragic Age of the Greeks,* one is compelled to set the beginning of the moral epoch, and hence of Western nihilism as far back as Anaximander. After translating the only extant sentence of Anaximander, Nietzsche characterized this puzzling saying as that of a "true

pessimist' and placed Anaximander in the spiritual vicinity of Schopenhauer and Kant. For "the origin of this world was no longer treated purely in terms of physics" by the Milesian; becoming seemed to him as a "punishable emancipation from eternal being . . . as a wrong that had to be atoned by perishing" (*Nachlaß*, X, pp. 26–30). Incidentally, in the same fragment of Nietzsche's a sharp dividing line is still drawn between Socrates (who there ranked among the representatives of the "republic of geniuses," which began chronologically with Thales) and Plato (*Nachlaß*, X, pp. 13–17). About the problems raised by Nietzsche's by no means unambiguous understanding of Socrates, see the work by H. J. Schmidt, *Nietzsche und Sokrates.*

12. *Nachlaß*, IX, p. 190.

13. *Nachlaß*, XII, p. 266.

14. "Neither does this [Jesus'] faith formulate itself—it *lives,* it resists formulas" (AC 32). Or even more drastically: "It is not a 'belief' which distinguishes the [real] Christian, . . . he is distinguished by a *different* mode of acting" (AC 33).

15. Jesus "denied any chasm between God and man; he *lived his* glad tidings" (AC 41).

16. E. Benz tried to make Nietzsche's image of Jesus *theologically* productive (especially in the closing remarks of his book on *Nietzsches Ideen zur Geschichte des Christentums;* cf. K. Jaspers, *Nietzsche und das Christentum,* pp. 25f., note, and Benz's response at the end of the revised version of his book [1956]). The portrayal, in part 2 of Benz's studies, of those who inspired Nietzsche's understanding of Christianity deserves some attention. But posthumous material first published in KGW requires modification of some of Benz's judgments, and attention was called to this, above, with regard to Dostoevsky. Thus the excerpts Nietzsche made from L. Tolstoy, *Ma religion,* 1885, and which were first printed in KGW, VIII/2, pp. 335–48, show clearly the untenableness of Benz's thesis that Tolstoy at least had not exercised direct influence on Nietzsche. The significance of his reading of Dostoevsky, and above all of Tolstoy, for Nietzsche's *Anti-Christ* cannot be pursued further in the present, for the most part "systematically" oriented book.

17. Karl Jaspers characterizes the decadence of the Nietzschean Jesus as "decadence without duplicity," but "yet with all the basic traits of décadence as . . . a form of perishing life" (*Nietzsche und das Christentum,* p. 23). This could be explained as follows: Jesus, in Nietzsche's understanding of him, does in his actual life deny reality. He is however not "duplicitous" in the sense that Nietzsche reproaches nearly all representatives of later Christianity: that they put on a pretense of unselfishness, whereas the feeling of revenge ultimately determines their behavior. The *historical problem* of Jesus' decadence has, of course, hardly been touched upon even approximatively in its significance for Nietzsche's thinking by this reference. See the following statements in the text, above.

18. In his time, i.e., in the late phase of European nihilism, Nietzsche sees the possibility that with the downfall of Christianity "Buddhism is silently gaining ground everywhere in Europe" (WP 240; cf. BGE 202 and GM, Preface, 5). In fact in the nineteenth century interest in Indian philosophy was constantly on the increase. Since according to Nietzsche nihilism must be intensified to the extreme before it can be overcome, "a European Buddhism" as a nihilistic late form "was perhaps indispensable" (WP 132).

19. Even before Buddha, namely in the Sankya philosophy, five centuries before Christ, in India that "decisive point was reached" where morality dissolves itself. This situation corresponds to that of contemporary Christianity (GM III:27). The self-dissolution of Christian morality will be discussed in more detail in the next pages.

20. On such tendencies of Buddhism, cf. Nietzsche's statements in WP 342, 159.

21. In the legends on Francis of Assisi, Nietzsche rediscovers the psychological type of the redeemer (AC 29). Cf. WP 212: "Christianity is still possible at any time. It is not tied to any of the impudent dogmas that have adorned themselves with its name: it requires neither the doctrine of a *personal God,* nor that of *sin,* nor that of *immortality,* nor that of *redemption,* nor that of *faith;* it has absolutely no need of metaphysics, and even less of asceticism, even less of a Christian 'natural science.' Christianity is a *way of life,* not a system of beliefs. It tells us how to act, not what we ought to believe. Whoever says today: 'I will not be a soldier,' 'I care nothing for the courts,' 'I shall not claim the services of the police,' 'I will do nothing that may disturb the peace within me: and if I must suffer on that account, nothing will serve better to maintain my peace than suffering'—he would be a Christian."

22. In the epilogue to *The Case of Wagner,* one reads: "The Gospels present us with precisely the same physiological types that Dostoevsky's novels describe."

23. "The Case of Wagner," p. 2.

24. The "irascible, envious tirades of Luther, who never felt quite well unless he could spit at someone with rage" (letter to P. Gast, dated October 5, 1879, Ges. Br., IV, p. 25) were the expression of "an insatiable need for revenge"; Nietzsche finds the same thing also in Rousseau (WP 347). Nietzsche's image of Luther as of 1879 was essentially influenced by J. Janssen's *Geschichte des deutschen Volkes,* to which J. Burckhardt had referred him (cf. the cited letter to Gast).

25. GS 358. However, Nietzsche here sees Luther's struggle directed only against "the dominion of 'the higher human beings' as conceived by the Church." The old Church is thus evaluated mainly positively, otherwise than in *The Anti-Christ:* as "a structure for ruling that secures the highest rank for the more spiritual human beings," as an anti-plebeian, relatively noble institution (GS 358).

26. *Nachlaß,* XI, p. 312.

27. A more precise analysis of Nietzsche's view of Christian pity would encounter more of the *ambivalency* that showed up in the discussion of the "ascetic ideal": it wants power, i.e., it affirms life and yet intends nothingness insofar as pity in its struggle against the strong turns against life and negates it. (On this last point, cf. GM, Preface, 5.)

Chapter 5: The Will to Truth and the Will to Power

1. *Nachlaß,* XI, p. 35.

2. "One anticipates the worse effects of lying to one another. That is the source of the *duty of truth*" (*Nachlaß,* X, p. 130).

3. *Nachlaß,* X, p. 149.

4. Ibid., p. 162.

5. Ibid., p. 163.

6. *Nachlaß*, XII, p. 84.

7. Cf. ibid.

8. Insofar as the world "on which alone the moral standard can be applied does not exist at all: there are *neither moral nor immoral actions*" (WP 786).

9. The truthful person understands himself to a certain extent as the personification of the will to truth. He demands of his behavior that it should conform to the criterion of truth. Therefore he wants to be "simple, transparent, not in contradiction with himself, durable, remaining always the same" (WP 543).

10. "On Truth and Lying in an Extra-Moral Sense," Kaufmann, ed., *Portable Nietzsche*, p. 47.

11. *Nachlaß*, X, p. 215.

12. "The will to truth here is merely the desire for a *world of the constant*" (WP 585A). The world as "something that becomes" presents itself in terms of this desire "as a falsehood always changing but never getting near the truth: for—there is no 'truth' in the desired sense" (WP 616).

13. Because they preserve the species, "*the falsest assumptions are precisely the most indispensable ones for us*" (*Nachlaß*, XIV, p. 16). See also, in addition to the following remarks, what was said above about the genealogy of logic.

14. Cf. also *Nachlaß*, XI, p. 162: "The feeling that something comes easy to us and links up with already present feelings is considered by us to be *evidence of* truth."

15. What was stated here as exemplified in the relation of individuals to one another also applies, of course, to the relations between social groups. Thus the cohesion of a ruling group is destroyed when it no longer has a common enemy to fight. Those who were formerly strong now are decimated by internecine warfare.

16. "In truth there are no *individual truths,* but rather sheer individual *falsehoods*" (*Nachlaß*, XII, p. 128).

17. *Nachlaß*, XII, p. 293; cf. HA I:518: "He who considers more deeply knows that, whatever his acts and judgments may be, he is always wrong."

18. Nietzsche has always been reproached with falling prey to the "error" of skepticism by his assertion that there is no truth. Thus A. Hanel, *Friedrich Nietzsche und sein Verhältnis zum Relativismus*, writes that by this proposition Nietzsche was "certainly setting up a 'truth' by denying all of us any truth. The denial of all truth is a possibility only under the presupposition of a generally valid transcendental 'truth'" (p. 133). This chapter will try to show that Nietzsche denies the *traditional understanding* of truth, but in such a negation arrives at a *more original* understanding of truth (in terms of his own intellectual presuppositions). Apart from that, the above-cited objection to skepticism is too formal and indefinite to be considered a serious argument. For instance, how is the "presupposition" that is spoken of to be understood? To what extent must what is presupposed be transcendental with universal validity? Anyway, such anemic attempts at refutation do not reach the *real* skeptic at all, because they have nothing to say to him (cf. M. Heidegger, *Sein und Zeit,* pp. 228f.). And finally: even if one pays any heed to the formal

argumentation, one must discover that it does not hold true. Heidegger, in his Nietzsche lectures showed this very nicely (*Nietzsche* I:501ff.; Eng.: III:27). He starts from the well-known attempts to refute Nietzsche's dictum that truth is an illusion. Heidegger writes: "And if Nietzsche wants to be 'consistent'—for there is nothing like 'consistency'—his statement about truth is an illusion, too, and so we need not bother with him any longer. The idle acumen that presents itself with this kind of refutation creates an illusion that everything is settled. However, in its refutation of Nietzsche's own statement about truth as an illusion it forgets one thing, to wit, that if Nietzsche's statement is true, then not only must Nietzsche's statement as true become an illusion but just as necessarily so must the true consequent statement that is brought forward as a refutation of Nietzsche be an 'illusion.' However, the defender of acumen will now answer, having meanwhile become *still* more clever, that our characterization of his refutation is also for its part illusion. Certainly—and such mutual refutation can be continued endlessly, only to confirm what it already made use of with the very first step: Truth is an illusion. This statement is not only not shattered by the argumentative *tour de force* of more acumen, it is not even touched by it." Heidegger, *Nietzsche* I:501ff.; Eng.: III:26.

19. *Nachlaß*, XII, pp. 70f.

20. *Anhang* to *Wille zur Macht*, GA XVI, pp. 416, 421.

21. "What does nihilism mean?—That the highest values devaluate themselves" (WP 1).

22. EH, "The Birth of Tragedy," 1.

23. The rhyming words are: *nihilist/Christ* [Trans.].

24. In the notes on a plan from the fall of 1888, Nietzsche summarizes as follows: "Nihilism as the *necessary* consequence of *Christianity,* morality and the truth concept of philosophy" (*Anhang* to *WzM*, GA XVI, p. 435).

25. Cf. also *Nachlaß*, XIV, p. 8.

26. *Nachlaß*, XII, p. 368.

27. Cf. WP 25: "It is only late that one musters the courage for what one really knows. That I have hitherto been a thorough-going nihilist, I have admitted to myself only recently: the energy and radicalism with which I advanced as a nihilist deceived me about this basic fact. When one moves toward a goal it seems impossible that 'goal-lessness as such' is the principle of our faith."

28. EH, "Daybreak," 2.

29. By now it must be clear that Nietzsche—as he thinks—brought together in a decisive way "the two greatest points of view (devised by Germans)": that of *becoming* and that of the *value of existence* (WP 1058, p. 545).

30. *Nachlaß*, XIV, p. 382.

31. *Nietzsche* I:620; Eng.: III:126.

32. Ibid.I:620ff., contrasts truth as harmony "with becoming chaos" with *the* truth that has its essence in the "fixation of the constant." The first is for Nietzsche the standard for the second: it unmasks it as error. It finds its expression in *art,* under which title Nietzsche sums up all higher possibilities of creative man. The "fixation of chaos in knowledge" and the "transfiguration in art" are combined in Heidegger's concept of "assimila-

tion" [*Eingleichung*]. It is the transfiguration that commands and poeticizes, establishes perspectival horizons and fixates (I:636; Eng.: III:140). As a condition for the possibility of assimilation Heidegger names *justice* (I:637; Eng.: III:141), whose going beyond the narrow moral perspectives (I:645; Eng.: III:147) is supposed to open a higher essential determination of the world (I:647; Eng.: III:149). A discussion of Heidegger's extensive analysis of Nietzsche's conception of truth cannot be presented here. It, too, is oriented to the history of metaphysics. It is determined, not least of all, by his teleologically oriented interpretation of the will to power, which was assessed in chapter 1 of this book. Cf., e.g., the explication of the factor of advantage that is constitutive of the concept of justice as what is allotted in advance (*Nietzsche* I:646f.; Eng.: III:148; and *Nietzsche* II:326f.). On the path taken by the understanding of truth as certainty to the point of harmony "as calculating transferral of being through letting go of beingness into machination," according to Heidegger, cf. *Nietzsche* II:25ff.

33. Within a complex power perspective, "errors" of varying stability are found. Many will be unavoidable, "insofar as an organic entity of our species could not live without [them]" (WP 535). But this does not diminish the necessity for the perspective *as a whole* to change constantly if the will is to survive the power struggle.

34. Cf. *Nachlaß*, XIII, p. 361 and WP 602.

35. A. Camus stated concerning Nietzsche's idea of intellectual freedom: "The essence of his discovery consists in the proposition that, if the eternal law is not freedom, then lawlessness is even less so. . . . To deny that something is forbidden in this world amounts to a renunciation of what is allowed" (*L'Homme révolté*, 1951, pp. 94f., translated from the German *Der Mensch in der Revolte*, 1953, p. 79.). That Camus' Nietzsche-interpretation is determined by a completely different intention than the present study, and that he does not view the complete context of the problem of truth in Nietzsche, does not prevent him from seeing the above-described "danger." It must become all the clearer to him, since he was preoccupied with the possibility of the indifference of all truths from early on (cf. *Le Mythe de Sisyphe*, 1942; cf. on this W. Müller-Lauter, "Thesen zum Begriff des Absurden bei Albert Camus," in: *Th. Viat.* VIII, 1961/62, pp. 203ff.).

36. "The Shadow."

37. Such "attempts to escape nihilism without revaluating our values" must remain unsuccessful. They "produce the opposite, make the problem more acute." Nietzsche speaks of them as *incomplete* nihilism (WP 28).

Chapter 6: The Way to the Overman

1. *Nietzsche. Einführung in das Verständnis seines Philosophierens*, p. 161.

2. "I teach that there are higher and lower men" (WP 997). "I distinguish between a type of ascending life and another type of decay, disintegration, weakness" (WP 867).

3. *Nachlaß*, XIV, p. 262.

4. Under the title *"New Appraisal of Man"* Nietzsche puts in the first place the questions: "How much power is in him? How much multiplicity of drives? How much ability to communicate and receive?" (*Nachlaß*, XII, p. 363). It will be seen that the more

positively an answer to the first of the questions raised turns out, the more negative is the answer to the second. And the amount of ability to communicate also ends, in his reflections, in a reciprocal relation to the amount of ability to receive contents.

5. "Even if all you want is *your* ideal, you must compel the whole world to accept it" (*Nachlaß*, XII, p. 281).

6. *Nachlaß*, XII, p. 400. Cf. Nietzsche's "Gesetz wider das Christenthum" (KGW, VI/3, p. 252).

7. "We desire that man should become more evil than he has ever been before" (WP 988).

8. "On Old and New Tablets," 29, p. 214. Cf. TI, "The Hammer Speaks."

9. Nietzsche is probably not thinking of direct destruction, but of encouragement to self-destruction.

10. *Nachlaß*, XII, p. 246.

11. Cf. TI, "Morality as Anti-Nature," 3: "The Church has at all times desired the destruction of its enemies: we, we immoralists and anti-Christians, see that it is to our advantage that the Church exist."

12. "*The conjuring up of enemies:* we *need* it for the sake of our ideal! To transform the enemies that are our equals into gods and thus to lift and transform ourselves" (*Nachlaß*, XIV, p. 274).

13. Carried to the extreme: "The highest men suffer most from existence—but they also have the greatest *counter-forces*" (*Nachlaß*, XIII, p. 37).

14. *Nachlaß*, XII, p. 168. Other statements of Nietzsche's also point in the same direction, e.g., *Nachlaß*, XII, p. 367: "Physical strength should be on the side of the greatest thought—as long as there must be war between the various thoughts!" In another passage "the exceptional situation and power position" of the future rulers is expressed in a formulation that highlights the antithesis: "the Roman Caesar with Christ's soul" (WP 983).

15. "To overcome *the past in us*: recombine the drives and direct them all together toward one goal: very difficult!" so Nietzsche notes (*Nachlaß*, XII, p. 360).

16. "Thus Spoke Zarathustra," 6.

17. *Nachlaß*, XIV, p. 271.

18. "The Magician," 2.

19. "Upon the Blessed Isles."

20. "On the Higher Men," 2.

21. *Nachlaß*, XII, p. 363.

22. Ibid., p. 362.

23. *Nietzsche* II:125f.

24. Ibid. II:304.

25. Ibid. II:125, cf. I:284.

26. "Why I Write Such Good Books," 1.

27. *Nachlaß*, XII, p. 413.

28. Nietzsche does not mean that the overman is supposed to bring mankind (in the sense of all humans) up to his level. The mediocre shall stay mediocre (WP 891). The

overman is the exception that presupposes the continued existence of the rule (WP 894). As an exception he must be concerned with keeping the mediocre in good heart (WP 893). They are, however, without any significance of their own for "mankind." For its goal lies, as Nietzsche said early on, "only *in its highest exemplars*" (HL 9). His doctrine of the overman stands in opposition to the socially oriented theories of progress. Georg Simmel (in *Schopenhauer und Nietzsche,* pp. 206–27) goes more deeply into this problem. He declares that neither of the two opposite theories can refute the other. Each appeals to axiomatic demands whose validity the other side denies. "Between the socialist and the Nietzschean theories of value . . . the fissure goes down to their foundation; there is no common ultimate principle whose proven harmony with one theory would convince the other; and therefore in them argument and counter-argument do not stand opposed, nor opinions, but rather facts, two human ways of *being,* which no longer can convince one another logically, but only persuade psychologically or overpower in practice" (p. 215).

29. *Nachlaß,* XIII, p. 74.

30. "Thus Spoke Zarathustra," 6.

31. The inconsistencies in Nietzsche's statements on the overman were discovered very early. Generally, one started with Nietzsche's alleged Darwinism. Theobald Ziegler sees in the Zarathustra idea of the overman "a poetic fiction," which "taken seriously is a misuse of Darwinism," which theory was "set up by its author only as a heuristic principle for natural scientists, not for prophets" (*Fr. Nietzsche,* p. 141). Adalbert Düringer finds in the doctrine of the overman nothing but the "reflex which Darwin's and Haeckel's publications on natural selection . . . provoked in the head of an eccentric, sickly enthusiast." "Nietzsche's fantasies" were scientifically "completely worthless," but this did not prevent "a number of overexcited or sensual women . . . from following Nietzsche's advice and busying themselves, awake or dreaming, with the problem of *giving birth to the overman*" (*Nietzsches Philosophie und das heutige Christentum,* pp. 42f.). Authors who deserve to be taken more seriously than Düringer express themselves more cautiously about Darwin's influence on Nietzsche, especially in view of his criticism of Darwinism. Raoul Richter pointed out that Nietzsche "did not discuss the natural scientific details of Darwinism" (*Fr. Nietzsche. Sein Leben und sein Werk,* p. 202). And contemporary discussion has become even more reserved in estimating this influence. H. M. Wolff finds that Nietzsche employs "Darwinistic thoughts or some that sound like Darwin" (*Fr. Nietzsche. Der Weg zum Nichts,* p. 181). Eugen Fink asks whether in Zarathustra's proclamation of the overman "in the last analysis the Darwinistic theory of evolution" was not being announced, and rejects this with the words: "The thinker was merely citing current, familiar notions to formulate his problem" (*Nietzsches Philosophie,* p. 69).

But whether one assigns greater or lesser significance to the influence of Darwinism on the idea of the overman, it remained unmistakable that many of Nietzsche's statements point in a completely different direction. Ziegler first alluded to the *contradiction* between the so-called naturalistic conception of the overman that called for the breeding of a *superior species* and the quasi-"idealistic" ideas that envisaged the rise of exceptional genius types (*Fr. Nietzsche,* esp. p. 141). Ziegler's elaboration of this problem was widely followed by Richter (*Fr. Nietzsche,* pp. 203f.), Vaihinger (*Nietzsche als Philosoph,* pp. 62ff.), and Grützmacher (*Nietzsche,* pp. 126ff.). Although these interpreters in part use different terms to describe the content (for instance, Vaihinger uses the concept "superior species" in contrast with Ziegler's "ideal overman") nevertheless the basic distinction is preserved between the overman as a violent *natural creature* that appeared in the past and the overman as a *cultural being* whom Nietzsche expects or dreams up for some future time and who is to have morality-forming traits. That Nietzsche chose the same name for two contradictory conceptions is considered to be inexcusable terminological "double talk" (*Doppelzüngigkeit*) by Richter, who reassures himself, however, with the suggestion that in other great philosophers, too, the main concepts are similarly contradictory. (pp. 203f.)

Ziegler's remarks are more differentiated than the interpretations that followed him; he sees that he does not hit the mark with the aforementioned dichotomy. Finally he must admit that the diverse lines of thinking that he culls from Nietzsche's text "mix and cross" and "often become entangled." "Nietzsche's doctrine of the overman is fissured and contradictory . . . shifting and Protean." In the end, all that remains in common is "only what is completley personal—the great desire beyond oneself, the unquenched and insatiable longing for an ideal, a superhuman, not to say, divine one" (*Fr. Nietzsche,* pp. 146f.). Accurate as it is that—as K. Löwith, among others, later states—"the overman appears when God is dead" and that "the death of God" requires "an overcoming of man" (*Von Hegel zu Nietzsche,* p. 349), such a general statement as this reference to Nietzsche's contradictory theses requires an explanation based on this philosopher's basic concerns and the presuppositions of his thought to make the multifariousness of his statements understandable. This chapter has tried to contribute to this endeavour.

32. *Nachlaß,* XIII, pp. 73f.

33. Ibid., XII, p. 359.

34. "On Priests," p. 93.

35. Nietzsche himself speaks of such faith in a note complaining about "the deep *unproductivity* of the nineteenth century": "I have met no person who really could have produced a new ideal. The nature of German music misled me to *hope* for the longest time. A *stronger type,* in whom our forces are bound synthetically—my belief" (*Nachlaß,* XII, pp. 367f.).

36. *Nietzsche,* pp. 167–69.

37. *Nietzsche und das Christentum,* p. 54.

38. For a fundamental critique of Jaspers's book on Nietzsche, cf. K. Ulmer's remarks in *Nietzsche. Einheit und Sinn seines Werkes,* pp. 9–11. How Jaspers's interpretations, even while realizing essential insights, themselves get lost in abstraction, and the abstraction that he imputes to the contents he is interpreting finally comes out into the open as nebulosity—this can be shown by his discussion of the antithesis-problem that he undertakes in *Nietzsche und das Christentum.* He rightly speaks of "the ultimate, most comprehensive polarity" of Nietzsche's "feeling of reality and value," shown by the fact that Nietzsche displays "the most abysmal antitheses." Nietzsche "takes a stand on one side of world-historically perceived battle fronts and he abolishes all antitheses in his suffering of the

counterpositions as of possiblities also proper to himself." The polarity of Nietzsche's philosophy of antitheses, however, consists precisely not in abolishing or, as Jaspers also formulates it, in "rejecting opposites," as must be said against this interpretation. Nietzsche does not exactly accept as his own principle Jesus' "good news" that there are no more opposites (p. 73). Jaspers finds in Nietzsche "the most astonishing attempts to retrieve back into a higher unity what was separate from himself and pushed into the mutual struggle" (p. 74). But he does not give a thorough investigation of Nietzsche's efforts at such syntheses. Rather, he challenges his reader to "abandon this entire level of alternative thinking and achieve a deeper *mode of thinking,* in which all states of the question change, space becomes wide, and truth deep, and the noise of screaming assertions falls silent" (p. 78). Jaspers does not catch sight of the *inescapableness* of the concrete antitheses in which Nietzsche's thinking consciously struggles. Precisely this allows him to escape. He can show that Nietzsche's thinking fails again and again. But—if I may cite a sentence of Heidegger's from a different context—Jaspers's "'philosophizing' about failure [is] separated by a chasm from a failed thinking" (*Ueber den Humanismus,* p. 30).

39. H. Vaihinger's statement that the idea of the overman is merely a "heuristic-pedagogical-utopian fiction" (*Die Philosophie des Als Ob,* p. 789) misses the seriousness of Nietzsche's state of the question, which is directed at the *realization* of the overman out of the distress of the time.

40. Karl J. Obenauer, referring to Nietzsche's statement that the overman is the goal, even writes: "The goal and the meaning . . . do not reside in my ego and self, nor in your ego and self. It lies far beyond, far in the future. This goal is farther from the ego and self and more beyond than any goal, than any beyond of any faith" (*Fr. Nietzsche, der ekstatische Nihilist,* p. 73).

Chapter 7: The Two Types of Overman and the Doctrine of Eternal Recurrence

1. "The Birth of Tragedy," 3.

2. For information on the most important contributions to this discussion until 1954, cf. K. Löwith's bibliographic report in *Nietzsches Philosophie der ewigen Wiederkehr des Gleichen,* Addendum, pp. 199ff..

3. *Nietzsches Lehre in ihren Grundbegriffen. Die ewige Wienderkunft des Gleichen und der Sinn des Uebermenschen,* pp. 18f.

4. *Nietzsche, der Philosoph und Politiker,* p. 80. Ernst Bertram's talk that "the pseudo-revelation of the Eternal Return" was a "deceitful, mocking, delusory mystery of the late Nietzsche" (*Nietzsche, Versuch einer Mythologie,* pp. 11f.) is beyond discussion.

5. Löwith, *Nietzsches Philosophie,* e.g., pp. 13f. and 25f.

6. Ibid., p. 204, cf. pp. 60, 113ff., and passim.

7. *Nietzsche* II:14. Heidegger describes the difference in such a metaphysical relationship as follows: "In the two main theses—being as a whole is will to power, and being as a whole is eternal return of the same—the 'is' means something different in each case. Being as a whole 'is' will to power means: being as such *consists of* what Nietzsche defines

as will to power. And being as a whole 'is' eternal return of the same means: being as a whole *is* being in the *mode* of eternal return of the same. The determination 'will to power' answers the question of being with respect to·*what it consists of;* the determination 'eternal return of the same' answers the question of being with respect to *its way of being*' (ibid. I:463f.). Based particularly on plans and drafts of Nietzsche's from the years 1884 to 1888, insofar as they were published in the *Großoktavausgabe,* Heidegger tries to elaborate more sharply on the connection of and the difference between the two doctrines. He asks: "Is the theory of recurrence not only compatible with the idea of 'will to power' but *its real and only basis?*" (I:414). Nietzsche's 1885 notes show that "the question of the will to power" is "inserted into the philosophy of eternal return" (I:416). The thought of eternal return would indeed need the interpretation of events as the will to power, which is the ultimate fact we can reach. The 1887 and 1888 plans showed that the thought of eternal recurrence was "the last thing to be portrayed . . . according to the matter and grounding context," but "the first thing reaching through from beginning to end" (I:417–19). That Nietzsche posits the will to power as the *precondition* for the eternal recurrence of the same is, according to Heidegger, only of limited, easily misleading significance. Yet the doctrine of eternal return asserted "its determining position." Nietzsche had not won "a clear and grounded concept" of the "relationship prevailing here" (I:425; cf. II:10). The metaphysical distinction between essence (W*as-sein*) and existence (*Daß-sein*) "came to the fore once again" in Nietzsche "in the perfection of Western metaphysics . . . but at the same time in such a way that this *distinction as such* is forgotten and the two fundamental determinations of being as a whole—the will to power and the eternal recurrence of the same—are, as it were, metaphysically without a home, but are posited and spoken into the unconditional" (II:15f.). But what fits so finally into Heidegger's sketch on the history of philosophy cannot lead to a convincing context oriented by Nietzsche's own thinking. The priority that he gives to the theory of return spares him from presenting an objectively grounded proof of the absolute necessity that compels Nietzsche to adopt this idea. That is possible only starting from a rightly understood doctrine of the will to power.

8. *Nachlaß,* XII, p. 400; cf. XIV, 265.

9. Ibid., XII, p. 397.

10. Ibid., p. 401.

11. "On Redemption": "The will to power must will something higher than any reconciliation."

12. "Thus Spoke Zarathustra," 1.

13. Nietzsche continues in this passage: ". . . and not only to a spectacle but at bottom to him who needs precisely this spectacle . . . and makes [it] necessary—What? And this wouldn't be—*circulus vitiosus deus?*"

14. *Nachlaß,* XII, p. 427.

15. Ibid., p. 63. [The word "*Schwergewicht*" (literally "heavy weight") as used by Nietzsche seems to connote some attributes of "*Schwerpunkt*" (center of gravity) and is sometimes so translated by Nietzsche's premier translator, Walter Kaufmann. In other contexts it seems to have the meaning "heavy burden."—*Trans.*]

16. Heidegger writes in a discussion of the thought of recurrence as a weight or burden (*Schwergewicht*): "What do we think of when we say the word 'burden'? A burden hinders vacillation, renders calm and steadfast, draws all forces to itself, gathers them and gives them definition. A burden also exerts a downward pull, compelling us constantly to hold ourselves erect; but it also embodies the danger that we will fall down, and stay down. In this way the burden is an obstacle that demands constant 'hurdling,' constant surmounting. However, a burden creates no new forces, while it does not alter the direction of their motion, thus creating for whatever force is available new laws of motion" (*Nietzsche* I:272; Eng.: II:22).

17. Cf. *Nachlaß*, XII, p. 425.

18. Ibid., p. 64.

19. *Nachlaß*, XII, p. 415.

20. "For this thought we do not want to have thirty years of jubilation with drums and fifes, and thirty years of grave-digger's work, followed by an eternity of dead silence, as is the case with so many famous thoughts" (*Nachlaß*, XII, p. 69).

21. *Nachlaß*, XII, pp. 68f.

22. *Nietzsche* II:12; I:321, 395; Eng.: II:65f., 132. Occasionally Nietzsche seems to speak of his philosophy as a pantheism (WP 55). More precise observation shows, however, that here too—as so often—he is "operating with traditional concepts, ready to cast them away again when they do not prove to be valid for doing justice to the basic fact." So writes E. Hefrich at the end of an impressive analysis of the aforementioned pantheism-passage in his book *Nietzsches Philosophie. Identität von Welt und Nichts,* pp. 247–62.

23. *Nietzsche* I:385; Eng.: II:123.

24. Here he refers to statements of Nietzsche's that are found in the *Nachlaß* at the time of *The Gay Science* (*Nietzsche* I:383). The following note, especially, deserves special mention: "The thought of thoughts (namely, of eternal recurrence) is a heavy weight that presses down on you as much as all other weights and more than them" (*Nachlaß*, XII, p. 64).

25. *Nietzsche* I:385–87; Eng.: II:123–25.

26. Ibid. I:391; Eng.: II:128. Heidegger's rejection of the view that "the doctrine of return is a personal confession of religious faith on Nietzsche's part" (I:384; Eng.: II:122) is directed mainly against Baeumler's Nietzsche-interpretation. Cf. I:29ff.; Eng.: I:21ff.

27. The relation of religion to art in the writings of the "enlightenment phase" cannot be elaborated here, since that would lead beyond the framework of this digression on Nietzsche's understanding of religion. The suggestion must suffice that the *essential* determinations of the artistic are derived from religion and remain oriented thereby. On "religion in music" in Richard Wagner, cf. WP 840.

28. *Nachlaß*, XIV, p. 270.

29. *Nietzsche contra Wagner,* "We Antipodes," VIII, pp. 193f. A more differentiated explanation of Nietzsche's concept of the Dionysian cannot be undertaken here; it could receive its complete concretization only in the determination of its relation to the Apollinian.

30. *Nachlaß*, XII, p. 65. That Nietzsche does not speak of endless, but rather of eternal recurrence, is for Jaspers—by way of a digression on S. Kierkegaard's Christian understanding of eternity as a moment that contains both the future and the past, i.e., the fullness of time—evidence that "Nietzsche with the completely un-Chriatian idea of recurrence" may have "preserved a remnant of Christian substance, distorted to unrecognizability." Jaspers states: "Nietzsche would have wanted the most radical break, but in fact he did not accomplish it: he wanted a philosophy of godlessness with an unhistorical transcendence; but the secret fulfillment would have brought him an Other, indeed out of the content of that which he rejected" (*Nietzsche*, p. 362).

31. *Nachlaß*, XII, p. 68.

32. Ibid., pp. 67f.

33. *Nachlaß*, XII, pp. 63f.

34. Ibid., pp. 66f.

35. Ibid., p. 68.

36. Ibid., p. 409.

37. Ibid., p. 369.

38. Ibid., p. 65.

39. Ibid., pp. 370f.; cf. also pp. 18f.: "A new doctrine finds its best representatives at the very last. . . . The weaker, more empty, more sickly, more needy are those who receive the new infection—the first adherents prove nothing *against* a doctrine."

40. *Nachlaß*, XII, p. 63.

41. Ibid., XIV, p. 264.

42. *Nachlaß*, XII, p. 412.

43. "On the Great Longing." There Zarathustra speaks to his soul: "I taught you the contempt that does not come like the worms gnawing, the great, the loving contempt that loves most what it despises most."

44. "The Convalescent," 2.

45. *Nachlaß*, XIV, p. 264.

46. On the active nihilists, Nietzsche writes "that they destroy in order to be destroyed," that they "also want power by *compelling* the powerful to become their hangmen" (WP 55).

47. *Nachlaß*, XIV, p. 295.

48. Ibid., XII, p. 369. WP 1060, states that "the enjoyment of all kinds of uncertainty, experimentalism, as a counterweight to this extreme fatalism" could be a necessary result of the idea of recurrence.

49. P. Gast even says in a letter dated November 29, 1913, that the thought of eternal recurrence "causes the pedantic person with the long pipe to rejoice more than the hero and innovator" (quoted according to E. Podach, *Gestalten um Nietzsche*, p. 121). Heidegger writes that "there is only a narrow gap . . . between two things that in one way look alike, so that they appear to be the same. On the one side stands the following: 'Everything is nought, indifferent, so that nothing is worthwhile—*it is all alike.*' On the other side: 'Everything recurs, it depends on each moment, everything matters—*it is all alike.*' The

smallest gap, the rainbow bridge of the phrase, *it is all alike,* conceals two things that are quite distinct: 'everything is indifferent' and 'nothing is indifferent.' The overcoming of this smallest gap is the most difficult overcoming in the thought of eternal return of the same as the essentiallly overcoming thought. If one takes the thought ostensibly 'for itself' in terms of its content—'Everything turns in a circle'—then it is perhaps sheer delusion. But in that case it is not Nietzsche's thought" (*Nietzsche* I:446; Eng.: II:182).

50. If one thinks the doctrine of eternal recurrence through "with full sharpness," Simmel remarks, every absolutely identical repetition of my conduct would have to occur again and again. This "would not be able to have the slightest significance for me" (*Schopenhauer und Nietzsche,* pp. 251f.).

51. "On the Vision and the Riddle," #2, p. 158.

52. "The Convalescent," pp. 215–18.

53. *Nietzsche* I:308f.

54. *Nachlaß,* XIV, p. 295.

55. Heidegger understands the entire passage cited above as the expression of Nietzsche's own struggle for assurance as well as for the truth of the doctrine of eternal recurrence (*Nietzsche* I:409f.). He pays no attention to the *composition* of Nietzsche's brief note, at the end of which both Zarathustra's doubts as well as his rejection of the doctrine are overcome in a "blissful maturing."

56. *Nietzsche* I:256; Eng.: II:6.

57. *Blätter für Deutsche Philosophie,* IX, pp. 368–87; reprinted in Becker's volume of collected philosophical essays, which appeared in 1963 under the title *Dasein und Dawesen,* pp. 41f.

58. *Nietzsche* I:368; Eng.: II:108.

59. *Dasein und Dawesen,* p. 41.

60. Ibid., p. 66.

61. Ibid., pp. 50f.

62. *Nietzsche* I:371.

63. *Dasein und Dawesen,* p. 42.

64. *Nachlaß,* XII, p. 57.

65. *Dasein und Dawesen,* p. 42.

66. *Nachlaß,* XIV, p. 320, cf. p. 37 ("mathematics is constantly contradicted in real events").

67. Ibid., p. 22.

68. *Dasein und Dawesen,* p. 42.

69. Ibid., p. 43.

70. Ibid.

71. Ibid., pp. 43–45.

72. Ibid., p. 50n.

73. *Dasein und Dawesen,* p. 50.

74. *Nachlaß,* XII, pp. 58f.

75. *Dasein und Dawesen,* pp. 50f.

76. Afterword, in *Fr. Nietzsche, Werke in drei Bänden* III:1441.

77. *Dasein und Dawesen,* p. 51.

78. Ibid., p. 53.

79. Ibid., p. 52.

80. Ibid., p. 66.

81. Ibid., pp. 51ff.

82. Ibid., p. 63.

83. Cf. comments above on Becker's first proof, and also *Dasein und Dawesen,* p. 64.

84. Ibid., p. 57.

85. In the following pages the lectures are cited as they appeared in a book by this title, *Die Geschichte der Natur,* 5th edition, 1962.

86. Cf. A. Mittasch, *Friedrich Nietzsches Naturbeflissenheit,* p. 22.

87. *Die Geschichte der Natur,* p. 37.

88. On Gast's discussion of Nietzsche's natural scientific ideas, see a passage in Gast's letter of November 29, 1913, already mentioned above: "The craziest thing for me is that against Robert Mayer, with whose theory of heat I first made him acquainted, Nietzsche champions the Ragusan Boscovich, an astronomer thinking merely mathematically, who as a consequence of his wrong idea of the nature of energy reaches the point that he denies the existence of matter: there exists *only* energy. From his atomistic speculations Boscovich arrives at this nonsense: and since there was method about it, it pleased Nietzsche all the more, for he lacked the physicist's instinctive insights as a controlling mechanism." Gast then writes further: "The doctrine of eternal recurrence, by which Nietzsche wants to set the powerful accent on his overman collapses with the transformation of chemical elements into one another, which has become very probable in recent years" (cited according to Podach, *Gestalten um Nietzsche,* p. 121). Gast's influence on Nietzsche's later natural scientific readings must not be underestimated, although this influence was very little able to budge Nietzsche's basic position. This cannot be gone into here in detail. It would require intensive study of the Peter Gast legacy, which has meanwhile been added to the Nietzsche files in the Goethe and Schiller Archives in Weimar (cf. KGW, VI/3, p. 161).

89. *Die Geschichte der Natur,* p. 43. On Weizsäcker's dispute with the theory of a constant new origination of matter, cf. ibid., p. 54.

90. Cf. *Nachlaß,* XII, p. 433 (not, as Becker wrongly states, p. 432).

91. Cf. Becker, *Dasein und Dawesen,* pp. 61f.

92. Ibid., p. 66.

93. *Schopenhauer und Nietzsche,* pp. 250f. note.

94. *Dasein und Dawesen,* p. 66.

95. Ewald already saw this problem. But this meaning is not worked out in a manner appropriate to Nietzsche, due to the generally Kantian orientation of Ewald's interpretation. Ewald writes: "The hypothesis that the totality of matter is contained in a countable quantum presupposes that it must at least physicially, objectively, not be impossible

to run through the entire scope of existing matter and bring the numerically fixable sequence to a close. But this says nothing about the boundary value extending in the opposite dimension. How far in this direction the indefatigable division leads, how far it
can lead, whether with the infinitely large also the infinitely small has been bracketed out,
whether the operations undertaken in both directions are subject to the same experien-
tial whole, to the same laws, are problems about which nothing has yet been decided.
Here perception and concept stand in stubborn conflict" (*Nietzsches Lehre in ihren
Grundbegriffen,* p. 26).

96. *Nachlaß,* XIV, p. 273.

97. Ibid., XII, p. 369.

98. "The Convalescent" 2.

99. Nietzsche is thinking in *his* sense when he writes: "Becoming must appear justified
at every moment. . . . The present must absolutely not be justified by reference to a future, nor the past by reference to the present" (WP 708).

100. One of Nietzsche's sketches by the title, "*The eternal recurrence. A prophecy,*" says:
"Its place in history as a *mid-point*" (WP 1057).

101. "On the Higher Man," 2.

102. *Nachlaß,* XII, p. 63.

103. Ibid., XIV, p. 267.

104. "On the Gift-Giving Virtue," 3.

105. *Nietzsche Philosophie der ewigen Wiederkehr des Gleichen,* p. 64.

106. Ibid., p. 66, cf. pp. 88ff.

107. Ibid., p. 64.

108. Ibid., pp. 90ff.

109. *Nachlaß,* XII, pp. 64f.

110. *Nietzsches Philosophie,* p. 91.

111. *Nachlaß,* XII, pp. 61f.

112. Ibid., p. 371.

113. Ibid., XIII, p. 62.

114. Ibid., XII, p. 369. Nietzsche's thesis, presented in chapter 1, that nothing is the same
applies only to events *within* a series. Cf. *Nachlaß,* XII, pp. 51f.: "Everything has existed
countless times, insofar as the total situation of all forces always recurs. Whether, *apart
from that,* anything the same has ever existed is completely indemonstrable. It seems that
the total situation reconstitutes the characteristics down to the smallest detail, so that two
different total situations can have nothing the same. Whether there can be anything the
same in *one* total situation, for example, *two leaves*? I doubt it: it would presuppose that
they had an absolutely identical origin, and thus we would have to assume that *back into
all eternity* something identical had existed despite all changes of the total situations and
the creation of new qualities—an impossible assumption!" Nietzsche's talk of the overman as the "destroyer" also makes sense only in the case of prerogatives of the series over
the circulation.

Chapter 8: Nietzsche's "Doctrine" of the Will to Power

1. My interpretation of the "will to power" has been delineated in its basic traits in earlier chapters. Extensive critiques have been made by the following scholars: W. Weischedel, in his article entitled "Der Wille und die Willen. Zur Auseinandersetzung Wolfgang Müller-Lauters mit Martin Heidegger," pp. 71–76; and P. Köster, "Die Problematik wissenschaftlicher Nietzsche-Interpretation: Kritische Überlegungen zu Wolfgang Müller-Lauters Nietzschebuch," pp. 31–60. In the following pages, I will deal with these critics in endnotes, insofar as they touch upon the problem of the will to power. When this is not done explicitly, I nonetheless believe I have taken their objections into account in my own treatment of the subject.

2. The following remarks come from a lecture by the title "Reflections on Nietzsche's Doctrine of the Will to Power," which I presented in Louvain on May 13, 1973, by invitation of the Wijsgerig Gezelschap.

3. The works published or prepared for publication by Nietzsche are cited as accurately as possible by work and section, aphorism, and so on, from the KGW. The literary remains (*Nachlaß*) are also cited from the KGW, insofar as this had been published at the time of writing, otherwise from the GA. Since in part no concordances are available for the *Nachlaß* published till now in the KGW of the 1980s (V 1 and 2), and in part only from the KGW to the GA (VIII 2 and 3) it is possible that one or another of the *Nachlaß* fragments that have appeared in the KGW was still cited according to the GA. Insofar as texts from the KGW that had appeared in the earlier editions of the *Nachlaß*-compilation, *The Will to Power*, were discovered, the aphorism-number of that compilation is given without treating of any differences in deciphering or demarking the aphorisms, or any changes of the text that the editors of the GA may have made.

4. *Nachlaß*, GA XIII, p. 61; Aug.–Sept. 1885, 40 [55]; KGW VII 3, p. 387.

5. *Nachlaß*, GA XIV, p. 327; cf. GA XVI, 415; Aug.–Sept. 1885, 40 [61]; KGW VII 3, p. 393.

6. *Nachlaß*, Nov. 1882–Feb. 1883, 4 [120]; KGW VII 1, p. 151.

7. *Nachlaß*, Fall 1887, 9 [188]; KGW VIII 2, p. 114.

8. Heidegger, *Nietzsche* I:17. That Nietzsche "hardly spoke of the will to power" in the works published by himself, is for Heidegger "a sign that he wanted to keep this innermost truth about being as such known by him to himself for as long as possible and wanted to place it under the protection of a uniquely simple speaking" (II:264).

9. K. Schlechta, *Der Fall Nietzsche*, p. 11, cf. p. 90, and in the afterword to Schlechta's edition of *Nietzsches Werke*, vol. III, p. 1433. That Schlechta does not exclude the possibility that important material might yet be found in the still unpublished *Nachlaß* is shown by a remark in the "philological afterword" to his Nietzsche edition: "When I said that *The Will to Power* presented nothing new, this remark referred only to the *Nachlaß*-anthology that goes by that name. However, the case does not seem any better with the materials published in the GA [*Großoktavausgabe*], XIIf. [1903 and after]—but my assertion does not extend to the entire *Nachlaß*. That cannot at all be the case because this

Nachlaß has in part not yet been deciphered or only defectively; thus there are still unknown texts in it" (SA III, p. 1405).

10. In a report on the preliminary reflections of the publishers of an Italian translation of Nietzsche's works and literary legacy, M. Montinari writes: "[We were able] to make no good use of the Schlechta edition for our purposes. In its first two volumes we did have a mostly faithful rendition of Nietsche's first editions before us, but in the third volume we had precisely the same material—although arranged in relatively chronological order—as became known in 1906 with publication of the second edition of *The Will to Power*. In Florence we would of course have been able to do something further beyond Schlechta: for we could with the help of Otto Weiss's apparatus on *The Will to Power* (in Volume XVI of the *Großoktavausgabe*) have eliminated many crude mutilations of the text; moreover we could have consulted the first one-volume *Will to Power* (1901) and retrieved a certain number of important fragments which in a peculiar fashion had disappeared from the much more compendious *Will to Power* (1906); finally, based on the list of manuscripts in Volumes XIII and XIV of the *Großoktavausgabe,* we could have complemented the manuscripts used for *The Will to Power* (i.e., those which were also listed in Volumes XV and XVI of the *Großoktavausgabe*). In this way we would have been able to produce more compendious *Nachlaß* from the 1880s in relative chronological order according to the manuscripts."

Montinari then goes into further editorial problems; he describes the path that led to the publishing of the KGW and names its objective. The quotation is taken from the original version of an essay by Montinari that the author was so kind as to make available to me. This essay has previously been published only in a translation into English by D. S. Thatcher by the title "The New Critical Edition of Nietzsche's Complete Works," in *The Malahat Review* 24 (1972):121–34.

11. A more thorough and detailed critique of Schlechta's procedure was presented by E. Heftrich in his book *Nietzsches Philosophie. Identität von Welt und Nichts,* pp. 291–95. It is strongly recommended.

12. K. Löwith, "Zu Schlechtas neuer Nietzsche-Legende," *Merkur* 12 (1958):782.

13. On the following statements quoted from Schlechta, cf. *Der Fall Nietzsche,* pp. 120–22.

14. Heftrich, *Nietzsches Philosophie,* p. 72.

15. *Nachlaß,* GA XIV, p. 349; Fall 1885–Fall 1886, 2 [17]; KGW VIII 1, p. 72.

16. A. Baeumler, "Nachwort zu Der Wille zur Macht," in *Die Unschuld des Werdens* [his edition of selections from the *Nachlaß*], vol. 2, p. 714.

17. On the problem of the relationship between the published and posthumous text, cf. Heftrich, *Nietzsches Philosophie,* pp. 69ff. Beyond that, another, earlier version of the ending of the aphorism WP 1067 printed in GA XVI, p. 515, can be cited. (It was printed as a preliminary stage of KGW VII 38 [12] in KSA 14, p. 727.) K. Löwith, in his book *Nietzsches Philosophie der ewigen Wiederkehr des Gleichen,* p. 97, compared the two versions in connection with a discussion with L. Klages. The first version brings to the foreground the "will to willing-again-and yet-once-more." It could be interpreted by including Nietz-

sche's doctrine of eternal return, which we cannot go into in this treatise. Löwith writes: "While in the first version the problem of a will for eternal return in the image of a reciprocal mirroring of a world-constitution and self-preservation finds an apparent solution from the fact that the wanting itself of the world is thought as a wanting of oneself again and again in terms of an eternal return and the human will as a wanting back-and-ahead moves in a circle, in the second version the dubiousness of a willing for fatality is rather concealed than expressed in the abrupt formulation of the 'will to power' that is supposed simply to be the same in man and in the world" (p. 98). Löwith finds that Nietzsche's doctrines of the will to power and of the eternal return contradict one another. In chapter 7, on the contrary, I have tried to prove that they are compatible. What I was concerned with there, among other things, was to show to what extent the highest will to power must want the eternal return of the same. In my interpretation the appearance of an objective discrepancy between the two versions of this text is resolved.

18. W. Weischedel, *Der Wille und die Willen*, pp. 76, 75.

19. K. Jaspers, *Nietzsche. Einführung in das Verständnis seines Philosophierens*, p. 310.

20. W. Schulz, *Der Gott der neuzeitlichen Metaphysik*, p. 101.

21. In *Der Wille und die Willen*, Weischedel asks: "Is Nietzsche a metaphysician, as Heidegger claims, or is he not, as Müller-Lauter asserts?" (p. 74). This question presupposes a common understanding of metaphysics between those questioned. Whether this is rightly assumed must be discussed at least in broad outlines.

According to Nietzsche, metaphysics arises from the fact that thinking "*mentally adds, invents the unconditioned in addition to the conditioned.*" Again and again Nietzsche tries to display the "nonsense of all metaphysics as a derivation of the conditioned from the unconditional" (WP 574). I orient myself by Nietzsche's own understanding of metaphysics when I deal with the genealogy of metaphysics from logic and when I distinguish Nietzsche's philosophy from that of Schopenhauer. For Nietzsche, metaphysics is involved when "a plurality is deduced from something first, simple." It is not accurate that my own understanding of metaphysics is exhausted in this formulation, as Weischedel apparently thinks (*Der Wille und die Willen*, p. 72). What matters to me is to highlight Nietzsche's understanding of metaphysics even in my discussion of other Nietzsche-interpretations. One cannot do Nietzsche justice if one imputes to him that he himself falls back into the form of metaphysics that he saw and criticized. Heidegger does this, as I try to show (in chapter 1). So does Weischedel, when he writes that Nietzsche could "indeed be considered the great destroyer of traditional metaphysics. But this merely means that he replaces it with his own metaphysics of the will to power. In his philosophical activity he too cannot forego replacing an absolute" (*Der Gott der Philosophen*, 1:455).

I speak of Nietzsche's non-metaphysical thinking only because in immanent description I make *his* understanding of metaphysics the basis. But if by metaphysics one understands far more comprehensively the question of being as a whole and as such, then one must, in my opinion, characterize Nietzsche as a metaphysician. Then of course the signs of dissolution in Nietzsche's metaphysics must be observed: "the whole" is still given only as "chaos"; being as such is no longer "determinable." If with Heidegger one interprets metaphysics in its "essence" as forgetfulness of being, then Nietzsche's philosophy, in which "being" is considered a mere fiction, proves to be a pronounced kind of metaphysics. In any case, I agree with Heidegger, insofar as I am not ready to remove Nietzsche from the history of metaphysics, not to say from the metaphysics of subjectivity. That subjectivity heightened to the extreme at the same time signals its own disintegration, is delineated more clearly here.

These few suggestions must suffice to delimit the question named by Weischedel at the beginning. Only insofar as Heidegger imputes to Nietzsche's thinking a metaphysics that he himself expressly opposed, does the distinction between myself and Heidegger assumed in the question rightly follow. Weischedel himself does not stop with that distinction. He points out that Heidegger's definition of the will to power as constitution of being and my statements on the will to power as sole quality "are closer to one another than it seems at first sight" (*Der Wille und die Willen*, p. 75). In fact, both Heidegger and I elaborate *the* will to power as *essence*. But even in this elaboration of what essence and existence mean in Nietzsche, our common ground ends.

22. "On the Happy Isles," KGW VI 1, p. 106.

23. G. Deleuze, *Nietzsche et la philosophie*, Paris 1970, p. 7.

24. M. Heidegger, *Nietzsche* I:73. Heidegger (II:36) states that "instead of 'will to power' Nietzsche says often and easily misunderstood '*Kraft*' [strength, force]."

25. Cf. *Nachlaß*, Spring–Fall 1881, 11 [115], KGW V 2, p. 380: "A drive, however complicated it may be, if it has a name, is considered a *unity* and tyrannizes all thinkers who seek its definition."

26. Köster criticizes the distinction I made concerning Nietzsche between a fixating concept and a referential word ("Die Problematik," p. 40). The questions raised in this context have been continued and deepened by J. Salaquarda (in "Der Antichrist," pp. 91ff). Salaquarda's remarks clarify how Nietzsche can give his "concepts," for example, "their own twilight color, an aroma both of depth and of mould" (*Nachlaß*, GA XIV, p. 355; June–July 1885, 37 [5]; KGW VII 3, pp. 305f.).

27. M. Heidegger, *Einführung in die Metaphysik*, Tübingen 1953, pp. 71ff.

28. Occasionally, however, Nietzsche also uses the word "being" in the sense of "life." Then being itself is understood as becoming. It also sometimes is used in the sense of "essence," "reality," "particular being," as well as "being as a whole."

29. If I reject the assumption that one could ascribe to Nietzsche's will to power a substantiality in the Leibnizian sense, this view does not conceal the idea that the will to power has substantiality in any other sense, as Köster suspects ("Die Problematik," pp. 43ff.). Nor do I run the danger of a reification when, following Nietzsche's trains of thought, I understand man as a unity of relatively independent components. "Man" does not in my interpretation thereby awaken "to new life" after his preceding "destruction," as Köster writes (p. 46). From the very start of my remarks on this topic, man is viewed as a plurality of forces organized into a unity.

30. *Nachlaß*, Spring 1888, 14 [37]; KGW VIII 3, p. 28.

31. Ibid., 14 [81]; KGW VIII 3, p. 53.

32. In GM I:2, one reads: "The rulers' right to give names goes so far that one should be permitted to grasp the origin of language itself as an expression of the rulers' power: they say 'that is that and that,' they imprint a seal on each thing and event with a sound and thereby take possession of it, as it were."

33. *Nachlaß*, GA XIII, p. 80; Spring 1882, 25 [96]; KGW VII 2, p. 19.

34. Ibid., XII, p. 156; Fall 1881, 12 [35]; KGW V 2, p. 480.

35. "*I* and *me* are always two different persons." Also my "*me*" is "fictitious and invented" (*Nachlaß*, GA XII, p. 304; Summer–Fall 1882, 3 [1], p. 352, and 3 [1] 333; KGW VII 1, pp. 96 and 93f.

36. *Nachlaß*, GA XIII, pp. 293f.; Spring 1884, 25 [401] KGW VII 2, p. 112.

37. Ibid., p. 249; June–July 1885, 37 [4]; KGW VII 3, p. 304.

38. Both Weischedel and Köster argue—against my interpretation of "will-to-power pluralism"—that Nietzsche after all again and again speaks of *the* will to power. The two critics both refer to Nietzsche's statement that this world is the will to power, and nothing besides. The question would arise, Weischedel writes, why Nietzsche "does not say—as Müller-Lauter would have it—: This world is an endless abundance of wills to power" (*Der Wille und die Willen*, p. 75). Köster states that the sentence, "according to Müller-Lauter, really should have been worded: 'This world is the (multiplicity of) wills to power'" ("Die Problematik," p. 39). In what sense Nietzsche can speak of *the* will to power as the world will be made clear in the following two sections.

The conclusion that Weischedel draws from that sentence is that it suggests "that Nietzsche in the last analysis thinks of the many concrete wills to power as manifestations of a unitary principle determining all reality," "of course in such a way that this comprehensive will takes shape in single wills to power" (*Der Wille und die Willen*, p. 75); this relegates Nietzsche's thinking to that metaphysical dimension that he has abandoned. Nietzsche himself would fall into that doubling of reality that he opposes: the will to power would consist first of a comprehensive principle and secondly of its particularizations. Weischedel, on the other hand, comes close to my view when he writes that the many power-wills are "connected insofar as they are all beings of the will to power" (p. 75), that the will to power has "its breadth of existence in the concrete wills, whose constitution it forms" (p. 76). Thus Weischedel is, after all, thinking the plurality of *the* will to power as something grounding it from the very first.

The problem of an interpretation that regards *the* will to power as a quasi-subject that desires itself, becomes clear in Köster's controversy with me. Köster finds in my "insistence on the plurality of 'ultimate givens'" a "onesidedness" ("Die Problematik," p. 48). The "no doubt constitutive aspect of plurality . . . in the will to power" must not "be emphasized at the expense of the equally constitutive aspect of unity" (41). In the course of interpreting a *Nachlaß* fragment from spring 1888 (which first became available unmutilated and complete in KGW VIII 3, pp. 49–51, Frgm. 14 [79]), he comes to the result: "The multiplicity of quanta (identical with it) thus seems to have its one ground in the will to power" (41 n. 22).

This seems questionable to me. The question that would have to be asked here is that of the relationship between "identity" and "ground." Köster runs the danger of falling into a dualism that is inadequate to the presuppositions of Nietzsche's thought when he distinguishes between the power-wills of the individual and *the* will to power. What applies to them, he writes, cannot "without further ado be generalized and applied to the will to power." My assertion that everything simple is the product of a real plurality, did indeed apply "to Nietzsche's destruction of the individual will, but it did not apply in the same way [*sic*] to the 'will to power,' which must not be confused [*sic*] with it" (p. 42).

On the other hand, Köster stresses that despite every distinction the two determinations belong together. But according to him they cannot be *thought together.* The "universal character of the world and hence the will to power manifests itself in the unthinkable and precisely so willed simultaneity of one and many," for which "Nietzsche used the concept of the Dionysian." In any case, "the Dionysian identity . . . was willed by Nietzsche despite and because of its impossibility" (pp. 42f.). Despite Köster's admonition (p. 36 n. 16) I cannot here go into Nietzsche's understanding of the Dionysian. In Köster's critique, in any event, the Dionysian is given the function of bringing the contradictions in the willed unthinkable into a synthesis (p. 36, cf. also p. 57), and from this unthinkable basis disqualifying my elaboration of Nietzsche's contradictions as rationalistic.

When Köster in his distinction between *the* will to power and *wills* to power calls attention to Nietzsche's use of quotation marks, this kind of argumentation contrasts with the subtlety of the topic. He points out that Nietzsche in two of the passages quoted by me puts the plural in quotation marks while the singular does not have them (pp. 48f. n. 33). This is supposedly "a fine point that should be noticed." When Köster then writes that "otherwise too in almost all the other *Nachlaß*-texts . . . the concept of the will to power is used first in the singular and not put in quotation marks," this is, to put it mildly, an exaggeration. There are many statements in which Nietzsche uses the plural without quotation marks. To list them here seems superfluous. But even disregarding Köster's statement with its tendency to generalize and taking seriously his demand that the meaning of the quotation marks used by Nietzsche "only emerges when one takes the (particular) text as a whole," it immediately turns out that one must go beyond the particular text to understand the meaning of this punctuation (p. 49).

An instructive example for this is Heftrich's effort to interpret the quotation marks in which Nietzsche enclosed the words "the world" at the beginning of WP 1067. It soon turns out that Heftrich must go far beyond the long aphorism: "For to interpret the quotation marks means naturally to define the term 'world'" (*Nietzsches Philosophie*, p. 54). The very interpretation that Köster holds up to me as a mode—Heidegger's exegesis of a dash—is only possible in terms of an understanding of the will to power that cannot be drawn from the interpreted aphorism.

If Köster's recommendation is further restricted, namely, to Nietzsche speaking of "two 'wills to power' in struggle," then one must discover that Köster does not draw his own interpretation exclusively from the cited aphorism (WP 401). That the will to power, out of the contradiction between life and nothingness, produces and at the same time takes back and abolishes within itself "the manifold contradictions of that empty appearance which is called 'world'" (p. 49) cannot be gathered from the text under examination, as one should expect from Köster's demand.

That my interpretation of the quotation marks in the expression of the two struggling "wills to power" also is based on a general understanding of Nietzsche's thinking is obvious. Here as elsewhere there are several reasons that make such punctuation suitable. In this case: the extreme simplification; the clarification that the will to nothingness too is will to power; the state of facts that the two wills to power (of the strong and the weak) are not *actual* power-wills, if one thinks them in their generality and not as particularizations within organizations. Why Nietzsche's philosophy in general must "always look like a philosophy in 'quotation marks'" would need a treatment of its own.

39. Heidegger, *Nietzsche* II:106.

40. *Nachlaß,* Spring 1888, 14 [72]; KGW VIII 3, p. 46. Immediately before this text is found the following list of Nietzsche's:

> Will to power as "natural law"
> Will to power as life
> Will to power as art
> Will to power as morality
> Will to power as politics
> Will to power as science
> Will to power as religion. (14 [71])

41. Here comparative "quotation-marks philosophy" is called for. The word "nature" is the only word in the list that is set in quotation marks. In Nietzsche's immediately prior note, only the word *Naturgesetz* (law of nature) was in quotation marks. It is therefore plausible to understand "nature" in the above-cited text as mechanically interpreted nature. This in turn would mean that therefore an interpretation of the series in the sense of the course of development of a metaphysically conceived will to power is excluded. What we have here is no quasi-Hegelianism.

42. *Nachlaß,* Spring 1888, 14 [136]; KGW VIII 3, p. 112. Nietzsche sets value on the statement that morphological descriptions cannot *explain* anything, but merely *describe* states of fact: cf. WP 645, *Nachlaß,* GA XVI, pp. 118f. and GA XIV, p. 331; June–July 1885, 36 [28]; KGW VII 3, p. 226 and Summer–Fall 1884, 27 [67]; KGW VII 2, p. 291.

43. *Nachlaß,* Spring–Summer 1888, 16 [86]; KGW VIII 3, pp. 311f.

44. "Truth is thus not something that exists and would have to be found or discovered—but something that *must be created* and that provides the name for a *process,* more yet for a will of overpowering that in itself has no end: to insert truth as . . . *an active determination, not* a becoming aware of something [that] would be fixed and determinate 'in itself.' It is a word for the 'will to power'" (*Nachlaß,* Fall 1887, 9 [91]; KGW VIII 2, p. 49).

45. Heidegger seeks to describe "how in Nietzsche's metaphysics the difference between *essentia* and *existentia* vanishes, why it must vanish at the end of metaphysics, how nonetheless precisely so the farthest distance from the beginning is reached" (*Nietzsche* II:475). In the context of his meditations on the history of metaphysics, Heidegger understands

the will to power as *essentia,* the eternal recurrence of the same as *existentia.* Such an as-cription is inappropriate to Nietzsche's thinking, but this cannot be treated further here. For the topic under discussion, it is essential that the relationship essence:existence must be thought even with regard to the will to power. Yet even here the distinction does seem to disappear: at least the prevalent Nietzsche-interpretations seem to provide evidence of this. If it is a matter of "disappearance," then to be sure Heidegger's statement within the cited context is true: that such a disappearance can "only be shown by trying to make the distinction visible." This will be attempted here.

To understand the essence of the will to power in a metaphysical sense, Heidegger sums up a few of the properties of the will, which can be found in Nietzsche: "will as that do-minion over . . . which reaches beyond itself, will as affect (the exciting outburst), will as passion (the outreaching rush to the distance of being), will as feeling (competency of the standing-to-oneself) and will as command." Heidegger rightly refuses to produce, out of these and other possible traits, "a formally neat" definition that would gather together all the cited information (*Nietzsche* I:70f.). In the course of this investigation I too will forego "definitions"; with them one would succumb to the logic that Nietzsche undermined.

As for the characteristics listed by Heidegger, the first one interests me the most. What is to be understood by the dominion that reaches out beyond itself? Heidegger interprets it as the self-overpowering of the will. "The one unitary essence of the will to power regu-lates the interweaving that characterizes it. Overpowering involves something that is over-come by the respective stage of power, and something that overcomes. What is to be overcome must put up resistance and for this must be something constant that maintains and preserves itself. But the overcoming too must have a status and be constant, other-wise it could neither go beyond itself, nor remain unwavering and certain of its possibil-ity of enhancement" (II:269f.). The overcomer needs the resistance of what must be over-come. I agree with Heidegger on this point. But when he understands the actual conflict of the overpowerer and that which is to be overpowered as stages of "something unitary" (cf. II:36 and 103), he elevates the essence of the will to power to an *absolute being* that develops itself into a plurality and yet remains in itself. This however misses Nietzsche's thought.

46. Nietzsche once also calls "apparent *purposefulness*" "the consequence . . . of the *will to power*" (WP 552). (On the problem of "interpretation," cf. section 9 of this chap-ter.)

47. "On the Thousand and One Goals."

48. *Nachlaß,* May–June 1888, 17 [4]; KGW VIII 3, p. 321.

49. "We should best be able to experience what we ourselves are by the guideline of the body"—as Nietzsche so often formulated it. It is "the much richer phenomenon, which allows of clearer observation" (WP 532, cf. 492).

50. *Nachlaß,* GA XIII, pp. 247f.; June–July 1885, 37 [4]; KGW VII 3, p. 302.

51. *Nachlaß,* GA XIII, pp. 248f.; June–July 1885, 37 [4]; KGW VII 3, p. 303.

52. *Nachlaß,* Spring–Fall 1881, 11 [316]; KGW V 2, p. 461.

53. Ibid. Nietzsche speaks of the last organisms in the plural: nations, states, societies.

For every will to power needs a counter-will in order to be able to be will to power. Concerning the three above-mentioned last structures it is therefore impossible to speak of a *very last one* as actually existing. Thus Nietzsche can say: "'Mankind' does not advance, it does not even exist" (WP 90). That he frequently uses the term "mankind" in delineating his own interests (e.g., in the sense of the masses, of the sum of all men, of the essence of all men) cannot be discussed here. Mankind is in any case not an organism for him and thus not a will to power. Cf. on this topic *Nachlaß*, Spring–Fall 1881, 11 [222], KGW V 2, p. 425, where Nietzsche opposes philosophical discussions "which transform mankind into an organism—that is the opposite of my tendency." He is concerned with "as many changing, different kinds of organisms as possible, which having reached maturity and rottenness let fall their fruit; the individuals, most of them perish, but what matters is only a few." Socialism is in this context seen by Nietzsche as a "fermentation" that announces "a great number of state-experiments, hence also of state-perishings and new seeds."

54. *Nachlaß*, GA XIII, p. 80; April–June 1885, 34 [247]; KGW VII 3, p. 223.
55. *Nachlaß*, Spring–Fall 1881, 11 [36]; KGW V 2, p. 352.
56. Ibid., 11 [148]; KGW V 2, p. 396.
57. Ibid., 11 [202]; KGW V 2, p. 421.
58. *Nachlaß*, Spring–Fall 1881, 11 [213]; KGW V 2, p. 423.
59. Ibid. Cf. also *Nachlaß*, GA XII, p. 60; Spring–Fall 1881, 11 [201]; KGW V 2, p. 420: "We must think it [i.e., the universe] as a whole precisely as far as possible from the organic!"
60. Cf. also, as early as *Nachlaß*, Spring–Fall 1881, 11 [201]; KGW V 2, p. 420: "The modern scientific counterpart to belief in god is belief in *the universe as an organism:* that disgusts me. Thus to make that very seldom, unspeakably derivative thing, the organic, which we perceive only on the crust of the earth, into the essential, universal, eternal! And the disguised polytheism in the monads, which together comprise the cosmic organism! . . . Sheer fantasy!—If the universe could become an organism, it would already have become so!"
61. Thus Nietzsche states, e.g. in WP 711, "that the world is not an organism at all, but chaos."
62. *Nachlaß*, GA XI, p. 235; Fall 1880, 6 [63]; KGW V 1, p. 540.
63. Ibid., pp. 541f. Here one reads: "The subject leaps around." There is no substantial difference.
64. *Nachlaß*, GA XIII, p. 245; Aug.–Sept. 1885, 40 [38]; KGW VII 3, p. 379. Another *Nachlaß*-note says of man "as multiplicity": "It would be false to deduce from a state necessarily to an absol[ute] monarch" (*Nachlaß*, GA XIII, p. 243; Summer–Fall 1884, 27 [8]; KGW VII 2, pp. 276f.). Nietzsche occasionally speaks of a "kind of aristocracy of 'cells'" in which dominion resides," WP 490; *Nachlaß*, GA XVI, p. 16; Aug.–Sept. 1885, 40 [42]; KGW VII 3, p. 382. Thus he highlights multiplicity also in the power-wills that are to be dominated.
65. *Nachlaß*, May–July 1885, 35 [59]; KGW VII 3, p. 259.
66. *Nachlaß*, GA XIII, p. 227; May–July 1885; 35 [58]; KGW VII 3, p. 259.

67. On segmentation and assimilation in the lowest animals up to the constitution of *castes* in the higher organisms, cf. also *Nachlaß*, Spring–Fall 1881, 11 [134], KGW V 2, pp. 388ff.

68. *Nachlaß*, GA XIII, p. 259, cf. XIV, 325; Fall 1885–Fall 1886, 2 [68]; KGW VIII 1, p. 90; cf. Fall 1885, 43 [2]; KGW VII 3, p. 439. *Nachlaß*, Fall 1887, 9 [98], KGW VIII 2, pp. 55f.: "*No* subject-'atoms.' The sphere of a subject constantly *growing* or *diminishing*—the central point of the system constantly *shifting*—; in case it cannot organize the appropriated mass it splits in two. On the other hand it can reshape a weaker subject into its functionary without destroying it and to a certain extent form a new subject together with it. No 'substance,' rather something that strives for enhancement; and that only indirectly wants to 'preserve' itself (what it wants is to *surpass* itself).

69. *Nachlaß*, GA XIII, p. 85; Summer 1886–Fall 1887, 5 [16]; KGW VIII 1, p. 194.

70. In the same note (WP 634) Nietzsche writes that it makes no difference whether we start with "the fiction of a little clump of an atom or even . . . its abstraction, the dynamic atom." In the latter, too, a thing is always thought "that produces effects—i.e., we have not got away from the habit into which our senses and language seduce us."

71. One must not misunderstand Nietzsche when he writes: "The victorious concept 'force,' by means of which our physicists have created God and the world, still needs to be completed: an inner will must be ascribed to it, which I designate as '*will to power*'" (WP 619). Deleuze calls this text "one of the most important texts that Nietzsche wrote to explain what he meant by will to power" (*Nietzsche et la philosophie*, p. 56). However, he takes Nietzsche's statement that the physical concept of force needs complementing by the will to power too literally. Yet he is right when he says: "The will to power . . . is never separable from such and such determinate forces." And one must agree with him when he states: "The will to power cannot be separated from force without falling into metaphysical abstraction" (p. 57).

The problematical character of Deleuze's interpretation comes to light, however, when Nietzsche adds: "Inseparable does not mean identical," and introduces the distinction: "Force is what can, will is what desires" (p. 57). Thus he draws a "distinction" where Nietzsche does not and *must* not distinguish if he does not want to surrender the inner coherence of his thinking. In this context, in addition to what has already been said, we can refer to Aphorism 36 from *Beyond Good and Evil,* which aims "to determine all efficient force univocally as—*will to power.*" "'Will,' of course, can affect only will. . . . One has to risk the hypothesis whether will does not affect will wherever 'effects' are recognized—and whether all mechanical occurrences are not, insofar as a force is active in them, will-force, effects of will" (KGW VI 2, p. 51).

In his writings Nietzsche uses the concept of force with two meanings: first in the sense of the mechanistic view, and second in the sense of 'will to power.' Genealogically the first meaning must be derived from the second. When he starts from the mechanistic way of thinking, Nietzsche can speak of the necessity of a *complement* for the physicists' concept of force, which Deleuze understands as a demand for an "addition of an inner will" (in this context he uses the word "*ajouter*" [add], p. 57). But here Nietzsche is not thinking "additively" any more than his call for the elimination of the popular mechanistic concept of necessity in another aphorism (WP 634) has a merely *subtractive* meaning. What results for the understanding of reality from the replacement of the mechanistic concept of force by Nietzsche's view makes a fundamental *re-thinking* of events in nature unavoidable, so that no truth can be ascribed to any "remnant" of mechanism. That Nietzsche does not deny the "usefulness" of mechanism is a different matter, which remains to be discussed.

P. Valadier states in the *Bulletin Nietzschéen* (*Archives de Philosophie* 36/1 (1973):141) that the works of Deleuze "have contributed not a little . . . to the interpretation of the will, which Müller-Lauter also defends." I agree with him with regard to the common ground of a few *tendencies* in Deleuze and myself in our statements about the problem of the will to power; Valadier's reference first brought this to my attention. The far-reaching *differences* of our interpretations must however not be overlooked. I was able to discuss them here only with a few examples. Meanwhile the aphorism cited at the beginning of this note has been published in KGW (*Nachlaß,* June–July 1885, 36 [31]; VII 3, p. 287). Instead of "inner will" it reads "an inner world." That to every physical force an *inner world* (i.e., a multiplicity of power-wills) must be ascribed, although one eventually never comes upon anything "simple," supports my interpretation. Cf. on this point, M. Bauer "Zur Genealogie von Nietzsches Kraftbegriff," in *Nietzsche-Studien* 13, pp. 222f., n. 34.

72. *Nachlaß,* Spring–Fall 1881, 11 [149]; KGW V 2, p. 452.

73. That there are really no qualities is stated at the end of the next-quoted text. For the only quality that exists is "will to power."

74. *Nachlaß,* Spring–Fall 1881, 11 [293]; KGW V 2, p. 397. On Nietzsche's mistake in the example, cf. A. Mittasch, *Nietzsches Naturbeflissenheit,* p. 25, who states that what we have "may be a transcription error as regards Schopenhauer's data, for he had spoken of one atom of hydrogen to nine atoms of 'oxygen,' when the correct statement would be 8 weight units of oxygen to 1 weight unit of hydrogen, 1 atom of oxygen to 2 atoms of hydrogen." The error is irrelevant to Nietzsche's fundamental statement that in the natural sciences we can speak only of *similar* "qualities" rather than of *identical* ones: "Nothing occurs twice; the oxygen atom is without any identical one; in truth for us the assumption that there are countless identical ones suffices" (*Nachlaß,* 11 [237], KGW V 2, pp. 429f.).

75. *Nachlaß,* GA XIII, p. 230; Summer 1883, 12 [27]; KGW VII 1, p. 442.

76. *Nachlaß,* GA XIII, pp. 227f.; May–July 1885, 35 [51], [52], [58], [59]; KGW VII 3, pp. 258f.

77. *Nachlaß,* GA XIII, p. 228; Fall 1885–Spring 1886, 1 [105]; KGW VIII 1, p. 31. Cf. *Nachlaß,* Spring–Fall 1881, 11 [70]; KGW V 2, p. 366: "Completely false valuations of the *perceiving* world toward the *dead* one. How we are it! *Belong* to it! And yet *superficiality,* deception begin with perception. . . . The '*dead*' world! eternally moved and without error, force against force! And in the perceiving world everything is false, arrogant! It is a feast to go out of this world into the 'dead world'—and the greatest lust for knowledge aims at opposing this false arrogant world with the eternal laws where there is no plea-

sure and no pain and deceit. . . . Let us *not* think of the return to non-perception as a retrogression! We become completely true, we are perfected. Death must be *reinterpreted*! We thus are *reconciled* with reality, i.e., with the dead world."

78. *Nachlaß*, GA XIII, p. 229; Summer 1883, 12 [27]; KGW VII 1, p. 422.

79. *Nachlaß*, GA XIII, p. 231; Summer 1883, 12 [31]; KGW VII 1, 424.

80. *Nachlaß*, Spring–Fall 1881, 13 [11]; KGW V 2, p. 518.

81. I call attention to Nietzsche's suggestion, cited earlier, that oxygen, for example, is something new at every moment.

82. *Nachlaß*, GA XIII, p. 227; May–July 1885, 35 [59]; KGW VII 3, p. 259.

83. This does not mean that no contradictions are to be found in Nietzsche's statements on the relationship inorganic/organic. If in one instance the organic is "derived," in another note one reads that the organic (in the narrower sense) has not originated (*Nachlaß*, GA XIII, p. 232; Spring 1884, 25 [403], KGW VII 2, p. 113). Evolution from the inorganic to man is sometimes understood as a rise and sometimes as a descent.

84. K. Jaspers, *Nietzsche,* p. 290.

85. Ibid., p. 296.

86. Ibid., p. 299.

87. Of course, we cannot go into this at this time. For Jaspers's understanding of Nietzsche's interpretation of interpretation, his remarks on the problem of "truth and life" would especially have to be examined (*Nietzsche,* pp. 184ff.).

88. Cf. *Nachlaß*, GA XIII, p. 64; Fall 1885–Spring 1886, 1 [115]; KGW VIII 1, p. 34: "The interpretative character of all occurrences. There is no event as such. What happens is that a group of appearances is *selected* and summarized by an interpreting being."

89. On the philosophical "analogy of interpretation" in Nietzsche, cf. Jaspers, *Nietzsche,* pp. 292ff.

90. *Nachlaß*, GA XIII, p. 69; Fall 1885–Spring 1886, 1 [120]; KGW VIII 1, p. 35.

91. Ibid.

92. *Nachlaß*, GA XIV, p. 40; April–June 1885, 34 [120]; KGW VII 3, p. 180.

93. *Nachlaß*, GA XIV, p. 31; Aug.–Sept. 1885, 40 [12]; KGW VII 3, p. 365.

94. "Of all the interpretations of the world attempted hitherto, the mechanistic one seems today to stand victorious in the foreground" (WP 618).

95. *Nachlaß*, GA XIII, p. 82; April–June 1885, 34 [247]; KGW VII 3, p. 224.

96. *Nachlaß*, GA XIII, pp. 83f.; Summer–Fall 1884, 26 [227]; KGW VII 2, p. 207.

97. Cf. *Nachlaß*, Spring–Fall 1881, 11 [338]; KGW V 2, p. 471: "Future history: *this* idea will become more and more victorious—and those who do not believe in it must finally *die out* according to their nature!"

98. *Nachlaß*, GA XIII, p. 82; April–June 1885, 34 [76]; KGW VII 3, p. 163.

99. *Nachlaß*, Spring–Fall 1881, 11 [234]; KGW V 2, p. 429.

100. *Nachlaß*, GA XIV, p. 31; Aug.–Sept. 1885, 40 [12]; KGW VII 3, p. 365.

101. M. Heidegger, *Sein und Zeit,* p. 153.

102. Jaspers, *Nietzsche,* 294.

103. Cf. already *Nachlaß*, Fall 1880, 6 [130], KGW V 1, p. 559: "The intellect is the in-

strument of our drives; it *never becomes free.* It sharpens itself in the struggle of the various drives and refines the activity of every single drive thereby." Later Nietzsche writes in reference to the possibility of self-knowledge by the intellect: "It is almost comical that our philosophers demand that philosophy must begin with a critique of the cognitive faculty. Is it not improbable that the organ of knowledge can critique itself when one has become distrustful about the previous results of cognition?" "An apparatus cannot carry out a *critique* of its own validity; the intellect cannot determine its own limits, nor its own success or failure." "A cognitive apparatus that wants to know itself!! One should be above the absurdity of this task! (The stomach that consumes itself!)" (*Nachlaß,* GA XIV, p. 3, Fall 1885–Spring 1886, 1 [60]; KGW VIII 1, p. 22. Fall 1885–Fall 1886, 2 [132]; KGW VIII 1, p. 131. Summer–Fall 1884, 26 [18]; KGW VII 2, p. 152).

104. Jaspers, *Nietzsche,* pp. 309f., cf. e.g., p. 330.

105. On the problem Nietzsche runs into when he tries to think the future great man and ultimately the overman as a synthesis of strength and wisdom, cf. chapter 6.

106. *Nachlaß,* GA XIII, pp. 48f.; Summer 1886–Spring 1887, 6 [23]; KGW VIII 1, pp, 246f.

107. Jaspers *Nietzsche,* p. 329.

108. At the beginning of his critical review, Köster calls it a "general characteristic" of my Nietzsche book that I take a stand "decisively on the ground of rational science which trusts in the arguments of logic" ("Die Problematik," p. 34). My interpretation could not be more completely misunderstood. This inappropriate prejudice colors all the objections Köster then presents. It is all the more incomprehensible since I begin my Nietzsche-portrayal with Nietzsche's destruction of logical contradiction, in order to display behind it the real oppositions of the power-wills.

Köster finds that I do not grasp Nietzsche's critique of logic radically enough (p. 40), "that Nietzsche's 'abolition' of the law of contradiction therefore remains in a peculiar fashion without thoroughgoing consequences" (p. 41). But since in the course of my investigation I *presuppose* Nietzsche's critique of logic, the question arises: What leads Köster to impute to me that logic that, like Nietzsche, I leave behind? Where I am concerned with the question of the possibility or impossibility of a philosophical proof of the synthesis of opposites in Nietzsche, Köster finds that "all signs indicate" that I expect "a rationally reasoning line of proof" from Nietzsche (p. 37). Must I say that I am not that foolish? When I discover antitheses in Nietzsche's thinking, according to Köster I merely hold firmly to their "*logical* incompatibility" (p. 37). Even the caution with which I choose my words (plausibility, incompatibility, philosophical demonstration), has not led Köster to question his accusation of rationalism. One gets the impression that he equates: displaying contradictions = rational = logical = scientific, and sees in such equation, which he groups under the rubric "conceivability," as "inconceivably wanted" by Nietzsche. As if there were no demonstrable thinking that leaves rationality behind, as if there were not—for example—Hegel's "science of logic," which contests the rightness-claim of formal logic.

It is grotesque to see my interpretation *in this regard* "as standing in clear contrast to the way Heidegger deals with Nietzsche" (p. 34). As if Heidegger were not likewise repeatedly concerned with showing the compatibility of Nietzsche's statements. Let us mention the question of the relationship between Nietzsche's doctrines of the will to power and the eternal recurrence as it is posed by Heidegger. He writes in a critique of Baeumler's Nietzsche-interpretation: "But supposing there is a contradiction between the two doctrines . . . : since Hegel we know that a contradiction is not necessarily [sic] a proof against the truth of a metaphysical proposition, but a proof in its favor. If the will to power and the eternal recurrence thus contradict one another, perhaps this contradiction is precisely a challenge to *think* [sic] these most difficult thoughts instead of fleeing to the 'religious.'"

But even granting that there is an irresoluable contradiction and that the contradiction compelled one to decide: either will to power or eternal recurrence, why does Baeumler then decide against "Nietzsche's most difficult thought and the pinnacle of contemplation for the will to power?" (*Nietzsche* I:30f.). Heidegger places Nietzsche without restriction under the claim of thinking; even fundamental contradictions are for him no challenge to flee to the "unthinkable"; he grants the possibility that there could be in Nietzsche an irresoluble contradiction that would compel one to decide. As is well known, Heidegger, as opposed to Baeumler, sees no contradiction between Nietzsche's two doctrines; he seeks rather—of course, in his own fashion—to demonstrate their compatibility, indeed, their "*inner unity*," and that, absolutely "within the horizon of metaphysics and with the help of its distinctions" (II:14).

Köster, however, claims to have discovered that (as opposed to Heidegger) I apply rational standards to Nietzsche when I ask about the compatibility of his fundamental statements. Does the radicalization of Nietzsche's denial of the law of contradiction consist for Köster in Nietzsche's supposedly being able to express himself only in contradictions? What I argued above against Jaspers applies in principle to Nietzsche's thinking. If Nietzsche, in the context of portraying his own position, must not permit any contradictions, that does not mean that he subjects himself to the truth-criterion of logic. The claim of the "rightness" of his thinking is of a fundamental kind; it is not affected by the formal demands of "logical coherence." In my book I interrogate Nietzsche's thinking only in terms of this claim.

Köster and I apparently agree about the inner incompatibility of Nietzsche's fundamental ideas. Köster's insinuation that I could believe that Nietzsche "did not see" their incompatibility ("Die Problematik," p. 58) is absurd: for I strive precisely to show how Nietzsche struggles for compatibility. When I state that the synthesis of strength and wisdom in the overman could still be kept open by Nietzsche only as a belief, I do not leap out of immanent critique by this "only," as Köster says (pp. 58f. n. 50). By such a "restriction" I also do not measure him by a "scientific claim," but I speak from the requirement that Nietzsche himself made on his thinking with admirable intensity. If one describes the incompatible in its full incompatibility, in my opinion one does greater justice to this intensity than if one brings the movement of his thinking to rest in the unthinkable. Precisely the latter would mean "to close one's eyes to dangers" (p. 60) that come toward us with Nietzsche's philosophy.

109. "The inorganic *determines* us completely: water, air, ground, terrain, electricity, etc. We are plants under such conditions," a note states (*Nachlaß,* Spring–Fall 1881, 11 [210],

KGW V 2, p. 423). The determining factor does not remain as a cause outside us, *we* are what determines us. —On the other hand, this is also true: "You say that food, place, air, society transform and determine you? Well, your opinions do so even more, for they determine you for this food, place, air, society" (*Nachlaß*, Spring–Fall 1881, 11 [143], KGW V 2, p. 394).

110. In Nietzsche transcendental and naturalistic thinking not only underwent a symbiosis, they interpenetrate and completely fuse together. Any emphasis on Nietzsche's naturalism needs correction by pointing out that *all being* interprets, *is* interpretation. And vice versa it is also true that every interpretation is "natural." It is inadequate and leads to misunderstandings in discussing Nietzsche's revision of the "concept of the transcendental" to come to a stop with his perspective doctrine of human affects, as J. Habermas does (cf. his "Afterword" to *Nietzsche: Erkenntnistheoretische Schriften*). This perspectivity must in turn be understood in terms of the multiplicity of "natural" perspectives that have been incorporated in the human being. Such an interpretation makes it possible for Nietzsche to make statements about the interpretative character of both inorganic and organic beings and at the same time to undermine the possible reproach that his philosophy of the will to power is dogmatic naturalism. Points of departure for a critique of Nietzsche are also given on the plane of understanding thus attained. But it must first be attained if an objectively grounded critique of Nietzsche's "theory of knowledge" is to be attempted.

111. "Perhaps indeed there was nothing more fearful and uncanny in the whole prehistory of man than his *mnemotechnique,*" Nietzsche writes in *On the Genealogy of Morals* (GM II:3). Starting with the question of the *ability to promise,* he there gives suggestions for his genealogy of the memory.

112. *Nachlaß,* GA XIV, pp. 40f.; June–July 1885, 38 [1]; KGW VII 3, pp. 323f.

113. "'I have no idea how I *am acting*! I have no idea how I *ought to act*!'—you are right, but be sure of this: you will be *acted upon*! at every moment! Mankind has in all ages confused the active and the passive: it is their everlasting grammatical blunder." "The struggle itself is hidden from me, and likewise the victory as victory; for, though I certainly learn what I finally *do,* I do not learn what motive has therewith actually proved victorious" (D 129, cf. D 124). Cf. also *Nachlaß,* Spring–Fall 1881, 11 [131]; KGW V 2, p. 387.

114. Nietzsche's "fatalism" does not conflict with his self-understanding as the one who must appeal to men to take upon themselves the truth of the will to power. "Appeal" and "proclamation" are in turn *necessitated,* just as the acceptance of the appeal by the future great men also would be.

Chapter 9: The Organism as Inner Struggle

1. "Human All Too Human," 3; cf. also "Why I Am So Clever," 2: "ignorance *in physiologicis—that damned 'idealism'*—that was the real calamity in my life, totally superfluous and stupid, something of which nothing good ever grew, for which there is no compensation, no counterbalance. The consequences of this 'idealism' provide my

explanation of all blunders, all great instinctual aberrations and 'modesties' that led me away from the task of my life; for example that I became a philologist—why not at least a physician or something else that opens one's eyes?"

2. A. Mittasch, *Frederich Nietzsches Naturbeflissenheit*, p. 7. Cf. K. Schlechta, "Nachwort," *Werke* III:1444: "I consider it permissible to blame parts of this admission on the coquetry typical of *Ecce Homo*. But with regard to the radical change of *direction* of his main interest, Nietzsche is no doubt saying the truth."

3. Schlechta, "Nachwort," pp. 1443f.

4. "Nietzsches Verhältnis zu Naturwissenschaft und Naturphilosophie," unpublished dissertation, Münster, 1951, p. 5.

5. I must agree with A. Mittasch, who states that "Nietzsche's natural philosophy to a considerable extent is the foundation also of his philosophy of culture and his final metaphysical thinking" (*F. Nietzsche als Naturphilosoph*, p. xiii). Yet the dependence of Nietzsche's natural philosophy on his reading of scientific writings should not be overestimated. Mittasch himself, citing H. Heimsoeth and C. A. Bernoulli, also points out that Nietzsche went his own way (pp. 31, 44). This applies both to his selection and to his use of the works he consulted.

6. Mittasch, in his book *Nietzsches Naturbeflissenheit*, alludes to Nietzsche's lack of knowledge of elementary chemistry, citing a note from the *Nachlaß* from the Spring–Fall of 1881, 11 [140] (KGW V, 2). If Nietzsche, apparently in reference to the composition of water, speaks there of 9 parts oxygen to 11 parts hydrogen, this could be "a copying error from Schopenhauer's statement which had spoken of '1 atom of hydrogen and 9 atoms of oxygen' . . . (Actually the figures are 8 weight units of oxygen to 1 weight unit of hydrogen, i.e., one atom of oxygen and 2 atoms hydrogen.)" (p. 25).

7. Mittasch writes that Nietzsche "was equipped with a rare ability, even without thorough technical studies, to see through the surface to the bottom of things—or to the 'background' of things" (*Nietzsche als Naturphilosoph*, p. 30).

8. *Nachlaß*, End of 1886–Spring 1887, 7 [25], KGW VIII 1, 312; 7 [9] KGW VIII, 1, p. 303.

9. *Nachlaß*, Spring 1888, 14 [95], KGW VIII, 3, 66. Cf. 14 [82], KGW VIII 3, p. 54; 14 [186], KGW VII 3, p. 165.

10. KGW III 1, pp. 247, 326.

11. *Nachlaß*, June–July 1885, 36 [31], KGW VII, 3, p. 287.

12. *Nachlaß*, End of 1886–Spring 1887, 7 [25], KGW VIII 1, p. 312. Cf. GM II, 12.

13. A clear influence of Nietzsche's reception of ideas or concepts from Roux is found in the following fragments of M III 1, which are published in KGW V, 2, under the numerals 11: [28], [130], [131], [132], [134], [182], [241], [243], [256], [284].

14. Cf. above all the following fragments from M III 4 b (VIII 1, notebook 7): [86]–[95], [98], [174], [178], [190], [194], [197], [211], [273].

15. GA XIII, Aph. 628, pp. 259f. The editors of this volume list sheet 20 of the notebook W II as the place where this fragment was found; but it is not to be found there. The editors of KGW have until now been unable to find its "location." Internal evidence

suggests that it is a note from the year 1884; this will be discussed below; VII 2, 26 [272], [275] [Meanwhile M. Montinari found the fragment and clarified the context. Two things are important here:—1. The editors of GA XIII erroneously refer to notebook W II as the source, whereas the cited text is located in W VII (sheet 20).—2. The text, together with GA 259 is the continuation of the preliminary version of BGE 12, as is noted by the editor of KGW in the critical apparatus to BGE 13]. The use of Roux's concepts occurs in VII 2, 25 [333], [426]; 26 [138] ("durability"). Nietzsche still speaks of "self-regulation" as an organic process even after he has polemicized against Roux's supposed understanding of this concept. Cf. *Nachlaß*, Aug.–Sept. 1885, 40 [37]; KGW VII 3, p. 378; BGE 36.)

16. Nietzsche obtained an essential orientation on Darwinism from F. A. Lange's *Geschichte des Materialismus,* 1866 (cf. his letter to C. v. Gersdorff dated February 2, 1868, KGB I 2, pp. 257f.). He first saw the considerably expanded version of Lange's book (1873–75) in the 4th edition dated 1882, as J. Salaquarda has shown. Lange goes into details on the discussion of Darwinism. Nietzsche may well have drawn suggestions for his own critique from there. However, in the fourth edition of Lange's book published by H. Cohen, the notes from which Nietzsche might have taken his source references, for example, were not printed (cf. Salaquarda, "Nietzsche und Lange," p. 240 n. 20). But even in his Basel period, Nietzsche had taken a lively interest in the discussion of evolutionary theory independently of Lange. Thus E. Förster-Nietzsche reports that in 1869, in the disputes between E. Haeckel, on the one hand, and L. Rütimeyer, C.E. von Baer, and C. v. Naegeli, on the other, Nietzsche had sided with the latter (*Das Leben Friedrich Nietzsches* II, book 2, pp. 521f.). Nietzsche also acquired and worked through v. Naegeli's later book *Mechanische-physiologische Theorie der Abstammungslehre,* 1884, in which he could find objections to Darwin's emphasis on external influence in the formation of organs, as well as in Roux (and in earlier statements of v. Naegeli, as well as in Lange, and elsewhere [pp. 326ff.]). On the significance of W. H. Rolph's abundance theory for Nietzsche's critique of Darwin in the 1880s, cf. note 169, below.

17. On the influence of Mayer's writings on Nietzsche's understanding of events in nature, cf. note 101, below. The beginning of the Fragment 11 [131], KGW V 2, p. 387, is cited from Foster's book (p. 524).

18. Peter Gast and August Horneffer in their commentary on GA XIII (pp. 367f.) referred to three books that had "most inspired" Nietzsche in 1883. Besides Roux's work they name G. H. Schneider, *Der tierische Wille* (1880) and E. v. Hartmann, *Phänomenologie des sittlichen Bewußtseins* (1879). With regard to Roux, they give the false impression that Nietzsche had not occupied himself with this book until late summer 1883. Charles Andler had already called attention to the fact that Nietzsche had consulted Roux "with predilection" in biological questions. Yet he could base his view neither on the completely published and chronologically reliable Nietzsche *Nachlaß,* nor did he have at hand the first edition of Roux's book, which Nietzsche had used. But from the second edition of 1895, he was able, despite Roux's revisions, to recognize that "Wilhelm Roux provided Nietzsche a great number of arguments which he would muster against vulgar Darwinism. He rooted him

in the neo-Lamarckism for which Rütmeyer had given him the first formulation" (*Sa vie et sa pensée,*pp. 1920ff., cited according to the 1958 edition, II, pp. 525f.).

19. For Nietzsche's first occupation with natural-scientific questions, cf. K. Schlechta and A. Anders, *Friedrich Nietzsche. Von den verborgenen Anfängen seines Philosophierens.*

20. *Nachlaß,* Spring 1880, 2 [55]; KGW V 1, p. 372.

21. *Nachlaß,* Spring–Fall 1881, 11 [12]; KGW V 2, p. 343.

22. Cf. Schlechta-Anders, pp. 55–59.

23. *Nachlaß,* Spring–Fall 1881, 11 [128]; KGW V 2, p. 385. Nietzsche cites "love" and "hate" as such intellectual interpretations. He is obviously referring to Roux's suggestion that the theoretical solution of the problem of purposefulness had already been found in Empedocles (Roux, *Der Kampf der Theile im Organismus,* p. 1). When KGW writes "annoyance" [*Ärger*], "love," and "hate," in the Nietzsche-fragment, I suspect a misreading; the word "*Ärger*" makes no sense in this context. Consulting the Roux text, the reading "*Kräfte*" [forces] seems plausible. (M. Montinari has meanwhile proven to my satisfaction that Nietzsche wrote "*Ärger.*" Cf. Montinari's statements in KSA 14, p. 645. I should have checked with him before publishing my text. As for the matter at hand, I now suspect—not out of obstinacy—a slip of the pen on Nietzsche's part. Otherwise I am unable to understand the formulation.)

24. *Nachlaß,* Spring–Fall 1881, 11 [134]; KGW V 2, pp. 388ff.

25. Ibid., 11 [132]; p. 388. Roux, *Der Kampf der Theile,* p. 65.

26. Ibid., 11 [128]; p. 385.

27. Ms. P I 20, 190, cited according to Schlechta-Anders, *Fr. Nietzsche,* p. 39.

28. Let us point out additionally only Nietzsche's effort in 1881 to understand man as the picture-shaper. His reflections once led him to conclude: "To reshape the ego-feeling! To weaken the personal inclination! To accustom one's eye to the reality of things! *Temporarily to disregard persons as much as possible*! What effects this must have! . . . To let ourselves be *possessed by things* (not by persons) and by as broad as possible a scope of *true things*! The result of this must be awaited: we are the *plowed land* for things. *Images of existence* must grow out of us and we should be such as fertility makes us be. . . . The images of existence have until now been the *most important* thing—they rule over mankind" (*Nachlaß,* Spring–Fall 1881, 11 [21]; KGW V 2, pp. 348f.). Just a little later, he writes: "To obtain the advantages of a dead person. . . . To think oneself away from mankind, to forget the desires of every kind: and to use up the entire excess of strength in *observing.* To be the *invisible observer*!" (11 [35]; p. 352). As so often, here we see Nietzsche's free-floating groping for the possibilities of human existence.

29. *Nachlaß,* Fall 1881, 14 [2]; KGW V 2, p. 521.

30. Schlechta-Anders, *Fr. Nietzsche,* p. 57.

31. *Nachlaß,* Fall 1881, 14 [3]; KGW V 2, p. 521.

32. "The purpose of science is world destruction. But in the process it happens that the first effect is that of small doses of opium: and intensification of world-affirmations" (GA IX, Aph. 30, p. 72). Cf. on this topic, Schlechta-Anders, esp. pp. 50ff.

33. *Nachlaß,* Spring–Fall 1881, 11 [173]; KGW V 2, p. 405.

34. Ibid., 11 [167]; p. 404.

35. Ibid., [130]; p. 386. On Nietzsche's idea of breeding, as developed in the contexts under discussion, cf. 11 [276]; 445.

36. Roux understands by mechanistic events "strictly lawful events," and influenced by his Jena philosophical studies under R. Eucken (1877–78), he based himself on Kant. On the misunderstandings that his concept of evolutionary mechanics provoked among his scientific colleagues, cf. his statements in *Die Medizin der Gegenwart in Selbstdarstellungen,* pp. 145f.

37. Ibid., pp. 152f.

38. Roux, p. iv.

39. Roux, p. 38.

40. Roux, p. 34, cf. p. 236.

41. "Über die Verzweigungen der Blutgefäße. Eine morphologische Studie."

42. Before Roux, W. His and F. Boll applied the struggle for existence to explain certain tissue processes, though without elevating struggle to the fundamental principle of interpretation. Cf. W. Roux, "Über die Selbstregulation der Lebewesen," p. 643.

43. Cf. Roux, *Der Kampf,* pp. 64f.

44. Ibid., pp. 2f.

45. Ibid., pp. 73ff.

46. *Nachlaß,* Spring–Summer 1883, 7 [86]; KGW VII 1, p. 280 (cf. Roux, pp. 73ff., 87, 76–78); 7 [95]; KGW, pp. 282f. (cf. Roux pp. 76, 73, 79, 80). On p. 283, line 5, instead of "*leichte*" (easy) the reading should be "*leichter*" (easier).

47. Ibid., 7 [95]; p. 282. Cf. Roux, p. 76.

48. Ibid., [93]; p. 282. Cf. Roux, p. 69.

49. Roux, *Der Kampf,* p. 69.

50. *Nachlaß,* Spring–Fall 1881, 11 [132]; KGW V 2, p. 388. Cf. Roux, *Der Kampf,* p. 71.

51. *Nachlaß,* Spring–Summer 1883, 7 [92]; KGW VII, 1, p. 282. Cf. Roux, *Der Kampf,* p. 65.

52. Ibid., pp. 65f.

53. *Nachlaß,* Spring–Summer 1883, 7 [92]; KGW VII, 1, pp. 310f. Cf. Roux, *Der Kampf,* pp. 97, 98, 102.

54. On the following passage, cf. ibid., pp. 215ff.

55. Ibid., pp. 219f.

56. Ibid., pp. 327f. Both Darwin and Haeckel received Roux's investigations with great recognition (S. R. Mocek, *Wilhelm Roux—Hans Driesch. Zur Geschichte der Entwicklungsphysiologie der Tiere,* p. 72). Darwin as early as 1881 called Roux's book "the most important book about evolution that has appeared in a long time" (Roux, *Ges. Abh.* I, 141).

57. *Nachlaß,* Spring–Summer 1883, 7 [89]; KGW VII 1, p. 281. Cf. Roux, *Der Kampf,* pp. 39ff.

58. *Nachlaß,* 7 [194]; p. 312. Cf. Roux, *Der Kampf,* p. 110.

59. *Nachlaß,* 7 [98]; p. 283. Cf. Roux, *Der Kampf,* pp. 81–83. Roux stressed the inde-

pendence of the struggle of the parts from Darwin's theory of natural selection in 1902 under the impression of critiques of Darwin's principles. Even if it were proven, he stated, that the struggle for existence and selective sexual breeding had played no part in the origin of species, "I must still stress that this would include *nothing against my derivations of the effect of the struggle of the parts in the organism.*" For these refer "to the origin of the *most general tissue* qualities, the self-preservation qualities and the resulting *most general formative capacities*" ("Über die Selbstregulation der Lebewesen," pp. 633ff.).

60. Roux, *Der Kampf,* p. 180, cf. p. 200.

61. Ibid., p. 81; Nietzsche, *Nachlaß,* 7 [98]; p. 283.

62. Nietzsche, *Nachlaß,* 7 [196]; p. 312.

63. Ibid., 7 [94], 7 [90]; cf. Roux, *Der Kampf,* p. 63; Nietzsche, *Nachlaß,* 7 [92]; cf. Roux, *Der Kampf,* pp. 107, 110; Nietzsche, *Nachlaß,* 7 [174]; cf. Roux, *Der Kampf,* p. 110.

64. Nietzsche, *Nachlaß,* 7 [86], [87]; pp. 280f.

65. Ibid., 7 [95]; pp. 281f.; cf. Roux, *Der Kampf,* p. 80.

66. Nietzsche, *Nachlaß,* 7 [88]; p. 281.

67. "This word must of course here not be understood as conscious feeling, but in the sense of a stronger affinity for food when there are stronger nutritional needs" (Roux, *Der Kampf,* p. 22).

68. Nietzsche, *Nachlaß,* 7 [98]; pp. 283f.; cf. Roux, *Der Kampf,* p. 84.

69. Nietzsche, *Nachlaß,* 7 [170]; p. 305.

70. Ibid., [97]; p. 283.

71. *Nachlaß,* Spring 1884, 25 [96]; KGW VII, 2, p. 29.

72. *Nachlaß,* Summer–Fall 1884, 26 [386]; KGW VII 2, p. 250.

73. *Nachlaß,* Spring 1884, 25 [336]; KGW VII 2, pp. 95f.

74. Ibid., 25 [427]; p. 121.

75. Ibid., [96]; p. 29.

76. Ibid., [314]; p. 89.

77. *Nachlaß,* June–July 1885, 36 [34]; KGW VII 3, p. 288.

78. *Nachlaß,* Spring 1884, 25 [316]; KGW VII 2, p. 89.

79. Ibid., 25 [356]; p. 102. Cf. Nietzsche's allusion to "the Darwinists and anti-teleologists among the physiological workers, with their principle of the 'least possible force' and the greatest possible stupidity" in BGE 14; also TI 9:14: "Darwin has forgotten the spirit (—that is English)."

80. Ibid., 25 [433]; p. 123.

81. *Nachlaß,* Summer–Fall 1884, 26 [68]; KGW VII 2, 164.

82. *Nachlaß,* Spring 1884, 25 [426]; KGW VII 2, 120.

83. Ibid., 25 [448]; p. 128.

84. GA XIII, pp. 259f. (cf. note 15, above). In the cited note Nietzsche lists additionally "self-regulation," "adaptation," and "division of labor" among the teleological determinations that still remain indispensable.

85. *Nachlaß,* 1884, 26 [272], KGW VII 2, p. 219.

86. Ibid., 26 [273]; p. 219.

87. A collection of the "distinctions and terms" that Roux later introduced can be found in D. Barfurth, "Wilhelm Roux zum 60. Geburtstag," in *Archiv f. Entwicklungsmechanik der Organismen* XXX:I, 1910.

88. Roux's 1881 book was determined by a Darwinism with a Haeckelian stamp, which included ideas of Lamarck's. Haeckel's conviction of the inheritability of acquired characteristics was expressed in Roux's doctrine of the inheritance of individually acquired functional adaptations. On Roux's change of standpoint on this problem, cf. R. Mocek, *Wilhelm Roux,* pp. 80ff.

89. For a more precise definition of the "self" in Roux, one would have to go into the distinction between determination factors and realization factors, which would lead beyond what is possible in the present context.

90. W. Roux, *Die Medizin der Gegenwart,* p. 187.

91. For a general summary and information on Driesch's beginning with Roux and going beyond him, cf. his book *Philosophie des Organischen,* 1921 (German edition), pp. 47ff. Driesch's point of departure from an entelechetic agent left no room for Roux's idea of a struggle of the parts. Cf. on this topic Driesch's book *Die organischen Regulationen* (1901). In addition, Roux's reply in "Über die Selbstregulation der Lebewesen," pp. 635, 639–43, in which he also opposes O. Hartwig, on whom Driesch bases himself.

92. On the sometimes very strong polemics waged by Roux against Driesch, cf. among others: "Über die Selbstregulation der Lebewesen," his review of Driesch's 1901 book *Die organischen Regulationen,* pp. 651ff.; on Roux's dispute over principles with the "entelechists" cf. his statements under the title "Prinzipielles der Entwicklungsmechanik," in *Annalen der Philosophie,* III, 1923, pp. 454–73. On the progress of the spreading controversies concerning the results of embryological experiments from Roux's standpoint, a summary of information can be found in D. Barfurth, "Wilhelm Roux,"pp. xivf. Roux's interpretation of the evolution of small whole embryos from the holistic potency [*Totipotenz*] of bifurcating cells and his interpretation of the whole formations as postgeneration, a theory first propounded by Roux in 1892, are especially important for his controversy with the "teleologists" (but not only with them). Here we can only refer to H. Spemann's "abolition" of the antithesis between Roux and Driesch. Cf. R. Mocek, *Wilhelm Roux,* pp. 104ff.

93. *Die Medizin in der Gegenwart,* p. 163.

94. *Prinzipielles der Entwicklungsmechanik,* p. 471. To what extent Roux's use of the prefix "self-" has worked against his own intentions is shown by A. Portmann's citing Roux in his elaboration of the organic "self-representation" as interiority expressing itself (*An den Grenzen des Wissens,* pp. 138–40).

95. *Nachlaß,* Summer–Fall 1884, 26 [272]; KGW VII 2, p. 219.

96. *Nachlaß,* Spring 1884, 25 [389]; KGW VII 2, pp. 109f.

97. Ibid., 25 [436]; p. 123; cf. BGE 19.

98. *Nachlaß,* 25 [411], p. 115.

99. *Nachlaß,* Summer–Fall 1884, 26 [276]; KGW VII 2, p. 220.

100. *Nachlaß,* 26 [277]; p. 220.

101. Nietzsche's understanding of release of energy [*Kraftauslassung* = "letting out, vent-

ing"] would need extensive treatment with regard to the concept of "release" [*Auslösung* = "triggering"]. It must be left aside here since Nietzsche's use of the term is not due to the influence of Roux, but rather is attributable to J. R. Mayer. Mittasch, with outstanding knowledge of both Nietzsche and Mayer, dealt in great detail with this influence in his book *Nietzsche als Naturphilosoph*. His remarks, which cast great light on essential aspects of Nietzsche's doctrine of the will to power, have not gotten the attention they deserve. Since 1881 Nietzsche used terms such as "triggering" (of power) and "explosion" again and again. What he means by them can be adequately understood only by referring to Mayer's essay "*Über Auslösung*" (1876), which Nietzsche discovered bound in his copy of Mayer's *Mechanik der Wärme* (1873). He wrote to P. Gast on April 16, 1881, in a postscript: "'*Über Auslösung*' is for me the most essential and useful part of Mayer's book" (*Fr. Nietzsches Briefe an P. Gast*, p. 63). In his essay Mayer traces all motion phenomena—from inorganic reality, through organic processes, all the way to psychology—back to triggerings that are not comprehensible mathematically (in numerical units). Nietzsche accepts Mayer's statements on the subject of "little causes—great effects," including the examples Mayer gives, for example, in GS 360. Cf. Mittasch, *Nietzsche als Naturphilosoph*, p. 119, who also lists a great number of further documentations for Nietzsche's adoption of Mayer's notion of triggering (pp. 120–26). Nietzsche also owes essential insights to Mayer's understanding of "stimulus" and "regulation." Mittasch sums it up: "Robert Mayer's theory of action [*Wirklehre*], including his theory of triggerings, found its only strong reception and extensive completion in Nietzsche's theory of energy (and drives)" (p. 127).

102. Nietzsche, *Nachlaß*, Fall 1887, 9 [151]; KGW VIII 3, p. 88; *Nachlaß*, Spring 1888, 14 [174]; KGW VIII 2, p. 152.

103. *Nachlaß*, May–July 1885, 35 [51]; KGW VII 3, p. 259.

104. Aversion as an inhibition or resistance is accordingly "a *necessary ingredient of all activity* (all activity is directed *against* something that must be overcome)." So he wrote as early as 1884 (*Nachlaß*, 26 [275], KGW VII 2, p. 220) that the will to power thus strives for resistances, for aversion. Of course a distinction must be drawn between "aversion as a stimulant for the enhancement of power and aversion after a waste of power." The latter is a symptom of exhaustion, or even more originally "incapacity for resistance" (*Nachlaß*, Spring 1888, 14 [174]; KGW VIII 3, esp. p. 153). The aversion striven for in the quest for resistances shows that "there is a will to suffering at the basis of all organic life" (*Nachlaß*, VII 2, p. 220). Therefore "the will to power is not a being, not a becoming, but a *pathos*." This is "the most elementary fact from which a becoming, an action first ensues" (*Nachlaß*, Spring 1888, 14 [79]; KGW VIII 3, p. 51).

105. *Nachlaß*, Summer 1883, 12 [51]; KGW VII 1, p. 424; cf. *Nachlaß*, Summer–Fall 1884, 26 [156]; KGW VII 2, p. 188.

106. *Nachlaß*, 25 [403]; KGW VII 2, p. 113.

107. On perception in the inorganic world, cf. *Nachlaß*, May–June 1885, 35 [53], [58], [59]; KGW VII 3, pp. 258f. Cf. also chapter 8 in this volume.

108. Nietzsche, *Nachlaß*, Fall 1887, 9 [151]; KGW VIII 2, p. 88.

109. *Nachlaß*, Summer–Fall 1884, 26 [276]; KGW VII 2, p. 220.

110. *Nachlaß,* Fall 1887, 10 [138]; KGW VIII 2, pp. 201f.

111. *Nachlaß,* Summer–Fall 1884, 26 [277]; KGW VII 2, pp. 220f.

112. *Nachlaß,* Aug.–Sept. 1885, 40 [55]; KGW VII 3, p. 387.

113. *Nachlaß,* April–June 1885, 33 [248]; KGW VII 3, p. 224. Cf. *Nachlaß* June–July 36 [18]; KGW 283; also *Nachlaß,* Aug.–Sept. 1885, 39 [13]; p. 353.

114. *Nachlaß,* Spring 1888, 14 [79]; KGW VIII 3, p. 50. Nietzsche characterizes the difference between the mechanistic interpretation of events and his own in *Nachlaß,* Fall 1885–Spring 1886 as follows: "The absolutely identical course but the higher interpretation of the course! The mechanistic indifference of strength, but the intensification of the feeling of power!" (1 [119]; KGW VIII 1, p. 34.)

115. *Nachlaß,* Spring 1888, 14 [81]; KGW VIII 3, p. 52.

116. *Nachlaß,* May–July 1885, 35 [15]; KGW VII 3, p. 236. Strictly speaking, it is true "that the concept of causality is completely unusable—a necessary sequence of circumstances does not necessarily result from a causal relationship (—that would mean to cause its *effective capacity* to leap from 1 to 2, to 3, to 4, to 5). *The causality interpretation [is] an illusion.* . . . There are neither causes nor effects. We do not know how to free ourselves of them in our language. But that is unimportant. . . . In sum, *an event is neither caused, nor does it cause*" (*Nachlaß,* Spring 1888, 14 [98]; KGW VIII 3, p. 67).

117. Cf. *Nachlaß,* Aug.–Sept. 1885, 40 [37]; KGW VII 3, pp. 378f.

118. *Nachlaß,* June–July 1885, 36 [31]; KGW VII 3, p. 287.

119. *Nachlaß,* Fall 1885–Spring 1886, 1 [58]; KGW VIII 1, p. 21.

120. *Nachlaß,* Spring 1884, 25 [452]; KGW VIII 2, p. 129.

121. *Nachlaß,* May–June 1885, 35 [15]; KGW VII 3, p. 236.

122. *Nachlaß,* Spring 1884, 25 [389]; KGW VII 2, pp. 109f.

123. Cf. *Nachlaß,* June–July 1885, 38 [8]; KGW VII 3, pp. 334ff.

124. *Nachlaß,* Summer–Fall 1884, 27 [24]; KGW VII 2, p. 282.

125. *Nachlaß,* Spring 1884, 25 [436]; KGW VII 2, p. 123. Cf., for example, *Nachlaß,* Spring–Fall 1881, 11 [135]; KGW V 2, p. 390: "The stimulation that one exercises, the incitement it gives, causing others to release their power . . . is usually mistaken for an *effect.*" Nietzsche here is referring to world-historical events (e.g., the founding of a religion), and he again refers to the relationship "small causes—big effects."

126. The inner spontaneity [*Von-Innen-Her*] gets its confirmation and concretization with the acceptance of the idea of release: "In the smallest organism strength is constantly being built up and it must then be released: either on its own, when *abundance* is there, or a stimulus comes from the outside. *Which way* should the force turn? Certainly in the *accustomed* direction: that is, *wherever the stimuli lead,* that is where the *spontaneous* release moves. The frequent stimuli also *train the direction of the spontaneous release*" (*Nachlaß,* Spring–Fall 1881, 11 [139]; KGW V 2, p. 391.

127. Mittasch points out that research in this century "has tended more and more toward the idea that the complicated physiological processes, such as fertilization and germination, can be untangled meaningfully and brought closer to an understanding only based on the assumption that one uses the *psychological analogy of giving instructions, com-*

manding and obeying based on an existing resonance as receptivity" (*Nietzsche als Naturphilosoph*, p. 187). He draws his examples from the works of H. Spemann (p. 336), who continued the evolutionary-physiological research of Roux and Driesch. We find here one evidence (among others) that Nietzsche's reflections on "natural philosophy" do not stand in opposition to later research but absolutely are "scientifically relevant."

128. *Nachlaß*, Aug.–Sept. 1885, 41 [42]; KGW VII 3, p. 382. We must take into account that not only the felt stimuli "act": they are "very seldom and scanty phenomena compared with the countless stimuli which a cell, an organ exercises on another cell, another organ" (*Nachlaß*, Winter 1883–84, 24 [16]; KGW VII 1, p. 696.

129. *Nachlaß*, June–July 1885, 38 [8]; KGW VII 3, pp. 334ff. Cf. BGE 19; KGW VI 2, pp. 25ff.

130. *Nachlaß*, Summer–Fall 1884, 27 [19], KGW VII 2, pp. 279f.

131. *Nachlaß*, Spring–Fall 1881, 11 [134]; KGW, V 2, p. 389. In this context, Nietzsche, following Roux, presents the *struggle* of "functions of similar degree" as the formative principle.

132. Ibid., 11 [284]; p. 448.

133. KGW VI 1, p. 35. Nietzsche's apotheosizing of the body as a great reason must at the same time be seen as connoting a "devaluation" of "mind" [*Geist*] as the "little reason." Zarathustra characterizes the mind as "a small tool and play thing" of the greater reason.

134. *Nachlaß*, Summer–Fall 1884, 27 [8]; KGW VII 1, pp. 176f. Cf. 17 [17]; p. 282.

135. *Nachlaß*, 27 [19]; p. 179. Nietzsche explains this statement: "i.e., over and over again there must be commanding (and obeying) down to the smallest detail and only when the command is broken down into the countless little sub-commands can the motion proceed, which *starts with the last and smallest obeyer.*"

136. Ibid., [59]; p. 289.

137. *Nachlaß*, April–June 1885, 34 [55]; KGW VII 3, p. 157. The word "freedom" of course does not mean arbitrariness. Only *mechanical* necessity is denied by this term. In spring 1884 Nietzsche notes: "Some things are commanded that cannot be completely achieved because the strength is insufficient" (*Nachlaß* 25 [432]; KGW VII 2, p. 122). Decisive is the power-ratio in the play of stimuli. As early as 1881 Nietzsche's psychological notes say: "For a stimulus to really have a triggering effect, it must be stronger than the counter-stimulus, which is also always present" (*Nachlaß*, 11 [131]; KGW V 2, p. 387).

138. *Nachlaß*, April–June 1885, 34 [113]; KGW VII 3, pp. 181f.

139. *Nachlaß*, Summer–Fall 1884, 26 [276]; KGW VII 2, p. 220.

140. *Nachlaß*, June–July 1885, 26 [22]; KGW VII 3, pp. 284f.

141. *Nachlaß*, June–July 1885, 37 [4]; p. 303.

142. *Nachlaß*, Aug.–Sept. 1885, 40 [21]; p. 370.

143. *Nachlaß*, Summer–Fall 1884, 27 [8]; KGW VII 2, p. 277.

144. *Nachlaß*, April–June 1885, 34 [123]; KGW VII 3, p. 182.

145. To what extent Nietzsche, by the fall of 1880, was predisposed for the Roux-reception that took place the next year, is shown by fragment 6 [70]; KGW V 1, pp. 541–43. He there describes "the ego . . . [as] a plurality of personlike forces, of which now one

now the other stands in the foreground as ego." "As the drives are engaged in a struggle, the feeling of the 'I' is always strongest where the superior power happens to be."

146. *Nachlaß,* June–July 1885, 37 [4]; KGW VII 3, p. 303.

147. *Nachlaß,* Aug.–Sept. 1885, 40 [42], p. 382.

148. In this context Nietzsche opposes H. Spencer, who "defines life itself as an ever more purposeful adaptation to external circumstances." He sees this as a misundertanding of life, which consists in the will to power.

149. *Nachlaß,* Spring 1884, 25 [520]; KGW VII 2, p. 145.

150. *Nachlaß,* Summer–Fall 1884, 26 [134], p. 183.

151. *Nachlaß,* June–July 1885, 37 [4]; KGW VII 3, p. 303.

152. Let us point out only the *shielding off* of our "'consciousness,' which is usually thought of as unique [*einzig*]," from the "many consciousnesses" that present to the first "only a *selection,*" and "moreover events that are simplified, made surveyable and comprehensible, that is *falsified.*" This occurs so that our apparently unique consciousness can prepare "acts of the will." "And precisely the same operation that takes place here, must continually occur on all deeper levels, in the behavior of all these higher and lower beings: this same selection and presentation of experiences, this abstracting and thinking together, this 'willing,' and finally this retro-translation of the always very indeterminate willing into a determinate activity" (*Nachlaß,* June–July 1885, 37 [4]; KGW VII 3, p. 304).

153. *Nachlaß,* Winter 1883–84, 24 [16]; KGW VII 1, pp. 695–98. Our goal-setting could under such a presupposition perhaps be "only a *sign-language for something essentially different—namely non-willing and unconscious*" (p. 697).

154. *Nachlaß,* Spring 1888, 14 [98]; KGW VIII 3, p. 66.

155. *Nachlaß,* End of 1886–Spring 1887, 7 [25]; KGW VIII 1, p. 312.

156. *Nachlaß,* Fall 1887, 9 [91]; KGW VII 2, p. 50.

157. *Nachlaß,* June–July 1885, 37 [4]; KGW VII 3, p. 303.

158. When Nietzsche in BGE 13 warns "against *superfluous* teleological principles (cf. *Nachlaß,* 2 [63]; KGW VIII 1, p. 87), he does not mean that it is indispensable but only that some teleological "interpretation" for the time being cannot be dispensed with (cf. GA XII, Aph. 628, pp. 259f.). "The apparent '*purposefulness*'" is "only an expression for an order of spheres of power and their interplay," he says in a note of Fall 1887 (*Nachlaß,* 9 [91]; KGW VIII 2, p. 50).

159. *Nachlaß,* June–July 1885, 37 [4]; KGW VII 3, p. 303.

160. *Nachlaß,* Spring–Fall 1881, 11 [316]; KGW V 2, p. 461.

161. *Nachlaß,* Fall 1881, 12 [163]; KGW V 2, p. 502.

162. That such "transposals" do not represent philosophical arbitrariness on Nietzsche's part, but rather that they guide natural scientific research even to the present hardly need be mentioned. But with regard to Roux, let us mention that Haeckel proposed to him as a completion of his title *Struggle of the Parts:* "breeding principle in the cell-state" (Mocek, *Wilhelm Roux,* p. 48).

163. *Nachlaß,* Spring 1888, 14 [81]; KGW VIII 3, p. 53.

164. *Nachlaß,* Summer–Fall 1884, 26 [277]; KGW VII 2, p. 221. On the drive for self-

preservation as a teleological breach of logic on Spinoza's part, cf. BGE 13. In the same text self-preservation is interpreted as "one of the indirect and most frequent *effects*" of life as the will to power.

165. Cf. *Nachlaß*, Spring 1884, 25 [427]; KGW VII 2, pp. 120f; also [430], [432]; pp. 123f.

166. *Nachlaß*, June–July 1885, 36 [22]; KGW VII 3, p. 284.

167. *Nachlaß*, End of 1886–Spring 1887, 7 [9]; KGW VIII 1, p. 303.

168. *Nachlaß*, Fall 1885–Fall 1886, 2 [76]; KGW VIII 1, p. 94.

169. *Nachlaß*, Summer 1886–Fall 1887, 5 [64]; KGW VIII 1, p. 213. Nietzsche's statements cited in this context are based on his acceptance of ideas of W. H. Rolph, whose book *Biologische Probleme zugleich als Versuch zur Entwicklung einer rationalen Ethik* (1882), he acquired in its second edition (1884). The following references should make this clear in the brief space available here:

A. Rolph replaces "Darwin's hunger from a lack of food" with an "eternal, insatiable hunger due to infinite receptivity" (1882, p. 71). Nietzsche accepts the trait of *insatiability* (see above); it is congruent with his understanding of will to power—but it should be mentioned that Rolph occasionally uses both terms, "will" (p. 102) and "power" (p. 133).

B. The insatiability of living creatures tends, according to Rolph, to *enclose* everything they "meet," not only their food. For amoebas this enclosing occurs as a flowing-around, e.g., of sand particles (pp. 42, 60). Nietzsche writes: "'Feeding' is only derived: the original tendency is to want to enclose everything" (*Nachlaß*, ibid.).

C. *Coupling* is for Rolph a "substitute for normal feeding" (p. 52, cf. pp. 100f.). Nietzsche writes: "Where the males seek the females out of hunger and merge with them, procreation is a result of hunger" (*Nachlaß*, Fall 1885–Fall 1886, 1 [118]; KGW VIII 1, p. 34). No doubt based on Rolph, he writes in BGE 36: The problem of "procreation and nourishment" is "one problem."

D. When the limit of possible growth is reached, according to Rolph, the splitting of the protoplasm begins; the parts begin their work anew (pp. 58, 89ff.). Nietzsche: "The *splitting* of a protoplasm in two occurs when the power is not sufficient to master the appropriated property: procreation is a result of impotence" (ibid.).

E. According to Rolph *all progeneration* is a partition; despite all differences sexual progeneration is not fundamentally different from a nonsexual one (p. 90); he regards sexual organs as "physiological organs for elimination of food" (p. 62). He carries this idea through to the full equation of male and female copulatory organs as "ovipositers" (p. 129). For Nietzsche, too, there are no *fundamental* differences within the organic gradations as regards "procreation and progeneration." Finally, I would like to point out that Nietzsche took up Rolph's theory of abundance into his critique of Darwinism, namely in GS 349 ("in nature it is not conditions of distress that are *dominant* but overflow and squandering, even to the point of absurdity"), as well as in TI 9:14: "The general aspect of life is not hunger and distress, but rather wealth, luxury, even absurd prodigality. . . . One should not mistake Malthus for nature." On the latter, cf. Rolph, p. 71.

170. KGW VI 1, p. 250.

171. *Nachlaß*, Fall 1885–Fall 1886, 2 [76]; KGW VIII 1, p. 95.

Works Cited

Andler, Charles. *Nietzsche. Sa vie et sa pensée,* 6 vols. Paris, 1920ff.

Andreas-Salomé, Lou. *Friedrich Nietzsche in seinen Werken.* Vienna, 1894.

Baeumler, Alfred. "Zur Einführung" and "Nachwort," in Fr. Nietzsche, *Die Unschuld des Werdens, Der Nachlaß,* 2 vols. Stuttgart, 1956, 1964.

———. *Nietzsche, der Philosoph und Politiker.* Leipzig, 1931.

Becker, Oakar. "Nietzsches Beweise für seine Lehre von der ewigen Wiederkunft," *Blätter für Deutsche Philosophie* IX, 1936, 368–87. Cited from rpt. in Becker, *Dasein und Dawesen. Ges. phil. Aufsätze.* Pfullingen, 1963.

Benn, Gottfried. "Nach dem Nihilismus," in *Ges. Werke in vier Bänden,* vol. 1. Wiesbaden, 1959. 151–61.

Benz, Ernst. "Nietzsches Ideen zur Geschichte des Christentums," in *Zeitschrift für Kirchengeschichte* 56, 1937, 169–313; rpt. Stuttgart, 1938.

———. *Nietzsches Ideen zur Geschichte des Christentums und der Kirche (Zeitschrift für Religions- und Geistesgeschichte,* Beiheft (Supplement) 3. Leiden, 1956.

Bertram, Ernst. *Nietzsche, Versuch einer Mythologie.* Berlin, 1919.

Biser, Eugen. *Gott ist tot. Nietzsches Destruktion des christlichen Bewußtseins.* München, 1962.

Bourget, Paul. *Essais de psychologie contemporaine,* 2 vols. Paris, 1887.

Bröcker, Walter. "Nietzsche und der europäische Nihilismus," in *Zeitschrift für philosophische Forschung* 3, 1949, 161–77.

Camus, Albert. *L'Homme révolté.* Paris, 1951.

———. *Le Mythe de Sisyphe.* Paris, 1942.

Deleuze, Gilles. *Nietzsche et la philosophie.* Paris, 1970.

Deussen, Paul. *Erinnerungen an Friedrich Nietzsche.* Leipzig, 1901.

Dickopp, Karl-Heinz. *Nietzsches Kritik de Ich-denke* (Phil. diss.). Bonn, 1965.

Driesch, Hans Adolph Eduard. *"Die organischen Regulationen."* Leipzig, 1901.

———. *Philosophie des Organischen.* Rev. ed., Leipzig, 1921.

Düringer, Adelbert. *Nietzsches Philosophie und das heutige Christentum.* Leipzig, 1907.

Ewald, Oskar. *Nietzsches Lehre in ihren Grundbegriffen. Die ewige Wiederkunft des Gleichen und der Sinn des Übermenschen.* Berlin, 1903.

Fink, Eugen. *Nietzsches Philosophie.* Stuttgart, 1960.

Förster-Nietzsche, Elisabeth, *Das Leben Friedrich Nietzsches,* 2 vols. in 3 books. Leipzig, 1895–1904.

Grau, Gerd-Günther. *Christlicher Glaube und intellektuelle Redlichkeit. Eine religionsphilosophische Studie über Nietzsche.* Frankfurt am Main, 1958.

Grützmacher, Richard Heinrich. *Nietzsche.* Leipzig, 1917.

Habermas, Jurgen. "Nachwort" ("Afterword"), in Friedrich Nietzsche, *Erkenntnistheoretische Schriften.* Frankfurt am Main: Suhrkamp, 1968. 237–61.

Hanel, Alfred. *Fr. Nietzsche und sein Verhältnis zum Relativismus* (Phil. diss.). Jena, 1923.

Häuptner, Gerhard. *Die Geschichtsansicht des jungen Nietzsche.* Stuttgart, 1936.

Heftrich, Eckhard. *Nietzsches Philosophie. Identität von Welt und Nichts.* Frankfurt am Main, 1962.

Heidegger, Martin. *Einführung in die Metaphysik.* Tübingen, 1953.

———. *Nietzsche,* 2 vols. Pfullingen, 1961.

———. *Sein und Zeit.* Tübingen, 1953.

———. *Über den Humanismus.* Frankfurt am Main, 1947.

Hillebrand, Karl. "Über historisches Wissen und historischen Sinn," in *Zeiten, Völker, Menschen,* vol. 2. Straßburg, 1891. 314–38.

Horneffer, Ernst. *Vorträge über Nietzsche. Versuch einer Wiedergabe seiner Gedanken.* Berlin, 1904.

Jaspers, Karl. *Nietzsche. Einführung in das Verständnis seines Philosophierens.* Berlin, 1946.

———. *Nietzsche und das Christentum.* Munich, 1952.

Klages, Ludwig. *Die psychologischen Errungenschaften Fr. Nietzsches.* Leipzig, 1926.

Köster, Peter. "Die Problematik wissenschaftlicher Nietzsche-Interpretation: Kritische Überlegungen zu Wolfgang Müller-Lauter's Nietzschebuch," in *Nietzsche-Studien* 1 (1973): 31–60.

Landmann, Michael. *Geist und Leben. Varia Nietzscheana.* Bonn, 1951.

Löwith, Karl. *Von Hegel zu Nietzsche. Der revolutionäre Bruch im Denken des 19. Jahrunderts.* Stuttgart, 1950.

———. *Nietzsches Philosophie der ewigen Wiederkehr des Gleichen.* Stuttgart, 1956.

Lukács, Georg. *Die Zerstörung der Vernunft.* Berlin, 1954.

Mayer, Julius Robert. *Mechanik der Wärme,* 1873.

———. *Die organische Bewegung in ihrem Zusammenhang mit dem Stoffwechsel,* 1845.

Minssen, Hans Friedrich. *Die französische Kritik und Dostojewski.* Hamburg, 1933.

Mittasch, Alwin. *Friedrich Nietzsche als Naturphilosoph.* Stuttgart: Kroner, 1952.

———. *Friedrich Nietzsches Naturbeflissenheit.* Heidelberg, 1950.

Mocek, S. R. *Wilhelm Roux—Hans Driesch, Zur Geschichte der Entwicklungsphysiologie der Tiere,* 1974.

Montinari, Mazzino. "Das Leben Fr. Nietzsches in den Jahren 1875–1879: Chronik," in KGW IV/4, 7–90.

Müller-Lauter, Wolfgang. "Thesen zum Begriff des Absurden bei Albert Camus," in *Theologia Viatorum* VIII. Berlin, 1962. 156–74.

———. *Briefe an Peter Gast. Friedrich Nietzsches Gesammelte Briefe,* vol. IV. Leipzig: Insel-Verlag, 1908.

Nietzsche, Friedrich. *The Portable Nietzsche.* Ed. and trans. Walter Kaufmann. New York: Viking, 1954.

Nohl, Hermann. "Eine historische Quelle zu Nietzsches Perspektivismus: G. Teichmüller, die wirkliche und die scheinbare Welt," in *Zeitschrift für Philosophie und philosophische Kritik* 149 (1913), 106–15.

Obenauer, Karl Justus. *Friedrich Nietzsche, Der ekstatische Nihilist. Eine Studie zur Krise des religiösen Bewußtseins.* Jena, 1924.

Platz, Hermann. "Nietzsche und Bourget," in *Neuphilologische Monatsschrift* 8, 1937, 177–86.

Podach, Erich F. *Gestalten um Nietzsche.* Weimar, 1932.

Portman, Adolf. *An den Grenzen des Wissens.* Düsseldorf, 1974.

Reinhardt, Karl. "Nietzsche und die Geschichte," in *Vermächtnis der Antike. Ges. Essays zur Philosophie und Geschichtsschreibung,* C. Becker, ed. Göttingen, 1960. 296–309.

Richter, Raoul. *Friedrich Nietzsche. Sein Leben und sein Werk.* Leipzig, 1903.

Riehl, Alois. *Fr. Nietzsche. Der Künstler und der Denker.* Stuttgart, 1923.

Rolph, W. H. *Biologische Probleme zugleich als Versuch zur Entwicklung einer rationalen Ethik,* 1882.

Roux, Wilhelm. *Der Kampf der Theile im Organismus. Ein Beitrag zur Vervollständigung der mechanischen Zweckmäßigkeitslehre,* 1881.

———. *Die Medizin der Gegenwart in Selbstdarstellungen,* L. R. Grote, ed., 1, 1923.

———. *Gesammelte Abhandlungen über Entwicklungsmechanik der Organismen.* 2 vols. Leipzig: Verlag von Wilheim Engelmann, 1895.

———. "Über die Selbstregulation der Lebewesen," in *Archiv für Entwicklungsmechanik* XIII, 1902.

———. "Über die Verzweigungen deourget," in *Neuphilologische Monatsschrift* 8, 1937, 177–86.

Salaquarda, Jörg. "Der Antichrist," in *Nietzsche Studien* 2 (1973).

———. "Nietzsche und Lange," in *Nietzsche Studien* 7 (1978).

Salin, Edgar. *J. Burckhardt und Niezsche.* Heidelberg, 1948.

Schlechta, Karl. "Philologischer Nachbericht," in *Nietzsches Werke in drei Bänden.* Munich, 1954ff. III:1381–1432.

———. "Nachwort," in *Nietzsches Werke in drei Bänden.* Munich, 1954ff.; rpt. as "*Das Werk und seine Intention,*" in *Der Fall Nietzsche: Aufsätze und Vorträge.* Munich, 1959. 15–43.

———. "Nietzsches Verhältnis zur Historie," in *Der Fall Nietzsche: Aufsätze und Vorträge.* München, 1959.

———, and Anders, Anni. *Fr. Nietzsche. Von den verborgenen Anfängen seines seines Philosophierens.* Stuttgart–Bad Rannstadt, 1962.

Schmidt, Hermann Josef. *Nietzsche und Sokrates. Philosophische Untersuchungen zu Nietzsches Sokratesbild.* Meisenheim, 1969.

Schopenhauer, Arthur. *Parerga und Paralipomena,* vol. 2. Leipzig, 1938.

———. *Die Welt als Wille und Vorstellung,* vol. 1. Leipzig, 1939.

Schulz, Walter. *Der Gott der neuzeitlichen Metaphysik.* Pfullingen: Neske, 1957.

Simmel, Georg. *Schopenhauer und Nietzsche.* Leipzig, 1907.

Stender-Petersen, Adolf. *Geschichte der russischen Literatur,* vol. 2. Munich, 1957.

Steverding, B. *Nietzsches Verhältnis zu Naturwissenschaft und Naturphilosophie* (Phil. diss.). Münster, 1951.

Ulmer, Karl. *Nietzsche. Einheit und Sinn seines Werks.* Bern and Munich, 1962.

Vaihinger, Hans. *Nietzsche als Philosoph.* Berlin, 1916.

———. *Die Philosophie des Als Ob . . . Mit emem Anhang über Kand und Nietzsche.* Leipzig, 1920.

Weischedel, Wilhelm. *Der Gott der Philosophen.* Darmstadt, 1971.

———. "Der Wille und die Willen. Zur Auseinandersetzung Wolfgang Müller-Lauters mit Martin Heidegger," in *Zeitschrift für philosophische Forschung* 27/1 (1973), pp. 71–76.

Weizsäcker, Carl Friedrich von. *Die Geschichte der Natur.* Göttingen, 1962. Eng.: *The History of Nature,* trans. Fred U. Wieck. Chicago: University of Chicago Press, 1976.

Windelband, Wilhelm. *Lehrbuch der Geschichte der Philosophie,* H. Heimseth, ed. Tübingen, 1957.

Wolff, Hans M. *Friedrich Nietzsche. Der Weg zum Nichts.* Bern, 1956.

Ziegler, Theobald. *Friedrich Nietzsche.* Berlin, 1900.

WOLFGANG MÜLLER-LAUTER is Professor Emeritus at Humboldt University of Berlin. Born in Weimar, Germany, in 1924, he studied philosophy at the Free University of Berlin from 1950 to 1958, writing his dissertation on Heidegger. In 1961 he was appointed Lecturer in Philosophy at the Kirchliche Hochschule in Berlin, and in 1963 he became a professor there, serving as Rektor from 1974 to 1976. In 1989 the Kirchliche Hochschule merged with the Department of Protestant Theology at Humboldt University, where he became a faculty member and, in 1990, Professor Emeritus. In 1996 he was awarded the first Nietzsche Prize by the Land of Sachsen-Anhalt.

DAVID J. PARENT, until his death in 1997, was a professor of German at Illinois State University, whose faculty he had joined in 1968, after studying at Heidelberg and receiving his M.A. and Ph.D. degrees from the University of Cincinnati. A scholar of recent German literature in his own right, with books and essays on Werner Bergengruen and Heinrich Böll, he also translated from the German a dozen books and monographs in philosophy and related disciplines, by and pertaining to such figures as Friedrich Nietzsche, Helmuth Plessner, Alfred Schutz, and Michael Landmann, with scores of essays and articles by and about these and other writers.